IN SEARCH OF LIGHT

The Broadcasts of Edward R. Murrow

1938-1961

Edited with an Introduction by Edward Bliss, Jr.

DA CAPO PRESS
NEW YORK

Library of Congress Cataloging in Publication Data

Murrow, Edward R.
  In search of light: the broadcasts of Edward R. Murrow, 1938–1961 / edited with
an introduction by Edward Bliss, Jr.—1st Da Capo Press ed.
    p.   cm.
  Originally published: New York: A. A. Knopf, 1967.
  Includes index.
  ISBN 0-306-80762-9 (alk. paper)
  1. History, Modern—20th century. I. Bliss, Edward, 1912– . II. Title.
D422.M8 1997   96-39079
909.82—dc21
                                                                        CIP

First Da Capo Press edition 1997

This Da Capo Press paperback edition of *In Search of Light* is an unabridged
republication of the edition first published in New York in 1967. It is reprinted
by arrangement with Alfred A. Knopf, Inc.

Published by Da Capo Press, Inc.
A Subsidiary of Plenum Publishing Corporation
233 Spring Street, New York, N.Y. 10013

For almost thirty years Blanche Knopf tried to persuade Ed to write a book. Somehow he was always too busy with an immediate project to undertake this work. After Ed's death I asked Blanche if she would be interested in publishing some of his broadcasts. Her response was enthusiastic. I wished that in some way her belief in Ed and his work might be recorded. Therefore, this volume is dedicated to

BLANCHE *with love and appreciation.*

Janet Murrow

CONTENTS

ILLUSTRATIONS

following page 142

CREDITS: *Photos* I *to* V, VII *to* XIII, XV *CBS;* VI *BBC*

INTRODUCTION

Ed Murrow made more than five thousand broadcasts, starting with an eyewitness report on Hitler's seizure of Austria and ending, twenty-three years later, with observations on the inaugural address of John F. Kennedy, in whose administration he was soon to serve. In addition to direct reports, documentaries, and news analyses, which he called "think pieces," there were the speeches made both as a broadcaster and as director of the United States Information Agency. To put all that is significant of this work between the covers of a less than encyclopedic book is not possible.

Obviously, in making these selections, hard choices were made. Some broadcasts have been omitted because the events that occasioned them proved of transitory interest or importance; others were not selected because they consist solely of what, in the trade, is called hard news—that is, straight reporting of facts which can be found in any good newspaper file or history. No effort is made to cover, in broadcast form, all that happened. Indeed, large events occurred while Murrow was vacationing or serving CBS News in a non-broadcasting capacity. On the night of December 7, 1941—on leave from London—he was at the White House, reporting to the President on the temper of the British people after two years of war. Franklin D. Roosevelt, in turn, informed him of the true damage inflicted by the Japanese at Pearl Harbor, a story the reporter considered privileged. There is, consequently, no Murrow broadcast on Pearl Harbor.

The broadcasts chosen are those that add dimension to history because of Murrow's perspective, or that show development of his reporting style and beliefs. A few light pieces are included. At the time, his excuse for occasional frivolity was change of pace. But, more than that, he loved a good story.

Hopefully, the reader will find here the essence of his philosophy as it emerges in what he had to say to a generation of Americans in the most revolutionary quarter century in the history of man. These were years that saw the bloodiest war ever fought, genocide without parallel, worldwide ideological warfare, the end of Western Colonialism, Africa's emergence, the founding of the United Nations, the Communist take-over in China, birth of the Atomic Age, and the first rocket probes of outer space. The United States scrapped its traditional policy of isolation in peacetime; it strove to adapt to the Negro revolution; McCarthyism imperiled freedom of the individual through fear. Contemplating the turbulence of this period, Murrow said, "I have lived through it as a reporter and can scarcely credit it."

When full assessment of Ed Murrow is taken, it may be said that he served his country best as unofficial ambassador to Britain in its finest hour; as head of the United States Information Agency, which he revitalized; as defender of the rights and dignity of Commonman, not just in the McCarthy era, but throughout his career. Murrow recognized McCarthyism long before the word was invented. He reported during the Battle of Britain that for two days, while London was being bombed, the House of Commons discussed conditions under which enemy aliens were detained—there were to be no concentration camps in England. In 1946, he suspected that the most important thing that had happened in Britain during the war had not been the demonstration of physical courage, or winning the Battle of Britain, or even the successful landings in Normandy. The most important thing, he believed, was that there had been no retreat from principles, that parliamentary procedure and equality before the law had survived.

Thus as early as 1947, with perfect consistency, he pointed out that no less an issue than the right of dissent was involved in the investigation of Hollywood Reds. "This reporter," he said, "approaches the matter with rather fresh memories of friends in Austria, Germany and Italy who either died or went into exile because they refused to admit the right of their government to determine what they should say, read, write or think." In 1948, he was disturbed when a member of Congress, albeit a leftist, was denied a passport. Such action may be wise, he said. "But when it is done without a vote by our elected representatives—without a law—it is dangerous." He believed, devoutly, in due process. In 1949, he was saying, "It is regrettable that individuals and some organs of opinion are disposed to convict people by association or before they have been tried." With these deep convictions, what other stand in relation to McCarthy could he conceivably have taken?

This book is composed, in the main, of Ed Murrow's radio broadcasts. Radio is where he began; his short-wave reporting of the Battle of Britain—"This Is London"—won him his reputation. Television was not established as a news medium until a decade later, and even then if he had something to say, he said it on his daily radio broadcast. There is another reason for relying largely on the radio broadcasts. In television, words are tied to pictures; each loses something without the other. Consequently radio scripts read better in book form than television scripts; they are written to stand by themselves.

Excerpts of three television broadcasts do appear. The first is taken from the "See It Now" program of March 9, 1954, in which Murrow and Fred W. Friendly, by means of film clips, demonstrated Senator McCarthy's ruthlessness. Another, longer excerpt, also from "See It Now," consists of a conversation that took place the same year between Murrow and Carl Sandburg at the poet-historian's goat farm in North Carolina. The excerpt ends with Sandburg reading his own question from *Remembrance Rock:* "When we say a patriot is one who loves his country, what kind of love is it we mean?" The third television script is from the premiere "Small World" broadcast of October 12, 1958, in which the participants, besides Murrow, were Aldous Huxley, Thomas E. Dewey, and Prime Minister Nehru of India. This was another first of a kind since the participants were thousands of miles apart. Two speeches are included in their entirety and have been placed in a special section at the back of the book. In these, Murrow expressed his belief that the first responsibility of broadcasting is to inform—and warned that there is no safety unless we remain free. The first speech was delivered before a meeting of radio and television news directors in Chicago; the second upon receiving the annual Freedom House Award in 1954.

Ed Murrow had a special respect for fliers, perhaps because of the gallant stand they made in the Battle of Britain and because he came to know them early. Murrow guessed that, in two wars, he flew about forty combat missions. He rarely spoke of this. He felt guilty, almost ashamed, that he could choose his missions, could ground himself whenever he felt like it, while the men he flew with had to keep going back. Three broadcasts based on these flights are included.

Murrow's career as director of the United States Information Agency is not covered, though he served in that post with distinction, as was his habit, until compelled to resign for reasons of health. In conferring on him the Medal of Freedom, the highest civilian award the government can bestow, President Johnson said, "He has brought to all his endeavors the conviction that truth and personal integrity are the ultimate persuaders of men and nations." In his history of the Kennedy Administration, *A Thousand Days,* Arthur Schlesinger, Jr., says, "Under Ed Murrow, the Voice of America became the voice, not of American self-righteousness, but of American democracy."

He never changed.

A personal word. I first became acquainted with Ed Murrow in New York in 1947. And in 1948, when I became night editor for CBS News, I got to know him better. Murrow had begun his series of nightly radio broadcasts, and it was policy, decreed by someone higher up possessed of great faith in young editors, that the night man must scrutinize scripts for all evening broadcasts, including Murrow's, before airtime. I was impressed by Murrow's wide knowledge of international affairs and his gentleness. On the rare occasion that error was discovered, his gratitude was tremendous. The dark, taciturn face (they said he carried the troubles of the world on his back) would light up in a marvelous way, and he would say, "Good catch." In 1955, Murrow asked me to join his staff. Until he went to Washington, I was privileged to work with him and Raymond Swing, who often assisted Murrow in the preparation of his broadcasts from 1954 to 1959.

Last year, when it was decided to publish a book of Ed Murrow's broadcasts, Janet Murrow suggested that I edit them for publication, which I have regarded as a high honor and fearsome responsibility.

There are many to whom I owe appreciation. Chief among them

are the Columbia Broadcasting System, which made texts of the broadcasts available; Miss Kay Campbell, who took most of the original dictation; Ashbel Green, of Alfred A. Knopf, Inc., publisher; Miss Louise Gimple, who typed the manuscript; and James M. Seward, executor of the Edward R. Murrow estate and long-time friend of Murrow, who gave unfailing counsel. Needless to say, I also am in debt to CBS News.

E. B., Jr.

November 1, 1966

IN SEARCH OF LIGHT

The Broadcasts of Edward R. Murrow

1 9 3 8 — 1 9 6 1

1938

1945

Edward R. Murrow's special, almost legendary association with England began, not with broadcasting, but with a visit he made to London in 1930 as the youthful, peripatetic president of the National Student Federation of America. He was arranging student tours, and his first impressions of England—it was not love at first sight—are described in a broadcast he did for the BBC in 1946. The broadcast was called "A Reporter Remembers."

I first came to England sixteen years ago in the summertime. It rained for two weeks. Being just out of the university, I wore a straw-boater and carried a cane. No one laughed at me, at least not openly. The boater did not survive the rigors of the English summer; the cane was jettisoned during the crossing from Dover to Ostend. I saw little of England, nothing of Scotland. What I did see did not impress me.

During the next seven years I was three times in England, always for a brief visit. I am Irish, French, English and German, a mixture that is not uncommon in my country. I knew something of your history and more of your literature. But, to me, England was a small, pleasant, historical but relatively unimportant island off the coast of Europe. It was different and therefore interesting. Your country was a sort of museum piece, pleasant but small. You seemed slow, indifferent and exceedingly complacent—not important. I thought your streets narrow and mean, your tailors overadvertised, your climate unbearable, your class-consciousness offen-

3

sive. You couldn't cook. Your young men seemed without vigor or purpose. I admired your history, doubted your future and suspected that the historians had merely agreed upon a myth. But always there was something that escaped me. Always there remained in the back of a youthful and undisciplined mind the suspicion that I might be wrong.

About nine years ago, being persuaded that war was inevitable, I came here to live. I spent a lot of time on the Continent. Young Germans, Czechs, Dutch, French, Poles and all the rest were repeatedly saying, "Tell us, you know the British, you have lived there. It is true, isn't it, that they are soft, decadent, have lost faith in themselves and their destiny?" And I always replied, "Gentlemen, you may be right. There is evidence to support your point of view. But I have a suspicion you are wrong. Perhaps you misjudge these young men who are rather languid and wear suede shoes and resolve that they will fight not for king or country."

I remember being in Warsaw when the Germans marched into Austria, flying to Vienna and finding that everyone there was asking the question: "What will the British do?" I remember my Austrian friend saying, "There they are, the British, living in the past. Their future is all behind them." And still I doubted.

March 13, 1938

When the German Army marched into Austria, the British did nothing. Like the rest of the world, they watched. On the day before Hitler's entry into Vienna to proclaim Anschluss with Germany, Murrow made his first news broadcast.

This is Edward Murrow speaking from Vienna. It's now nearly 2:30 in the morning and Herr Hitler has not yet arrived. No one seems to know just when he will get here, but most people expect him sometime after 10 o'clock tomorrow morning. It's, of course, obvious after one glance at Vienna that a tremendous reception is being prepared.

I arrived here by air from Warsaw and Berlin only a few hours ago. There was very little excitement apparent in Warsaw. People went quietly about their work. The cafes were full. The drivers of

4

those horse-drawn cabs were muffled up in their fur coats and they seemed pretty remote from the crisis. A Polish friend of mine said to me, "You see, we Poles have seen so many headlines during the past twenty years that they no longer excite us." There were rumors in Warsaw that the frontier guard had been strengthened, but these were officially denied. Foreign correspondents there seemed to agree that there was very little probability of Poland making a protest in any form concerning recent developments in Austria. I saw the Minister of War at luncheon yesterday and he certainly seemed calm and unworried, and just as I left Warsaw a distinguished Polish gentleman said to me, "This is a time for cool heads and calm decisions." Perhaps that sums up Poland's position. And then a few hours ago, in Berlin, I saw many couples walking along the Unter den Linden. Their primary interest seemed to be enjoying a brisk walk in the clear sunshine of a March afternoon.

From the air, Vienna didn't look much different than it has before, but, nevertheless, it's changed. The crowds are courteous as they've always been, but many people are in holiday mood; they lift the right arm a little higher here than in Berlin and the "Heil Hitler" is said a little more loudly. There isn't a great deal of hilarity, but at the same time there doesn't seem to be much feeling of tension. Young storm troopers are riding about the streets, riding about in trucks and vehicles of all sorts, singing and tossing oranges out to the crowd. Nearly every principal building has its armed guard, including the one from which I am speaking. There are still huge crowds along the Ringstrasse and people still stand outside the principal hotels, just waiting and watching for some famous man to come in or out. As I said, everything is quiet in Vienna tonight. There's a certain air of expectancy about the city, everyone waiting and wondering where and at what time Herr Hitler will arrive.

> *It was Murrow's first broadcast. It was also a "first" for broadcast journalism, for participating with him on the 35-minute program, aired at 8 p.m., New York time, were William L. Shirer in London, Edgar Ansel Mowrer in Paris, Pierre Huss in Berlin, Frank Gervasi in Rome, and Robert Trout in New York. Never before had the American public heard a news program consisting of a series of short-wave reports direct from European capitals. The broadcast was*

the culmination of a year's planning in which Ed Klauber, executive vice president at CBS, and Paul W. White, director of CBS News, along with Murrow and Shirer, took an important part.

September 16, 1938

During the Munich crisis—it was called the Czechoslovakian crisis then—Murrow's short-wave reports from London were prototypes of all his broadcasts of the war years to come: what is happening, how does it relate to America, how does Commonman feel? His love of London already shows, though the famous salutation "This is London" did not occur in the first broadcasts.

Hello, America, this is London calling. I'm speaking from a little balcony on the third floor of Grindley's Bank in Whitehall. Now Whitehall is that broad flagstone street running behind Trafalgar Square and Parliament Square. And, incidentally, it's lit with gas and not with electricity. Down to my right, at the end of the street, I can see Nelson's Monument. Beyond that I can see the reflection of the lights in Piccadilly Circus. At the other end of the street is Westminster Abbey, and it's outlined against the midnight sky.

It's just about 12:15 in London. Everything is quiet. Not a soul at the entrance of Downing Street. The usual amount of traffic is passing along Whitehall. You can probably hear in the background the roar of those big, double-deck red buses as they pass along this broad street between Trafalgar Square and Westminster Bridge. For the last four hours I've been going about London, riding in buses, talking with cab drivers, talking with doormen of hotels and clubs, and while it may be true that London isn't typical of England—and perhaps the people that I talked with haven't been typical of London—nevertheless I've been very impressed with the unanimity of support for Prime Minister Chamberlain. A number of people said to me, "Well, the only way to settle this business is man to man, and the Prime Minister has gone out and had a try at it." I talked with one ex-serviceman, and I said, "What do you think is going to happen?" And he said, "Well, sir, about thirty or forty

6

years ago I was in your country, out in Colorado, and I saw those big poker games going on in the gold mines, and the events here have reminded me of those games I saw out in Colorado many years ago."

September 17, 1938

The British cabinet met this morning for two hours and a half. They rose without issuing any statement. The American ambassador, Mr. Joseph Kennedy, called at the Foreign Office while the cabinet was in session. The King is remaining in London during the weekend.

At times like this, one tries to get information by talking with people who are involved in negotiations and with other people who have established reputations as experts in foreign affairs. When I followed this course during the past week, I was told, first, that there aren't any experts on European affairs any more. Things are moving too fast. Primary and secondary issues are all mixed up, and one man's guess is as good as another's. And as soon as that has been said, everyone asks, "What about the United States? What will their attitude be if Britain advocates a plebiscite? Or if she goes so far as to sanction actual dismemberment of Czechoslovakia?" And then they ask, "Do the Americans think the Czechs will really fight, even if they are deserted by England and France?" And *always* they ask, "If a war starts, how long will it be before America comes in?"

Americans who have lived twenty years in London tell me that never in their memory has there been such concern expressed about the state of American feelings.

September 22, 1938

For the first time Murrow started his broadcast by saying, "This is London."

This is London.

Just about three or four minutes ago I spoke with the Foreign Office on the telephone concerning the rumor of Mr. Chamberlain's return to England tonight. I was told that according to one press association the discussions were to be continued tomorrow. Beyond that, I was given no information. Now the latest information here is that Mr. Chamberlain talked for about three and three-quarters of an hour this afternoon with Herr Hitler. No one was present other than Dr. Schmidt, the interpreter. Dr. Schmidt will have interesting memoirs to write sometime because he was also at one time interpreter for Mr. Stresemann [the former German chancellor].

There is still no information concerning the calling of Parliament, although one press association reports that it will probably be called early next week.

So far as conditions in London are concerned, it seems tonight we remain in the state of what has been called "collective insecurity" that has been maintained for the last several days. The opinion, I think, is general that we're just entering the critical phase of the crisis. When Mr. Chamberlain left this morning, the general atmosphere was considerably different from what it was when he left for Berchtesgaden last week. At that time people were saying, "What is Mr. Chamberlain taking with him in the way of a plan?" Today they're saying, "What is he going to bring back?" The conviction seems to be growing that Herr Hitler will, in the vernacular, raise the ante.

September 28, 1938

The early morning papers in London carried large headlines concerning the mobilization of the British fleet. It has also been announced that certain subway stations have been closed for what has been termed officially "urgent constructional work."

A certain number of school children are leaving London today. War risk insurance rates were doubled yesterday. Last night, about three in the morning, I was watching the news tickers here in London. Normally by that time of night they're quiet, but last night at three in the morning they were still typing out their story of moves and countermoves in this diplomatic game that's going on in Europe. I was impressed by one thing: Not a single news agency reported war fever in any single country in Europe.

Throughout most of last night, trucks loaded with sandbags and gas masks were to be seen. Trenches were being dug in the parks by the light of flares and automobile headlights. The surface calm of London remains, but I think I noticed a change in people's faces. There seems to be a tight strained look about the eyes. It reminded me a little of the expression I saw on people's faces in Vienna at the time of the Anschluss. Occasionally one sees a smile that seems to have been stuck on. But this country is certainly calm. It hasn't lost its sense of humor. Even in this morning's papers one finds certain rather humorous comments about the experience of the air raid precaution men as they've gone about various parts of England fitting gas masks.

Practically every morning paper in London today has at least one page of pictures. I have before me one page from the *Telegraph and Morning Post* which shows, of course, the launching of the *Queen Elizabeth* on the Clyde Bank yesterday. But it shows also a group of the territorial army manning an antiaircraft gun. It shows an antiaircraft listening post, and there's a rather large picture of a group of men digging trenches in the parks. Of course, as you will expect, everyone is waiting for the announcement to be made by the Prime Minister this afternoon at 2:35, London time. In the meanwhile all we can do is to wait as well.

September 29, 1938

Reports have been circulating in Berlin and Rome for the last two hours that agreement has been reached. There was a certain amount of jubilation in the streets of London when the first report was issued. At public gatherings, three cheers went up. Bands struck up the national anthem. Crowds of women who were happy and relieved by the news, which is not yet officially confirmed, made Mrs. Chamberlain the center of an affectionate demonstration when she left St. Michael's Church tonight.

During the last few weeks Europe has been like a man in a darkened house throwing open door after door in search of light. Last night it appeared that at least a faint glimmer of light and hope had been found. Tonight the light still seems to be faint, but it's there, and we're still standing by in London for an official confirmation of the reported agreement in Munich.

9

It has just been reported by the Munich wireless that Herr Hitler, Signor Mussolini, Mr. Chamberlain, and Mr. Daladier at 12:30 this morning signed an agreement regarding the terms of the cession of the Sudeten German areas. Further news is expected later.

Now when Mr. Chamberlain left Heston airport this morning he said he hoped when he returned to be able to say as Hotspur says in *Henry IV,* "Out of this nettle, danger, we pluck this flower, safety." Mr. Chamberlain's opponents say, "But don't forget that the nettle is still there." His opponents are still wondering how much of the nettle will remain when they have learned the terms of the agreement that has been signed in Munich tonight. The opposition parties continue to watch developments with what might be termed suspicion.

An official statement from Prague: "At this critical juncture the Czech government is placing the interest of civilization and world peace before the distress of its own peoples and is resolved to make sacrifices which never in history were expected from an undefeated state with such concentrated effort."

All London now waits to learn the contents of the agreement reported to have been signed in Munich tonight.

September 30, 1938

> *At Munich, Britain and France agreed to surrender Czechoslovakia's Sudetenland to Hitler, and Chamberlain returned to London with his pronouncement of "Peace in Our Time."*

Thousands of people are standing in Whitehall and lining Downing Street, waiting to greet the Prime Minister upon his return from Munich. Certain afternoon papers speculate concerning the possibility of the Prime Minister receiving a knighthood while in office, something that has happened only twice before in British history. Others say that he should be the next recipient of the Nobel Peace Prize.

International experts in London agree that Herr Hitler has scored one of the greatest diplomatic triumphs in modern history. The average Englishman, who really received his first official information concerning the crisis from Mr. Chamberlain's speech in the House of Commons on Wednesday, is relieved and grateful. Men who predicted the crisis and the lines it would follow long before it arrived did not entirely share that optimism and relief. One afternoon paper carried this headline: WORLD SHOWS RELIEF—BUT WITH RESERVATIONS.

August 28, 1939

> *Hitler was not satisfied with occupying the Sudetenland. On March 15, 1939, he took the rest of Czechoslovakia. Then, amid threats against Poland, he and Stalin arranged their nonaggression pact. Britain warned Hitler that it was committed to come to the aid of Poland if attacked.*

I have a feeling that Englishmen are a little proud of themselves tonight. They believe that their government's reply was pretty tough, that the Lion has turned and that the retreat from Manchukuo, Abyssinia, Spain and Czechoslovakia and Austria has stopped. They are amazingly calm; they still employ understatement, and they are inclined to discuss the prospects of war with, oh, a casual "bad show," or, "If this is peace, give me a good war." I have heard no one say as many said last September, "I hope Mr. Chamberlain can find a way out."

There is not much thinking going on over here. People seem to revert to habit in times like this. Nothing seems to shake them. They lose the ability to feel. For instance, we had pictures in today's papers, pictures of school children carrying out a test evacuation. For them it was an adventure. We saw pictures of them tying on each other's identification tags, and they trooped out of the school building as though they were going to a picnic, and for them it was an adventure.

There is a feeling here that if Hitler does not back down, he will probably move against the Poles—not the French and British in the first instance. Then the decision must be made here and in France, and a terrible decision it will be. I will put it to you with the brutal frankness with which it was put to me by a British politician this afternoon: "Are we to be the first to bomb women and children?"

11

The military timetable has certainly been drawn up, but so far as we know in London the train for an unknown destination hasn't started. Within the last two hours, I have talked to men who have a certain amount of first-hand information as to the state of mind in Whitehall, and I may tell you that they see little chance of preserving peace. They feel that Herr Hitler may modify the demands, that the Italians may counsel against war, but they don't see a great deal of hope. And there the matter stands, and there it may stand until Parliament meets tomorrow in that small, ill-ventilated room where so many decisions have been made. I shall be there to report it to you.

Well, if it is to be war, how will it end? That is a question Englishmen are asking. And for what will it be fought, and what will be the position of the U.S.? Of course, that is a matter for you to decide, and you will reach your own conclusions in the light of more information than is available in any other country, and I am not going to talk about it. But I do venture to suggest that you watch carefully these moves during the next few days, that you further sift the evidence, for what you will decide will be important, and there is more than enough evidence that the machinery to influence your thinking and your decisions has already been set up in many countries.

And now, the last word that has reached London concerning tonight's developments is that at the British Embassy in Berlin all the luggage of the personnel and staff has been piled up in the hall, and it is remarked here that the most prominent article in the heavy luggage was a folded umbrella, given pride of placement amongst all the other pieces of baggage.

August 31, 1939

It was the last day of peace. Quietly Britain prepared for the worst.

Tomorrow we shall see the children, the halt, the lame, and the blind going out of Britain's cities. Six hundred fifty thousand will leave London tomorrow. The exodus will start at 5:30 in the morning. In all, there are three million people to be evacuated in the

12

crowded areas—one million three hundred thousand from London alone. Nine roads out of London and only one-way traffic. It's not going to be a very pleasant sight.

This afternoon we learned that the Navy has been fully mobilized; all reservists have been called up for the Army, and the Royal Air Force has called up part of its reserves. They are being called up by radio. There's none of the usual business of individual notices. Now this does not represent complete mobilization, but it certainly calls up all the men that can be handled immediately. One thing incidentally: One evidence of the state of preparedness is that within two hours after the evacuation announcement was made, newspapers appeared in the streets with complete maps and detailed instructions for any who might care for them. Women and children have been helping the men dig trenches today.

So far, Whitehall stands by its statement that war is not regarded as inevitable. We in London know, as you know, of the various diplomatic moves that have gone on in Europe during the day. We know nothing of their outcome, but the conviction has grown that we shall have a decision before very long.

Those of you who are familiar with military terminology will understand what I mean when I say that in London last night the command seemed to be: "Stand steady." Tonight it seems to be: "Prepare for action."

Germany invaded Poland during the night.

September 1, 1939

I should like to recapitulate a few things said from here on an earlier broadcast. First, that the British ultimatum without a time limit has been handed to Von Ribbentrop, and it is believed that the communication will be discussed with Hitler before a reply is given. Second, that Poland has been hammered by the German military machine for nearly twenty-four hours, and the pledges of France and Britain which were to come into force at once have not become operative. Third, it has been expected in certain quarters that the Prime Minister would speak to the nation by radio tonight. He has not done so.

Britain is not yet at war, but tomorrow morning's press speaks of war in the present tense. Here is the comment of the London *Times*. Last September, it was the first British newspaper to advocate the dismemberment of Czechoslovakia, and since that time it has consistently defended the policy embodied in the Munich agreement. Here is the quotation: "Since Herr Hitler has chosen war in spite of the many chances given to him up to the last hour to avoid it, war there must be." Then here is just one sentence from *The Times* which will give you some indication of the style of journalistic writing that still is employed, even at a time like this, in the newspaper that has been called "The Thunderer." Here is the sentence: "All the preparations made on the chance that the inhuman egotism of the ruler of Germany would rush blindly to catastrophe have proved adequate so far as they have yet been tested." In other words, *The Times* believes that so far Britain has done very well.

The Times concludes as follows: "The whole of the proceedings in Parliament yesterday were inspired by the conviction that a great evil must be erased from the world. That evil is the spirit of faithlessness, of intolerance, of bullying, and of senseless ambition which is embodied in Herr Hitler and those who surround him. The conviction overrides the horror of the thought that civilized man has had to tackle the same task twice in twenty-five years. The task will be done again, no matter what the effort required, and it will be done this time in a way which will insure that our children will not have to repeat it."

In general, tomorrow morning's press is unaminous in its support of the government. You have been told of the hardening of public opinion here, the unity in the House of Commons, and the calm steadiness of the British public. You have been told that many expected a declaration of war tonight, and you have been told that there has been delay because a final appeal has been made to Herr Hitler to withdraw—an appeal which the Prime Minister has said he does not expect to succeed.

I suggest that it is hardly time to become impatient over the delayed outbreak of a war which may spread over the world like a dark stain of death and destruction. We shall have the answer soon enough. If war comes tomorrow or the next day, most folks here believe that it will be a long war, and it is the historical belief of Britishers that wars are won at the end, not at the beginning.

14

September 2, 1939

Some people have told me tonight that they believe a big deal is being cooked up which will make Munich and the betrayal of Czechoslovakia look like a pleasant tea party. I find it difficult to accept this thesis. I don't know what's in the mind of the government, but I do know that to Britishers their pledged word is important, and I should be very much surprised to see any government which betrayed that pledge remain long in office. And it would be equally surprising to see any settlement achieved through the mediation of Mussolini produce anything other than a temporary relaxation of the tension.

Most observers here agree that this country is not in the mood to accept a temporary solution. And that's why I believe that Britain in the end of the day will stand where she is pledged to stand, by the side of Poland in a war that is now in Progress. Failure to do so might produce results in this country, the end of which cannot be foreseen. Anyone who knows this little island will agree that things happen slowly here; most of you will agree that the British during the past few weeks have done everything possible in order to put the record straight. When historians come to sum up the last six months of Europe's existence, when they come to write the story of the origins of the war, or of the collapse of democracy, they will have many documents from which to work. As I said, I have no way of ascertaining the real reason for the delay, nor am I impatient for the outbreak of war.

What exactly determined the government's decision is yet to be learned. What prospects of peaceful solution the government may see is to me a mystery. You know their record. You know what action they've taken in the past, but on this occasion the little man in the bowler hat, the clerks, the bus drivers, and all the others who make up the so-called rank and file would be reckoned with. They seem to believe that they have been patient, that they have suffered insult and injury, and they certainly believe that this time they are going to solve this matter in some sort of permanent fashion. Don't think for a moment that these people here aren't conscious of what's going on, aren't sensitive to the suspicions which the delay

15

of their government has aroused. They're a patient people, and they're perhaps prepared to wait until tomorrow for the definite word. If that word means war, the delay was not likely to have decreased the intensity or the effectiveness of Britain's effort. If it is peace, with the price being paid by Poland, this government will have to deal with the passion it has aroused during the past few weeks. If it's a five-power conference, well, we shall see.

The Prime Minister today was almost apologetic. He's a politician; he sensed the temper of the House and of the country. I have been able to find no sense of relief amongst the people with whom I've talked. On the contrary, the general attitude seems to be, "We are ready, let's quit this stalling and get on with it." As a result, I think that we'll have a decision before this time tomorrow. On the evidence produced so far, it would seem that that decision will be war. But those of us who've watched this story unroll at close range have lost the ability to be surprised.

September 3, 1939

Forty-five minutes ago the Prime Minister stated that a state of war existed between Britain and Germany. Air raid instructions were immediately broadcast, and almost directly following that broadcast air raid warning sirens screamed through the quiet calm of this Sabbath morning. There were planes in the sky. Whose, we couldn't be sure. Now we're sitting quite comfortably underground. We're told that the "all clear" signal has been sounded in the streets, but it's not yet been heard in this building.

In a few minutes we shall hope to go up into the sunlight and see what has happened. It may have been only a rehearsal. London may not have been the objective—and may have been.

I have just been informed that upstairs in the sunlight everything is normal, that cars are traveling through the streets. There are people walking in the streets and taxis are cruising about as usual.

The crowd outside Downing Street received the first news of war with a rousing cheer, and they heard that news through a radio in a car parked near Downing Street.

16

September 4, 1939

For several days I've reported, or repeated to you, calls for ambulance drivers, stretcher bearers, and personnel of the civilian defense. It might be useful to request the services of a good sociologist because if this business of repeated air alarms goes on, the sociological results will be considerable. This is a class-conscious country. People live in the same small street or apartment building for years and never talk to each other. The man with a fine car, good clothes and perhaps an unearned income doesn't generally fraternize with the tradesmen, day laborers and truck drivers. His fences are always up. He doesn't meet them as equals. He's surrounded with certain evidences of worldly wealth calculated to keep others at a distance, but if he's caught in Piccadilly Circus when the sirens sound, he may have a waitress stepping on his heels and see before him the broad back of a day laborer as he goes underground. If the alarm sounds about four in the morning, as it did this morning, his dignity, reserve and authority may suffer when he arrives half-dressed and sleepy, minus his usual defenses and possessed of no more courage than those others who have arrived in similar state. Someone, I think it was Marcus Aurelius, said something to the effect that "death put Alexander of Macedon and his stable boy on a par." Repeated visits to public air raid shelters might have produced the same results. Maybe I'm wrong—I'm not a very good sociologist—but I can tell you this from personal experience, that sirens would improve your knowledge of even your most intimate friend.

London, as usual, is black tonight. One gets accustomed to it, but it can hardly be called pleasant. I don't know how you feel about the people who smoke cigarettes, but I like them, particularly at night in London. That small, dull red glow is a very welcome sight. It prevents collisions and makes it unnecessary to heave to until you locate the exact position of those vague voices in the darkness. One night several years ago I walked bang into a cow, and since then I've had a desire for man and beast to carry running lights on dark nights. They can't do that in London these nights, but cigarettes are a good substitute.

17

For a moment tonight I thought I was back in the London of Mr. Pickwick's time. I heard a voice booming through these stark London streets. It said, "28 Portland Place. All's well!" It was an air raid warden; he had shouted to someone an order to cover their window. They had done so, and so he was telling them that no more light came through.

September 9, 1939

Now here's one item that was given at the end of tonight's news broadcast. "Motorists who claim in the future to have seen zebras in the forests should not be disbelieved. The New Forest Common Earth Defense Association advocated today that wild ponies should have white stripes painted on them so that they may be more easily seen by motorists in blackouts."

And that's London at 11:45, all quiet and all calm.

September 29, 1939

Poland, the first victim of Blitzkrieg, *lay beyond relief. On September 17, Russia occupied the eastern part of the country, and Hitler and Stalin ratified partition by formal treaty. Then an ominous lull—*Sitzkrieg—*which was to last for six and a half months.*

I went to the country today for the first time in seven weeks. Whatever you may think of English politics, Englishmen's clothes or Englishmen's hats, you would, I think, agree with me that the beauty of the English countryside has not been overadvertised. The light green of the fields outlined by the darker green hedges, city children playing in village streets, white clouds occasionally obscuring a brilliant autumn sun. But I went to the country not to enjoy its beauty but to look at one of the largest aviation training centers in Britain. I saw the art of camouflage raised to a new level of effectiveness, and I've seen camouflaged airports in half a dozen different countries in Europe.

18

Upon arrival, a sunburned youngster in a RAF uniform suggested that he'd be willing to show us around. He was diffident and almost shy. This, I thought, is very nice. They have assigned someone from their press section to take us about. It wasn't until twenty minutes later that I realized we were being shown over the field and hangars by a young squadron leader, responsible for the most advanced phases of blind flying, different types of bombing and formation flying.

Since the outbreak of war the training period has been somewhat telescoped, but the officials seem to be confident of their ability to turn out fully qualified pilots in the shortest period. All of the men at this particular station had plenty of hours in the air before reporting for their advanced training. They apparently were not very much concerned about the progress of the war. Their job was to learn to fly, bomb, shoot and navigate in the shortest possible time. Everything seemed clear cut and decisive. No confusion. After spending days and nights trying to understand the political side of this war, the military side seemed very efficient and straightforward. The youth of those pilots gives one a very strange feeling. But as I was walking along today I heard a maintenance sergeant say, "There's one of those noisy Americans." That, I thought, was a little blunt but quite clear, though perhaps not in the British tradition of courtesy to foreigners.

I was somewhat relieved, upon talking with him, that he referred to one of the Harvard training ships that happened to be power diving at that moment. Those Harvards are American training ships purchased before the outbreak of the war and assembled over here, and they do make a noise that is quite individual.

Now coming back to London, traveling on a train without lights of any kind, I felt as though we were passing through an endless tunnel. In my compartment there were two Air Force pilots. We sat there in the dark and talked—not about the war or flying or yet the American Neutrality Act. Nothing was said about the burden of the war budget. I happened to know the part of England from which they came, and we talked about that; about the single clump of trees that stands on the top of the hill like an Indian-feather headdress, about the local pub and the vicar who seems to be having trouble navigating his bicycle along the winding country lanes these dark nights.

December 1, 1939

A few hours after I finished talking with you last night, I left London for a British seaport. I can't tell you its name, but early this morning I saw a harborful of small ships—tough-looking, rusty little ships, they were—trawlers that had been scarred and hammered by North Atlantic gales. Black smoke was pouring from their funnels. Many of them old, some still with fish scales in their holds. I saw some of them arriving from Grimsby, Hull, Aberdeen, Fleetwood and the other fishing ports of Britain. They were coming in answer to the Navy's call for more trawlers to meet the German mine menace. Many of them still flew that familiar red duster—the flag of the British merchant navy. They had not yet been commissioned. Some of them had already been transformed into mine sweepers. They carried a small gun on top of a toadstool-like steel structure forward. Depth charges, looking like squat milk cans, were chained up now, ready to be dropped overboard by the flick of a lever.

The men in those ships are small. They are of all ages and voices. Some of them come from the rocky coast of Scotland and others from the quiet, dark waters on the coast of Essex. Often they have trouble understanding one another. They wear no uniform, but their ships, after they have been commissioned, fly the white ensign of the British Navy. I saw weather-beaten skippers talk to the port captain with hands in pockets and pipe in mouth. All of them were fishermen in peacetime and their job now is to fish for mines.

I went aboard one of those trawlers, and they nosed her out beyond the breakwater. There was a stiff breeze blowing and those ships are not dry. When we were well clear of the harbor something that looked like a medium-sized door was flung out from the gallows, or steel bow, through which so many trawling lines have run in peacetime. Attached to it is a light steel float with red flag on top of it. It looks very much like an oversize tuna fish that has been speared by a red flag. A three-by-four-inch cable was paid out from a steel winch and the float drifted astern and to port. That steel cable, called the sweepline, is rough in order that it will saw through the anchor line of a mine. After about five hundred yards of sweepline had been paid out, the heavy piece of steel, which looked like an overgrown window shutter and was attached to the

20

line, was dropped into the water and it immediately forced the sweepline about thirty feet below the surface. Thus we have five hundred yards of steel cable cutting through the water on our port side about thirty feet below the surface, feeling for mines. The float with its little red flag bounces along the way to port and just a little astern. The sweepline throbs and hums in the blocks as we move out to sea and swing down the commercial shipping lanes. We stand and watch the float because if the sweep wire does not saw the mine anchor in two, it slides along until it hits a big knifelike affair just beneath the float and then the mine bobs to the surface and after that it's exploded by shellfire. I was told that we had a reasonable chance of picking up a mine, but nothing happened.

It was rough and wet out there today, and I wasn't particularly sorry when we saw the white cliffs of England, looking like a dirty white sheet hanging from the edge of a green roof, just before dusk. I crawled behind the forward gun support with two seamen. The wind had freshened and our little trawler was taking plenty of water aboard. Brown, cold water it was, too. For me the day was interesting and represented a new adventure, but those fishermen sailors do it every day and many nights. All for about sixty cents a day, plus family allowance. Heroes aren't expensive in Britain's most famous mine-sweeping patrol, but it takes plenty of four-o'clock-in-the-morning courage to do that job.

December 31, 1939

Tonight Britain says farewell, without regret, to this year of grace nineteen hundred thirty-nine. When the year began there seemed some reason for hope. Mr. Chamberlain was claiming that peace in our time was assured. He was preparing to go to Rome for conferences with Signor Mussolini. Editorial writers were telling us one year ago today that Britain had been near to war in 1938, but there were brighter prospects for 1939. The big news in London at this time last year was that Germany had decided to build more submarines, that she would seek parity with Britain. London papers told their readers that this action need cause no alarm. Germany was acting in accordance with existing treaties, and anyway she probably wanted more submarines to met the threat of Russian naval expansion.

One year ago today many writers were predicting a year of peace and prosperity. The new year was greeted with horns, sirens and bells. There were gay parties in London's hotels, and families were together. Mr. Douglas Fairbanks left London for New York. American ships were still sailing from British ports. Unemployed men hung a huge banner on a London monument, asking that they should not starve during the new year. Astrologers predicted a year of peace and prosperity. Of course, there was war news a year ago, but it all seemed very remote to Londoners. There were pictures of exploding mines in our papers, but they were halfway around the world—in the war between China and Japan. Franco's bombers raided Barcelona twice, Italian forces south of Lerida were forced to retreat. But even the war in Spain seemed remote.

The end of 1939 finds Britain near the end of the fourth month of a war which has confounded the experts. Roughly, one million men are under arms in Britain and hundreds of thousands more will probably be asked to register on Tuesday of next week. Homes have been broken up by evacuation. The cost of this war cannot be conveyed by mere figures. Not only the bank clerks are working this year. There are tens of thousands of men and women manning searchlights and antiaircraft guns, fire engines and ambulances, all over Britain. Many businesses have been ruined. Prices continue to rise. There are no bright lights this year, and there will be no sirens or horns sounded at midnight tonight, lest they be confused with air raid warnings.

This is the only opportunity I shall have to extend New Year's greetings to my friends at home. Here they are: "The new year is at the door. I wish for the stupid a little understanding and for the understanding a little poetry. I wish a heart for the rich and a little bread for the poor. But, above all, I wish that we may blackguard each other as little as possible during the new year."

Those words were written by a German, Heinrich Heine—a great man—who died in 1856.

April 9, 1940

Hitler invaded neutral Norway and Denmark, posing new strategic problems for the Allies.

22

I was in the House of Commons this afternoon, and it was a tense and expectant House. Members became a little impatient as the big clock above the speaker's chair ticked off the minutes, while no less than one hundred and eleven questions were answered by various cabinet ministers. Everyone wanted to hear the Prime Minister. When Mr. Chamberlain rose briskly to his feet, silence settled over the House. He began by quoting, almost with satisfaction, from his speech made at the end of the Finnish war, in which he predicted that the policy of Sweden and Norway would not in the end save them from aggression.

The Prime Minister went on to say that the Allies were going to the assistance of Norway and that heavy units of the fleet were now at sea. The speech was brief and added nothing to reports that had been published. The Prime Minister proved to his own satisfaction, and apparently to the satisfaction of the House as well, that the German smash into Denmark and Norway was well under way before the Allies began laying mines in the Norwegian waters. No one suggested the possibility that the Germans, through clever intelligence work, may have had advance information concerning Allied moves.

Military correspondents in London do not underestimate the difficulty involved in the landing of an Allied expeditionary force in Norway. Such an operation presents one of the most difficult of all military maneuvers, since it involves the combined operation of the Army, Navy and Air Force. Staff work and weather conditions will probably be the determining factors, when and if a British expeditionary force is dispatched.

> *Anglo-French forces reached Norway within five days but were soon withdrawn because, in Churchill's phrase, "Dunkirk was upon us."*

May 10, 1940

> *After a seven-month delay, due to bad weather and repeatedly revised strategy, German air and ground forces invaded the Netherlands, Belgium and Luxembourg.*

History has been made too fast over here today. First, in the early hours this morning, came the news of the British unopposed landing in Iceland. Then the news of Hitler's triple invasion came rolling into London, climaxed by the German air bombing of five nations. British mechanized troops rattled across the frontier into Belgium. Then at 9 o'clock tonight a tired old man spoke to the nation from No. 10 Downing Street. He sat behind a big oval table in the Cabinet Room where so many fateful decisions have been taken during the three years that he has directed the policy of His Majesty's government. Neville Chamberlain announced his resignation.

Winston Churchill, who has held more political offices than any living man, is now Prime Minister. He is a man without a party. For the last seven years he has sat in the House of Commons, a rather lonesome and often bellicose figure, voicing unheeded warnings of the rising tide of German military strength. Now, at the age of sixty-five, Winston Churchill, plump, bald, with massive round shoulders, is for the first time in his varied career of journalist, historian and politician the Prime Minister of Great Britain. Mr. Churchill now takes over the supreme direction of Britain's war effort at a time when the war is rapidly moving toward Britain's doorstep. Mr. Churchill's critics have said that he is inclined to be impulsive and, at times, vindictive. But in the tradition of British politics he will be given his chance. He will probably *take* chances. But if he brings victory, his place in history is assured.

The historians will have to devote more than a footnote to this remarkable man no matter what happens. He enters office with the tremendous advantage of being the man who was right. He also has the advantage of being the best broadcaster in this country. Mr. Churchill can inspire confidence. And he can preach a doctrine of hate that is acceptable to the majority of this country. That may be useful during these next few months. Hitler has said that the action begun today will settle the future of Germany for a thousand years. Mr. Churchill doesn't deal in such periods of time, but the decisions reached by this new prime minister with his boyish grin and his puckish sense of humor may well determine the outcome of this war.

May 30, 1940

Recalling that disastrous month of May, 1940, Murrow said, "The British watched the German scythe cut through Holland, Belgium and northern France with a dazed feeling of unbelief. The channel ports were lost; the Belgians capitulated. We were told that the British and French were falling back on Dunkirk."

The battle around Dunkirk is still raging. The city itself is held by marines and covered by naval guns. The British Expeditionary Force has continued to fall back toward the coast and part of it, including wounded and those not immediately engaged, has been evacuated by sea. Certain units, the strength of which is naturally not stated, are back in England.

On the home front, new defense measures are being announced almost hourly. Any newspaper opposing the prosecution of the war can now be suppressed. Neutral vessels arriving in British ports are being carefully searched for concealed troops. Refugees arriving from the Continent are being closely questioned in an effort to weed out spies. More restrictions on home consumption and increased taxation are expected. Signposts are being taken down on the roads that might be used by German forces invading this country. Upon hearing about the signposts, an English friend of mine remarked, "That's going to make a fine shumuzzle. The Germans drive on the right and we drive on the left. There'll be a jolly old mix-up on the roads if the Germans do come."

One of the afternoon papers finds space to print a cartoon showing an elderly aristocratic Englishman, dressed in his anti-parachute uniform, saying to his servant, who holds a double-barrel shotgun, "Come along, Thompson. I shall want you to load for me." The Londoners are doing their best to preserve their sense of humor, but I saw more grave solemn faces today than I have ever seen in London before. Fashionable tearooms were almost deserted; the shops in Bond Street were doing very little business; people read their newspapers as they walked slowly along the streets. Even the newsreel theaters were nearly empty. I saw one woman standing in line waiting for a bus begin to cry, very quietly. She didn't even bother to wipe the tears away. In Regent Street there was a sandwich man. His sign in big red letters had only three words on it: WATCH AND PRAY.

June 2, 1940—8:00 a.m.

We are told today that most of the British Expeditionary Force is home from Flanders. There are no official figures of the number saved, but the unofficial estimates claim that as much as two thirds or perhaps four fifths of the force has been saved. It is claimed here that not more than one British division remains in the Dunkirk area. It may be that these estimates are unduly optimistic, but it's certainly true that a week ago few people believed that the evacuation could have been carried out so successfully.

There is a tendency on the part of some writers in the Sunday press to call the withdrawal a victory, and there will be disagreement on that point. But the least that can be said is that the Navy, Army and Air Force gilded defeat with glory. Military experts here agree that the operation has been the most successful in British military history. The withdrawal from Gallipoli during the last war does not compare with the removal of these troops from the pocket in northern France. The Gallipoli withdrawal was done in secrecy. There was no threat of air attacks. The action was spread over twenty-one nights. One hundred and twenty thousand men were removed at that time. During this operation it is reliably reported that a considerably larger number was taken off in five days under incessant bombing and during the last two days under long-range German artillery fire.

The Navy is pleased with its share in the operation and sees substantiation for its claim that the German fleet was badly mauled in the Norwegian campaign. They see confirmation of this in the fact that the German navy did not attempt serious interference during the withdrawal. Naval experts here say that the sea action offered an ideal opportunity for the use of German submarines, but there has been no mention of U-boat action in official or unofficial reports. The German air arm was apparently entrusted with the job of stopping the British withdrawal. Goering's fliers had plenty of planes and no lack of targets. But according to the British view, they were unable to interfere seriously with sea-going movement.

The main subject of speculation here today is what will Hitler do next? He still has the initiative and a choice of several alternatives. He may hold the line of the Somme and the Aisne and launch his attack against this country. He may re-form his tank divisions and attempt to smash through to Paris, perhaps with his good friend Mussolini hitting the French in the south. He may do both of these things simultaneously or he may offer peace terms to Paris. The best opinion here seems to be that he will not attempt two operations at once, since the whole history of German strategy seems to prove that he will concentrate upon a single objective. His strength so far has lain in the cooperation of his mechanized units and his air force. The Somme-Aisne line, now held by the Allies, is longer and less well defended than the line on the Belgian frontier through which he smashed three weeks ago.

As a result of these considerations, the weight of the guessing here today is that a supreme effort will be made to knock France out of the war during the next few weeks.

June 2, 1940—7:00 p.m.

Yesterday I spent several hours at what may be tonight or next week Britain's first line of defense, an airfield on the southeast coast. The German bases weren't more than ten minutes flying time away—across that ditch that has protected Britain and conditioned the thinking of Britishers for centuries. I talked with pilots as they came back from Dunkirk. They stripped off their light jackets, glanced at a few bullet holes in wings or fuselage and, as their ground crews swarmed over the aircraft, refueling motors and guns, we sat on the ground and talked.

I can tell you what those boys told me. They were the cream of the youth of Britain. As we sat there, they were waiting to take off again. They talked of their own work, discussed the German Air Force with all the casualness of Sunday morning quarterbacks discussing yesterday's football game. There were no nerves, no profanity and no heroics. There was no swagger about those boys in wrinkled and stained uniforms. The movies do that sort of thing much more dramatically than it is in real life.

They told me of the patrol from which they'd just returned. "Six

Germans downed. We lost two." "What happened to Eric?" said one. "Oh, I saw him come down right alongside one of our destroyers," replied another. "The Germans fight well in a crowd. They know how to use the sun, and if they surprise you, it's uncomfortable." They all told the same story about numbers. "Six of us go over," they said, "and we meet twelve Germans. If ten of us go, there's twenty Germans." But they were all anxious to go again.

When the squadron took off, one of them remarked quite casually that he'd be back in time for tea. About that time a boy of twenty drove up in a station wagon. He weighed about 115 pounds. He asked the squadron leader if he could have someone fly him back to his own field. His voice was loud and flat; his uniform was torn, had obviously been wet. He wore a pair of brown tennis shoes three sizes too big. After he'd gone I asked one of the men what was the matter with him. "Oh," he replied, "he was shot down over at Dunkirk on the first patrol this morning, landed in the sea, swam to the beach, was bombed for a couple of hours, came home in a paddle steamer. His voice sounds like that because he can't hear himself. You get that way after you've been bombed for a few hours," he said.

June 4, 1940

I sat in the House of Commons this afternoon and heard Winston Churchill, Britain's tired old man of the sea, sum up the recent operations. He tried again, as he has tried for nearly ten years, to warn this country of the threat that impends. He told of the 335,-000 troops—British and French—brought back from Dunkirk. British losses exceed thirty thousand killed, wounded and missing. Enormous material losses were sustained. He described how the eight or nine German armored divisions swept like a sharp scythe to the right and rear of the northern armies. But the thrust did not reach Dunkirk because of the resistance put up at Boulogne and Calais. Only thirty unwounded survivors were taken off from the port of Calais.

He then paid his tribute to the Royal Air Force. It decisively defeated the main strength of the German Air Force, inflicting losses of at least four to one. As he talked of those young fliers, greater than Knights of the Round Table, crusaders of old, Mr. Churchill needed only wings and an engine to take off. But wars, he said, are not won by evacuations. Nearly one thousand guns had been lost. All transport and all armored vehicles with the northern armies had been lost. A colossal military disaster had occurred, and another blow must be expected immediately. Mr. Churchill believed that these islands could be successfully defended, could ride out the storm of war and outlive the menace of tyranny. If necessary, alone.

There was a prophetic quality about that speech. We shall go on to the end, he said. We shall fight in France; we shall fight on the seas and oceans; we shall fight on the beaches, in the fields, in the streets and in the hills; we shall never surrender. If this island or a large part of it were subjugated and starving, then the empire beyond the seas, armed and guarded by the British fleet, would carry on the struggle until, in God's good time, the New World with all its power and might sets forth to the rescue and liberation of the Old.

With these words, the Prime Minister sat down. I have heard Mr. Churchill in the House of Commons at intervals over the last ten years. I heard his speech on the Norwegian campaign, and I have some knowledge of his writings. Today, he was different. There was little oratory; he wasn't interested in being a showman. He spoke the language of Shakespeare with a direct urgency such as I have never before heard in that House. There were no frills and no tricks. Winston Churchill's speeches have been prophetic. He has talked and written of the German danger for years. He has gone into the political wilderness in defense of his ideas. Today, as Prime Minister, he gave the House of Commons a report remarkable for its honesty, inspiration and gravity.

The evacuation of Dunkirk, according to Paris reports, has been completed. No more men will be taken off from those blood-stained beaches. There was little air activity in that area yesterday. The Royal Air Force has continued its effort to destroy fuel tanks captured by the Germans in Belgium and Holland. Reconnaissance aircraft have been busy on both sides. There is a breathing space tonight, but no one here expects it to last long.

France surrendered on June 22. Now Britain truly stood alone. Murrow reported, "We await undismayed the impending assault."

August 18, 1940

I spent five hours this afternoon on the outskirts of London. Bombs fell out there today. It is indeed surprising how little damage a bomb will do unless, of course, it scores a direct hit. But I found that one bombed house looks pretty much like another bombed house. It's about the people I'd like to talk, the little people who live in those little houses, who have no uniforms and get no decorations for bravery. Those men whose only uniform was a tin hat were digging unexploded bombs out of the ground this afternoon. There were two women who gossiped across the narrow strip of tired brown grass that separated their two houses. They didn't have to open their kitchen windows in order to converse. The glass had been blown out. There was a little man with a pipe in his mouth who walked up and looked at a bombed house and said, "One fell there and that's all." Those people were calm and courageous. About an hour after the all clear had sounded, people were sitting in deck chairs on their lawns, reading the Sunday papers. The girls in light, cheap dresses were strolling along the streets. There was no bravado, no loud voices, only a quiet acceptance of the situation. To me those people were incredibly brave and calm. They are the unknown heroes of this war.

This afternoon I saw a military maneuver that I shall remember for a long time, a company of women dressed in Royal Air Force blue marching in close order. Most of them were girls with blond hair and plenty of make-up. They marched well, right arms thrust forward and snapped smartly down after the fashion of the Guards. They swung through a gate into an airdrome that had been heavily bombed only a few hours before. Some of them were probably frightened, but every head was up. Their ranks were steady and most of them were smiling. They were the clerks, the cooks and waitresses going on duty. I was told that three members of the Women's Auxiliary Air Force were killed in a raid there this morning.

After watching and talking with those people this afternoon I am more than ever convinced that they are made of stern stuff. They can take what is coming. Even the women with two or three children clustered about them were steady and businesslike. A policeman showed me a German machine-gun bullet he had picked up in the street. He said, "I was certainly frightened. Look at my hand. It's still shaking." But it wasn't shaking, and I doubt that it had been.

There is room for many opinions about the diplomatic, economic and military policy of the British government. This country is still ruled by a class, in spite of Miss Dorothy Thompson's broadcast to this country the other night in which she informed Mr. Churchill that he is the head of a socialist state. If the people who rule Britain are made of the same stuff as the little people I have seen today, if they understand the stuff of which the people who work with their hands are made, and if they trust them, then the defense of Britain will be something of which men will speak with awe and admiration so long as the English language survives.

September 8, 1940

For two months the Luftwaffe attacked British shipping, air bases and aircraft plants. Then, on September 7, Marshal Goering sent three hundred bombers, escorted by six hundred fighters, against London. It was the beginning of the blitz.

Yesterday afternoon—it seems days ago now—I drove down to the East End of London, the East India Dock Road, Commercial Road, through Silvertown, down to the mouth of the Thames Estuary. It was a quiet and almost pleasant trip through those streets running between rows of working-class houses, with the cranes, the docks, the ships and the oil tanks off on the right. We crossed the river and drove up on a little plateau, which gave us a view from the mouth of the Thames to London. And then an air-raid siren, called "Weeping Willie" by the men who tend it, began its uneven screaming. Down on the coast the white puffballs of antiaircraft fire began to appear against a steel-blue sky. The first flight of German bombers was coming up the river to start the twelve-hour attack against London. They were high and not very numerous. The Hurricanes and Spitfires were already in the air, climbing for altitude above the nearby airdrome. The fight moved inland and out of sight. Things were relatively quiet for about half an hour. Then the British fighters returned. And five minutes later the German bombers, flying in V-formation, began pouring in. The antiaircraft fire was good. Sometimes it seemed to burst right on the nose of the leading machine, but still they came on. On the airdrome, ground crews swarmed over those British fighters, fitting ammunition belts and pouring in gasoline. As soon as one fighter was ready, it took the air, and there was no waiting for flight leaders or formation. The Germans were already coming back, down the river, heading for France.

Up toward London we could see billows of smoke fanning out above the river, and over our heads the British fighters, climbing almost straight up, trying to intercept the bombers before they got away. It went on for two hours and then the all clear. We went down to a nearby pub for dinner. Children were already organizing a hunt for bits of shrapnel. Under some bushes beside the road there was a baker's cart. Two boys, still sobbing, were trying to get a quivering bay mare back between the shafts. The lady who ran the pub told us that these raids were bad for the chickens, the dogs and the horses. A toothless old man of nearly seventy came in and asked for a pint of mild and bitters, confided that he had always, all his life, gone to bed at eight o'clock and found now that three pints of beer made him drowsy-like so he could sleep through any air raid.

Before eight, the siren sounded again. We went back to a haystack near the airdrome. The fires up the river had turned the moon blood red. The smoke had drifted down till it formed a canopy over the Thames; the guns were working all around us, the bursts looking like fireflies in a southern summer night. The Germans were sending in two or three planes at a time, sometimes only one, in relays. They would pass overhead. The guns and lights would follow them, and in about five minutes we could hear the hollow grunt of the bombs. Huge pear-shaped bursts of flame would rise up into the smoke and disappear. The world was upside down. Vincent Sheean lay on one side of me and cursed in five languages; he'd talk about the war in Spain. Ben Robertson of *PM* lay on the other side and kept saying over and over in that slow South Carolina drawl, "London is burning, London is burning."

It was like a shuttle service, the way the German planes came up the Thames, the fires acting as a flare path. Often they were above the smoke. The searchlights bored into that black roof, but couldn't penetrate it. They looked like long pillars supporting a black canopy. Suddenly all the lights dashed off, and a blackness fell right to the ground. It grew cold. We covered ourselves with hay. The shrapnel clicked as it hit the concrete road nearby, and still the German bombers came.

Early this morning we went to a hotel. The gunfire rattled the windows. Shortly before noon we rang for coffee. A pale, red-eyed chambermaid brought it and said, "I hope you slept well, sirs." This afternoon we drove back to the East End of London. It was like an obstacle race: two blocks to the right, then left for four blocks, then straight on for a few blocks and right again—streets roped off, houses and shops smashed; a few dirty-faced, tow-headed children standing on a corner, holding their thumbs up, the sign of the men who came back from Dunkirk; three red buses drawn up in a line waiting to take the homeless away; men with white scarfs around their necks instead of collars and ties, leading dull-eyed, empty-faced women across to the buses. Most of them carried little cheap cardboard suitcases and sometimes bulging paper shopping bags. That was all they had left. There was still fire and smoke along the river, but the fire fighters and demolition squads have done their work well.

September 10, 1940

This is London. And the raid which started about seven hours ago is still in progress. Larry LeSueur and I have spent the last three hours driving about the streets of London and visiting air-raid shelters. We found that like everything else in this world the kind of protection you get from the bombs on London tonight depends on how much money you have. On the other hand, the most expensive dwelling places here do not necessarily provide the best shelters, but certainly they are the most comfortable.

We looked in on a renowned Mayfair hotel tonight and found

many old dowagers and retired colonels settling back on the over-stuffed settees in the lobby. It wasn't the sort of protection I'd seek from a direct hit from a half-ton bomb, but if you were a retired colonel and his lady, you might feel that the risk was worth it because you would at least be bombed with the right sort of people, and you could always get a drink if you were a resident of the hotel. If you were the sort of person I saw sunk in the padding of this Mayfair mansion, you'd be calling for a drink of Scotch and soda pretty often—enough to keep these fine uniformed waiters on the move.

Only a couple of blocks away we pushed aside the canvas curtain of a trench cut out of a lawn of a London park. Inside were half a hundred people, some of them stretched out on the hard wooden benches. The rest huddled over in their overcoats and blankets. Dimmed electric lights glowed on the whitewashed walls, and the cannonade of antiaircraft and reverberation of the big stuff the Germans were dropping rattled the dust boards underfoot at inter-vals. You couldn't buy a drink there. One woman was saying sleep-ily that it was funny how often you read about people being killed inside a shelter. Nobody seemed to listen. Then over to the famous cellar of a world-famous hotel, two floors underground. On uphol-stered chairs and lounges there was a cosmopolitan crowd. But there wasn't any sparkling cocktail conversation. They sat, some of them with their mouths open. One of them snored. King Zog was over in a far corner on a chair, the porter told me. The woman sleeping on the only cot in the shelter was one of the many sisters of the former king of Albania.

The number of planes engaged tonight seems to be about the same as last night. Searchlight activity has been constant, but there has been little gunfire in the center of London. The bombs have been coming down at about the same rate as last night. It is impossible to get any estimate of the damage. Darkness prevents observation of details. The streets have been deserted, save for a few clanging fire engines during the last four or five hours. The planes have been high again tonight, so high that the searchlights can't reach them. The bombing sounds as though it was separated pretty evenly over the metropolitan district. In certain areas there are no electric lights.

Once I saw *The Damnation of Faust* presented in the open air at

34

Salzburg. London reminds me of that tonight, only the stage is so much larger. Once tonight an antiaircraft battery opened fire just as I drove past. It lifted me from the seat and a hot wind swept over the car. It was impossible to see. When I drove on, the streets of London reminded me of a ghost town in Nevada—not a soul to be seen. A week ago there would have been people standing on the corner shouting for taxis. Tonight there were no people and no taxis. Earlier today there were trucks delivering mattresses to many office buildings. People are now sleeping on those mattresses, or at least they are trying to sleep. The coffee stalls, where taxi drivers and truck drivers have their four-in-the-morning tea, are empty.

As I entered this building half an hour ago, one man was asking another if he had a good book. He was offered a mystery story, something about a woman who murdered her husband. And as he stumbled sleepily down the corridor, the lender said, "Hope it doesn't keep you awake."

And so London is waiting for dawn. We ought to get the all clear in about another two hours. Then those big German bombers that have been lumbering and mumbling about overhead all night will have to go home.

September 13, 1940

This is London at 3:30 in the morning. This has been what might be called a "routine night"—air-raid alarm at about nine o'clock and intermittent bombing ever since. I had the impression that more high explosives and few incendiaries have been used tonight. Only two small fires can be seen on the horizon. Again the Germans have been sending their bombers in singly or in pairs. The antiaircraft barrage has been fierce but sometimes there have been periods of twenty minutes when London has been silent. Then the big red buses would start up and move on till the guns started working again. That silence is almost hard to bear. One becomes accustomed to rattling windows and the distant sound of bombs, and then there comes a silence that can be felt. You know the sound will return. You wait, and then it starts again. That waiting is bad. It gives you a chance to imagine things. I have been walking tonight—there is a full moon, and the dirty-gray buildings appear white. The stars, the empty windows, are hidden. It's a beautiful and lonesome city where men and women and children are trying to snatch a few hours' sleep underground.

In the fashionable residential districts I could read the TO LET signs on the front of big houses in the light of the bright moon. Those houses have big basements underneath—good shelters—but they're not being used. Many people think they should be.

The scale of this air war is so great that the reporting of it is not easy. Often we spend hours traveling about this sprawling city, viewing damage, talking with people and occasionally listening to the bombs come down, and then more hours wondering what you'd like to hear about these people who are citizens of no mean city. We've told you about the bombs, the fires, the smashed houses and the courage of the people. We've read you the communiques and tried to give you an honest estimate of the wounds inflicted upon this, the best bombing target in the world. But the business of living and working in this city is very personal—the little incidents, the things the mind retains, are in themselves unimportant, but they somehow weld together to form the hard core of memories that will remain when the last all clear has sounded. That's why I want to talk for just three or four minutes about the things we haven't talked about before; for many of these impressions it is necessary to reach back through only one long week. There was a rainbow bending over the battered and smoking East End of London just when the all clear sounded one afternoon. One night I stood in front of a smashed grocery store and heard a dripping inside. It was the only sound in all London. Two cans of peaches had been drilled clean through by flying glass, and the juice was dripping down onto the floor.

Talking from a studio with a few bodies lying about on the floor, sleeping on mattresses, still produces a strange feeling, but we'll probably get used to that. Today I went to buy a hat—my favorite shop had gone, blown to bits. The windows of my shoe store were blown out. I decided to have a haircut; the windows of the barbershop were gone, but the Italian barber was still doing business. Someday, he said, we smile again, but the food it doesn't taste so good since being bombed. I went on to another shop to buy flashlight batteries. I bought three. The clerk said, "You needn't buy so many. We'll have enough for the whole winter." But I said, "What if you aren't here?" There were buildings down in that street, and he replied, "Of course we'll be here. We've been in business here for a hundred and fifty years."

September 18, 1940

There are no words to describe the thing that is happening. Today I talked with eight American correspondents in London. Six of them had been forced to move. All had stories of bombs, and all agreed that they were unable to convey through print or the spoken word an accurate impression of what's happening in London these days and nights.

I may tell you that Bond Street has been bombed, that a shop selling handkerchiefs at $40 the dozen has been wrecked, that these words were written on a table of good English oak which sheltered me three times as bombs tore down in the vicinity. But you can have little understanding of the life in London these days—the courage of the people, the flash and roar of the guns rolling down streets where much of the history of the English-speaking world has been made, the stench of air-raid shelters in the poor districts. These things must be experienced to be understood.

September 22, 1940

I'm standing again tonight on a rooftop looking out over London, feeling rather large and lonesome. In the course of the last fifteen or twenty minutes there's been considerable action up there, but at the moment there's an ominous silence hanging over London. But at the same time a silence that has a great deal of dignity. Just straightaway in front of me the searchlights are working. I can see one or two bursts of antiaircraft fire far in the distance. Just on the roof across the way I can see a man wearing a tin hat, a pair of powerful night glasses to his eyes, scanning the sky. Again, looking in the opposite direction, there is a building with two windows gone. Out of one window there waves something that looks like a white bed sheet, a window curtain swinging free in this night breeze. It looks as though it were being shaken by a ghost. There are a great many ghosts around these buildings in London. The search-lights straightaway, miles in front of me, are still scratching that sky. There's a three-quarter moon riding high. There was one burst of shellfire almost straight in the Little Dipper.

Down below in the streets I can see just that red and green wink of the traffic lights; one lone taxicab moving slowly down the street. Not a sound to be heard. As I look out across the miles and miles of rooftops and chimney pots, some of those dirty-gray fronts of the buildings look almost snow-white in this moonlight here tonight. And the rooftop spotter across the way swings around, looks over in the direction of the searchlights, drops his glasses and just stands there. There are hundreds and hundreds of men like that standing on rooftops in London tonight watching for fire bombs, waiting to see what comes out of this steel-blue sky. The searchlights now reach up very, very faintly on three sides of me. There is a flash of a gun in the distance but too far away to be heard.

October 10, 1940

This is London, ten minutes before five in the morning. Tonight's raid has been widespread. London is again the main target. Bombs have been reported from more than fifty districts. Raiders have been over Wales in the west, the Midlands, Liverpool, the southwest and northeast. So far as London is concerned, the outskirts appear to have suffered the heaviest pounding. The attack has decreased in intensity since the moon faded from the sky.

All the fires were quickly brought under control. That's a common phrase in the morning communiques. I've seen how it's done, spent a night with the London fire brigade. For three hours after the night attack got going, I shivered in a sandbag crow's-nest atop a tall building near the Thames. It was one of the many fire-observation posts. There was an old gun barrel mounted above a round table marked off like a compass. A stock of incendiaries bounced off rooftops about three miles away. The observer took a sight on a point where the first one fell, swung his gun sight along the line of bombs and took another reading at the end of the line of fire. Then he picked up his telephone and shouted above the half gale that was blowing up there, "Stick of incendiaries—between 190 and 220—about three miles away."

Five minutes later, a German bomber came boring down the river. We could see his exhaust trail like a pale ribbon stretched straight across the sky. Half a mile downstream there were two eruptions and then a third, close together. The first two looked like some giant had thrown a huge basket of flaming golden oranges high in the air. The third was just a balloon of fire enclosed in black smoke above the housetops. The observer didn't bother with his gun sight and indicator for that one. Just reached for his night glasses, took one quick look, picked up his telephone, and said, "Two high explosives and one oil bomb," and named the street where they had fallen.

There was a small fire going off to our left. Suddenly sparks showered up from it as though someone had punched the middle of a huge campfire with a tree trunk. Again the gun sight swung around, the bearing was read, and the report went down the telephone lines: "There is something in high explosives on that fire at 59."

There was peace and quiet inside for twenty minutes. Then a shower of incendiaries came down far in the distance. They didn't fall in a line. It looked like flashes from an electric train on a wet night, only the engineer was drunk and driving his train in circles through the streets. One sight at the middle of the flashes and our observer reported laconically, "Breadbasket at 90—covers a couple of miles." Half an hour later a string of fire bombs fell right beside the Thames. Their white glare was reflected in the black, lazy water near the banks and faded out in midstream where the moon cut a golden swathe broken only by the arches of famous bridges.

We could see little men shoveling those fire bombs into the river. One burned for a few minutes like a beacon right in the middle of a bridge. Finally those white flames all went out. No one bothers about the white light; it's only when it turns yellow that a real fire has started.

I must have seen well over a hundred fire bombs come down and only three small fires were started. The incendiaries aren't so bad if there is someone there to deal with them, but those oil bombs present more difficulties. As I watched those white fires flame up and die down, watched the yellow blazes grow dull and disappear, I thought what a puny effort is this to burn a great city.

Finally we went below to a big room underground. It was quiet. Women spoke softly into telephones. There was a big map of London on the wall. Little colored pins were being moved from one point to another and every time a pin was moved it meant that fire pumps were on their way through the black streets of London to a fire. One district had asked for reinforcements from another, just as an army reinforces its front lines in the sector bearing the brunt of the attack. On another map all the observation posts, like the one I just left, were marked. There was a string with a pin at the end of it dangling from each post position; a circle around each post bore the same markings as I had seen on the tables beneath the gun sight up above. As the reports came in, the string was stretched out over the reported bearing and the pin at the end stuck in the map. Another report came in, and still another, and each time a string was stretched. At one point all those strings crossed and there, checked by a half-dozen cross bearings from different points, was a fire. Watching that system work gave me one of the strangest sensations of the war. For I have seen a similar system used to find the exact location of forest fires out on the Pacific coast.

We picked a fire from the map and drove to it. And the map was right. It was a small fire in a warehouse near the river. Not much of a fire, only ten pumps working on it, but still big enough to be seen from the air. The searchlights were bunched overhead, and as we approached we could hear the drone of a German plane and see the burst of antiaircraft fire directly overhead. Two pieces of shrapnel slapped down in the water and then everything was drowned in the hum of the pumps and the sound of hissing water. Those firemen in their oilskins and tin hats appeared oblivious to everything but the fire. We went to another blaze—just a small two-story house down on the East End. An incendiary had gone through the roof and the place was being gutted. A woman stood on a corner, clutching a rather dirty pillow. A policeman was trying to comfort her. And a fireman said, "You'd be surprised what strange things people pick up when they run out of a burning house."

And back at headquarters I saw a man laboriously and carefully copying names in a big ledger—the list of firemen killed in action during the last month. There were about a hundred names. I can now appreciate what lies behind that line in the morning communiques: "All fires were quickly brought under control."

November 27, 1940

I should like to tell you about a completely unimportant incident that occurred in a small village I know down in Essex. A thin man, wearing a big, loose overcoat and a black hat with the trim brushed down till it nearly hit his right eye, walked into the bar of a public house. In a husky voice he asked for dry sherry. Sitting down in a fire-shadowed corner, he took out a notebook and began to write with the stub of a pencil. The regular customers, standing near the dartboard, looked him over carefully and in whispers urged one of their number to make contact with the mysterious stranger. And so, ignoring the big clock over the bar, one of the locals went over and asked for the time. And he also tried to see what the stranger was writing. The stranger exhibited a watch, and the local couldn't make anything of the strange scrawls and convolutions in the notebook. "Is that the right time?" he said. "Yah," replied the man in the black hat.

Back at the dartboard there were whispers of "German" and "spy." One member of the team eased out into the dusk in search of a policeman. When he returned with a tin-hatted representative of the law, the stranger was engaged in a game of darts with two members of the local Home Guard. The policeman came in, viewed the situation and, being by nature cautious, did not arrest the suspicious stranger immediately. For he was no Fifth Columnist, just a reporter. The "yah" was the American monosyllable "yeah," and the strange hieroglyphics in the notebook, believed to be code, turned out to be nothing but shorthand.

December 3, 1940

A theory advanced by certain British and American journalists in the weeks preceding the American presidential election has perished. That theory was that the United States would be of greater help to Britain as a nonbelligerent than as a full-fledged ally. The British, in spite of surface impartiality, wanted President Roosevelt to win the election. They encouraged this theory that American assistance, based on peacetime organization, would be more effective than full-scale belligerant aid. It had the advantage of reassuring those American voters who feared that the country might be involved in a war. Since the election, we have heard nothing of this thesis. It's a dead and dynamited fish, and you would have difficulty in finding any responsible British official with a desire to revive it. It's possible that for a time certain Britishers believed that American aid on a neutral basis would be adequate and effective. If they thought so, their disillusionment has been rapid. Ask any member of Parliament or any member of the government whether he prefers a neutral America or a belligerent America, and you will get only one answer. Some would express a preference for winning the war without American aid, but most would admit that it can't be done.

I'm reporting what I believe to be the dominant informed opinion in this country. Later on, you may hear it expressed by responsible British spokesmen. There are no indications that any British minister is going to urge you to declare war against the Axis, but you must expect repeated references in the press and in public statements to the British belief that a democratic nation at peace cannot render full and effective support to a nation at war, for that is what the majority of thinking people in this country have come to believe. As a reporter I'm concerned to report this development, not to evaluate it in terms of personal approval or disapproval.

December 24, 1940

Christmas Day began in London nearly an hour ago. The church bells did not ring at midnight. When they ring again, it will be to announce invasion. And if they ring, the British are ready. Tonight, as on every other night, the rooftop watchers are peering out across the fantastic forest of London's chimney pots. The antiaircraft gunners stand ready. And all along the coast of this island, the observers revolve in their reclining chairs, listening for the sound of

German planes. The fire fighters and the ambulance drivers are waiting, too. The blackout stretches from Birmingham to Bethlehem, but tonight over Britain the skies are clear.

This is not a merry Christmas in London. I heard that phrase only twice in the last three days. This afternoon as the stores were closing, as shoppers and office workers were hurrying home, one heard such phrases as "So long, Mamie" and "Good luck, Jack" but never "A merry Christmas." It can't be a merry Christmas, for those people who spend tonight and tomorrow by their firesides in their own homes realize that they have bought this Christmas with their nerve, their bodies and their old buildings. Their nerve is unshaken; the casualties have not been large, and there are many old buildings still untouched. Between now and next Christmas there stretches twelve months of increasing toil and sacrifice, a period when the Britishers will live hard. Most of them realize that. Tonight's serious Christmas Eve is the result of a realization of the future, rather than the aftermath of hardships sustained during the past year. The British find some basis for confidence in the last few months' developments. They believe that they're tearing the Italian Empire to pieces. So far, shelter life has produced none of the predicted epidemics. The nation's health is about as good now as it was at this time last year. And above all they're sustained by a tradition of victory.

Tonight there are few Christmas parties in London, a few expensive dinners at famous hotels, but there are no fancy paper hats and no firecrackers. Groups determined to get away from the war found themselves after twenty minutes inspecting the lastest amateur diagram of the submarine menace or the night bombers. A few blocks away in the underground shelters entire families were celebrating Christmas Eve. Christmas carols are being sung underground. Most of the people down there don't know that London is not being bombed tonight. Christmas presents will be unwrapped down underground before those people see daylight tomorrow. Little boys who have received miniature Spitfires or Hurricanes will be waking the late sleepers by imitating the sound of whistling bombs, just as we used to try to reproduce the sound of a locomotive or a speeding automobile.

I should like to add my small voice to give my own Christmas greeting to friends and colleagues at home. Merry Christmas is somehow ill-timed and out of place, so I shall just use the current London phrase—so long and good luck.

This appears to be the origin of the phrase "Good night and good luck" with which Murrow concluded his broadcasts after the war.

March 9, 1941

Soon it will be spring in England. Already there are flowers in the parks, although the parks aren't quite as well kept as they were this time last year. But there's good fighting weather ahead. In four days' time the moon will be full again, and there's a feeling in the air that big things will happen soon.

The winter that is ending has been hard, but Londoners have many reasons for satisfaction. There have been no serious epidemics. The casualties from air bombardments have been less than expected. And London meets this spring with as much courage, though less complacency, as at this time last year.

Many ancient buildings have been destroyed. Acts of individual heroism have been commonplace. More damage has been done by fire than by high explosives. The things cast down by the Germans out of the night skies have made hundreds of thousands of people homeless. I've seen them standing cruel cold of a winter morning with tears frozen on their faces looking at the little pile of rubble that was their home and saying over and over again in a toneless, unbelieving way, "What have we done to deserve this?" But the winter has brought some improved conditions in the underground shelters. It has brought, too, reduced rations, repeated warnings of the imminence of invasion, shorter restrictions upon the freedom of the individual and organizations.

When spring last came to England the country was drifting and almost dozing through a war that seemed fairly remote. Not much had been done to give man power and machinery to the demands of modern war. The story of the spring, summer and fall is well known to all of you. For the British it was a record of one disaster after another—until those warm, cloudless days of August and September when the young men of the Royal Air Force beat back the greatest air fleet ever assembled by any nation. Those were the days and nights and even weeks when time seemed to stand still. At the beginning they fought over the English Channel, then over the coast of Kent, and when the German bombers smashed the advance fighter bases along the coast the battle moved inland. Night after night the obscene glare of hundreds of fires reddened the bellies of the big, awkward barrage balloons over London, transforming them into queer animals with grace and beauty. Finally the threat was beaten off. Both sides settled down to delivering heavy blows in the dark. Britain received more than she gave. All through the winter it went on. Finally there came bits of good news from the western desert. But even Tobruk and Bengazi seemed far away. Victories over the Italians are taken for granted here. Even the children know that the real enemy is Germany.

It hasn't been victories in the Middle East or promises of American aid that have sustained the people of this island during the winter. They know that next winter, when it comes, will probably be worse, that their sufferings and privations will increase. Their greatest strength has been and is something that is talked about a great deal in Germany but never mentioned here—the concept of a master race.

The average Englishman thinks it's just plain silly for the Germans to talk about a master race. He's quietly sure in his own mind that there is only one master race. That's a characteristic that caused him to adopt an attitude of rather bored tolerance toward all foreigners and made him thoroughly disliked by many of them. But it's the thing that has closed his mind to the possibilities that Britain may be defeated.

The habit of victory is strong here. Other habits are strong, too. The old way of doing things is considered best. That's why it has taken more than a year and a half to mobilize Britain's potential strength, and the job is not yet finished. The other day, watching a farmer trying to fill in a twenty-foot-deep bomb crater in the middle of his field, I wondered what would happen before he harvested the next crop from that bomb-torn soil. I suppose that many more bombs will fall. There will be much talk about equality of sacrifice which doesn't exist. Many proud ships will certainly perish in the western approaches. There will be further restrictions on clothes and food. Probably a few profiteers will make their profits.

No one knows whether invasion will come, but there are those who fear it will not. I believe that a public opinion poll on the question "Would you like the Germans to attempt an invasion?" would be answered overwhelmingly in the affirmative. Most people, believing that it must be attempted eventually, would be willing to have it come soon. They think that in no other way can the Germans win this war, and they will not change their minds until they hear their children say, "We are hungry."

So long as Winston Churchill is Prime Minister, the House of Commons will be given an opportunity to defend its traditions and to determine the character of the government that is to rule this country. The Prime Minister will continue to be criticized in private for being too much interested in strategy and too little concerned with the great social and economic problems that clamor for solution. British propaganda aimed at occupied countries will continue to fight without its heavy artillery, until some sort of statement on war aims or, if you prefer, peace aims has been published.

And in the future, as in the past, one of the strangest sensations for me will be that produced by radio. Sometime someone will write the story of the technical and military uses to which this new weapon has been put; but no one, I think, will ever describe adequately just what it feels like to sit in London with German bombs ripping through the air, shaking the buildings, and causing the lights to flicker, while you listen to the German radio broadcasting Wagner or Bavarian folk music. A twist of the dial gives you Tokyo talking about dangerous thoughts; an American senator discussing hemisphere defense; the clipped, precise accent of a British announcer describing the proper method of photographing elephants; Moscow boasting of the prospects of the wheat harvest in the Ukraine; each nation speaking almost any language save its own, until, finally, you switch off the receiving set in order that the sounds from the four corners of the earth will not interfere with the sound of the German bombs that come close enough to cause you to dive under the desk.

There was no dancing in the streets here when the Lend-Lease Act was passed, for the British know from their own experience that the gap between legislation and realization can be very wide. They remember being told that their frontier was on the Rhine, and they know now that their government did very little to keep it there. The course of Anglo-American relations will be smooth on the surface, but many people over here will express regret because they believe America is making the same mistakes that Britain made. For you must understand that the idea of America being of more help as a nonbelligerent than as a fighting ally has been discarded, even by those who advanced it originally. Maybe we shall do some frank, forthright talking across the Atlantic instead of rhetoric, but I doubt it. One thing that is not doubted is that the decisions taken in Washington between now and the time the crops are harvested will determine the pattern of events for a long time to come.

There's still a sense of humor in the country; the old feeling of superiority over all other peoples remains. So does class distinction. There is great courage and a blind belief that Britain will survive.

The British aren't all heroes; they know the feeling of fear; I've shared it with them. They try to avoid thinking deeply about political and social problems. They'll stand any amount of government inefficiency and muddle. They're slow to anger, and they die with great dignity. They will cheer Winston Churchill when he walks through block after block of smashed houses and offices as though he'd brought them a great victory. During a blinding raid when the streets are full of smoke and the sound of the roaring guns, they'll say to you, "Do you think we're really brave, or just lacking in imagination?"

Well, they've come through the winter; they've been warned that the testing days are ahead. Of the past months, they may well say, "We've lived a life, not an apology." And of the future, I think most of them would say, "We shall live hard, but we shall live."

June 22, 1941

> *The British persevered, and Hitler turned East. In* Operation Barbarossa *he planned, optimistically, to cut Russia to pieces in five months. Then it would be England's turn again. Churchill warned that ideology notwithstanding, Russia must be given aid.*

As you know, the Prime Minister made a broadcast this evening. Never before has he been so violent is his denunciation of Hitler, whom he termed a bloodthirsty guttersnipe. Mr. Churchill made a solemn and sober prophecy that there would be misery and famine without equal in history; India and China were next on the Nazi list. He said a thousand million more human beings were menaced.

The Prime Minister brought all his oratorical power to the appeal for aid to the Soviet Union, which he has always hated—and still does. His plea was based on a combination of humanitarian principle and national self-interest. What he implied was that the Russians, after all, are human but the Germans aren't. Russia's danger, he said, is our danger. And he believed that the German plan was to destroy Russia in the shortest possible time and then throw her full weight against Britain in an attempt to crush this island before winter comes. And, reaffirming Britain's determination to destroy the Nazi regime, the Prime Minister promised that there would be no parley and no contract with Hitler and his gang. Any man or state who fights Nazidom will have our help, he said.

The announced policy of His Majesty's Government is to give the Russians all possible technical and economic assistance. Mr. Churchill said nothing about military aid, other than to reaffirm Britain's intention of bombing Germany on an ever-increasing scale. There is no suggestion in London that any direct military aid can, or will, be supplied. It is worth noting that the Prime Minister said nothing about the fighting qualities of the Russian Army and gave no optimistic forecast about the duration of this new German campaign.

A few days ago, Mr. Churchill in a broadcast to the States used the sentence: "But time is short." If Russia is beaten quickly and decisively, time will be much shorter.

> *Before the year was out, Japan precipitated the United States into the war with its attack on Pearl Harbor. Britain now had allies, but their wounds would be grievous. As Murrow expressed it much later, "We were paying for a geography lesson with blood, from Anzio to the Aleutians, Long Stop Hill to Leyte, Oran and Okinawa; Red Beach and red skies over burning cities, boys from Hannibal flying the Hump."*

48

July 12, 1942

The urgent business for the United Nations [*i.e.*, the Allies] is not victory but survival. Russia and China must be kept in the war, the Middle East defended, and somehow the Battle of the Atlantic must be won. About that vital battle we are told next to nothing, but it is clear that we are not winning it and may not even be holding our own. If I were permitted to give you the figures of the British merchant seamen who have lost their lives in this war, and to show you the men in shiny blue serge suits and Derby hats waiting to sign on in Liverpool and Glasgow, it might serve as a partial answer to those who have concluded finally and fecklessly that the British won't fight. The other day a little Scotsman from one of the Western Isles was brought ashore—eighteen days he had had in an open boat. He came down the rope ladder, dodged the port doctor, bought a bottle of whiskey, went to a movie and was at sea again four days later.

There are those who conclude that after the war Britain will go Communist. Such conclusions are hasty and incorrect. There is at the moment a considerable emotional allegiance to Russia. But it is a sentiment that has been swept forward on a tide of gratitude and admiration for the fighting qualities of the Red Army. Never has the ground been better prepared for political propaganda than it has for the Communists in this country by the bloodshed in Russia. In the newsreels and at public meetings, Russia is more loudly cheered than the United States. That's not only because the Russians are killing more Germans. It's because there is a feeling that the Russians are sacrificing more, much more even than the British. What happens in this country after this war will be determined by the United States and by Russia, and certainly by the native caution and political stability of the people of this island. Already there are people here who are concerned about the trend of some of the discussion in America about postwar organization. Anything approaching American economic imperialism would certainly drive this country into radical political and economic experiments in concert with one or more European powers. Alliances are not always lasting, as this war and earlier wars have demonstrated.

Some effort to explain America to the British people might smooth the path of Anglo-American relations now and in the future. But it is so far no part of our government policy to do so. Everyone agrees that there has never been a time when the British have been more anxious and willing to learn about American affairs and institutions, but we do nothing about it. You would find no outspoken anti-American sentiments over here. But the British themselves sat surrounded by their oceans, filled with pride and ignorance, for too long not to resent it when another country adopts the same attitude.

August 30, 1942

Before this weary week wanders off the calendar and its events become the stuff with which historians work, Britain will have ended three years of war. How long is three years? I don't know. It's long enough for people to marry and have children, long enough for a revolution, long enough for small boys to be able to put their elders to shame when it comes to identifying aircraft. And it's plenty of time for big English breakfasts, thick Devonshire cream, good cigarettes and good wine to be lost in the mists of memory. Three years is long enough for you to forget what it was like to be able to buy and drive a new car, buy a new suit of clothes whenever you wanted it and travel whenever you had the money and the inclination. Three years is long enough for schoolboys to grow up and become soldiers but not long enough to permit you to forget the friends who have died. It's plenty of time for empires to change hands, for the reputation of generals to be made and unmade and for the social, economic and political fabric of nations to be ripped to shreds. More damage can be done in three years than can be measured in dollars. Millions of people can be made into slaves; hundreds of thousands may starve or be butchered. There's plenty of time for a civilization to die but not enough for a new one to be born.

Three years, or three hours, is plenty of time to see timid, cautious, careful men and women turned into heroes. After all, it requires only a few months, or even a few weeks, for physical courage to become commonplace; war seems to become almost the normal existence. Americans newly arrived in Britain almost invariably say things aren't the way they expected them to be. There's a casualness, a lack of tension—little feeling of imminent danger or nearness to the enemy. That's because these are a veteran people. Three years of war have done that. But the old spirit that caused the world to watch with a kind of horrified admiration while these people went through their ordeal by fire and high explosive is still here.

Maybe this is a good time to consider what's happened to Britain since that act of mechanized murder was committed against Poland. In the beginning there was a lack of preparation; there was confidence and business as usual. There was much talk about how the steel ring of the navy would starve the Germans into submission. The first shock came with Norway, and it jarred a complacent government out of office. After that came the collapse of France and the miracle at Dunkirk. Then the Battle of Britain, when it seemed the sky was filled with bits and pieces of German aircraft. That was a long time ago. Practically none of the boys who fought that battle are now flying. For a year Britain stood alone, the last that dared to grapple with the foe. Since then, with the exception of actions against the Italians, the record of this war has been one disaster after another, each followed by a debate in the House of Commons, which in turn was followed by a vote of confidence. No amount of talk could overtake the seven years' start the Nazis had. No debate could disguise the fact that there weren't enough Britishers to win this war. And during that entire time I heard no man or woman suggest that the price of continued resistance was too high. Finally the Germans attacked Russia, and Russian resistance startled everyone, including the Germans. Japan attacked the United States, but that brought no end to British reverses. The Far Eastern empire was lost in a hundred days. And later the hard-won gains in Libya were erased by the tracks of Rommel's tanks.

But this is no history of three years of war crowded into a few minutes. We ought to examine Britain's position at the beginning of the fourth year. It would not have been surprising had they sat back and waited for powerful allies to come fully into the fight. But the other morning the news of Dieppe went sweeping through the factories and down into the coal pits. Some believed that it was the opening of a second front. And in one mine at least, production for the day was more than doubled. In the first quarter of this year Britain produced more than two times the volume of army munitions as America did, and about twice the weight of combat aircraft. Out of every one hundred occupied men and women in this country, about fifty-five are working for the government, either in the armed forces, in the factories or in other services. To reach that level America would need almost forty million people working for the government. Britain could not have survived without Lend-Lease, and people here are not likely to forget it. But the minister of production said the other day that Britain has still paid for the greater proportion of what she has received from the United States. Moreover, British orders for aircraft and munitions made it possible for us to start ahead of the game in getting into full production. This country has discovered that money is as nothing compared with sacrifice. It has learned that the prices of essential commodities must be controlled, and that if production is to proceed, both management and labor must accept restrictions. Conscription of women has been demonstrated to be the only equitable and effective means of mobilizing the maximum labor force of the country.

Certainly there is still some cynicism and frustration in this country. It is true that some Englishmen sought refuge in the relative security of the United States, but few here mourned their going. There has certainly been a lamentable lag in adjusting production to conform with the lessons taught on the battlefield. There is, I think, a widespread willingness to accept a more ruthless and exacting direction of the war. The political complexion of the country is uncertain. There has been no general election for seven years, and there are men and women of twenty-eight who have never voted in a general election. The hard core of the Tory Party, which gave Mr. Chamberlain a considerable majority on the day he resigned, still wields decisive power in the House of Commons. The Prime Minister is the titular head of that party, but he is not in the public mind associated with its previous and, in some cases, its present policy.

Much progress has been made in leveling social and economic barriers. Something like 85 per cent of the purchasing power of this country is now in the hands of people making less than two thousand dollars a year. There still exists a full measure of spiritual frustration, with very little indication of the channels into which it may flow. Organized religion has, on the testimony of some of its own leaders, failed to achieve any substantial advance and has in some cases lost ground. Responsible leaders in this country have given up any belief that they might have held that Germany will collapse as a result of anything short of the defeat of her military power.

It would be a bold man who would venture to predict what may happen in the fourth year of the war, but for the British the future is not likely to be fraught with more danger and disappointment than the past. I have seen some of them meet death with dignity, and those who lived refused to give up hope. The coming winter will be the worst that Europe has ever seen. There will be cold and famine and pestilence and despair and degradation. How many more such winters must pass depends to a large extent upon the United States. We are the only people fighting this war with plenty of food, clothing and shelter, with an undamaged productive system that can work in the light. We aren't tired, and Europe is—all of it. We lack the incentive of the imminence of immediate danger. Our sacrifices must be made at long range and in cold blood. We have not had a doorstep demonstration of the one great truth that has brought Britain through years of war and which causes her people to face the future, however dark and dismal it may be, with courage and confidence undiminished. And that truth, learned through bitter experience and from the lips of those who have sought sanctuary on this island, is that free men fear death less than they fear life under the conditions that would be imposed by those who planned and prepared this war.

November 15, 1942

American troops, led by General Eisenhower, landed in North Africa on November 8. Almost simultaneously the British Eighth Army was winning the Battle of El Alamein.

This morning I stood on a London rooftop looking out over the miles of chimney pots and dull grey slate roofs. The air was filled with the sound of church bells—the first time we had heard them in twenty-nine months. The sound was pleasant, although some of the bell ringers were sadly out of practice. As the notes from the bells wandered up the crooked streets and were lost in the cavities where proud buildings once stood, one realized that this war has been going on for a very long time. When the bells were silenced it was announced that they would speak again only to announce invasion. For more than a year the bell ropes were in Hitler's hands. But the church bells of England remained silent. Today they sounded in tribute to the first clear-cut victory over German arms, won on the sands of Egypt.

Standing on that rooftop where I had spent so many nights during the blitz, I realized for the first time the comfort that comes from the homely sound of church bells on a Sunday morning. They seemed to jar the very building as it was often jarred by high explosives when the street below was filled with smoke and the clamor of bells from fire engine and ambulance. This was in a way Thanksgiving Day over here, a day set aside in tribute not only to the Eighth Army but to the civilian defenders of the country who with fire hose and buckets of sand fought the terror that came out of the night sky, and in so doing gained new confidence and dignity. One almost expected to see the smoke-stained banners of Coventry, Plymouth, Hull and all the rest pass by in the street below. But the bells were really being rung to celebrate the victory in Egypt, where American supplies gave weight to Montgomery's hammer, just as the British Navy took the Americans through to North Africa on schedule.

I came down from the roof and asked a man what he thought of the bells, and he replies, "Tempting Providence, that's what it is." The week has been crowded with excellent and astonishing news, but the people of this island, like veteran troops, are not disposed to magnify the importance of the victories won. They realize that it is a long way from Bizerte to Berlin. Brilliant as the achievements have been at both ends of the Mediterranean, it should be remembered that we went to North Africa because we didn't have the stuff to go directly onto the continent of Europe.

The North African campaign has buttressed Winston Churchill's political hold upon this country. It has improved relations with Russia. And the fact that British paratroops have been spilling out of American planes—American Rangers going ashore [in French

North Africa] under the guns of British ships—has given body to the phrase "United Nations." Not since the closing days of the Battle of Britain has a week brought such news. Most of it has been good, but one item was astonishing. That was the announcement that Admiral Darlan is to be in effect high commissioner for French Africa. Let us look at the man's record. On February 10, 1941, he became vice president of the council, secretary of state for foreign affairs, the Interior and the Navy. One of his first acts was to turn over political refugees to the Germans. He began at once to adopt Gestapo methods. His government was responsible for the sending of foreigners, mostly Spanish Republicans, from internment camps in France to slave-gang labor on the Trans-Sahara Railway. He intensified anti-Semitic measures. His police force helped the Germans round up Alsatian refugees in Unoccupied France who were wanted by the Germans. In July, his government practically turned over Indo-China to the Japanese, thereby opening the back door to Singapore. And now this man is given political dominion over North Africa, with American support.

The British press and radio, acting under guidance, take the line that for the time being military considerations dominate. One can only wonder if this answer would impress the Fighting French who died trying to stop Rommel's advance at Bir Hacheim. And one wonders whether or not we may stand dishonored in the eyes of the conquered peoples on the Continent. This is a matter of high principle in which we carry a great moral burden which we cannot escape. Wherever American forces go they will carry with them food and money and power, and the Quislings will rally to our side if we permit it. This decision about Darlan was, I believe, a political decision, and it has puzzled many people here. General Eisenhower did not go to North Africa as a politician. He was sent to occupy certain territory and to carry out certain military operations, which he has done. But some at least of his political advisers have been consistently sympathetic with the Vichy regime.

We have made a choice in North Africa. It may or may not have been dictated by military necessity. But there is nothing in the strategic position of the allies to indicate that we are either so strong or so weak that we can afford to ignore the principles for which this war is being fought.

December 13, 1942

One of the nice things about talking from London on Sunday night is that one can sit down, review the events of the week, study the reports coming in from all over the world, and then talk about whatever seems interesting. Sometimes it's like putting letters in a hollow log or talking to yourself in a dark room. But tonight it's a little different. One is almost stunned into silence by some of the information reaching London. Some of it is months old, but it's eye-witness stuff supported by a wealth of detail and vouched for by responsible governments. What is happening is this: Millions of human beings, most of them Jews, are being gathered up with ruthless efficiency and murdered.

Some of you will remember the days when we used to bring you broadcasts from Vienna, from Warsaw and from all the other capitals of Europe. Now from that continent there is only silence, but still the information gets out. And when you piece it all together— from Holland and Norway, from Poland—you have a picture of mass murder and moral depravity unequaled in the history of the world. It is a horror beyond what imagination can grasp.

Let me tell you a little about what's happened in the Warsaw ghetto. It was never a pleasant place even in peacetime. The business started in the middle of July. Ten thousand people were rounded up and shipped off. After that, thousands more went each day. The infirm, the old and the crippled were killed in their homes. Some of them were driven to the Jewish cemetery, and they killed them there. The others were put in freight cars; the floors were covered with quicklime and chlorine. Those who survived the journey were dumped out at one of three camps, where they were killed. At a place called Treblinka a huge bulldozer is used to bury the bodies. Since the middle of July these deportations from the Warsaw ghetto have been going on. For the month of September 120,-000 ration cards were printed for the ghetto; for October only 40,000. The Jews are being systematically exterminated throughout all Poland. Nobody knows how many have committed suicide; nor does anyone know how many have gone mad. Some of the victims ask their guards to shoot them, and sometimes the guards demand a special fee for doing so. All this information and much more is contained in an official report issued by the Polish government. And few people who have talked as I have with people who have escaped from Poland will doubt its accuracy. The phrase "concentration camps" is obsolete, as out of date as "economic sanctions" or "non-recognition." It is now possible to speak only of extermination camps.

Information coming out of Holland proves that each week four thousand Dutchmen are being sent to Poland, and that is no guess. It is based upon one of the best secret service organizations in Europe. Do you remember the "state of emergency" declared in the Trondheim area of Norway in October? Detailed and documented information about it has now reached the Norwegian government in London. At noon on October 6, the German dictator of Norway and his Gestapo chief drove through the town of Trondheim, together with police on motorcycles with mounted machine guns. At eight o'clock that night the local radio announced that ten hostages had been shot. The ten men heard of their own death over the radio, for they were not in fact shot until the following morning. At Falstad concentration camp, Russian prisoners of war were made to dig an open grave. No one knew who was to be killed. Then at eight o'clock in the morning a group of fifteen men were brought out and ordered to stand at attention. They stood there for eleven and a half hours until 7:30 in the evening. Then they were invited to listen to the announcement of their deaths. The following day they were taken to the edge of the big grave, stripped naked and shot.

It seems that the Germans hope to escape retribution by the sheer magnitude of their crimes. They are exterminating the Jews and the potential leaders of the subject people with ruthless efficiency. That is why newspapers, individuals and spokesmen of the Church in this country are demanding that the government make a solemn statement that retribution will be dealt out to those responsible for the cold-blooded massacre of Jews in Poland. The Archbishop of York insists that there shall be punishment, not only for those who gave the orders, but also for the underlings who seem to be gladly carrying them out.

57

December 27, 1942

Thus ends the first year of global war. Last December the whole world became one vast battlefield, a contest between the two greatest military coalitions known to history. A year ago all the separate wars became one, and the two groups of powers began to plan and practice world strategy. Germany and Japan were to link up across the Indian Ocean, and for a while their chances looked good; but they allowed themselves to be diverted from their primary objective. The Japanese tried for Australia and for India, and failed in both places. The Germans drove for Suez with the Afrika Korps, threw one army across the Don against Stalingrad and another into the Caucasus, and today all three are gravely threatened. They might have achieved victory in one or even two theaters. But they divided their forces, overreached themselves, and are now everywhere on the defensive.

While the Axis, east and west, tried to do too much too quickly, the Allies held their hand in the face of a rising clamor for action. The fact that we were not led into some premature diversionary move and the fact that the Russians agreed, however reluctantly, to that policy are impressive evidence of the strength of the Allied coalition. The military planning of the North African campaign—both ends of it—was carried out by men who worked harder and in closer harmony than has ever before been achieved. And when our men and the British set out in that great convoy, the oceans must have been proud to bear them. There were differences of opinion between London and Washington over our handling of the political situation in North Africa—there may well be similar divergence of views in the future—but nothing has happened to diminish British confidence in the military leadership of General "Ike" Eisenhower. There was no criticism of his appointment, and there has been none of his conduct of operations. The fact—and it is a fact—that Eisenhower, commanding land, sea and air in the biggest combined operation, continues to enjoy the respect and confidence of the British is a definite item on the credit side of the ledger. So is the steadily rising curve of manpower and production of the Allies.

Here in Britain the first year of global war has produced many changes. The Luftwaffe has been employed elsewhere, and that has meant an almost complete absence of raids. British factories and shipyards have had to contend with the blackout but not with bombs. Civilian consumer goods have gradually disappeared from the shops; more millions of women have gone into industry or into the armed forces; the draft age has been lowered to eighteen; people are more tired and less well-dressed. Traveling is more difficult, food more monotonous, but everyone is working. There is plenty of money, even if there isn't much to spend it on. People appear cheerful and confident. In cities that were derelict and dying you never see a beggar on the street. Movies and theaters are full; more books are being read. In other words, wartime existence has come to seem almost normal. Curiosity about America has grown by leaps and bounds; any American over here could spend his whole time lecturing about home. American expressions are becoming part of the common currency of English speech. A year ago you seldom saw an English girl chewing gum; now if you visit a town where American troops are stationed, the girls seem to be chewing as though trying to make up for lost years. The first year of global war brought the Americans to Britain, and the place will never be the same again.

As the year ends more people are thinking about the future. The governments in exile are making estimates of the food, medicine and raw material required to rehabilitate their countries. Some of them, but not all, may be hoping to ride back to power on Allied food trains. What happens in the liberated countries will be largely decided by the United States. Many of the weapons and men that free them will be American. Most of the food that will feed them will be American; most of the merchantmen carrying the stuff will fly the Stars and Stripes.

I believe that any American who watched the first year of global war from London would have at the end of it one dominant impression, and that would be the power and responsibility of his own country. It is fashionable, and probably true, to speak of this war as a revolution. When the French made their revolution more than a hundred years ago, they hoped to regulate the destiny of nations and found the liberty of the world. That is the task that now confronts America and her allies.

A little more than a year ago I stood in that crowded room under the big dome in Washington and heard the President ask for a declaration of war. And as I watched those men and women, as I had watched other men and women in London more than two years before trying so hard to be casual while making history, I realized that Congress had decreed the freedom of the world. We are yet far from achieving it. On occasion we have done less than our allies expected. But we have done more than our enemies believed possible. We have not fought and suffered as the Russians, nor have we sacrificed as the British, but we have brought hope and confidence to a world that was waiting. The years of trial may be many, but the sunrise gates of fulfillment are opening before us. Thus ends the first year of global war.

April 11, 1943

This is Edward Murrow at Allied Force Headquarters, North Africa. To reach the front you fly for hours over country of infinite variety, over what might be the Badlands of the Dakotas cut by valleys as rich and green as the Willamette. Then again you can imagine yourself high above the Blue Ridge or the Cascade Mountains. For hours you look down at winding roads and the railroad clinging to the side of the mountains, and you begin to realize that the problem of getting men and material up to that northern front is much tougher than you had thought.

The plane finally touches down at an advance airdrome. You climb into a car, drive x number of miles and bed down in an olive grove. You lie there till midnight. The ground trembles as the big trucks loaded with ammunition, gasoline and food drop down into second gear for the long pull to the top of the pass and you think of young boys pushing heavy transports over that road where Roman legions marched more than fifteen hundred years ago. At one in the morning you roll out of your blankets and start for the front. It's dark and cold; the road might be in New Mexico. The sky is clear and the stars seem to come down to the very top of a ragged stone mountain off to the right. A shooting star stencils its way across the heavens and the driver remarks, "Whenever there is a shooting star a baby is born." And he adds, "My wife is having a baby in Glasgow next week, would you take her a letter when you go back?"

Under the scrubby little trees beside the road you can see the ambulance drivers stripping the camouflage nets from their vehicles, getting ready to move up. The order is given to turn out all lights. You pull up beside the road and watch the long lines of trucks and ambulances glide forward. They have no headlights, no tail lights, only one small white light hitting the road directly under the rear axle. The wheels scarcely seem to touch the ground. The whole long line is supported by those little white lights. A truck pulls up alongside to ask directions. From the back comes heavy snoring—it's loaded with German prisoners. Someone suggests it might be a good idea to talk with them, but the sergeant driving the truck says, "Let the poor unmentionables sleep, they're tired."

You drive on and reach a point a couple of miles behind the British gun positions. You climb a hill. It is 3:30 on Wednesday morning. Twenty minutes later a trail of chain lightning seems to run along the ground, stretching for five miles on either side of you; the barrage opening the British attack is under way. It is designed to clear the high ground north and west of the road running to Medjez El Bab. The German reply is not long delayed; in four minutes you see their shrapnel bursting over the British guns. Along the whole front the guns rave and roar, more than a hundred of them. Up on the left the twenty-five-pounders are being worked so fast that a steady stream of fire seems to fan out towards the German positions across the valley. The infantry moved off at 4 a.m. to face mines, mortar fire and heavy machine guns firing on fixed lines. A quarter of an hour later the first green Very light plopped in the night sky; that meant someone had reached somewhere. The Germans filled the sky with flares; the red, blue and green signal lights kept drifting in the slight breeze above the valley. It was cold—you shiver—but it isn't that cold. The attack is making progress, and later you'll learn that the whole ridge overlooking the road has been cleared, more than a thousand prisoners taken.

You decide to go back to camp. The road winds white before you, the edge of the rising sun touches the fields and the ambulances going toward the front. There are dead and wounded men in the valley behind you. To get down to the other part of the front you drive through country that pleases neither the mind nor the eye, a country fit only for fighting. And as you approach Pichon and the

61

valley leading down to Fondouk, it gets worse. There is a cold, cutting wind. When the clouds hit the mountain tops you expect them to make a noise. There is dust and cactus and thorn bushes and bad roads. It is a cold country with a hot sun. Tanks and trucks have cut through the dust and left bare rock exposed; a dispatch rider is thrown from his motorcycle and its wheels spin in the air. Everything is covered with that white, tired dust; men's red-rimmed eyes look like smoldering holes in a grey blanket. The dust blows from right to left. You begin to meet ambulances coming back. They are taking the dust as drivers nurse them carefully over those terrible roads. You can see them lift on the wheel, trying to ease the shock for the wounded back behind.

If you had gone into the little town of Pichon a few hours after it had been retaken, here are a few things you would have noticed. A fairly good road leading down to a stream. It is pockmarked with holes where the sappers have removed landmines. A batch of Austrian prisoners being herded along. They are obviously well fed, but their shoes are not good. They don't look particularly sullen, just tired. Where the road cuts down to meet the stream there is a knocked-out tank, two dead men beside it and two more digging a grave. A little farther along a German soldier sits smiling against the bank. He is covered with dust and he is dead. On the rising ground beyond a young British lieutenant lies with his head on his arm as though shielding himself from the wind. He is dead, too. Near him is a German antitank gun, its muzzle pointing at the sky. Pichon itself is a miserable dirty little town with a few whitewashed houses, their sides scarred and chipped with machine-gun bullets. Much of the firing was high. The Germans seem to have taken with them every piece of removable metal, including door knobs.

No one seems to doubt that we shall have to throw the Germans out of here—they aren't going to cut and run. The other day I saw a long line of tank carriers moving over narrow mountain roads, through country covered with cork trees. They looked grand, each tank on a trailer wearing twenty-four rubber tires and the truck pulling it had ten tires and I thought that's where the tires of American automobiles have gone. Then I remembered the hundreds of miles those tanks must travel before they moved against the enemy under their own power. It's not an easy problem. But I do wish that the people who make those Sherman tanks could see

62

them when they charge through a field of cactus, could see the boys driving them, how they look out through the slot like schoolboys who should be riding their first bicycle with a coaster brake.

May 16, 1943

London witnessed a parade of heroic irregulars—the doughty Home Guard.

Some of the women wore wooden-soled shoes. They were dressed in the spring clothes that were new four or five years ago; many of them had those cheap silver fox furs slung slantwise across their shoulders like a bandolier. The hats were, and ever have been, indescribable. The men, most of them, wore the summer civilian uniform—grey flannel trousers and well-worn tweed coat. There were a few children. The crowd formed a thin, unsteady fence on each side of the street. There was little animation in the faces. But it was a crowd waiting for a parade; there was no question about that.

Dim and distant down the dingy street there came the sound of an uncertain brass band; some of the notes seemed to stagger into the blasted and gutted buildings as they traveled up the street. Five London policemen came into view. They were riding white horses. Behind them came an impressive demonstration of the strength of England. For forty minutes it flowed past. Perhaps "flow" isn't just the right word, for there were some ripples in the ranks of the Home Guard. They didn't march like American Marines or like British Guardsmen, but the sight was impressive and no rifles were dropped.

There were some fine faces there, the kind you see in the old prints of the men who came to America—lean and long-jawed with steady eyes. Some of them were pale from too much time behind desks; others were browned by sun and wind. There were men who looked like stevedores and men who were obviously City brokers. There were faces wearing the scars of the last war.

It was a military parade all right, but the men taking part have been doing their essential civilian jobs, devoting their one day a week to training, fighting mock battles on golf courses, firing on the

63

range (now that there is ammunition to spare), spending long nights on lonesome moors watching for the parachutists that haven't come. There was a story, after Dunkirk, that a member of the Home Guard was asked by a regular what the Home Guard was supposed to do. He replied, "You fellows have evacuated so many places, we have been formed to see you don't leave England." Whenever the regulars are ready to leave for the Continent again, the Home Guard will be here to replace them.

May 24, 1943

It is of the utmost importance that we understand one thing about the political complexion of Europe. There is little appetite to go back to where they were. There is a certain "sense of guilt" about the systems that didn't work. There is bound to be a demand for more control of industry and of finance, more security for the state and for the individual. It isn't possible to predict that will happen, but the evidence is overwhelming—everyone who comes out of Europe confirms it, that there will be no return to the old order unless the Allies try to reimpose it. The old allegiances, like the old institutions, have gone. That's true to a certain extent in this country. It is astonishing the number of people who say to you, "I was a member of the Labor Party" or "I was a Conservative." Now they aren't sure what they are.

The passing of the Comintern won't make Communism on the Continent either more or less likely, and it won't reduce the chances of revolution when the war is over. We are committed to certain broad and fundamental policies; they were stated in the Atlantic Charter and they still stand. We have said there will be no territorial changes which do not accord with the freely expressed wishes of the people concerned—all people to choose the form of government under which they will live, victors and vanquished, great and small, to have access on equal terms to the trade and to the raw materials of the world which are needed for their economic prosperity. And we have promised the disarmament of all aggressor nations pending the establishment of a permanent system of security. These broad and sweeping principles we have promised to apply when we have secured the unconditional surrender of our enemies.

64

It will not be easy. It is not true that war settles nothing. But it is true that victory isn't going to settle the old problems of Europe; it will merely provide a chance to settle them. Take the example of East Prussia and Danzig. A pretty strong case has been made for their transfer to Poland, but the inhabitants of those territories could invoke the Atlantic Charter against any such action.

The peace isn't going to be plain sailing. But what happens to Allied adherence to principles, not by whether the Comintern is Europe, whether it moves to the right or left, will be determined by liquidated. Communism is an item for export; so is democracy. The two are bound to compete. The realization of that fact is the basis of German propaganda, and it is also the basis of the Allied efforts to reach agreement with Russia about matters other than those directly connected with killing Germans. People who have had much talk with Stalin tell me that he isn't interested in acquiring more territory, or in the spread of his version of Communism. But Russia's neighbor nations aren't so sure about that. They would like to learn that Britain and America had come to some agreement with Russia which would insure them that they could, in fact, count on the blessings promised in the Atlantic Charter.

July 11, 1943

These are memories of a great ship, her voyage from a port somewhere in the United States to another port in Great Britain. In wartime it's forbidden to do much talking about ships; I can't even tell you her name, the port from which she cleared, or the place and time where passengers disembarked. But such things aren't very important. It is important only that a troop transport shall arrive and that the men shall be landed with dry feet.

A troop transport is like a community built to house and feed and sleep, say, three thousand people. The community must now hold fifteen thousand men; its size can't be increased. The men must be fed, and they must have a place to sleep. And the whole community must be moved across the Atlantic; naturally things are crowded. As you stand on the deck watching those long lines of brown, bent figures come aboard, it's like one of those old movies where twenty men emerge from a single taxicab; it seems that the ship must burst her sides, or the men must spill into the harbor. Even to one

65

who has done some traveling on crowded cruise ships the thing seems impossible; someone must have made a mistake, forgot to give the order to stop that long twisting line of boys coming aboard, bent double under field packs and barrack bags.

There is no noise, only the sound of shuffling feet; and when the line stops for a moment you can hear soft sighs as they ease the packs to a new position. One private reaches inside his shirt to adjust two sponges he has placed so they will keep the straps from cutting into his shoulders, and you think, "That private will be a sergeant soon." You walk up to the boat deck and lean on the rail beside a big corporal who has Iowa written all over him. He looks down at the oil-streaked water wandering along the port side of the gray-painted ship. He turns to you and says, "Man, it's higher than the silo back home."

There is no smoking during the embarkation. You wander down into the maze of decks and corridors. The long lines are twisting about down there, the whole inside of the ship seems to writhe. You notice that the cabins have been stripped—no running water, triple-decker bunks. The partitions between staterooms have been torn out; everything has been done to make more room. The ship is a mere shell filled with men. She is being double loaded. That means that the men will have twenty-four hours below decks with some kind of bed, then they will have twenty-four hours without any bed. You stop and talk with an M.P. stationed at the head of a flight of stairs. He says, "Sure would like to catch someone smoking." You ask what he'd do if he did. He grins and says, "Just stand and inhale the smoke for a bit, and then take him to the lieutenant, who'd probably show him where they peel potatoes."

The long lines keep moving. There are numbers chalked on every man's helmet, and the faces beneath them are frozen with fatigue. One man drops his duffle bag and it splits open; he looks down at it, the contents spilling out onto the floor, and sighs, "For a minute I didn't know whether it was me or the barracks bag what split open." Finally, as happens with all ships, the gangplanks were pulled ashore and the great ship eased away from the pier. As the lights of the city faded astern you hear a boy who must have come from the Texas panhandle say, "Never liked that place much anyhow." There is no cheering, no singing, no bands, and no crowds to see the boys off.

When we are clear of the harbor, the loud-speakers located all over the ship come to life. A steady confident voice from Scotland talks to all officers and other ranks. It's the staff captain of the ship. You know at once that he's spent his life at sea, knows what he's doing. He welcomes everyone to the ship, regrets that it can't be under more pleasant circumstances, appreciates the conditions under which we will live, but war is no respecter of persons and every ship we possess must be used to its fullest capacity. He goes on: "I am well aware that the ship is crowded, but you will, I hope, have two reasonable meals per day and somewhere to sleep." The staff captain reminds them that they are no longer in a safe area—enemy attack may come at any time—but if it does, it must not find us unprepared. He tells them that the ship is equipped with every modern safety device; she has crossed the ocean many times in safety. Even one glowing cigarette, carelessly smoked on an open deck at night, may bring attack from an unseen enemy vessel. After all, lights do not grow upon the ocean. All ports and windows must remain closed and secured during blackout hours. The orders for emergency stations are explained and a practice muster is held. When the men have all found their stations, the staff captain chuckles through the loud-speaker and says, "You did that so well that as soon as you've had some food we'll do it again."

By the end of the first day out the ship begins to settle down, but it's still crowded. A warrant officer remarks he thinks he'll go and see the dentist. Someone says, "Trouble with your teeth?" And he says, "Not a bit, but they tell me the dentist's chair is the only place on this boat where you can sit down!" You ease up and listen to a red-headed corporal talking to his squad. He has them well forward on the promenade deck and you hear him say, "Look fellows, this whole thing is just like crossing the street." The siren sounds for boat drill, and a young citizen from Pittsburgh says, "Sounds just like the factory whistle back home." He's a trifle homesick. You stand on one deck looking down at another, the men are standing closer than the pickets on a fence. The soldier beside you says, "Anybody who gets a sunburn on this ship will have to be bald-headed. There isn't room to turn your face up!"

There is much talk of where we are going. After x number of days they tell us officially we are going to England. There was much talk about what wives or mothers would say when they heard we were overseas. We saw some whales and then some porpoises, and there were rumors about submarines. After a couple of days there was singing—lots of it—mostly old songs. The singing swept round the ship like a crown fire in the western woods. The guitars and banjos and saxophones came up on the deck. Forward, she was coming round the mountain; amidships, down on B deck, she was on the sidewalks of New York; on the deck below she was truly loved, while aft two boys dolefully avowed their love for the little brown jug. By the way, the ship was dry—no beer, no whiskey. But there were two stout meals every day. There was plenty of gambling, and the stakes were high. But there were plenty of boys who thought it wasn't so smart to put your month's salary on a pair of dice. Once I saw eight straight passes made, which is something to see on a troop ship, or anywhere else for that matter.

These boys on this ship were just like they are at home. They argued the relative merits of California and Pennsylvania—they came from all over the country—and their names were English, Dutch, Scandinavian, Polish and all the rest. They endured considerable discomfort, and they did it without complaining. They slept on the floor in the corridors when their buddies had their twenty-four hours below in the bunks. You could see them any night, sprawled out like khaki-clothed dolls thrown aside by some petulant child. Sometimes they smiled in their sleep; at other times they were expressionless and relaxed—like dead soldiers I have seen. During their waking hours they wanted to talk about England: What would the weather and the girls be like? Could they get any food when they were on leave? And what would they do about this English tea and warm beer?

Shortly before we landed, the pictures of folks at home began to appear. By that time home was a long way away and hearts were turning west again. These boys with whom I crossed the Atlantic are not to be described. They were healthy; they were curious and courageous. The discipline was excellent. There were no heroics; the boys were serious, and they seemed to know more of what this war is all about than did the men in North Africa. We sat and talked about everything. One second lieutenant, talking about politics at home, remarked, "It's all a matter of perspective, whether you are interested in the next election or the next generation." When we saw Britain's shore, the hills were green; there were white

68

sheep on the hills and white clouds overhead. A soldier from California said, "Boy, that's a nice piece of real estate." A Scotsman standing beside him answered, "Aye, we've spent a thousand years improving it."

The long lines moved out of the ship. The men looked more confident than when they came aboard. After all, they had crossed the big ocean, hadn't been seasick, and the big adventure was beginning. There was a band playing on the quayside. The troop trains were waiting. The Red Cross was there with tea and doughnuts. The men started stowing their baggage aboard the train. Pockets were stuffed with chocolate for British kids. The band was playing "It's a Long Way to Tipperary." As the men stood in line waiting to go aboard the train, I heard one say, "I'm going to write my mother and tell her I crossed the ocean standing in line!" Finally the lines quivered and moved. The commands were crisp, not loud. The men went aboard and flopped into their seats. The engine gave a little toot, and the train began to roll.

I stood on the platform with a British friend and watched car after car slide past. Every window was filled with brown, grinning faces. It seemed to me that the whole of America was on that train. The faces were from the mountains of West Virginia, from the Far West coast. There were Negroes and Indians, Swedes, Poles and Italians. As the train gathered speed the windows were filled with a blur of brown faces, white teeth and close-cropped hair. My British friend remarked, "*There* is a grand advertisement for your country." A snatch of song floated out of the last car, something about "the second lieutenants would win the war, so what the hell are we doing here." I turned and looked at that great ship lying in the harbor. The men were still coming ashore. Looking down at those brown tin hats was like looking down from a second-story window at the cobblestones on a street. I hope never again to cross in that ship. Someday, if she lives, she will be luxurious. There will be thick carpets, richly decorated staterooms, soft music and good service. There will be men in evening clothes and women in elaborate dresses. But for me that ship will always carry the ghosts of men who slept on the floor, ate out of mess tins twice a day, carried their lifebelts with them night and day—the ghosts of men and boys who crossed the ocean to risk their lives as casually as they would cross the street at home.

The unnamed ship in this broadcast was the Queen Elizabeth. *Murrow did cross the Atlantic on one of the Queens
after the war, but it was the* Queen Mary.

December 3, 1943

*Before dawn on December 3, 1943, Murrow returned to
England from a bombing mission over Berlin. The same
afternoon he reported the flight by short wave to America.*

Yesterday afternoon, the waiting was over. The weather was right;
the target was to be the big city. The crew captains walked into the
briefing room, looked at the maps and charts and sat down with
their big celluloid pads on their knees. The atmosphere was that of
a school and a church. The weatherman gave us the weather. The
pilots were reminded that Berlin is Germany's greatest center of
war production. The intelligence officer told us how many heavy
and light ack-ack guns, how many searchlights we might expect to
encounter. Then Jock, the wing commander, explained the system
of markings, the kind of flare that would be used by the Path-
finders. He said that concentration was the secret of success in these
raids, that as long as the aircraft stayed well bunched, they would
protect each other. The captains of aircraft walked out.

I noticed that the big Canadian with the slow, easy grin had
printed "Berlin" at the top of his pad and then embellished it with
a scroll. The red-headed English boy with the two weeks' old moustache was the last to leave the room. Late in the afternoon we
went to the locker room to draw parachutes, Mae Wests and all the
rest. As we dressed, a couple of the Australians were whistling.
Walking out to the bus that was to take us to the aircraft, I heard
the station loud-speakers announcing that that evening all personnel would be able to see a film, *Star Spangled Rhythm,* free.

We went out and stood around a big, black, four-motored Lancaster *D for Dog.* A small station wagon delivered a thermos bottle
of coffee, chewing gum, an orange and a bit of chocolate for each
man. Up in that part of England the air hums and throbs with the
sound of aircraft motors all day. But for half an hour before take-
off, the skies are dead, silent and expectant. A lone hawk hovered

over the airfield, absolutely still as he faced into the wind. Jack, the tail gunner, said, "It would be nice if *we* could fly like that."

D for Dog eased around the perimeter track to the end of the runway. We sat there for a moment. The green light flashed and we were rolling—ten seconds ahead of schedule! The take-off was smooth as silk. The wheels came up, and *D-Dog* started the long climb. As we came up through the clouds, I looked right and left and counted fourteen black Lancasters climbing for the place where men must burn oxygen to live. The sun was going down, and its red glow made rivers and lakes of fire on tops of the clouds. Down to the southward, the clouds piled up to form castles, battlements and whole cities, all tinged with red.

Soon we were out over the North Sea. Dave, the navigator, asked Jock if he couldn't make a little more speed. We were nearly two minutes late. By this time we were all using oxygen. The talk on the intercom was brief and crisp. Everyone sounded relaxed. For a while the eight of us in our little world in exile moved over the sea. There was a quarter moon on the starboard beam. Jock's quiet voice came through the intercom, "That'll be flak ahead." We were approaching the enemy coast. The flak looked like a cigarette lighter in a dark room—one that won't light. Sparks but no flame. The sparks crackling just above the level of the cloud tops. We flew steady and straight, and soon the flak was directly below us.

D-Dog rocked a little from right to left, but that wasn't caused by the flak. We were in the slip stream of other Lancasters ahead, and we were over the enemy coast. And then a strange thing happened. The aircraft seemed to grow smaller. Jack in the rear turret, Wally, the mid-upper gunner; Titch, the wireless operator—all seemed somehow to draw closer to Jock in the cockpit. It was as though each man's shoulder was against the other's. The understanding was complete. The intercom came to life, and Jock said, "Two aircraft on the port beam." Jack in the tail said, "Okay, sir, they're Lancs." The whole crew was a unit and wasn't wasting words.

The cloud below was ten tenths. The blue-green jet of the exhausts licked back along the leading edge, and there were other aircraft all around us. The whole great aerial armada was hurtling towards Berlin. We flew so for twenty minutes, when Jock looked up at a vapor trail curling across above us, remarking in a conversational tone that from the look of it he thought there was a fighter up there. Occasionally the angry red of ack-ack burst through the clouds, but it was far away, and we took only an academic interest. We were flying in the third wave. Jock asked Wally in the mid-upper turret and Jack in the rear turret if they were cold. They said they were all right, and thanked him for asking. Even asked how I was, and I said, "All right so far." The cloud was beginning to thin out. Up to the north we could see light, and the flak began to liven up ahead of it.

Boz, the bomb aimer, crackled through on the intercom, "There's a battle going on on the starboard beam." We couldn't see the aircraft, but we could see the jets of red tracer being exchanged. Suddenly there was a burst of yellow flame, and Jock remarked, "That's a fighter going down. Note the position." The whole thing was interesting, but remote. Dave, the navigator, who was sitting back with his maps, charts and compasses, said, "The attack ought to begin in exactly two minutes." We were still over the clouds. But suddenly those dirty gray clouds turned white. We were over the outer searchlight defenses. The clouds below us were white, and we were black. *D-Dog* seemed like a black bug on a white sheet. The flak began coming up, but none of it close. We were still a long way from Berlin. I didn't realize just how far.

Jock observed, "There's a kite on fire dead ahead." It was a great golden, slow-moving meteor slanting toward the earth. By this time we were about thirty miles from our target area in Berlin. That thirty miles was the longest flight I have ever made. Dead on time, Boz, the bomb aimer, reported, "Target indicators going down." The same moment the sky ahead was lit up by bright yellow flares. Off to starboard, another kite went down in flames. The flares were sprouting all over the sky—reds and greens and yellows—and we were flying straight for the center of the fireworks. *D-Dog* seemed to be standing still, the four propellers thrashing the air. But we didn't seem to be closing in. The clouds had cleared, and off to the starboard a Lanc was caught by at least fourteen searchlight beams. We could see him twist and turn and finally break out. But still the whole thing had a quality of unreality about it. No one seemed to be shooting at us, but it was getting lighter all the time. Suddenly a tremendous big blob of yellow light appeared dead ahead, another to the right and another to the left. We were flying straight for them.

Jock pointed out to me the dummy fires and flares to right and left. But we kept going in. Dead ahead there was a whole chain of red flares looking like stop lights. Another Lanc was coned on our starboard beam. The lights seemed to be supporting it. Again we could see those little bubbles of colored lead driving at it from two sides. The German fighters were at him. And then, with no warning at all, *D-Dog* was filled with an unhealthy white light. I was standing just behind Jock and could see all the seams on the wings. His quiet Scots voice beat into my ears, "Steady, lads, we've been coned." His slender body lifted half out of his seat as he jammed the control column forward and to the left. We were going down.

Jock was wearing woolen gloves with the fingers cut off. I could see his fingernails turn white as he gripped the wheel. And then I was on my knees, flat on the deck, for he had whipped the *Dog* back into a climbing turn. The knees should have been strong enough to support me, but they weren't, and the stomach seemed in some danger of letting me down, too. I picked myself up and looked out again. It seemed that one big searchlight, instead of being twenty thousand feet below, was mounted right on our wing tip. *D-Dog* was corkscrewing. As we rolled down on the other side, I began to see what was happening to Berlin.

The clouds were gone, and the sticks of incendiaries from the preceding waves made the place look like a badly laid out city with the street lights on. The small incendiaries was going down like a fistful of white rice thrown on a piece of black velvet. As Jock hauled the *Dog* up again, I was thrown to the other side of the cockpit, and there below were more incendiaries, glowing white and then turning red. The cookies—the four-thousand-pound high explosives—were bursting below like great sunflowers gone mad. And then, as we started down again, still held in the lights, I remembered that the *Dog* still had one of those cookies and a whole basket of incendiaries in his belly, and the lights still held us. And I was very frightened.

While Jock was flinging him about in the air, he suddenly flung over the intercom, "Two aircraft on the port beam." I looked astern and saw Wally, the mid-upper, whip his turret around to port and then look up to see a single-engined fighter slide just above us. The other aircraft was one of ours. Finally, we were out of the cone, flying level. I looked down, and the white fires had turned red. They

73

were beginning to merge and spread, just like butter does on a hot plate. Jock and Boz, the bomb aimer, began to discuss the target. The smoke was getting thick down below. Boz said he liked the two green flares on the ground almost dead ahead. He began calling his directions. And just then a new bunch of big flares went down on the far side of the sea of flame and flare that seemed to be directly below us. He thought that would be a better aiming point. Jock agreed, and we flew on. The bomb doors were open. Boz called his directions, "Five left, five left." And then there was a gentle, confident, upward thrust under my feet, and Boz said, "Cookie gone." A few seconds later, the incendiaries went, and *D-Dog* seemed lighter and easier to handle.

I thought I could make out the outline of streets below. But the bomb aimer didn't agree, and he ought to know. By this time all those patches of white on black had turned yellow and started to flow together. Another searchlight caught us but didn't hold us. Then through the intercom came the word, "One can of incendiaries didn't clear. We're still carrying it." And Jock replied, "Is it a big one or a little one?" The word came back, "Little one, I think, but I'm not sure. I'll check." More of those yellow flares came down and hung about us. I haven't seen so much light since the war began. Finally the intercom announced that it was only a small container of incendiaries left, and Jock remarked, "Well, it's hardly worth going back and doing another run-up for that." If there had been a good fat bundle left, he would have gone back through that stuff and done it all over again.

I began to breathe and to reflect again—that all men would be brave if only they could leave their stomachs at home. Then there was a tremendous whoomp, an unintelligible shout from the tail gunner, and *D-Dog* shivered and lost altitude. I looked at the port side, and there was a Lancaster that seemed close enough to touch. He had whipped straight under us, missed us by twenty-five, fifty feet, no one knew how much. The navigator sang out the new course, and we were heading for home. Jock was doing what I had heard him tell his pilots to do so often—flying dead on course. He flew straight into a huge green searchlight and, as he rammed the throttles home, remarked, "We'll have a little trouble getting away from this one." And again *D-Dog* dove, climbed and twisted and was finally free. We flew level then. I looked on the port beam at the target area. There was a sullen, obscene glare. The fires seemed to have found each other—and we were heading home.

For a little while it was smooth sailing. We saw more battles. Then another plane in flames, but no one could tell whether it was ours or theirs. We were still near the target. Dave, the navigator, said, "Hold her steady, skipper. I want to get an astral site." And Jock held her steady. And the flak began coming up at us. It seemed to be very close. It was winking off both wings. But the *Dog* was steady. Finally Dave said, "Okay, skipper, thank you very much." And a great orange blob of flak smacked up straight in front of us. And Jock said, "I think they're shooting at us." I'd thought so for some time.

And he began to throw *D for Dog* up, around and about again. And when we were clear of the barrage, I asked him how close the bursts were and he said, "Not very close. When they're really near, you can smell 'em." That proved nothing, for I'd been holding my breath. Jack sang out from the rear turret, said his oxygen was getting low, thought maybe the lead had frozen. Titch, the wireless operator, went scrambling back with a new mask and a bottle of oxygen. Dave, the navigator, said, "We're crossing the coast." My mind went back to the time I had crossed that coast in 1938, in a plane that had taken off from Prague. Just ahead of me sat two refugees from Vienna—an old man and his wife. The co-pilot came back and told them that we were outside German territory. The old man reached out and grasped his wife's hand. The work that was done last night was a massive blow of retribution for all those who have fled from the sound of shots and blows on the stricken Continent.

We began to lose height over the North Sea. We were over England's shore. The land was dark beneath us. Somewhere down there below American boys were probably bombing-up Fortresses and Liberators, getting ready for the day's work. We were over the home field. We called the control tower, and the calm, clear voice of an English girl replied, "Greetings, *D-Dog.* You are diverted to Mule Bag." [Code for an airfield.] We swung around, contacted Mule Bag, came in on the flare path, touched down very gently, ran along to the end of the runway and turned left. And Jock, the finest pilot in Bomber Command, said to the control tower, "*D-Dog* clear of runway."

When we went in for interrogation, I looked on the board and saw that the big, slow-smiling Canadian and the red-headed English boy with the two weeks' old moustache hadn't made it. They were missing. There were four reporters on this operation—two of them didn't come back. Two friends of mine—Norman Stockton, of Australian Associated Newspapers, and Lowell Bennett, an American representing International News Service. There is something of a tradition amongst reporters that those who are prevented by circumstances from filing their stories will be covered by their colleagues. This has been my effort to do so.

[*Bennett survived the raid. He parachuted and was held prisoner by the Germans until May 1945.*]

In the aircraft in which I flew, the men who flew and fought it poured into my ears their comments on fighters, flak and flares in the same tones they would have used in reporting a host of daffodils. I have no doubt that Bennett and Stockton would have given you a better report of last night's activities.

Berlin was a kind of orchestrated hell, a terrible symphony of light and flame. It isn't a pleasant kind of warfare—the men doing it speak of it as a job. Yesterday afternoon, when the tapes were stretched out on the big map all the way to Berlin and back again, a young pilot with old eyes said to me, "I see we're working again tonight." That's the frame of mind in which the job is being done. The job isn't pleasant; it's terribly tiring. Men die in the sky while others are roasted alive in their cellars. Berlin last night wasn't a pretty sight. In about thirty-five minutes it was hit with about three times the amount of stuff that ever came down on London in a night-long blitz. This is a calculated, remorseless campaign of destruction. Right now the mechanics are probably working on *D-Dog,* getting him ready to fly again.

December 26, 1943

It's something of a problem to know what to do with your fifth wartime Christmas. I spent mine with the American Air Corps— Marauders and Liberators—nearly the whole of last week. I listened to the accents of boys who come from the West Coast, from the Deep South, from the flatlands of the Middle West and from the states that edge into the Atlantic. It was a warming, wonderful week. It wasn't until I returned to London a few hours ago that I heard of the appointment of General "Ike" Eisenhower as supreme commander in this theater.

When he first came over here a couple of years ago, he was wearing three stars. They looked very much like the three pips worn by an English captain. There was a lot of saluting then, and majors and colonels seemed to expect a salute from Ike. Walking back from luncheon one day, I mentioned this to him, and he said, "I'd trade these three stars for a captain's rank any day if I could trade years as well." Like most good generals, Eisenhower would trade his rank for a place at the front. Today he is receiving salutes— wholehearted, enthusiastic ones—from the British press.

There was a time when Allied policy in North Africa was strongly attacked by many people in this country. Officially, General Eisenhower was responsible for the policy, but anybody who knew anything about the general or the policy knew that that just wasn't so. General Eisenhower is about as non-political as a general could possibly be. He doesn't know anything about European politics, and he would be the first to admit it. Europe to him is a place where the German Army must be defeated, and one is entitled to hope that he will not be given the official responsibility for political decisions that may be taken in Washington or London. It just happens that Eisenhower has a certain genius when it comes to reconciling different points of view. He is a chairman—a coordinator—one who has the ability to weld a fighting organization together. The overadvertised English reserve hasn't bothered him in the least. He is quick and generous with his praise of subordinates, but when things go wrong the big grin disappears and he becomes as bleak as a Kansas cornfield in midwinter. Shortly after Ike came to London, I tried to do a small broadcast about him on the BBC. As soon as I had finished, the general rang up and said it was all right, but the war wasn't being fought to make a hotshot out of Ike Eisenhower.

April 30, 1944

You will have heard about mounting invasion fever on the Continent and in this country. You will probably hear much more in the same vein—more stories out of Helsinki by way of Stockholm and Berne—to the effect that the great effort is to be made in a matter of hours or days. It is true that a great many private persons in this country are studying the moons and the tides, and some are placing bets on the day. But while the tension is mounting, there is a disposition to remember Mr. Churchill's words: "There will be many false alarms, many feints and many dress rehearsals." Two great myths have been destroyed. The first that the Russians could win the war on their own. The second, that bombing would be enough. Today no serious observer doubts that the forces massed in this island must be flung onto the Continent in the face of able and determined German resistance. The Germans say that they have been bombing concentrations of Allied shipping in English ports, but neither their bombers nor their U-boats have caused sufficient damage to upset the timetable.

The planning of this operation is complex beyond description. Nothing like it has ever been seen. It is not just a matter of coordinating land, sea and air forces. It involves the loading of ships so that the things that are needed first will be the first to be unloaded. It means careful calculation of weather and tides, constant reconnaissance of enemy dispositions. And it means security, thousands of people knowing small bits of the plan but only a very few having knowledge of how the whole thing fits together. At no time in this war have I seen the planning officers work harder or talk less. As a matter of fact, there is less loose talk amongst civilians than ever before. It's as though everyone realized the importance of guarding the plans, even when most of the movements must be carried out within sight of the enemy's air reconnaissance. But in the end of the day all the plans, all the preparations, must depend upon the men who execute them, and personal boasting by British or American generals will not alter that fact.

Here then are a few personal impressions of Americans in Britain as they wait for D day. The Army is training harder, is tougher than ever before. There is none of the casualness that preceded the North African invasion—you can even find public relations officers in their offices on Sundays. The percentage of petty crime and of venereal disease has gone down. Mostly it's a homesick army, but I have yet to hear a man say he'd be willing to go home before the job is finished. No matter how shy a man may be, he'll always begin to talk if you know, or have even passed through, his home state or town. The nearer you can pinpoint common geographical knowledge, the easier the conversation becomes. The other night, talking with a second lieutenant, it developed that we both knew and had patronized the same hot dog stand. The fact that he longed for a certain stretch of the Connecticut River while I preferred the Columbia or the Snake didn't make any difference. We had that hot dog stand in common. This is a tough, tinkering Army. They'll tinker with anything, have more mechanical know-how than any army in the world. Homemade shower baths, indirect lighting in Nissen huts, new and faster methods of repairing flak damage, or a faster way of stringing telephone lines, it's all the same. In a showroom here in London there's a Rolls Royce engine with the side cut away. Any time during the day you can see a bunch of GIs standing around discussing it. The length of the piston stroke and the way the valve tappets work. It fascinates them. Most other Allied troops pass it by with scarcely a glance.

Out at the airfields, the pilots and bombadiers stand around and discuss the photographs of bomb strikes as though they were surgeons consulting about a delicate and difficult operation. When something goes wrong, they want to know why. When a ship fails to come back, they wonder what happened and how it could have been avoided. When someone gets in a tough spot and then gets out, the rest want to know how he did it, just so they'll have that bit of extra knowledge. The crew chiefs and the ground crews are proud of the performance of the ships they service; they have grease under their fingernails but dignity and competence in their bearing. It's a resourceful army, too. I'm indebted to *Stars and Stripes* for this story from Scotland. A GI was supposed to meet his girl at a theater in a nearby town. At the last minute he was slapped on K.P. So he sent a pal in to meet the girl. The friend didn't know the girl, so he rigged up two sandwich signs and paraded up and down in front of the theater, a large sign on front and back reading: "Mary, I have been a bad boy and can't come to town tonight—Tom." The substitute met the girl all right.

There are men who used to be city auditors and civil engineers trying to learn German, figuring out methods of getting the municipal water supply or the finances of some German city going again. There are fliers whose fathers or grandfathers left Europe in the steerage who are now flying over European cities the name of which they can't pronounce. Their curiosity is unlimited. Most of them have never been to Europe—they've only looked down at it from a bomber. A few days ago I was looking at pictures of a small French town with a group of them. I happen to have known the town in peacetime. They have seen it from the air twenty or thirty times. But they wanted to know what the houses were like along this big street, what the church really looked like and where the good restaurants were.

It seems to me that both the army and the civilians are more interested in things than in ideas. Most of them believe that Europe is a much simpler place than it is. They are courteous; many of them are shy. They haven't much respect for things that are old. The army—what I have seen of it—doesn't talk very much about politics; it wastes a lot of food; it spreads the habit of chewing gum wherever it goes. It isn't much of a singing army, preferring the tunes it danced to in peacetime to the so-called war songs. There doesn't seem to be much sentiment about small nations, except the old-fashioned American attitude that big bullies should pick on somebody their own size. The feeling seems to be that the chip has been knocked off our shoulder, and that we are sizeable enough and just about ready to make the proper response.

Something is happening to the Americans who have spent a couple of years abroad. I have the idea that when these men return home they will greatly influence American policy toward Britain and the rest of Europe, that the man who has been in Britain or Italy or Germany and returns to his own town to work in the bank or the service station may do more to influence opinion than the editors or the radio commentators. And who can say that that will be a bad thing?

June 6, 1944

> "Under the command of General Eisenhower, Allied naval forces, supported by strong air forces, began landing Allied armies this morning on the northern coast of France."
> The official announcement by Supreme Headquarters, Al-

*lied Expeditionary Forces in Europe, came at 3:32 a.m.,
New York time. Five minutes later, America heard Murrow
in London read Eisenhower's order of the day. At 3:47 a.m.
Eisenhower himself was heard reading his message to the
captive peoples of western Europe, instructing them to be
patient and await the signal to strike.*

*Murrow on D day was more coordinator than correspondent, ordering circuits, testing beachhead transmitters, checking by short wave with newsmen in Normandy and with Paul
White, director of CBS News, in New York. But at 10:07 a.m.,
speaking through heavy static, he made this report:*

This is London.

Early this morning we heard the bombers going out. It was the
sound of a giant factory in the sky. It seemed to shake the old gray
stone buildings in this bruised and battered city beside the Thames.
The sound was heavier, more triumphant than ever before. Those
who knew what was coming could imagine that they heard great
guns and strains of the *Battle Hymn of the Republic* well above the
roar of the motors. We were told that General Montgomery is
commanding the ground forces, while [Sir Trafford] Leigh-Mallory
directs the air offensive. His bombers put eight thousand tons onto
the target area in the course of ten hours.

Here in London, the steadiness of the civilian populace is one of
the most remarkable things I've ever seen. People go about their
business calmly. There was no excitement. Walking along the
streets of London, you almost wanted to shout at them and say,
"Don't you know that history is being made this day?" They realized
it all right, but their emotions were under complete control. For
weeks and months, the long lines of khaki-colored tank forces had
been riding down to the coast. Everyone, including the enemy,
knew what was coming. But when it came, it didn't seem to break
the tension.

The Germans have been fishing for information all day. They
must not only try to anticipate our next move; they must think
constantly of the coming Russian offensive. The eyewitness accounts of correspondents who landed with the assault troops have
not yet reached London, but a careful survey of every report by air

81

and naval observers reveals a strong note of surprise and amazement at the absence of the Luftwaffe.

A great race against time has been started. We are attempting to consolidate our positions to withstand the inevitable German counterattack, while the Germans are attempting to regroup their forces and prepare to strike before we are well established. That appears to be the position at the moment.

June 11, 1944

In Normandy, the battle is raging furiously. It is a swaying struggle, but so far as we know the day has brought no important change in position. Troops are in continuous contact from east of the River Orne to a point northeast of Sainte Mère Église. This is a distance of something like fifty miles, but at no point is the penetration deeper than eleven miles. About five hundred square miles of the Continent has been occupied by the Allies, but two million more are still controlled by the enemy. We have made a beginning, and a brilliant one, but it is still only a beginning. The battle has started, but it has not been fully joined—far from it.

I should like to tell you a story brought back by my colleague Charles Collingwood, who went across on an LST on D day. He says the last word from shore that the men on his ship had was a signal from a Wren, one of the girls serving with the Royal Navy. I should say that in this port there are a lot of British Wrens who help run the shore base. They live in dormitories up above the harbor, and it is a constant pastime among men of the LSTs in port to keep the girls under a continual inspection through their glasses. When the boys caught on that there were girls up there who knew semaphore, there was a sudden interest in the technique of signaling, and many a man learned to wave his way through a halting alphabet. They used to signal "Hello" and "How are you?" and "How about a date?" This never did them any good, but they felt very dashing, and it made them happy.

The signaling was finally stopped on security grounds, but the boys used to keep the girls under constant observation just the same. Collingwood says the night before they sailed, just as it was getting dark, a girl came out of the Wren house where they all live and began to signal. She made just one word. The amateur signalers on the LST spelled it out. The one word was "Courage." And then, because she knew it was against the rules, the Wren turned around and ran back into the house.

September 17, 1944

It was the war's greatest airborne operation. More than four thousand gliders and planes landed thirty-five thousand British and American fighting men in Holland in a leapfrog action designed to turn the German flank. Murrow rode a C-47 loaded with paratroopers to the drop zone.

Early this morning, the paratroopers, laden down with equipment, walked out across a green field and climbed into the C-47s of the 9th Troop Carrier Command. After we took off we seemed to gather more ships as we passed over a series of airfields and the pilot said, "We're gathering in all the little chickens before we cross the big water." Before we crossed the English coast the ships were in formation as far as the eye could see. The paratroops sat there completely relaxed—two of them were asleep. Another told me that flying always made him sleepy. The door of the rear of the plane had been removed; all the belts and hinges had been covered with tape to prevent the parachute harness fouling. The big fellow near the door looked down and said: "Look at them land girls down there, picking potatoes!"

As we went out over the North Sea there were British gliders on our right, heavy bombers to port, and ahead of us the C-47s stretched out mile after mile. They were going in to drop their parachutists at no more than four or five hundred feet. They didn't carry an inch of armor plate, no guns, no self-sealing gas tanks. Bob Masell, of the Blue Network, was handling the recording gear in our C-47. We returned to London only an hour or two ago and there has been no time to edit or polish the recording. But this is what it was like when we crossed the Dutch coast.

RECORDING
Now, we are over Holland and I'm going to move forward, up to the pilot's compartment, and I've got my parachute harness hung

on the door. We're flying over country that has been inundated. I can see a railway which seems to be still in operation, but some of the most civilized countryside in Europe now lies under water. I can see the red roofs of the houses just protruding. The sun is shining very brightly, and I can see the shadows of the formation ahead of us on the water. I'm just going to ask the skipper now if he's seen any flak yet.

MURROW: Seen any flak?

VOICE: Very small amount over on our left, about five hundred yards.

MURROW: What did it look like? 20 mm. stuff?

VOICE: Yes, it was either 20 mm. or 37.

MURROW: Right!

The skipper is sitting there very calmly, flying with one hand. This country has been flooded as far as my eye can reach. There is no traffic on this one railway which stands well above the water. It seems to have been built along the top of a dyke. It has also been broken in one or two places. This countryside below looks like the area around the Mississippi during flood time, except that all the houses seem to be covered with red tile. The country is desolate. It isn't possible that people are living down there, because in most cases the water is right up to the eaves.

We're now passing out of the flooded area, every ship still in perfect formation. The fighters are swirling around below us, going down to have a look at every hedgerow and every small wood that might possibly conceal an ack-ack emplacement. Bob Masell, of the Blue Network, is sitting here, working on the recording gear, just as calm and cool as any of the paratroopers, but perhaps both of us should be because they're going to jump and we aren't. But in a few minutes now these boys will be walking out of that back door.

I'm standing here, looking down the length of the ship now. The crew chief is on his knees back in the very rear, talking into his intercom, talking with the pilot. The rest of the men are folding up their Mae Wests, but there's certainly no possibility that we're pitching into the water on this trip. They're looking out the window rather curiously, almost as if they were passengers on a peacetime airline. You occasionally see a man rub the palm of his hand across his trouser leg. There seems to be a sort of film over some of the faces, as though they were just on the verge of perspiring, but they aren't.

There go the parapacks of a formation ahead of us—yellow, brown, red, drifting down gently, dropping the containers. I can't see—they're a little too far away—I can't see the bodies of the men. Yes, I can! I look back at the door, and the pilot gives me the clenched-hand salute, like a boxer about to jump. The ships ahead of us are still going on. There's a burst of flak. You can see it right from the side. It's coming from the port side just across our nose, but a little bit low. I think it's coming from a railway embankment just down to the left and was certainly considerably under us and just ahead of us. This is the first flak we've seen. There's one burst of light flak; there's another. More tracers going across us, in front of our nose. I think it's coming from that little village just beside the canal. More tracer coming up now, just cutting across in front of our nose. A lovely orange color it is.

More ships ahead of us are now dropping. Nine ships ahead of us have just dropped and you can see the men swinging down. In just about forty seconds now our ship will drop the men; the men will walk out onto Dutch soil. You can probably hear the snap as they check the lashing on the static line. There they go! Do you hear them shout? Three! . . . four! . . . five! . . . six! . . . seven! . . . eight! . . . nine! . . . ten! . . . eleven! . . . twelve! . . . thirteen! . . . fourteen! . . . fifteen! . . . sixteen! Now every man is out. I can see their chutes going down now. Every man clear. They're dropping just beside a little windmill near a church, hanging there. Very gracefully. They seem to be completely relaxed, like nothing so much as khaki dolls hanging beneath a green lampshade. I see the men go down just north of a little road. The whole sky is filled with parachutes. They're all going down so slowly; it seems as though they should get to the ground much faster. We're now swinging about, making a right-hand turn.
END OF RECORDING

That's the way it was.

September 24, 1944

Allied forces had entered Paris on August 25.

Coming back from Paris, I sat in the plane making some notes—all about impressions and a few facts. It seemed at the time that forty-eight hours in Paris might add up to a broadcast. There was the absence of transport; the fantastic prices of luxury goods; the fact that the city had suffered practically no physical damage when compared with London; the reports of malnutrition in the working class districts; the problem of what to do with the French Forces of the Interior. There was the memory of those familiar, well-fed but still empty-looking faces around the fashionable bars and restaurants—the last four years seemed to have changed them very little. There was the memory of very well-dressed women in the central part of Paris, and of those who were less well-dressed and certainly less well-fed in the suburbs. There was the fact that most of the Allied bombing, particularly around the airfields, was very accurate indeed. There were French newspapers which reflected a toughness and independence of view which seemed encouraging. There was the memory of conversations about who had collaborated, how much and with whom. None of the impressions, none of the facts was particularly new or startling, but they might have been whipped together into a rather nostalgic, perhaps slightly emotional broadcast about the most civilized city in Europe. But when we came down through the English mist, searched for the airfield and finally found it, ten minutes of conversation made it perfectly clear that no one could talk from London about Paris. There was, and there still is, an atmosphere that reminds one of the days of Dunkirk. No one is interested in Paris or in Brussels. The newspapers and the radio are not devoting much space to the presidential election at home or to the long-range plans about what to do with Germany. All attention, much hope and many prayers are centered on the fighting round the Dutch town of Arnhem.

Arnhem is today taking its place in British folklore, and it may in future stand alongside Waterloo and Trafalgar. British imagination has been captured by the daring of this great Allied airborne army which was thrown into Holland a week ago today, and there appears to be a widespread appreciation of what it may achieve. The

86

plan was very simple. Whatever progress our First and Third Armies might make through the natural defenses and through the Siegfried Line, they would still have to cross the Rhine. The Germans were depending upon the water barriers in Holland. The airborne army went in to hold crucial crossings at Eindhoven, Nijmegen, and Arnhem. The first two were taken and held. The third, the apex of the drive, would have made it possible for Allied armor to burst through into the great German plain, smash the enemy's right flank and turn the end of the German defensive system, somewhat as the Germans turned the end of the Maginot Line in 1940.

The opening of the attack last Sunday went well. The armor of the British Second Army was soon at Eindhoven and thrusting up the cobbled causeways towards Nijmegen. Some of the American paratroopers who had been dropped there crossed the river, and by hard fighting and excellent coordination they took the bridge intact. The British had been dropped about ten to twelve miles farther on, around Arnhem. The armor and supply columns could not get through to them. As you know, the success of any airborne operation depends upon their prompt linking up with the advancing ground forces. In the landings in Normandy the estimated time for this was about twenty hours. The men at Arnhem have now been fighting for seven days and seven nights. The weather has been consistently bad, and it has not only slowed down resupply from the air; it has also hindered the work of Allied dive bombers and fighter bombers. The glider landing zones and the paratroop drop zones are now covered with heavy ack-ack concentrations. A week ago, German resistence was only moderate, but they have reacted promptly and vigorously, and they now know exactly where the supplies and reinforcements must be dropped. During the last week, in parts of England, you could hear the transport planes roaring out and occasionally catch a glimpse of a glider slipping silently away. Allied air losses have been mounting, and there are squadrons of the Transport Command who check the operations room to find out who has got back, just the way the bomber crews used to do.

These airborne soldiers are an entirely unique group of fighting men. I sat through six or seven briefings with them before we flew last Sunday. They put them behind barbed wire enclosures—like prisoners—two or three days before the operation is ready to take off. They pitch horseshoes, shoot craps and play touch football in full fighting clothes. They wade through the English mud in the mess line. I saw one American outfit that had its own jazz band of paratroopers, playing in a muddy company street. There was an Englishman who dropped in last Sunday with a darts board slung round his neck, and an American who had a mouth organ in his hand. All the time a mission is being prepared the tension mounts, until a couple of minutes before the drop it is almost unbearable. These airborne troops might be called "sprint" fighters. They are lightly equipped, trained to fight with great ferocity for a day or two, and then be relieved by the ground troops with the heavy weapons. The men round Arnhem, what's left of them, have now been there for a week.

> *The next day, the British 1st Airborne, its ammunition exhausted, received orders to retreat. The Americans at Eindhoven and Nijmegen held their ground, but the over-all operation was a failure. The desired bridgehead on the lower Rhine was not secured.*

November 12, 1944

I shall try to say something about V-2, the German rockets that have fallen on several widely scattered points in England. The Germans, as usual, made the first announcement and used it to blanket the fact that Hitler failed to make his annual appearance at the Munich beer cellar. The German announcement was exaggerated and inaccurate in some details, but not in all. For some weeks those of us who had known what was happening had been referring to these explosions, clearly audible over a distance of fifteen miles, as "those exploding gas mains." It is impossible to give you any reliable report on the accuracy of this weapon because we don't know what the Germans have been shooting at. They have scored some lucky and tragic hits, but as Mr. Churchill told the House of Commons, the scale and the effects of the attack have not hitherto been significant.

That is, of course, no guarantee that they will not become so. This weapon carries an explosive charge of approximately one ton. It arrives without warning of any kind. The sound of the explosion is not like the crump of the old-fashioned bomb, or the flat crack of the flying bomb; the sound is perhaps heavier and more menacing because it comes without warning. Most people who have experienced war have been saved repeatedly by either seeing or hearing; neither sense provides warning or protection against this new weapon.

These are days when a vivid imagination is a definite liability. There is nothing pleasant in contemplating the possibility, however remote, that a ton of high explosive may come through the roof with absolutely no warning of any kind. The penetration of these rockets is considerably greater than that of the flying bomb, but the lateral blast effect is less. There are good reasons for believing that the Germans are developing a rocket which may contain as much as eight tons of explosives. That would be eight times the size of the present rocket, and, in the opinion of most people over here, definitely unpleasant. These rockets have not been arriving in any considerable quantity, and they have not noticeably affected the nerves or the determination of British civilians. But it would be a mistake to make light of this new form of bombardment. Its potentialities are largely unknown. German science has again demonstrated a malignant ingenuity which is not likely to be forgotten when it comes time to establish controls over German scientific and industrial research. For the time being, those of you who may have family or friends in these "widely scattered spots in England" need not be greatly alarmed about the risks to which they are exposed.

The significance of this demonstration of German skill and ingenuity lies in the fact that it makes complete nonsense out of strategic frontiers, mountain and river barriers. And, in the opinion of many able scientists, it means that within a few years present methods of aerial bombardment will be as obsolete as the Gatling gun. It serves to make more appalling the prospect or the possibility of another war, and may thereby inject an added note of urgency into the rather casual conversations that have been going on between the Allied nations.

November 26, 1944

America, in the shape of soldiers on the ground, planes in the sky, ships on the ocean, represents the hope and the fear of an awful lot of little people in Europe. Most of us probably have no desire that it should be so, but it is, and we now carry—whether we like it or not—the responsibility for what happens to a lot of people other than Americans.

At home, we fought this war in the light. Such homes as we had we still have. Our whole industrial plant is undamaged by war. Our nerves have not been tested and twisted by bombs and doodlebugs [pilotless, explosive-laden planes] and things that arrive without warning. We are—we must be—less tired than the peoples of Europe. And as our strength is greater, so must our responsibility be.

There is a dim light in Europe now. The blackout is gradually lifting. And when I leave this studio tonight I shall walk up a street in which there is light, not much, but more than there has been for five and a half years. You come to know a street pretty well in that time—the holes in the wooden paving blocks where the incendiaries burnt themselves out, the synagogue on the right with the placard which has defied four winters, although it's a little tattered and smoke-stained. Tonight, there will be a street lamp just near there, and I shall be able to read the legend: "Blessed is he whose conscience hath not condemned him and who is not fallen from his hope in the Lord." It is a street where in '40 and '41 the fires made the raindrops on the window look like drops of blood on a mirror. It's an unimportant street where friends died, and those who lived had courage to laugh.

Tonight, I suppose the air-raid shelters will be empty, but it will be possible for a man to walk this street without fear of hitting a lamppost or stumbling over a curb—five years and three months since they turned out the lights in the streets. There won't be anything brilliant about the illumination tonight, but each shaded street lamp will, for this reporter, be like a cathedral candle for those whose faith was greatest when the nights were darkest.

April 15, 1945

During the last week, I have driven more than a few hundred miles through Germany, most of it in the Third Army sector— Wiesbaden, Frankfurt, Weimar, Jena and beyond. It is impossible to keep up with this war. The traffic flows down the super-highways, trucks with German helmets tied to the radiators and belts of machine-gun ammunition draped from fender to fender. The tanks on the concrete roads sound like a huge sausage machine, grinding up sheets of corrugated iron. And when there is a gap between convoys, when the noise dies away, there is another small noise, that of wooden-soled shoes and of small iron tires grating on the concrete. The power moves forward, while the people, the slaves, walk back, pulling their small belongings on anything that has wheels.

There are cities in Germany that make Coventry and Plymouth appear to be merely damage done by a petulant child, but bombed houses have a way of looking alike, wherever you see them.

But this is no time to talk of the surface of Germany. Permit me to tell you what you would have seen, and heard, had you been with me on Thursday. It will not be pleasant listening. If you are at lunch, or if you have no appetite to hear what Germans have done, now is a good time to switch off the radio, for I propose to tell you of Buchenwald. It is on a small hill about four miles outside Weimar, and it was one of the largest concentration camps in Germany, and it was built to last. As we approached it, we saw about a hundred men in civilian clothes with rifles advancing in open order across the fields. There were a few shops; we stopped to inquire. We were told that some of the prisoners had a couple of SS men cornered in there. We drove on, reached the main gate. The prisoners crowded up behind the wire. We entered.

And now, let me tell this in the first person, for I was the least important person there, as you shall hear. There surged around me an evil-smelling horde. Men and boys reached out to touch me; they were in rags and the remnants of uniform. Death had already marked many of them, but they were smiling with their eyes. I looked out over that mass of men to the green fields beyond where well-fed Germans were ploughing.

A German, Fritz Kersheimer, came up and said, "May I show you round the camp? I've been here ten years." An Englishman stood to attention, saying, "May I introduce myself, delighted to see you, and can you tell me when some of our blokes will be along?" I told him soon and asked to see one of the barracks. It happened to be occupied by Czechoslovakians. When I entered, men crowded around, tried to lift me to their shoulders. They were too weak. Many of them could not get out of bed. I was told that this building had once stabled eighty horses. There were twelve hundred men in it, five to a bunk. The stink was beyond all description.

When I reached the center of the barracks, a man came up and said, "You remember me. I'm Peter Zenkl, one-time mayor of Prague." I remembered him, but did not recognize him. He asked about Benes and Jan Masaryk. I asked how many men had died in that building during the last month. They called the doctor; we inspected his records. There were only names in the little black book, nothing more—nothing of who these men were, what they had done, or hoped. Behind the names of those who had died there was a cross. I counted them. They totalled 242. Two hundred and forty-two out of twelve hundred in one month.

As I walked down to the end of the barracks, there was applause from the men too weak to get out of bed. It sounded like the hand clapping of babies; they were so weak. The doctor's name was Paul Heller. He had been there since 1938.

As we walked out into the courtyard, a man fell dead. Two others—they must have been over sixty—were crawling toward the latrine. I saw it but will not describe it.

In another part of the camp they showed me the children, hundreds of them. Some were only six. One rolled up his sleeve, showed me his number. It was tattooed on his arm. D-6030, it was. The others showed me their numbers; they will carry them till they die.

An elderly man standing beside me said, "The children, enemies of the state." I could see their ribs through their thin shirts. The old man said, "I am Professor Charles Richer of the Sorbonne." The children clung to my hands and stared. We crossed to the courtyard. Men kept coming up to speak to me and to touch me, professors from Poland, doctors from Vienna, men from all Europe. Men from the countries that made America.

We went to the hospital; it was full. The doctor told me that two hundred had died the day before. I asked the cause of death; he shrugged and said, "Tuberculosis, starvation, fatigue, and there are many who have no desire to live. It is very difficult." Dr. Heller pulled back the blankets from a man's feet to show me how swollen they were. The man was dead. Most of the patients could not move.

As we left the hospital I drew out a leather billfold, hoping that I

92

had some money which would help those who lived to get home. Professor Richer from the Sorbonne said, "I should be careful of my wallet if I were you. You know there are criminals in this camp, too." A small man tottered up, saying, "May I feel the leather, please? You see, I used to make good things of leather in Vienna." Another man said, "My name is Walter Roeder. For many years I lived in Joliet. Came back to Germany for a visit and Hitler grabbed me."

I asked to see the kitchen; it was clean. The German in charge had been a Communist, had been at Buchenwald for nine years, had a picture of his daughter in Hamburg. He hadn't seen her for almost twelve years, and if I got to Hamburg, would I look her up? He showed me the daily ration—one piece of brown bread about as thick as your thumb, on top of it a piece of margarine as big as three sticks of chewing gum. That, and a little stew, was what they received every twenty-four hours. He had a chart on the wall; very complicated it was. There were little red tabs scattered through it. He said that was to indicate each ten men who died. He had to account for the rations, and he added, "We're very efficient here."

We went again into the courtyard, and as we walked we talked. The two doctors, the Frenchman and the Czech, agreed that about six thousand had died during March. Kersheimer, the German, added that back in the winter of 1939, when the Poles began to arrive without winter clothing, they died at the rate of approximately nine hundred a day. Five different men asserted that Buchenwald was the best concentration camp in Germany; they had had some experience of the others.

Dr. Heller, the Czech, asked if I would care to see the crematorium. He said it wouldn't be very interesting because the Germans had run out of coke some days ago and had taken to dumping the bodies into a great hole nearby. Professor Richer said perhaps I would care to see the small courtyard. I said yes. He turned and told the children to stay behind. As we walked across the square I noticed that the professor had a hole in his left shoe and a toe sticking out of the right one. He followed my eyes and said, "I regret that I am so little presentable, but what can one do?" At that point another Frenchman came up to announce that three of his fellow countrymen outside had killed three S.S. men and taken one prisoner. We proceeded to the small courtyard. The wall was about eight feet high; it adjoined what had been a stable or garage. We entered. It was floored with concrete. There were two rows of bodies stacked up like cordwood. They were thin and very white. Some of the bodies were terribly bruised, though there seemed to be little flesh to bruise. Some had been shot through the head, but they bled but little. All except two were naked. I tried to count them as best I could and arrived at the conclusion that all that was mortal of more than five hundred men and boys lay there in two neat piles.

There was a German trailer which must have contained another fifty, but it wasn't possible to count them. The clothing was piled in a heap against the wall. It appeared that most of the men and boys had died of starvation; they had not been executed. But the manner of death seemed unimportant. Murder had been done at Buchenwald. God alone knows how many men and boys have died there during the last twelve years. Thursday I was told that there were more than twenty thousand in the camp. There had been as many as sixty thousand. Where are they now?

As I left that camp, a Frenchman who used to work for Havas in Paris came up to me and said, "You will write something about this, perhaps?" And he added, "To write about this you must have been here at least two years, and after that—you don't want to write any more."

I pray you to believe what I have said about Buchenwald. I have reported what I saw and heard, but only part of it. For most of it I have no words. Dead men are plentiful in war, but the living dead, more than twenty thousand of them in one camp. And the country round about was pleasing to the eye, and the Germans were well fed and well dressed. American trucks were rolling toward the rear filled with prisoners. Soon they would be eating American rations, as much for a meal as the men at Buchenwald received in four days.

If I've offended you by this rather mild account of Buchenwald, I'm not in the least sorry. I was there on Thursday, and many men in many tongues blessed the name of Roosevelt. For long years his name had meant the full measure of their hope. These men who had kept close company with death for many years did not know that Mr. Roosevelt would, within hours, join their comrades who had laid their lives on the scales of freedom.

Back in 1941, Mr. Churchill said to me with tears in his eyes,

"One day the world and history will recognize and acknowledge what it owes to your President." I saw and heard the first installment of that at Buchenwald on Thursday. It came from men from all over Europe. Their faces, with more flesh on them, might have been found anywhere at home. To them the name "Roosevelt" was a symbol, the code word for a lot of guys named "Joe" who are somewhere out in the blue with the armor heading east. At Buchenwald they spoke of the President just before he died. If there be a better epitaph, history does not record it.

April 22, 1945

"Tell them resistance was slight!" That's what a GI shouted to us as we entered Leipzig. There were two tankers dead at the corner. Somebody had covered them with a blanket. There was a sniper working somewhere in the next block. Four boys went out to deal with him, then there was silence.

The Gestapo headquarters has been evacuated in a great hurry, but they had taken all their files with them. Down in the air-raid shelter the floor was covered with money—Belgian, Polish, Hungarian—wherever the Germans had been. The money was ankle deep, and it was dirty. And it had no meaning.

The Germans were fighting for a bridge. They were doing what they have done for many days, firing off a few bazookas, killing a few boys, and then surrendering. There is no desperation about this German defense; they shoot till they are about to be killed and then they give up. I have seen them do it at Leipzig and in Nuremberg.

Let me tell you about the taking of Leipzig—the town hall. At 16:45 on Wednesday they lined up the tanks. The boys draped themselves around them; they were part of the 69th Division. It was about a thousand yards to the city hall. There were 185 men on the outside of the tanks. They started down the main street. There were thirteen tanks and five tank destroyers. They were in a column, moving down a single street.

When they began to roll, they were hit with bazookas and machine guns. When they turned a corner, the wounded slipped off. The medium tanks were traveling about 30 miles an hour, and no man turned back. Lieutenant Ken Wilder started with a total of 39 men, and when they reached the city hall he had eight. They had a company of infantry riding on the tanks—185 men. Sixty-eight reached the city hall. The tanks were marked with machine-gun fire, and they were splattered with blood.

An hour after reaching the city hall, those boys were driving German cars and motorcycles about the streets. In the place where we were sitting, a sniper's bullet broke a pane of glass in a window. A doughboy said, "My! My! Somebody done broke a window. Things are getting rough round here. Folks are destroying things." The Germans had given up. A few had shot themselves. One said he couldn't be taken prisoner by the Americans. He *must* commit suicide. A young lieutenant said, "Here's a gun." The German took it and shot himself, just under the right ear.

May 8, 1945

> *This was the official day of victory in Europe—V-E day—a slightly anticlimatic occasion because of the premature Associated Press story of Germany's surrender on May 7. Minutes after the formal announcement, delayed for twenty-four hours by Stalin, Murrow reported from London.*

The police are badly outnumbered, but for the last hour most Londoners have all wanted to go in the same direction, so it doesn't matter very much. They've been streaming towards Buckingham Palace, the Houses of Parliament, Trafalgar Square and Piccadilly. There are soldiers in paper hats, boys perched on lampposts. When an Army truck stops at an intersection it is swamped with men and women in uniform. They don't know where the truck is going and they don't care. They just want to ride.

In the center of London there is only one street with a NO ENTRY sign; that's one leading to a police station. The ambulances are standing by to pick up the casualties; the movie houses are all closed and barricaded; the managers don't want anyone tearing up the seats and throwing them out in the street. So far the crowd is wonderfully good natured. Today on the streets of London there are soldiers and sailors of all the nations that have made victory possible, and mixed with the uniforms are civilians; many of them are carrying their mackintoshes and umbrellas. They believe in peace, but not in the steadiness of the weather.

As you walk down the street you hear singing that comes from open windows; sometimes it's a chorus, and sometimes it's just a single voice raised in song. *Roll Out the Barrel* seems to be the favorite. Only the pigeons, walking along the ledges of blitzed buildings, seem unperturbed and unaware.

Many women are wearing flags in their hats; some are even draped in flags. At times, someone will start to shout. There's no obvious reason for the shout, but it's taken up at once. There are no words; just a sort of rumbling roar. London is celebrating today in a city which became a symbol. The scars of war are all about. There is no lack of serious, solemn faces. Their thoughts are their own. Some people appear not to be part of the celebration. Their minds must be filled with memories of friends who died in the streets where they now walk, and of others who have died from Burma to the Elbe. There are a few men on crutches, as though to remind all that there is much human wreckage left at the end. Six years is a long time. I have observed today that people have very little to say.

There are no words.

Murrow broadcast from London again that evening.

Tonight, walking through familiar side streets in London, trying to realize what has happened, one's mind takes refuge in the past. The war that was seems more real than the peace that has come. You feel a depression in the wooden paving blocks and remember that an incendiary burned itself out there. Your best friend was killed on the next corner. You pass a water tank and recall, almost with a start, that there used to be a pub, hit with a two-thousand-pounder one night, thirty people killed. You're walking north. If you walk far enough, you'll reach an airfield where you landed after leaving Vienna with the sounds of shots and the screams in the night still ringing in your ears, the same field where you saw Mr. Chamberlain step out of his plane from Munich, speaking of "peace in our time." You pass a pile of familiar rubble and recall Mr. Churchill's remark when he walked down that street the morning after a raid. When the people came out to cheer him and he said, "They act as though I had brought them a great victory."

There are little streets where you might meet anyone, and tonight it's easy to imagine that old friends are walking there. Some of the boys you watched jump at Remagen. Fliers you watched go down in flames over Berlin or a dozen other targets. And you wonder what's happened to the American boys who used to stand on those street corners far from home and rather lonesome. The soldiers who trained for D day and who since demonstrated that they were not living on the revolutions made by their grandfathers.

The price of victory has been high. We don't yet know just how high—how many twisted minds, how much loss of faith and hope. The first task is to bury the dead and feed the living. The formal declaration of victory will not return the wandering millions to their homes, or provide food for the hungry, or clothes for the ill clad. The economy of Europe is in shreds. The political structure is unstable. There is still danger of famine and plague. Unknown millions have lost everything—home, families, clothes, even their very countries. Perhaps we should remember, even tonight in the midst of the celebration, that the suffering will continue for many years. And that unspeakable crimes are still unpunished and, above all else, that power carries with it great responsibility. We have the power. Europe has no doubt that America is mighty in battle. Our nation, which was created by men who wanted to leave Europe, is the center of the hopes and some of the fears of millions who are in Europe today.

May 27, 1945

On Tuesday, the House of Commons will reassemble. Men who sat side by side on the leather-covered bench representing the British government for five dangerous years will be facing each other across the floor of the House. There will be debate and interruption, conducted in tones of formal conversation. During the dark days they sat shoulder to shoulder, and none but the Germans opposed them. On Tuesday, about twelve feet of green carpet will separate Churchill and Bevin, Eden and Morrison, and all the other politicians who in time of dire peril placed the state above the party. They have now disagreed about who should conduct the nation's business in the future. They have determined to place the matter in the hands of the electorate and to abide by their decision.

There may be involved, as undoubtedly there is, personal pride, desire for power and profit and prestige. But there has developed a fundamental difference of opinion as to the relationship between the state and the individual. It involves education as well as economics. The outcome will affect privilege as well as profits. But it is proposed by all parties that these decisions should be made by the people, no matter how ill informed or intelligent they may be.

This election is unlikely to interfere with the prosecution of the war against Japan. It will not prevent a meeting of the Big Three, if one should be called before the date of the election. But it will be powerful proof that all of this talk about democracy—the right of the individual to speak his mind and register his vote—was one of the things about which this war was fought. This political campaign may have been ill timed; it may uncover mean motives. But it will demonstrate democracy in action, even though it be only in a small island off the coast of Europe.

June 10, 1945

As Britain returned to "politics as usual," an international conference for organizing the United Nations was getting under way in San Francisco.

The announcement that the San Francisco deadlock had been broken, and that small nations may now air their grievances, did not cause a sensation here in London. There were a few mild expressions of satisfaction that the conference would now in all probability be able to reach agreement. But most of the diplomatic correspondents in London remember all too well that the road that led them to this war is littered with conferences and documents expressing "complete agreement." And those who remember Haile Selassie exercising his right to appeal to the conscience of the world by appearing at Geneva are not thoroughly convinced that the San Francisco compromise is heavy with promise for the future.

President Truman [after Roosevelt] does not loom large in the imagination or affection of the British people, but he has succeeded in establishing a relationship with the British government which is altogether remarkable. He is respected, and in so short a time, as a

99

man who conducts the business of his nation with this nation in a manner which officials here respect and admire, even when they disagree with him. Some of them even suspect when a message comes from President Truman he has written it himself!

August 5, 1945

> *Less than four months after Roosevelt's death, President Truman met Stalin and Churchill (and, upon Churchill's defeat in the British elections, Clement Attlee) at the Big Three conference in Potsdam. Partition of Germany was agreed upon.*

The Potsdam communique was not greeted with unquestioning enthusiasm over here. The comment was restrained. There was a tendency to point out the many matters that were not solved—the Middle East, the Dardanelles, the Italian colonies, Germany's western frontiers, and all the rest. But most British comment recognizes the overwhelming importance of the fact that the three nations met and mastered the most massive problem in Europe today. They did agree about what is to be done with Germany. And even those who do not approve of some of the detailed provisions—those who recognize how many problems remain to be solved, how beset with dangers and difficulties this three-lane highway is going to be— admit that the progress recorded was encouraging and that the announcement did not try to conceal the areas where agreement was not possible. Any critic can find plenty of things to complain about. Peformance undoubtedly will not measure up to some of the promises. There is still a residue of mistrust and suspicion. But a question which might have caused the Grand Alliance to come unstuck was solved, however imperfectly.

Now that the conference is ended it has been possible to see a few people who were there. One of them said to me: "We got some work done. At times it was a tough job. At the beginning there was some needling from all sides. But what we finally achieved was a good beginning, if only people will realize that it's that and nothing more." There doesn't seem to be any doubt that President Truman acquitted himself well. Several of those present were impressed with his ability to register his opposition to a proposition with a single word—No. The substitution of Attlee and Bevin for Churchill and Eden did not delay the proceedings. Generalissimo Stalin raised with Mr. Bevin the question of Rudolf Hess, Hitler's deputy who flew to this country in 1941. Stalin has raised this question with Sir Archibald Clarke-Kerr, the British ambassador in Moscow, each time the two men have met, and the Russian press has persistently demanded that Hess be tried as a war criminal. When the Generalissimo raised the matter with Mr. Bevin, Britain's foreign secretary demonstrated that his years spent in blunt labor negotiations had not been wasted. He said, "You can 'ave 'Ess, but you'll have to pay for his board and keep." Generalissimo Stalin laughed and did not pursue the matter.

I have heard no reports to indicate that this meeting was marked by complete unity or unfailing friendship. But the fundamental decisions cover sufficient territory for them to be accepted as a guarantee that the three nations are capable of, and concerned about, settling the affairs of Europe by discussion and compromise, rather than by force. It is true that the small nations were ignored, that the conference adjourned with much unfinished business, that the frontier decisions are unlikely to be reversed later on and that most reporters will be impressed by the assurances of free access to Eastern Europe when that happens. But the progress was considerable if not remarkable.

The events leading up to this war covered a considerable number of years, and history proves that it is much easier to make war than to make peace. This Potsdam Conference gave no guarantee of lasting peace, but it did demonstrate that the victors had elected not to quarrel over the prostrate body of a defeated foe. They have agreed on a major problem; they have created a machinery for continuing consultation, and they have demonstrated that the solution of the problems posed by victory in Europe cannot be either easy or quick. It seems to me that the real significance of the Potsdam communique, for Americans, ought to be that it is proof of the magnitude of the task that lies ahead. Most of the Americans who came over here to fight this war didn't want to come. We thought after the last war that we had secured a Europe that wouldn't bother us. Now it is clear that whether we like it or not, American power and American policy will be a major influence in the Europe that emerges. Those who believe that Russia got everything she wanted out of Potsdam while we got nothing might consider the possibility that perhaps we didn't know what we wanted. We created a continent and a civilization by turning our backs on Europe; then the New World returned to save the Old from a form of tyranny much worse than that from which our ancestors had escaped. It is difficult to see how we are going to escape from Europe again.

August 12, 1945

> *On August 6 Hiroshima was destroyed in history's first atomic raid. Thereupon the Soviet Union declared war on Japan. Another atomic bomb hit Nagasaki, and Japan sued for peace.*

There have been premature victory celebrations in London, but the whole temper of the people reflects a combination of relief and fear. No one is trying to assess the relative influence of the atomic bomb and the Russian declaration of war in bringing about the Japanese offer of surrender. People are content to leave that argument to the historians. The editorial writers have been much more concerned about control of the bomb than about control of Japan.

Secular history offers few, if any, parallels to the events of the past week. And seldom, if ever, has a war ended leaving the victors with such a sense of uncertainty and fear, with such a realization that the future is obscure and that survival is not assured. There is a widespread recognition that the agreement reached at San Francisco is obsolete and that the Big Four will have to think again if they are to devise any system which has even a reasonable chance of maintaining peace. President Truman's declaration that Britain and America will not reveal the secret of the bomb until means have been found for controlling it brought no great reassurance. It does for the moment alter the balance of power, but such a solution is only temporary. Other nations by research and espionage are likely to solve the problem before we have mastered the countermeasures. The editorial writers who have been saying that we are faced with a choice between a new world or none at all do not

102

feel that they are exaggerating. No one has expressed any confidence that an international agreement not to use this weapon would have any lasting effect. For it is impossible to ignore the fact that it has been used.

Science has presented statesmanship with a problem, and its successful solution implies a revolution in the relations between nations. It is not a new problem. Thoughtful writers have been presenting it for decades. It has merely gained an urgency. And it may be that fear, particularly on the part of those who have experienced even old-fashioned bombing, may spur governments to a solution.

September 2, 1945

Japan formally surrendered to the Allied powers on board the U.S. battleship Missouri *in Tokyo Bay.*

And now there is peace. The papers have been signed. The last enemy has given up—unconditionally. There is a silence you can almost hear. Not even the distant echo of guns or the rumble of bombers going out with a belly full of bombs, no more crisp or circuitous communiques. There are white crosses, and scrap iron, scattered round the world, and already some of the place names that will appear in the history books are fading from memory. (They will remain real only to those who were there.) Six years is a long time—and it was more than twice as long for the Chinese.

Today is so much like that Sunday six years ago today. There is sun; the streets are empty. There is just enough breeze to fill the sails of small boats on the Thames. People are sitting in deck chairs in the parks. People *and* chairs are shabbier than they were six years ago. It is a long time, long enough for nations to disappear and be recreated. Long enough for the whole moral and material complexion of a continent to be altered, for cities that were a thousand years in the building to be destroyed in a night, long enough for a way to be found that may destroy humanity.

But there is a fundamental difference between the atmosphere today and six years ago. Then the assumption was that this war was just taking up where the last one left off. The French had a power-

103

ful army; the iron ring of the blockade would strangle Germany. The tired voice of Neville Chamberlain announcing the declaration of war came as something of a relief. The recurring crises were over. The issue was to be fought out. There would probably be some bombing, but it wouldn't be long before the world returned to something like business as usual. There was some talk of total war, but no one really knew what it meant. Few, if any, foresaw what the price of victory would be. I doubt that any single individual can grasp it now. The world of six years ago is gone, and there is a widespread realization that there can be no return. The problems of peace are the more clear because so few appreciated the problems of war. For tens of millions of people the whole basis of existence has gone. They are without homes or hope. People who have lived dangerously lose their fear of change. Those who thought this would be an old-fashioned war when it started six years ago do not believe that peace can be made in the old-fashioned mold. It will require daring and perhaps even sacrifice equal to that displayed by the victors in war, and the constant knowledge that victory is no guarantee of peace.

We seem to be in a condition where there are few fixed, firm standards, so many of the old landmarks have been destroyed. There is even confusion about the meaning of familiar words. For example, General MacArthur said on board the *Missouri*, "Democracy is on the march today, in Asia as well as in Europe. The unshackled peoples are tasting the full sweetness of liberty and relief from fear." That is certainly acceptable as rhetoric, but it employs one word which is more in use today than at any previous time and which is subject to more different interpretations. The word is *democracy*. You see it in print and hear it on the radio in almost every country in the world. Russia refuses to help supervise free and secret elections in Greece because such action would be "a violation of democratic principles." The Rumanian premier refuses to give up his office and justifies his unconstitutional conduct by saying he is defending the democratic spirit. Democracy is used to defend policies pursued in Belgrade and Sofia and Budapest. It is clear that the word has a different meaning in different parts of the world but is still found useful as a slogan. Maybe we should start by redefining the word and settle for a written constitution, freedom of speech, a secret ballot and no secret police.

September 16, 1945

Murrow flew to New York for a month's visit, the fourth time he had come home from London in nine years.

I suppose that anyone can pose as an expert if he's far enough from home. I've been home for a little more than a week and haven't really seen anything except Washington and New York. But there has been time for a lot of reading and much listening and an astonishing amount of eating. The impressions created by this country at peace are so strong that I want to talk about them. It'll probably be old stuff to you, but it is at least possible that one who has spent a few years abroad, wondering what was happening in his own country, often longing to be there, might see or sense something that you have come to regard as commonplace. During the last few years I have tried to talk from various places in the world about something that was to me interesting and perhaps important. What is happening in America now is of tremendous importance to the rest of the world, and there's nothing that interests me more. So, with full knowledge that the impressions are superficial and may be mistaken, I should like—to use one of Mr. Churchill's favorite words—to "descant" for a few minutes upon the American scene.

You all look very, very healthy. You're not as tired as Europeans, and your clothes—well, it seemed to me for the first few days that everyone must be going to a party. The color, the variety and, above everything else, the cleanliness of the clothing is most impressive. And what can be said about the food? The other morning, flying from Washington to New York, the hostess asked if I would care for breakfast. She brought fruit juice, scrambled eggs, bacon, rolls and coffee and cream and sugar. That meal in Paris would have cost about ten dollars; it would have been unobtainable in London. On the outside, the plane was just like the C-47s in which I've ridden so many thousands of miles during the war. But inside there was comfort. No signal lights for the paratroopers, no racks for stretchers. It was very nice.

I conclude that this country is going to do as great a job in the air in peace as it did in war. An Englishman once said to me, "The greatest thing about your country is that no one has ever told it that a thing can't be done." I've thought of that while reading the stories about reconversion, comparing them with what's happening in Europe. And, without knowing any of the details, it seems to me to be a headlong, driving, confident business. The advertisements for new radios, cars, refrigerators, furniture, clothes, travel, drink—everything—speak a loud language of confidence.

In Washington this week there were signs on the lampposts reading "Welcome, Skinny." And it occurred to me that we're the only member of the victorious coalition that would call a great general "Skinny," and we're the only nation with paper to spare for the printing of signs. Incidentally, when General Wainwright spoke to the House of Representatives, only about half the members were there. Maybe they were busy on state business. But I was sorry all of them didn't see and hear the General. He reminded me of thousands of men I've seen coming out of concentration camps in Germany.

One day there was time to stand for ten minutes beside a service station. Cars drew up, were filled up and drove away. There's no country in Europe where that can happen. I thought it remarkable, but no one else seemed to. In New York it is possible to have laundry done in three days. In most Europen capitals it takes near to three weeks. You get soap with your hotel room here—two little cakes. That's currency in most of Europe. It'll get you more food than two five-dollar bills. There's a lot of fresh paint about. The houses seem so neat and undamaged. You must have lived in Europe these last six years to understand just how pleasing and almost exciting fresh paint can be. The other day a friend of mine just back from the Continent said, "You know, walking into a grocery store here is exciting, like going into a jeweler's used to be."

When I first came back, I spent some time listening to the radio. At first, the commercial advertising came as a shock, but that soon wore off and was replaced by the realization that the radio was telling me what to buy but not what to think. There is more news, more discussion of public issues, more controversy on the air here than in any European country. There is plenty of debate about ideas. The listener has a wide field to choose from, and I've heard no one say that the broadcaster is always right. Personally, I object to some of the advertising, but I prefer it to any system under which the government uses the power of broadcasting to tell me what to think.

By the accident of geography and the unfolding of history, we've had world leadership thrust upon us. Some of us are disposed to accept that leadership reluctantly. But during the last week I've heard a great deal of serious talk about American policy—economic and political—many expressions of real desire to aid our allies in Europe uncertainty as to how it can be done without demanding unfair sacrifices of ourselves. There is no easy, ready-made answer. But from these conversations and from the press and radio, I conclude that there has occurred, or is occurring, a change in our attitude toward Europe.

We fought the last war in an effort to secure a Europe that wouldn't bother us—and we failed. Another terrible war has been concluded, and many seem to realize that our future is bound up with that of Europe, that our self-interest is involved in what happens over there. There would seem to be one important test to apply to any and all American commitments in Europe, whether they be about Italian colonies or Trieste or the Dardanelles and that is this: Once the agreement has been made and agreed to by those powers concerned, are we prepared, in concert with other powers, to use force, to go to war, if those decisions are upset by force of arms? Our commitments should not extend beyond the areas where we are prepared to sustain and support them by all means at our disposal. We cannot, powerful as we are, do it alone.

It seems to me that our State Department is facing a test second only to that which confronted our Army after Pearl Harbor. We are all at the moment concerned about the policies pursued by the armies of occupation. Certainly, mistakes have been made. We haven't much experience in occupying countries. It seems a healthy sign that the public should be so concerned and vigilant about this matter of the treatment of defeated nations. But isn't there some chance that we may pay more attention to the defeated enemies than to the cultivation of our friends? We should make available to them, through libraries and the exchange of students and professors, through broadcasts and publications, information about this country. Many Europeans are curious and more than a little apprehensive about this great power in the West. Often our ways are not their ways. But a fuller exchange of information and ideas might result in both sides learning something of mutual advantage.

September 23, 1945

According to an article in Life, *Japan's attack on Pearl Harbor was not the surprise it had been represented as being.*

I have been reading a thoughtful magazine article by a friend of mine, John Chamberlain. He deals with an event which affected the lives of all of us—the attack at Pearl Harbor and the events that led up to it. He concludes that valuable lessons can be learned as the result of a thoroughgoing investigation. That is probably true, for the people have a right to know what was done in their name. But Mr. Chamberlain states, "To say that we were slugged without warning is a radical distortion of the truth. Roosevelt, the chief executive of the nation and the commander-in-chief of its Army and Navy, knew in advance that the Japanese were going to attack us and," he adds, "there is even grounds for suspicion that he elected to bring the crisis to a head, when it came." And Mr. Chamberlain continues, "More than 15 hours before Pearl Harbor, Roosevelt and the members of the Washington high command knew that the Japanese envoys were going to break with the United States the next day. The only thing they did not know was the precise point of the military attack."

These are serious charges and, presumably, will be investigated in due course. I should like to make some comment upon them. I dined at the White House on that Pearl Harbor Sunday evening. The President did not appear for dinner but sent word down that I was to wait. He required some information about Britain and the blitz, from which I had just returned. I waited. There was a steady stream of visitors—cabinet members and Senate leaders. In the course of the evening I had some opportunity to exchange a few words with Harry Hopkins and two or three cabinet members when they emerged from conference. There was ample opportunity to observe at close range the bearing and expression of Mr. [Henry L.]

Stimson, Colonel [Frank] Knox, and Secretary [Cordell] Hull [secretaries of Army, Navy and State]. If they were *not* surprised by the news from Pearl Harbor, then that group of elderly men were putting on a performance which would have excited the admiration of any experienced actor. I cannot believe that their expressions, bearing and conversation were designed merely to impress one correspondent who was sitting outside in the hallway. It may be that the degree of the disaster had appalled them and that they had known for some time, as Mr. Chamberlain asserts, that Japan would attack, but I could not believe it then and I cannot do so now. There was amazement and anger written large on most of the faces.

Some time after midnight—it must have been nearly one in the morning— the President sent for me. I have seen certain statesmen of the world in time of crisis. Never have I seen one so calm and steady. He was completely relaxed. He told me much of the day's events, asked questions about how the people of Britain were standing up to their ordeal, inquired after the health of certain mutual friends in London. In talking about Pearl Harbor he was as much concerned about the aircraft lost on the ground as about the ships destroyed or damaged.

Just before I left, the President said, "Did this surprise you?" I replied, "Yes, Mr. President." And his answer was, "Maybe you think it didn't surprise us!" I believed him. He had told me enough of the day's disaster to know that there was no possibility of my writing a line about that interview till the war was over. I have ventured to recount part of that interview now because it seems to me to be relevant to a current controversy.

1946

1952

January 13, 1946

A great trial began this week, an event more important than any judging of war criminals. That is one way to consider the first assembly of the United Nations Organization. It is the view of the most hopeful idealists, for to them the meeting in London of some seven hundred representatives of fifty-one nations is more than just another effort to do well what the men at Versailles did badly.

It is the last chance, the beginning of what may be the final test of modern man himself. These hopeful idealists agree with Prime Minister Attlee that the atomic bomb was only the last of a series of warnings. And they see at the bar of judgment the intelligence and conscience of mankind.

The future, rather than the past, is at stake. Not the warmakers but the peacemakers are in the dock. The jury is the world's public opinion, and the judge of success or failure will be history. Or, in the words of King George's address of welcome to the delegates, "the millions yet unborn."

March 10, 1946

During the past week the voice from Fulton, Missouri, was the loudest in the land. Mr. Churchill's speech has been digested, interpreted and commented upon. The reactions have fallen into an altogether predictable pattern. The extreme left accuse him of advocating an anti-Russian alliance. The extreme right give a warm welcome to the speech. And the majority, in the middle, continue in a state of confusion. Britain's leading government spokesmen have been careful to refrain from comment, but that should not be taken to mean that they had advance knowledge of the contents of the speech, or that it had in any sense government sanction or approval. It did not.

There appears to be a tendency on both sides of the Atlantic to regard the solution of the ideological, economic and geographical conflict between Russia and the Western world as being soluble only by creating a world in the image of Mr. Churchill or in the image of Mr. Stalin. In this connection, it is useful to remember that Mr. Churchill and his party were decisively beaten and turned from office by the ballots of the British people. After full and free debate, they decided that their gratitude to the great wartime leader was not sufficient to cause them to return him and his party to power. The British, in common with many peoples on the Continent, sought for middle ground between the conservatism of Mr. Churchill and the suppressive collectivism of Mr. Stalin.

It was customary during the war to say that democracy was on trial, as indeed it was. It survived, but the trial is not yet ended. The outcome will be determined, not by dollars, not by American battleships showing a flag in the Mediterranean, not by luxury or productivity at home. It will, I think, be determined by the degree to which Americans understand the role in world affairs that has been thrust upon them. And the importance, not only of our decisions but of our example. We have, whether we like it or not, come into our full inheritance, our full strength. The rest of the world knows it, if we do not. We can no longer mediate, or non-intervene. Our influence and our interests spread round the world. We have emerged from this war into a precarious peace with great power. Indeed, with a power which fills our friends with a mixture of admiration and fear.

It's difficult to get any idea of size, the dimensions of a skyscraper or a powerhouse, if you're inside it. I spent the past several years looking at America from the outside. Tomorrow I'm coming home to stay. That is why I have ventured to speak as I have about how America appears from Europe. For it would seem that we are

112

confronted with a choice. A choice between leadership and isolation. Not isolation of our own choice but the isolation which will be imposed upon us if we travel in one direction and the rest of the world in another.

During the last few years I have seen a considerable number of people die with great dignity, but the thing that impressed me most was not the demonstration of physical courage; that's been a cheap commodity in this war. Many people of many nations, the Spaniards, the Poles, the Dutch, the British, and the Germans, were brave under the bombs. I doubt that the most important thing was Dunkirk, or the Battle of Britain, El Alamein or Stalingrad, perhaps not even the arrival of the American troops and American power in Europe. Historians may decide that any one of these events was decisive. But I am persuaded that the most important thing that happened in Britain was that this nation chose to win or lose the war under the established rules of parliamentary procedure. It feared Nazism but did not choose to imitate it. Mr. Churchill remained the servant in the House of Commons. The government was given dictatorial power, but it was used with restraint. And the House of Commons was ever vigilant.

I remember that while London was being bombed in the daylight, the House of Commons devoted two days to discussing conditions under which enemy aliens were detained on the Isle of Man. Though Britain fell, there were to be no concentration camps here. I remember that two days after Italy declared war an Italian citizen convicted of murder in the lower court appealed successfully to the highest court in the land, and the original verdict was set aside. Representative government, equality before the law, survived. Future generations who bother to read the official record of proceedings in the House of Commons will discover that the British Army retreated from many places. But that there was no retreat from the principles for which our ancestors fought.

This reporter, who has not always been right and who on occasion had the high privilege of sharing the dangers and discomforts of the American Army and of the British people, saw Americans and Britons give the reply to tyranny that their history, their traditions and their ancestors demanded of them. It would be churlish for any reporter to leave this land without acknowledging his debt to the many people who have given him tea, hospitality and information. And, on occasion, inspiration. It would be equally unmannerly to fail to acknowledge the debt to those people at home who have written or cabled praise, condemnation or condolences. And now for the last time . . . this is Edward R. Murrow in London.

Murrow was returning to New York to take up new duties as a CBS vice president and director of public affairs. However, this was not to be his last London broadcast. Murrow felt ill at ease in the executive suite and returned to active reporting in September 1947.

September 29, 1947

Released from his non-reportorial duties, Murrow began the series of weekday evening radio broadcasts that was to run without interruption for twelve years and become radio's most cited news program. The first broadcast concluded:

I should like to say a personal word about this series of broadcasts. Perhaps the best way to do it is to read you a paragraph from my contract. It says there that news programs are broadcast

solely for the purpose of enabling the listeners thereto to know facts—so far as they are ascertainable—and so to elucidate, illuminate and explain facts and situations as fairly as possible to enable the listener to weigh and judge for himself. In other words, Columbia endeavors to assist the listener in weighing and judging developments throughout the world, but refrains particularly with respect to all controversial, political, social and economic questions from trying to make up the listener's mind for him. News periods therefore should be devoted to giving the facts emanating from an established news-gathering source, to giving all the color in the proper sense of the word, and interest, without intruding the views of the analyst. The news-analyst further can, and very often should, give as much light as possible on the meaning of events; the news-analyst should not say that they're good or bad in his opinion but should analyze their significance in the light of known facts, the results of similar occurrences and so on. And in this he, of course, should always

114

be fair. He is fully entitled to give, and should give, the opinions of various persons, groups or political parties when these are known, leaving the listener to draw his own conclusions after he has been, as well as possible, informed about the event, its meaning, the attitude of persons or groups toward it, and the known results of similar things in the past.

Now that's pretty complicated language, the kind that lawyers like to write. My own interpretation of it is that this program is not a place where personal opinion should be mixed up with ascertainable facts. We shall do our best to identify sources and to resist the temptation to use this microphone as a privileged platform from which to advocate action. It is not, I think, humanly possible for any reporter to be completely objective, for we are all to some degree prisoners of our education, travel, reading—the sum total of our experience. And we shall try to remember that the mechanics of radio which make it possible for an individual voice to be heard throughout the entire land don't confer great wisdom or infallibility on that individual.

It's unwise to predict what will happen on a news program because that will be determined by the nature of the news. But I think it is safe to say that no considerable amount of time will be devoted to news originating in divorce courts and maternity wards.

There's another thing that should be made clear at the outset. This is not a one-man show. It enjoys the support and active cooperation of radio's best news-gathering organization. From time to time you'll hear my colleagues, both in this country and abroad. And, believe me, it's a privilege to be working with them again. Being human, we will probably make mistakes, and the only thing that can be said about that in advance is that we shall do our utmost to be the first to correct them.

> *At 12:45 a.m., New York time, Murrow repeated the broadcast for the West Coast. For the inhabitants of that region, which was his own, he added a nostalgic note: "For several years this reporter sat behind microphones in various European capitals. Nine or ten hours separated him from friends on the western slopes. Now it's nearly one in the morning here in New York. Only three hours separate us. It's a good feeling, like nearing home."*

115

October 1, 1947

Much newsprint and a lot of radio time is being devoted to the discussion of what this nation can, and should, do to help less fortunate nations, those scarred by the red-hot rake of battle. Certainly the situation in Europe is desperate. Around the world a few hundred millions are shopping around for new allegiances, questioning old beliefs, asking themselves the old question, "What must we do to be saved?" Many of them are prepared to live dangerously and to risk desperate experiments. They are looking for food and warmth and security, looking for rather simple things which many of us take for granted. Not long ago I heard a European cabinet minister put it in these words. He said, "What I want for my country is this, that honest men may sleep peacefully in their beds at night, certain that nothing will come through the roof and explode and certain that no one will come through the door without a search warrant." That is a simple objective but difficult to achieve. And those who are trying to achieve it are looking to this country.

But in many countries, including Western Europe, we are regarded with a mixture of fear and admiration. In a curious way, the situation reminds this reporter of the condition that existed in that cold and desperate winter of 1940 when people all over Europe were asking, "What will America do?" That was the leading question because the answer to all other questions depended upon the answer to that one. Much the same thing is true today. We have, whether we like it or not, come into our full inheritance. We have had leadership thrust upon us. But that does not mean that foreign nations will accept that leadership just because we are powerful, just because we have the dollars. The war, after all, was something more than a game of marbles in which one boy ended up with most of the marbles. You will remember that winter of '40. We were spending many dollars then—remember —all aid short of war? It wasn't enough. Now we are talking about what can be spared for the support of our way of life in Europe. The estimates are being drawn up, and the debate continues. Any estimate of what we could have spared at the time

116

of Pearl Harbor would probably have been sufficient to have lost the war.

I want to make it quite clear that this is not an appeal for dollars for Europe. It is rather an attempt to point out that dollars were not in the past, and are not in the future, likely to be decisive. Something vastly more important is involved. Dollars may save civilized people from hunger and chaos and despair for a few months. Dollars may divert for a time the channels down which political history is flowing, but there aren't enough dollars to make dollar-democrats out of enough Europeans. Something more is needed, and it can be said in a word, and the word is a fair distillation of many years of conversations with Europeans who view us with that mixture of fear and admiration. The word is *example*. What we do here in this country—the example we set—will in the end of the day determine the terms of our bargain with destiny, will do more than dollars to persuade those who are shopping about for new allegiances that our concept of justice, of relation between the individual and the state, is something they should strive to imitate.

There is now in progress in the market places of the world a great debate. There are many who believe that our system cannot last, that we are unable to provide the security, justice, tolerance and stability, the economic and social equality that is written into our great documents. There are many who predict our economic collapse and not a few who hope for it. Here in this country we are much concerned about foreign affairs, matters of international moment. The demands upon us are heavy and likely to increase, but it would perhaps be useful to remember that here, in this provident land, is the real proving ground of our principles.

We are fat and the rest of the world is lean; we are not greatly loved abroad. Gratitude is not an emotion that determines the actions of nations. If you will read the press of the world and listen to the radio of foreign nations, you will quickly discover that we are being watched. Often our motives are distorted; we are under almost constant attack. Oratory at the UN or elsewhere is not an effective reply. But example—the example of a nation strong, tolerant and stable where men may live in dignity under established law, where civil liberties are secure and where economic security is expanding—that might prove to be the clinching argument in the great debate. If we can do it.

117

October 27, 1947

The House Un-American Activities Committee was conducting hearings on Communist infiltration of the film industry. Movie stars, as well as producers and directors, had testified. Murrow saw in the hearings a threat to the basic right of individuals to their beliefs.

I want to talk for a few minutes about the Hollywood investigation now being conducted in Washington. This reporter approaches the matter with rather fresh memories of friends in Austria, Germany and Italy who either died or went into exile because they refused to admit the right of their government to determine what they should say, read, write or think. (If witnessing the disappearance of individual liberty abroad causes a reporter to be unduly sensitive to even the faintest threat of it in his own country, then my analysis of what is happening in Washington may be out of focus.) This is certainly no occasion for a defense of the product of Hollywood. Much of that product fails to invigorate me, but I am not obliged to view it. No more is this an effort to condemn congressional investigating committees. Such committees are a necessary part of our system of government and have performed in the past the double function of illuminating certain abuses and of informing congressmen regarding expert opinion on important legislation under consideration. In general, however, congressional committees have concerned themselves with what individuals, organizations or corporations have or have not done, rather than with what individuals think. It has always seemed to this reporter that movies should be judged by what appears upon the screen, newspapers by what appears in print and radio by what comes out of the loudspeaker. The personal beliefs of the individuals involved would not seem to be a legitimate field for inquiry, either by government or by individuals. When bankers, or oil or railroad men, are hailed before a congressional committee, it is not customary to question them about their beliefs or the beliefs of men employed by them. When a soldier is brought before a court martial he is confronted with witnesses, entitled to counsel and to cross-questioning. His reputation as a soldier,

118

his prospects of future employment, cannot be taken from him unless a verdict is reached under clearly established military law.

It is, I suppose, possible that the committee now sitting may uncover some startling and significant information. But we are here concerned only with what has happened to date. A certain number of people have been accused either of being Communists or of following the Communist line. Their accusers are safe from the laws of slander and libel. Subsequent denials are unlikely ever to catch up with the original allegation. It is to be expected that this investigation will induce increased timidity in an industry not renowned in the past for its boldness in portraying the significant social, economic and political problems confronting this nation. For example, Willie Wyler, who is no alarmist, said yesterday that he would not now be permitted to make *The Best Years of Our Lives* in the way in which he made it more than a year ago.

Considerable mention was made at the hearings of two films, *Mission to Moscow* and *Song of Russia*. I am no movie critic, but I remember what was happening in the war when those films were released. While you were looking at *Mission to Moscow* there was heavy fighting in Tunisia. American and French forces were being driven back; Stalin said the opening of the Second Front was near; there was heavy fighting in the Solomons and New Guinea; MacArthur warned that the Japanese were threatening Australia; General Hershey announced that fathers would be called up in the draft; Wendell Willkie's book *One World* was published. And when *Song of Russia* was released, there was heavy fighting at Cassino and Anzio; the battleship *Missouri* was launched, and the Russian newspaper *Pravda* published, and then retracted, an article saying that the Germans and the British were holding peace talks. And during all this time there were people in high places in London and Washington who feared lest the Russians might make a separate peace with Germany. If these pictures, at that time and in that climate, were subversive, then what comes next under the scrutiny of a congressional committee? Correspondents who wrote and broadcast that the Russians were fighting well and suffering appalling losses? If we follow the parallel, the networks and the newspapers which carried those dispatches would likewise be investigated.

Certain government agencies, such as the State Department and the Atomic Energy Commission, are confronted with a real dilemma. They are obligated to maintain security without doing violence to the essential liberties of the citizens who work for them. That may require special and defensible security measures. But no such problem arises with instruments of mass communication. In that area there would seem to be two alternatives: either we believe in the intelligence, good judgment, balance and native shrewdness of the American people, or we believe that government should investigate, intimidate and finally legislate. The choice is as simple as that.

The right of dissent—or, if you prefer, the right to be wrong—is surely fundamental to the existence of a democratic society. That's the right that went first in every nation that stumbled down the trail toward totalitarianism.

I would like to suggest to you that the present search for Communists is in no real sense parallel to the one that took place after the First World War. That, as we know, was a passing phenomenon. Those here who then adhered to Communist doctrine could not look anywhere in the world and find a strong, stable, expanding body of power based on the same principles that they professed. Now the situation is different, so it may be assumed that this internal tension, suspicion, witch hunting, grade labeling—call it what you like—will continue. It may well cause a lot of us to dig deep into both our history and our convictions to determine just how firmly we hold to the principles we were taught and accepted so readily, and which made this country a haven for men who sought refuge. And while we're discussing this matter, we might remember a little-known quotation from Adolf Hitler, spoken in Königsberg befor he achieved power. He said, "The great strength of the totalitarian state is that it will force those who fear it to imitate it."

November 20, 1947

Murrow was in London on the occasion of Princess Eliza-beth's wedding.

This was rather more than a wedding, more than an opportunity for hundreds of thousands who couldn't see to cheer. The few hundred who fainted and were hauled away in ambulances, designed for air raid casualties, were just unlucky. It was a fairy book wedding of an almost diminutive princess to a blonde duke. It meant stability, continuity and an opportunity for a very considerable emotional outburst before another hard winter grips this island.

This reporter saw this day a strange sight—the Princess walking the three hundred feet on the red carpet in the sanctuary was more than life size. Before she came into the abbey, Queen Mary, Mr. Winston Churchill, Field Marshal Smuts of South Africa, King Peter of Yugoslavia, Michael of Rumania, and other familiar figures had all walked that distance and they seemed just normal. But when the fanfare roared around the pillars and arches of the abbey, when we could see silhouetted in the west door the King and the Princess, something happened. It may have been just the shimmer of ivory satin and crystals and pearls, the fitted bodice and flowing skirt, the long tight sleeves, the huge veil held in place by a tiara of pearls and diamonds—it may even have been the huge bouquet of white orchids—nevertheless, the King remained the same size, but the Princess, moving down the red carpet, was scarcely recognizable.

The one thousand five hundred hours of embroidery on her gown, the crystal flowers around the heart-shaped neckline, the roses and the orange blossoms, plus the way she carried herself, made her appear a good foot taller than she is. Maybe it was just the shoes, ivory satin sandals, platform soles, open toes, but I don't think so. Perhaps it was the way all the light in the abbey seemed to bounce off that tiara and white satin. Perhaps she only seemed taller because of the two pages—five-year-old boys, Prince William of Gloucester and Prince Michael of Kent—who were doing their serious best to manage that fifteen-foot train. It seemed to me that the Life Guards and the Beefeaters in scarlet and gold, all of them six-footers, were looking up at the Princess when she passed. I talked with her two nights ago at a party and can assure you that she is not more than five foot two. It may be that my perspective from the organ loft was somewhat distorted, but I can only report what I saw.

When the royal couple left the abbey, cheers pursued them all the way to Buckingham Palace. Anthony Eden told me later in the afternoon that he had never seen such an enthusiastic crowd in London. Only an hour ago, around Parliament Square, people were still trying to find buses and subway trains. They were tired after a day of standing, seemed almost as tired as the people who used to come up out of the air-raid shelters after a night-long raid seven years ago, but these people were happy even though most of them hadn't seen very much.

It was a damp, dreary, overcast day. The coal smoke and the mist from the Thames, that great river of liquid history, seeped into the abbey and wrapped itself around the lampposts in the late afternoon. It wasn't a pleasant day. But as I left Westminster the bus conductor said, "I'm so happy for them that it turned out fine today!"

March 10, 1948

The new Communist government of Czechoslovakia announced that Jan Masaryk, foreign minister since the end of the war and son of the founder of the Czech republic, had committed suicide.

This reporter would attempt to say a few words about an old friend. They say he committed suicide. I don't know. Jan Masaryk was a man of great faith and great courage. Under certain circumstances he would be capable of laying down his life with a grin and a wisecrack. For more than two years he had hidden a heavy heart behind that big smile and his casual, sometimes irreverent, often caustic comment on world affairs. I knew Jan Masaryk well before, during and after the war. I say that, not in any effort to gain stature in your eyes, but rather as a necessary preface to what follows. I sat with him all night in his London embassy the night his country was sacrificed on the altar of appeasement at Munich. He knew it meant war, knew that his country and its people were doomed. But there was no bitterness in the man, nor was there resignation or defeat.

We talked long of what must happen in Europe, of the young men that would die and the cities that would be smashed to rubble. But Jan Masaryk's faith was steady. As I rose to leave, the gray dawn pressed against the windows. Jan pointed to a big picture of Hitler and Mussolini that stood on the mantle and said, "Don't worry, Ed. There will be dark days, and many men will die, but

122

there *is* a God, and He will not let two such men rule Europe." He had faith, and he was a patriot, and he was an excellent cook. One night during the blitz he was preparing a meal in his little apartment. A bomb came down in the middle distance and rocked the building. Jan emerged from the kitchen to remark, "Uncivilized swine, the Germans. They have ruined my soufflé."

I once asked him what his war aim was, and he replied, "I want to go home." He always knew that in a world where there is no security for little nations there is neither peace nor security for big nations. After the Munich betrayal, the British made a conscience loan to Czechoslovakia. Beneš and Masaryk used a considerable part of the money to set up an underground news service. It was functioning when the Germans overran the country, and all during the war those two men were the best informed in London on matters having to do with Middle Europe. They had information out of Prague in a matter of hours from under the noses of the Germans. Jan Masaryk took to the radio, talking to his people, telling them that there was hope in the West, that Czechs and Slovaks would again walk that fair land as free men. When the war was over he went home. Certain that his country had to get along with the Russians or, as he used to say, "they will eat us up," his faith in democracy was in no way diminished. He became foreign minister in a coalition government. As the Communist strength increased, Jan saw less and less of his friends when he came to this country. His music gave him no comfort; no more were there those happy late night hours with Masaryk playing the piano, hours of rich, rolling Czech and Slovak folksongs. I asked him why he didn't get out, come to this country where he had so many friends. He replied, "Do you think I enjoy what I am doing? But my heart is with my people. I must do what I can. Maybe a corpse but not a refugee."

Did he make a mistake in this last crisis? I do not know. He stayed with Beneš. Who knows what pressures he was subjected to? It is unlikely that he could have altered the course of events. Perhaps it was in his mind that he could save some of his friends, some small part of liberty and freedom, by staying on as non-party foreign minister. I talked to him on the telephone on the third day of the crisis, before the Communists had taken over. He thought then that Beneš would dissolve parliament, call a national election, and the Communist strength would decrease. It would appear that the Communists moved too fast.

Did the course of events during the last two weeks cause Masaryk to despair and take his life, or was he murdered? This is idle speculation. Both are possible. But somehow this reporter finds it difficult to imagine him flinging himself from a third-floor window, which, as I remember and as the news agencies confirm, is no more than thirty-five or forty feet above the flagged courtyard. A gun, perhaps poison or a leap from a greater height would have been more convincing. It may be, of course, that Jan Masaryk made the only gesture for freedom that he was free to make. Whichever way it was, his name with that of his father will be one to lift the hearts of men who seek to achieve or retain liberty and justice.

March 12, 1948

> *The Senate was debating the Marshall Plan. Senator Taft, of Ohio, said he recognized no obligation to help Europe beyond one year. Senator Vandenberg, of Michigan, pressed for long-term assistance. It was an historic dialogue between two of the most powerful Republicans in Congress and a complete about-face for Vandenberg.*

Today in Washington the son of a president—Taft—and the son of a harness maker—Vandenberg—were again on opposite sides of an issue. As they have often been in recent years. Senator Taft wants to cut one billion, three hundred million from the Marshall Plan. He says the program threatens the economic stability of this country. He is in favor of aid for Western Europe, but only for specific programs necessary for subsistence or helpful in increasing their production, especially for export. He thinks the promise of unlimited American aid might discourage Europeans from trying to help themselves.

Senator Kem, a Republican from Missouri, said America should stop meddling abroad and arm itself so heavily that Russia, or any other aggressor, will not dare to attack. He suggested that the Marshall Plan might as well be called the Vandenberg Plan.

Certainly the Senator from Michigan has been the chief strategist in the campaign in the Senate. It is more than remarkable that a man who has spent most of his twenty years in the Senate as an ardent isolationist should devote his skill and his oratory to the passage of legislation without which the Administration just wouldn't have any foreign policy. Senator Vandenberg is a master of political timing. Either he has changed his mind or he has concluded that the mind of the country has changed.

Let's look briefly at his record. He voted against the repeal of the arms embargo after the last war began. He was against conscription in 1940. He didn't want to renew the reciprocal tariff act. In 1941, he voted against the extension of conscription. He cast his vote against Lend-Lease in the same year, and he also cast his ballot against the transfer of destroyers to Great Britain. Back in 1939, after the Germans had rolled into Poland, the Senator thought the war was nothing but "about twenty-five people and propaganda." He thought they wanted our money and men.

Compare those sentiments and those votes with what he said on the floor of the Senate in January of 1945: "The progress of science has made isolation impossible. No nation hereafter can immunize itself by its own exclusive action. Our oceans have ceased to be moats." He wanted the big powers to sign a treaty guaranteeing to keep Germany disarmed. The Senator lent strong support for the Bretton-Woods agreement, for the British loan in 1946. He spoke eloquently and often in support of the United Nations and the Truman Doctrine.

Senator Vandenberg, at sixty-four, is a big, six-foot-one two-hundred-pounder who wants to be liked. He was once a newspaper man himself, spent twenty-one years as editor of the *Grand Rapids Herald*. He writes his own speeches, and when he delivers them he sort of indicates, with his voice, what the lead of the story should be in tomorrow's papers. And he lifts the quotable quotes out of the text with his voice. He is given to rather old-fashioned, florid rhetoric, handles big words with ease. The Senator from Michigan had only one year of college training, but unlike some of his colleagues he gives the impression that he did not quit studying when he quit college.

Foreign diplomats who have dealt with Senator Vandenberg have told me that he is pretty much their idea of what an American senator would be like—informal, direct, smokes cigars, tells a good story, a comfortable and competent "sort of bloke," as one of them put it.

Today, Senator Arthur Vandenberg has what can only be described as a first-class sounding board, probably a better sounding board than any of the Republicans who are seeking the presidential nomination in a rather more active fashion. It is pretty difficult to write or broadcast a story about American foreign policy without including his name and his views. Of course, repetition of a man's name and his opinions may not help much in getting him the presidential nomination, but there is no evidence that it does any harm.

April 8, 1948

And now let's examine the case of Mr. Leo Isaacson and his passport. First, the facts. Mr. Isaacson was recently elected to the House of Representatives from the Bronx. He was the candidate of the American Labor Party. He had the support of Mr. Henry Wallace. There have been no charges of corruption, intimidation or coercion in connection with the election. Representative Isaacson applied to the State Department for a passport. He said he planned to attend a conference on aid to Greece to be held in Paris. The State Department refused to issue the passport. A spokesman for the department said the conference will include members of committees which have been organized in most Eastern European countries for the purpose of furnishing material and moral assistance to the guerrilla forces in Greece. The spokesman recalled that the United Nations General Assembly had passed a resolution calling on Greece's northern neighbors to do nothing to assist the guerrilla forces. Our own government is assisting the government of Greece to maintain its sovereignty against attack from guerrilla forces. And so the State Department concluded that the issuance of a passport for Mr. Isaacson would not be in the interest of the government of the United States. Mr. Isaacson renewed his request for a passport and was again refused by Acting Secretary of State Lovett, again on the grounds that Isaacson's presence at the Paris conference would not be in the best interest of this country.

This is the first time a member of Congress has ever been denied a passport by our State Department. Mr. Isaacson has accepted the decision as final but says it is an example of the book-burning mentality which now controls our government. He further claims that the department is limiting what information he may gather and where he may go as a congressman in search of facts. Now, under the law, any American citizen may apply for a passport to any country, but the decision as to whether it will be issued is solely within the power of the Secretary of State. The secretary can refuse to issue a passport, and under the law he is not required to state his reasons. So there is no question that under the existing law the Department of State acted in a wholly legal manner in refusing to give Mr. Isaacson his passport. Generally the issuance of a passport is a purely routine matter, but in this case it was denied on the grounds that Mr. Isaacson's presence at the Paris meeting would not serve the interests of this country. This position has received editorial support from *The New York Times,* which has stated, "No citizen is entitled to go abroad to oppose the policies and the interests of his country." The case of Mr. Isaacson and his passport has not aroused any considerable controversy in Congress or in the press. Those are the facts of the case.

This reporter would like to suggest a few considerations that are relevant to it. Mr. Isaacson is a follower of Henry Wallace. Had he been permitted to go to Paris, he might well have been expected to make speeches critical of American policy, similar to those made by Mr. Wallace on his European trip. However, the thesis that no citizen is entitled to go abroad to oppose the policies of his own country can be expanded. By denying him a passport, he can be prevented from expressing those views in person. But should he likewise be prevented from expressing them in print or on the air? For example, should the Voice of America in its broadcast to Europe report that there *is* complete unity in this country in support of our foreign policy? If it does so, it would not be telling the truth, and confidence in the honesty of our statements would be reduced. Also, are we to ban the export of publications containing material critical of our foreign policy?

Another question is raised by this decision. It is this: Should a government department be given sole power to determine who shall be free to travel abroad? If it is deemed to be in the best interest of this country to prevent those who oppose our foreign policy from going abroad, would it not be better to pass a law? For the only protection an individual has against other individuals or against the State is law, duly passed by his elective representatives and tested in the courts. The individual's freedom of movement, or, to put it another way, any restrictions placed upon the individual's freedom of movement are less likely to be abused under law than under a system where an individual in a government department makes the final decision.

The decision to keep Mr. Isaacson at home was made at the time when our representatives were making speeches about the freer movement of news and persons. The conference he's supposed to attend is to be held in Paris, is permitted to be held there by a government that has had the Communist Party at its throat but still has a deep tradition of personal and political freedom. The voters in this country are free to elect whom they will, mastermind or moron, conservative or radical. Candidates for public office, unlike persons wishing to enter many other professions, need pass no examination. They make decisions, enact laws for the rest of us. If after free and open debate they choose to limit the action of an individual or a group of individuals, that's one thing. But if the limitation is imposed by a single individual, by a single government department, that's something else again. In terms of the impact upon foreign opinion, it is doubtful whether any oratory or intrigue in which Mr. Isaacson might have engaged would have been more damaging to the interest of this country than the fact that he has been denied permission to leave.

This issue is, I suggest, considerably bigger than Mr. Isaacson, his passport or his political philosophy. It has to do with whether or not, in the absence of law, a duly elected representative, or any other citizen for that matter, shall be confined to the country because he opposes our foreign policy. Such action may be wise; it may even be necessary. But when it is done without a vote by our elected representatives, without a law, it is dangerous. And if this formulation is correct, it is as dangerous to apply such restrictions to those who occupy the extreme left of the political spectrum as it would be to apply them to those on the extreme right. For the act itself endangers the freedom of all of us. Probably the most significant and serious aspect of the Affair Isaacson is that it has pro-

128

duced so little controversy in Congress and in the country. It's surely a matter worth arguing about.

The State Department did not issue the passport.

April 14, 1948

> *Democracy was challenged in Italy, where it appeared that the Communists might win their first free parliamentary election. Murrow flew to Rome a few days before the voting and visited an old battlefield.*

Do you remember a place called Anzio, the beachhead where the Americans and British hung on from January till May of 1944, while the big German guns pounded them from the hills above? Anzio isn't far from Rome. You can drive it in less than an hour. As you approach the beachhead, the few buildings are all new. The fields are uneven because the bomb and shell holes have left their mark. There is plenty of barbed wire originally designed to contain men, not cattle. The usual political signs line the roads. A group of three men are painting red stars on a white wall, but with the countryman's wisdom they're doing it the easy way, using a spray gun. Just cut a star in a big piece of cardboard, hold it against the wall, let fly with the spray gun, and there you have it—modern mass production on the Appian Way.

In Anzio, you talk with the mayor. He's a Communist, has been since he was seventeen. He's in the new municipal building. The old one was smashed. There is that sweet, pleasing smell that is peculiar to fresh Italian plaster. Anzio has a population of nine thousand: three thousand fishermen, two thousand peasants, the rest scattering. There are about fifty families with relatives in the United States. The mayor tells you the Left coalition, led by the Communists, will win the election in Anzio. The fishermen are already socialized, have a long-standing cooperative deal with the men who own the boats. The peasants will vote Left because in the last couple of years some uncultivated land has been taken away from the two princes who own most of the land around there and turned over to the peasants—and they like that.

129

The mayor thinks the campaign has been orderly up to now, but he's afraid that he and a few other Communist leaders will be picked up the night before the voting. The mayor is a Catholic as well as a Communist. He shows you his saints' pictures and small religious medals, asserts that the Communists object only to the Church entering politics, never attack its spiritual teachings. He tells you that only a couple of Sundays ago, twenty Communist Party members went to church in a body for the first Communion of their children. The mayor grows a little bitter when he tells you that only two days ago one of the leaders of the Communist Party died. The Communists wanted to follow his coffin to the church, carrying their flags, but the priests refused to permit it. The Catholic Democrats were permitted to carry their banners. The mayor didn't think that was fair.

You go to see the parish priest, climbing up the two stories on cleated boards over loose brick and scaffolding. They're trying to rebuild his church. The priest is an old man. He confirms the mayor's story about that funeral parade. And he says two Communist leaders have died in the last few days from natural causes. One had been making political speeches all day, went home, suffered some sort of paralysis and died. The parish priest offers this comment: "I think he talked too much." He thinks the Christian Democrats of De Gasperi will win because their propaganda has been good and because the Communists in Anzio have promised much but done little, have taken some of the best villas for themselves. The parish priest agreed with the Communist mayor on one point, saying that the Communists bring their children to Confirmation, come to church, confess and have always treated him with respect. He spoke warmly of the packages and presents that have come to Anzio from America.

We decided to find one of the citizens of Anzio who has received a letter from America concerning the election. He's living in the one room that's left of a house—cardboard over the windows, no running water, no carpets, one chair, a small wardrobe with a ragged piece of cloth instead of a door and a small battered chest. He's a gray, tired little man. Had a letter from his older brother in Providence, Rhode Island. Fumbled around in the little chest and found it, a long letter telling him not to vote Communist because that would mean loss of freedom and loss of American aid. We asked the little man if the letter has changed his mind, and he says, "Yes." He had planned to vote Communist, but now he won't because, he says, his brother is older than he is and, therefore, the head of the family. He scrabbled around in that little chest again and came up with a picture of his brother, a fine, healthy-looking man, well dressed, obviously a successful American businessman. The little brother in Anzio is a night watchman, when he's working. Did that letter really change the vote of the little brother in Anzio? I don't know. That's his business. But Germans, Japanese and Italians have something of a habit of telling Americans what they think they would like to hear.

Anzio, like the rest of Italy, is rebuilding for an uncertain future. Today the sky was blue. The scars of battle are being removed. The children appear healthy. Their babies seem all to have been freshly oiled. The whole beachhead was unnaturally quiet. The white clouds stood steady in the blue sky, almost as though they were at attention for the 7,500 American boys in the cemetery. That cemetery is surrounded by big curtains of canvas, for arrangements are being made to bring home all that is mortal of the soldiers who were as steady and brave as any Roman legionnaire who ever trod the Appian Way. That's the way it was in Anzio today, three days before the election.

The election was won by the Christian Democrats, giving De Gasperi's pro-Western party a mandate to govern for five years. The Communists polled nearly one third of the vote.

May 17, 1948

In paying tribute to his colleague George Polk, who was slain while on assignment in Greece, Murrow revealed the ethos of reporting he demanded of himself.

And now this reporter would attempt to say something about George Polk. He is dead. His body—hands and feet tied with twine, a bullet hole in his head—was taken from Salonika Harbor yesterday. He had been missing for one week.

George Polk had been for more than two years the chief Middle East correspondent for the Columbia Broadcasting System. It is believed that he had gone from Athens to Salonika for the purpose of arranging an interview with the guerrilla leader, General Markos, although precise information on this point is lacking. The police in Salonika have said that they are hunting for "suspected Communists" with whom Mr. Polk might have been in contact in his efforts to interview the guerrilla leader. According to the Associated Press, twenty or more Communists have been questioned; the record does not show that any *non*-Communists have been questioned. The Premier of Greece has ordered the entire police force of the country to uncover details of the murder. One leading government spokesman, who declined to allow the use of his name, stated, "We are one thousand per cent sure it was the work of the Communists." He offered no support for this statement.

Polk, in common with many other good American correspondents, was not popular with the Greek government. Such men as Raymond Daniel of *The New York Times* (when he was stationed in Greece), Seymour Freidin of the New York *Herald Tribune,* Robert Vermillion of the United Press, Homer Bigart of the *Herald Tribune,* Constantine Argyros of the *Christian Science Monitor,* have all been attacked either openly or by indirection as Communists or "pinks." This is a device that is frequently used in Europe and is not altogether unknown in this country. As far back as February 3, George Polk in a private letter said there were a number of vague hints that "somebody is likely to get hurt." But he was inclined to think then that it was more likely that correspondents writing material critical of the present regime in Athens might be framed on some black market charge as an excuse to expel them from the country.

There is nothing in the record to show that Polk feared physical violence, either from the Communists or from the right-wing government forces. Indeed, his whole record shows that he didn't fear anything. This was a reporter who had worked in half a dozen capitals and flown both fighters and bombers for the Navy during the war, was wounded in the Solomons and decorated for bravery. George Polk had that honesty and integrity—the reverence for fact and indifference to criticism—which gave him the respect of the men in his trade.

Since this reporter returned to broadcasting nine months ago, much of the material about the Middle East, and particularly about Greece, carried on this program came from Polk. Invariably it was clean, hard copy, well documented. And his stories stood up—every last one of them. He spared neither the corruption, inefficiency and petty political maneuvering of the Greek government, nor the vacillation of American policy, nor the atrocities committed by the Communists. What happened he reported, without fear and in language that all could understand.

And now that he is dead, the question is not whether he might have had cause to fear from the Greek government *or* the Communists. The question is: who killed him? And that would seem to be a matter with which our government might concern itself with full vigor. Certain it is that you have lost one of the ablest, most conscientious and courageous reporters who has ever served you.

> *On April 21, 1949, three Greeks were convicted in the Polk case—a professed ex-Communist was sentenced to life imprisonment for complicity in the crime; two Communists were found guilty in absentia and received sentences of death. The annual George Polk Memorial Awards for Outstanding Achievement in Journalism were established at Long Island University.*

September 20, 1948

> *The blockade of Berlin, begun by the Russians in June, was not broken by the Allied airlift until May 12, 1949. With the blockade in its fourth month, Murrow did a broadcast from Berlin on what riding the airlift was like. The flight started at Westover Field in Massachusetts.*

You stand around waiting to take off. There're a dozen GIs going along. They're the new addition. No battle ribbons. Real youngsters, just finished their basic training. They horse around out there by the desk, full of vitamins. Their talk is like soldiers' talk you heard on so many airfields before. But they seem awfully young. And then it hits you. When this last war started these were nine- and ten-year-old boys playing with electric trains. They couldn't even drive an automobile. Now they're there in their brown suits and heavy boots about to fly a big ocean. And a few questions convince you that they know where they're going and why. This is a small section of a volunteer army and it's pretty good.

133

The flight, of course, is like all flights—down to Bermuda and over the pink coral in the first light of dawn. Then twelve hours to the Azores, where the C.O. tells you they've trained local talent to service the planes and do practically everything needed on the base. Relations with the local population is good. No banana republic here. Sounds good, and there doesn't seem to be any reason to doubt the story. Then off from the Azores into the face of a full moon. A GI informs you the beer there wasn't so good. One of six American girls, bound for Germany to do secretarial work for the Army, tells you "it just seemed like a good idea," and, anyway, her grandmother maybe crossed the plains in a covered wagon. But she'd never flown the Atlantic Ocean to run a typewriter for an army of occupation.

Finally, you touch down at Rhine-Mainz, a little more than thirty hours from home. The big field is only a few miles from Frankfurt. Things look better than they did a couple of years ago. The shops are full. They're rebuilding. Here you see part of the magnet that's supposed to attract the East to the West. And you see that things are looking up. And then over on the far side of the field you see the big trucks lined up. The sad, somber colonel commanding the wing briefs you on the flight. He tells you the crews fly two trips and have four trips off; three crews to each plane; each one makes four trips every day. He says maintenance of the aircraft will be tough during the winter weather, but it can be done. And he runs the whole show from a little white-washed ten-by-ten room. He explains how the planes take off at three-minute intervals, go up to Tempelhof at set speed and designated altitudes, unload, come out on a fixed course and then sort of coast home. It all sounds simple.

You go out and climb over the coal stacked in a C-54. You find three youngsters up front—pilot, co-pilot and flight engineer. And that's all. Plus about twenty-six thousand pounds of coal. The pilot says with great pleasure, "We're the first ones off." And then the motors roll. You taxi to the end of the strip and wait for a plane incoming from London to land, and then the tower gives it to us. The three boys do their jobs, and you and the coal get up off the runway and start the grind up through the overcast. Three minutes behind you the same thing happens again. And then again and again and again. And that coal doesn't seem to list any easier than the bombs did a few years back.

The pilot levels out at five thousand. The clouds clear off, and over to port there is a Russian maneuver area, and you can see the gunnery range. Russian tanks and half-tracks are parked around the edge of a wood. Off to the right, there's a fighter strip and dead ahead another field with some twin-engined stuff parked around the perimeter. And you get the feeling you used to get when crossing the enemy coast in a bomber with a bellyful of bombs, and then you remember you've got only coal aboard. You fly level and straight for about an hour and a half. The pilot calls the tower at Tempelhof, and he's told it's a cross-wind of twenty-five miles, gusting up to fifty miles. The motor sputters, and the mixture is changed. And the crew chief says, "If you run out of gas, I can throw in a shovelful of coal." And then the pilot lines up the runway, and a cross-wind hits you and you remember a night back in 1944. You were over Berlin in an RAF Lancaster when it was whipped around by a flak burst, and the city below was a symphony of flame and smoke.

The approach to the field is over a graveyard. And that fifty-mile gust that they reported is accurate. And as you come in the co-pilot laughs and points to the graveyard and says, "That would be a fine place to end up, all because you're carrying coal." The landing was smooth. And when the ship stopped rolling, a truck was there to unload it. The work was done by solemn, surly-looking Germans. Many of them were in Rommel's Afrika Korps, but they bend to the job with a will. The three boys who flew in the coal had a quick sandwich from the mobile canteen that drew up alongside their plane. You thank them for the ride and they start the motors rolling again, back to Rhine-Mainz for another load. That cross-wind whips dust off the rubble as you drive away from the field, through those familiar streets where the rubble is only hip high.

This small island of uncertainty is a long finger reaching out from Westover Field in Massachusetts. Right now, at midnight, the sky is heavy with the rumble of motors. The coal and flour and all the rest continue to come in.

November 3, 1948

Truman upset Dewey, winning occupancy of the White House in his own right with a national plurality of 2, 135,-747 votes.

It would be possible to exhaust all the adjectives in the book in an effort to describe what happened yesterday—why it happened and what consequences may be expected to flow from the decision freely taken by the American people. For weeks and months, both the analysts and apologists will be busy examining the labor vote, the farm vote, the size of the total vote and the strategy of the two major parties. There will be many explanations—much second guessing, considerable sympathy for those whose high hopes of office and honors have been frustrated. Not much of this outpouring will be significant, except insofar as it may serve to guide the conduct of future political campaigns.

I do not pretend to know why the people voted as they did, for the people are mysterious and their motives are not to be measured. This election result has freed us to a certain extent from the tyranny of those who tell us what we think, believe and will do without consulting us. No one, at this moment, can say with certainty why the Republicans lost or why the Democrats won. Certainly the Republicans did not lose for the lack of skillful, experienced, indeed, professional politicians. They did not lose for lack of money or energy. They lost because the people decided, in their wisdom or their folly, that they did not desire the party and its candidates to govern this country for the next four years. Maybe they lost because, as some claim, their policy was based upon expediency, rather than principle, or because they refrained from striking shrewd blows at points where the Democrats were vulnerable; maybe it was the labor vote that did them in, or the fact that the farmers are prosperous, or that too many Republicans were made complacent and didn't vote because of the predictions of easy victory. I do not know, and I do not think it matters, for the people are sovereign, and they have decided.

It will be equally difficult—indeed, more difficult—to explain the Democratic victory. President Truman was beaten to the floor by his own party, even before they nominated him, and he got up, dressed in the ill-fitting cape of Franklin Roosevelt. He was a man who seemed unimpressive to many even when they thought he was right. He waged what was, in effect, a one-man campaign. Just try to call to mind the nationally known names who stood with him in this campaign, and you'll realize what a lonely (some said ridiculous) effort it was. He was just doing the best he knew how and saying so, and whatever the reasons, the people went with him and gave him a House and a Senate to work with.

This is the overwhelmingly important fact that confronts us, not the reasons why it came about. For President Harry S. Truman now occupies a position that is wholly unique in American history. It is not only that he has won it on his own; it is that he has given few hostages in the process. He is free from the conservative southern wing of his party; he is free, if he wants to be, from any of the big-city Democratic bosses. His policies, if they are wise, may free him from any recurrence of the threat from the extreme Left. By tomorrow he will have, if tradition and precedent is followed, the resignations of his entire cabinet on his desk. That will mean that he will be free to choose new human instruments with which to carve out his policies. His prestige abroad, his power of negotiation with foreign countries, will have been immeasurably increased. He will, obviously, find no necessity to trim his sails to the varying winds of public opinion polls. He will have a freedom of maneuver seldom granted to the head of a constitutional state.

The presidency of this country is more difficult, more complicated, more exacting than any other political office in the world. The President is not only the formal but the functioning chief of state. He must make decisions on matters about which he knows little or nothing, must sign documents that he hasn't read. He must, if he is to function efficiently, surround himself with a corps of men who are able honest, industrious and devoted to the welfare of the nation. President Truman now has the freedom to do precisely that.

High office produces changes in all men. It has never been possible to predict with any accuracy what kind of President a man will turn out to be. Who could have foretold for sure the course that would be followed by Lincoln, a Grant, a Hoover or a Franklin Roosevelt? With Mr. Truman we know some of the things to expect, for he has, so to speak, been in a showcase for quite a while. But his position now is completely altered. The people have given him directly the highest honor in the land; he has great freedom and great power *and* is beset by massive problems. I do not know whether the next four years will reveal him to be a great President. But they had better.

November 5, 1948

It's open season on pollsters, but it ought to be pointed out that they are accused of nothing except being wrong. No one claims, so far as I know, that they were "bought" or that they deliberately attempted to influence the outcome by contributing to despondency and alarm, or by inducing complacency in the Republican ranks. They were just wrong, and in the field of information and ideas this is no crime. Those newspapers that are pointing the finger at the polls should look at their own records and their own columns. Did the editors abdicate their job of reporting and analyzing in favor of Messrs. Roper and Gallup? As a matter of fact, the press of this country, if you figure in terms of percentage, has gone to bat five times without getting a hit. During the last five presidential elections the majority of them, generally a substantial majority, have advocated the election of the losing candidate. Radio officially remained neutral during the campaign, but in general the most and the best time went to the party with the most money, and that may not be the best way of conducting a national debate over the air.

However, I believe that there are certain results that may stem from this upset of the experts and the polls. Ours is a highly mechanized country. Our clothes are largely standardized; we tell pretty much the same stories, use the well-advertised goods of mass production. Much of our information is mass-produced, superimposed upon the country by syndicated columns written in New York or Washington, or by broadcasts originating in those two cities. We know now that during recent months many of us were taken in by something that wasn't true. We had almost come to believe that the hopes, the fears, the prejudices, the aspirations of the people who live on this great continent could be neatly measured and pigeonholed, figured out with a slide rule. What has happened is that a bit of current mythology has been destroyed. That is probably a good thing. For if we draw from this experience the obvious lesson, it ought to lead to more critical reading of newspapers, more critical and sceptical listening to the radio, a decrease in the willingness to accept predigested opinions and conclusions. The experts and the pollsters have, in fact, restored to us an appreciation of the importance, and the purely personal character, of our own opinions. From here on it will be easier to doubt the persuasive or hysterical voice that reaches us through the radio or the columnist who writes with power or persuasiveness but who divulges few facts. This experience may well cause many of us to doubt anew, to question the more things that we have in the past taken for granted. Certainly the experience will cause many of us who write and talk to approach the task with more humility, to consider always the possibility that we may be wrong and to search more diligently for facts upon which the reader or listener may base his opinion.

The pollsters are reexamining their figures and their techniques and hope as a result to improve their service. In many areas it has been, and will continue to be, a socially useful service. But I, for one, hope that they never achieve perfection. What a dreary prospect it would be to know with certainty precisely what we, as individuals or as a nation, believe or will do, or refuse to do, under given circumstances at some future date. Such a state of affairs would reduce us to robots and eliminate the adventure, the uncertainty and the romance of living and doing. Fortunately, I think, we have fresh evidence that, for the foreseeable future at least, we are to be saved from any such fate.

November 9, 1948

The news coming out of China grows more and more somber. Experienced Far Eastern correspondents are speaking of the collapse of Chiang Kai-shek's government and Nationalist China as being not only inevitable but imminent. Government efforts to control prices in Shanghai and Nanking have been abandoned. General Chiang's son has been thrown out of his job as the economic czar in Shanghai. The city of Soochow is menaced by three Chinese Communist columns apparently trying to break the Nationalist defenses on the Yangtze River. There are reliable reports that six Nationalist regiments deserted to Chinese Communists on the Soochow front today. Shanghai is facing its most critical food situation in modern times. The shops are shut; there are transport strikes. The farmers in the outlying districts have lost confidence in the new currency and refuse to deliver their crops. Workmen in Shanghai had less food today than at any time during the recent war. There are unconfirmed reports that Chiang Kai-shek will ask foreign powers to resume control over the Shanghai international settlement. If that is true, it would represent an unparalleled confession of failure by the Nationalist government. Chiang Kai-shek has predicted another eight years of war, and American citizens have been advised to leave the country.

William C. Bullitt left by plane for China today as the representative of a joint congressional committee watching over Marshall Plan expenditures. His presence in that land of four hundred million persons is not likely to affect the outcome.

It is an old lesson of war that an army cannot operate successfully against guerrilla tactics unless it has the support of the local population. Clearly, on the record, in vast areas of China, Chiang Kai-shek's armies do not enjoy that support. In addition to military failures, the Nationalist government failed to introduce effective economic reforms; Shanghai and other large cities were centers of graft and corruption. And so today in the midst of economic chaos the Central Government's best armies have been destroyed. There remain several pockets of effective resistance near Peiping and Tientsin, along the northern fringe of the Yangtze Valley. North China is isolated and economically valueless. Central and South China are economically chaotic and militarily impotent. The conditions for the rapid spread of Communism are there. And the time when this country must make a fateful decision is here.

Since the end of the war, this country has provided about one and one-half billion dollars for Chiang Kai-shek's regime. Things have gone from bad to worse. His government is due to get four hundred million this year under the Marshall Plan. Obviously this is not enough if we purpose to stop the spread of Communism. No one can say how much *would* be enough. We have put 440 millions into Greece, with its nearly eight million people, and that has saved the country from going Communist. But it has not appreciably improved either the military or the economic situation, and the problem in Greece is puny compared to the one presented by China. It seems to me that we face at least three possible courses of action. We can abandon China, give it up completely as a hopeless task and face squarely the prospect of not only China but most of Southeast Asia coming under Communist control. We can continue

140

to temporize, giving to China some help—all aid short of what is effective. The third alternative would be an all-out assistance effort, costing unknown billions of dollars during the next few years, coupled with an effort at careful supervision and an insistence upon economic, military and political reforms.

The choice between these three alternatives may be as fateful as any we have made since the end of the war. It may be in peace as in war that we cannot exercise decisive strength at all points simultaneously. I do not know. But the pattern of events in China seems to be forcing us toward an immediate decision. We must either get in, and in a big way, or we must get out.

November 12, 1948

For thirty long months the trial of Japan's principal war criminals dragged on before the international military tribunal in Tokyo. The eleven black-robed judges sat on a raised platform at one side of the War Ministry auditorium; the twenty-five defendants sat on the opposite side. Down in the well between, the lawyers, interpreters, pages and experts did their work. There were two sessions every day, five days a week, for thirty months. Reporters dozed; the galleries were generally empty. More than four thousand documents were introduced in evidence. There were nearly seven hundred witnesses for the prosecution, more than five hundred for the defense.

Today, it took Sir William Webb, the Australian who was president of the tribunal, exactly twenty-one minutes to pronounce sentence on all twenty-five defendants: death by hanging for Tojo and six of his fellow conspirators; sixteen got life imprisonment, one a twenty-year term, and another seven years. No execution date was set. The sentences will be reviewed by General MacArthur, who has set the deadline for appeals at one week from today. The court's decision was couched in the strongest possible language, branding the Japanese and their leaders with a consistent and calculated policy of aggression since 1936, declaring them responsible for the death of millions, perpetrators of every manner of outrage and torture.

This trial, and the ones at Nuremberg, have established certain precedents for the future. The first is that nations have the power to set up such a tribunal under international law. Thus it is established that in the case of future aggressive war, the aggressors can assume from the beginning that they will be subject to prosecution—provided, of course, they don't win the war. It is now established that planning, preparing and initiating aggressive war constitutes an international crime. And it is also established that atrocities—crimes against humanity—are not merely the responsibility of those who commit them, but also the responsibility of the highest level of government officials. These rulings mean that war has been taken off its special pedestal, out of a special category, and placed alongside all other crimes involving the use of force to settle disputes. Nations, like individuals, must pay the penalty for aggressive violence; but obviously, if they do plan and perpetrate war, not until they have been beaten into submission.

The court in its judgment said that most of the witnesses for the defense were guilty of equivocations, evasions, a lack of candor. Clearly the court regarded many of the witnesses appearing before it as being guilty of the same duplicity and hypocrisy as had marked the activities of seventeen successive cabinets during the period of Japan's conspiracy. There were no signs of any moral regeneration on the part of the Japanese who testified. Tojo, the principal criminal, said he wanted to take the entire responsibility for the war, but unfortunately others were involved, much to his regret. He added that the spirit of the Japanese people is certain to rise again. From the beginning of the trial he said he had been worried lest Emperor Hirohito might be involved. But now that it is clear that he will not be, Tojo says, his mind is at rest.

Sir William Webb filed a minority opinion. He said Hirohito couldn't evade responsibility for Japanese aggression, although he enjoys political immunity. He added that the Emperor's authority was required for the war. If he did not want war, he should have withheld his authority. Webb's minority opinion revives a fundamental conflict in views. He held, from the beginning, that it was absurd to hold a trial without Emperor Hirohito in the dock as the principal war criminal. The American chief prosecutor was under strict orders from Washington not to involve the emperor in any way. Even the American attorneys supplied for the defendants were forbidden to involve him.

Emperor Hirohito was not tried for reasons of high policy or

Ed Murrow's habit of accompanying fliers into combat—forty missions in two wars—worried his home office. Ten missions were flown with the 386th Bomb Group, U. S. Eighth Air Force, led by Colonel Joe W. Kelly, shown here with Murrow in late 1944 after a raid on a German missile site. The airplane in background is a B-26.

In April 1942 Murrow and William L. Shirer did a broadcast from New York in which they discussed Hitler's Russian campaign and prospects for a second front. Shirer, in 1937, was the first correspondent Murrow recruited to cover Europe for CBS.

By 1942 Murrow had built a team of war correspondents that was to become renowned. Here, outside the CBS office in Hallam Street, London, Murrow posed—one foot on his Bentley—with Paul Manning, John Daly, and Robert Trout. Other CBS correspondents covering the European theater included Charles Collingwood, Richard C. Hottelet, Eric Sevareid, Howard K. Smith, Bill Downs, and Larry LeSueur.

Murrow's boss at CBS was William S. Paley, president and later chairman of the board. During World War II, Paley served as deputy director of the Psychological Warfare Division, SHAEF (Supreme Headquarters Allied Expeditionary Force). In 1945, shortly after V-E Day, they conferred in Bad Homburg, in western Germany, where Paley was stationed.

In June 1948 Thomas E. Dewey was again seeking the Republican nomination for president. On the eve of the Republican convention in Philadelphia, Murrow interviewed Dewey for his broadcast.

From a temporary platform on the memorial to Queen Victoria, outside Buckingham Palace, Murrow in 1953 described the coronation procession of another British queen, Elizabeth II.

Confrontation at Glen Arden Farm, Murrow's home in Pawling, New York. In the mid-1950's the dairy farm operated with a registered herd of ninety Holstein-Friesian cattle in which Murrow took personal pride.

In April 1953 Speaker Joseph W. Martin of Massachusetts (center) and former Speaker Sam Rayburn of Texas took Murrow on a television tour of the House of Representatives.

Murrow made three trips to Korea, where he reported the fighting with the same involvement that distinguished his wartime broadcasts from London. Here, at Christmastime 1953, wearing a borrowed helmet, he talks to soldiers of the 25th Infantry Division.

It was to Glen Arden Farm that Murrow turned for relaxation. Preparatory to a morning of trout fishing, he instructs his son, Charles Casey, aged 10, on attaching a fly. A stream, once stocked with brook trout, crosses a corner of the farm.

In 1957 on Islamorada, in the Florida Keys, Janet Murrow joined her husband during the filming of an informal interview with Harry S. Truman in which the former President reviewed his political career on the documentary series "See It Now." It was agreed that other portions of the interview would not be made public during Mr. Truman's lifetime.

The Fund for the Republic, in memory of dramatist Robert E. Sherwood, in 1958 presented Marian Anderson with a special award for her contribution to freedom and justice on the autobiographical program " The Lady from Philadelphia," produced by Murrow and Fred W. Friendly. Eleanor Roosevelt was a delighted witness to the presentation.

The annual "Years of Crisis" broadcasts on CBS, in which correspondents, foreign and domestic, debate events of the year past, were presided over by Murrow for nine years. Here Murrow enjoyed a joke during rehearsal of the program on January 2, 1955. With him, left to right, are Howard K. Smith, Eric Sevareid, and David Schoenbrun.

Murrow was sworn in as director of the United States Information Agency on March 21, 1961, at a White House ceremony attended by his family. President Kennedy gave the ex-broadcaster a voice in the making of policy decisions that the U.S.I.A. would have to explain to the world. "Whatever is done," Murrow said, "will have to stand on a rugged basis of truth."

Ed Murrow as millions remember seeing him. Of the broadcaster, James Reston said, "He had courage, and he had style." Said Eric Sevareid, "He was an original, and we shall not see his like again."

expediency. If he isn't as guilty as the other twenty-five, at least he would seem to be a likely suspect. His immunity may have been politically advantageous; some might even call it an act of statesmanship. But it was not, under any definition of the word with which I am familiar, an act of justice. The American chief prosecutor, Joseph Keenan, formally cleared Hirohito of involvement in the conspiracy and was careful to keep from the record any information that might have proved the emperor's participation. I do not assert that Hirohito was guilty, or that he is not extremely useful to the occupying powers, but only that he was a prime suspect and was not tried. And that it is unfortunate that justice and expediency should walk hand in hand even in a conqueror's court.

February 14, 1949

> *Buried in President Truman's State of the Union message was his proposal for a medical insurance program which came to be called Medicare.*

"It is a shocking fact that tens of millions lack adequate medical care. We are short of doctors, hospitals and nurses. We must remedy these shortages. Moreover, we need, and must have without further delay, a system of pre-paid medical insurance which will enable every American to afford good medical care." Those sentences are lifted from President Truman's State of the Union message. Most of us would agree that a lot of us need better medical care. The question is, how do we get it?

The President's plan, roughly and briefly, is this: The health insurance scheme would cover doctors' fees, hospital care, medicines and appliances. Patients would have the right to choose their own doctors. Doctors would be free to join, or not to join, in the federal program. It would be open, in the beginning at least, only to those covered by Social Security. This medical program would be paid for by special taxes on wages and salaries, starting with one-half to one per cent on the first forty-eight hundred dollars of income. Later on, the tax might reach four per cent, with employer and employee each paying part. State and local officials would be in full charge of the program, with a federal board providing over-all supervision.

In general, the Republicans are against the scheme. Governor Dewey thinks universal health insurance is an evil invention which would reduce our doctors to servitude. "It's no good, and it won't work," he says. Senator Vandenberg thinks the plan would produce "wholesale mediocrity in the skills which serve the sick, and saddle us with a new and appalling bureaucracy." The American Medical Association, which can, I hope without offense, be referred to as a medical labor union, doesn't like the plan. It has voted to tax each of its members twenty-five dollars to raise a three-and-a-half-million-dollar fund to fight it. But the AMA's discipline isn't as tight as it is in some labor unions, since doctors who refuse to pay the assessment can continue to practice. Spokesmen for the American Medical Association have in the past opposed old age and unemployment insurance as a step toward Communism or totalitarianism. They have also opposed workmen's compensation laws. Back in 1932, when a committee headed by Dr. Ray Lyman Wilbur recommended the establishment of medical centers where physicians and surgeons pooled their skill and equipment in one building, the medical association said that would be setting up something like "medical soviets." The AMA has issued a twelve-point plan to counter President Truman's proposal. It favors the creation of a Federal Health Department with cabinet status, a national foundation for medical research, health centers in rural areas and greater emphasis on industrial medicine.

Federal Security Administrator Ewing has been feuding with the medical association and claims that only twenty per cent of us can afford anything approaching adequate medical care. He points out that, under the plan, the government wouldn't own or operate the hospitals; that pre-paid medical insurance wouldn't own or operate the hospitals, that pre-paid medical insurance wouldn't be any more compulsory than old age insurance and that the quality of medical service as a whole would, in his opinion, improve. Last May, the Brookings Institution made a survey. It showed that there are not enough doctors in this country to carry out President Truman's compulsory health insurance plan. It isn't just a matter of our needing more doctors; the distribution is spotty. In some states there is one doctor for every seven or eight hundred people; in others, one doctor has to care for a couple of thousand. Young doctors are reluctant to settle in rural communities and engage in

144

general practice. They prefer the larger centers where both consulting experts and research facilities are available.

Few people will dispute that we need more doctors and more hospitals, and a better distribution of both. The nation's health is perhaps second only in importance to the nation's education. (No one has raised recently the claim that our system of compulsory education is a form of socialism or Communism.) The questions of health and education are not by any means analogous, but this matter of how more people are to get better medical care is worth arguing about. That is why I have tried to summarize some of the arguments for and against the proposed health insurance program. We'll be hearing more from both sides.

March 18, 1949

Remember the phrase "all aid short of war"? Remember the controversies about destroyers for bases, Lend-Lease—all part of the great debate as to whether the domination of Western Europe by a totalitarian state represented a threat to this country? Even when Britain stood alone we couldn't reach a decision. The debate never was resolved; the Japanese at Pearl Harbor relieved us of the necessity of making a decision. Now, in peacetime, the decision has been made. If the Senate approves, as approve it will, we shall put all our chips on the table; into the discard will go the tradition against foreign commitments that is as old as this nation. The argument in Congress will revolve around the size of the guns to be worn by our allies, who likewise have staked their all in this fateful contest against the Soviet Union and its satellites.

The North Atlantic Treaty, published this morning, is very much as advertised. It reaffirms the purposes and principles of the United Nations. It denies aggressive intent. It promises that the member nations will strengthen their free institutions, try to eliminate conflict in their international economic policies, will develop their individual and collective capacity to resist armed attack and consult together whenever the territorial integrity, political independence or security of any one of the parties is threatened. The meat of the matter is to be found in Article Five, where it is agreed "that an armed attack against any member, in Europe or North America,

145

shall be considered an attack against them all." If such an attack occurs, each nation will assist the nation attacked by "taking forthwith individually, and in concert with the other parties, such action as it deems necessary, including the use of armed force."

There is to be a council on which each nation shall be represented. A defense committee is to be established immediately. Other European nations may be invited to join by unanimous agreement. The treaty is to last for at least twenty years, although after it has been in force for ten years it may be reviewed. It will come into force when it has been ratified by a majority of the nations involved.

Under this pact we are pledged to defend slightly more than one quarter of the world, including our own territory. This Atlantic alliance will have an area and population about equal to that of the Soviet Union and its satellites. The language of this treaty is more precise and binding than is that of the treaty that ties us to the Latin American countries. While it reserves for Congress its constitutional right of declaring war, it means that if an attack is launched against any of our partners under this treaty, we must either go to war or welsh on a promise. In commenting upon this treaty, Secretary of State Acheson was forthright. His words will be interpreted in Europe as committing this government. He points out that nobody can force us to take action. But he believes that if Western European members should sustain an attack, we should go to war. He draws a distinction between minor border incidents and major attacks, saying, "You don't use a sledge-hammer to kill flies." He points out that obligations between nations are moral and that decent people carry out their contracts. He says that the terms of the treaty might be called into play "in the case of internal Communist uprising against one of the member nations, if it is inspired and assisted from the outside."

What is happening is clear enough. Both the East and the West are doing what they can to bunch themselves into one fist. Each side is labeling that fist as purely defensive. In viewing this cleavage in Europe we may be inclined to think that nearly everybody has chosen sides, or is about to. But there is a third force of great wealth and potential power: India, Pakistan, the countries of Southeast Asia, Indonesia, the richest archipelago in the world, and the Arab countries—all hoping to stand aloof, to occupy the middle

146

ground. It seems reasonable to expect that the forces contending in
Europe will use their fists—economic, political and propaganda-
wise—to drive those areas into one camp or the other. If the position is stabilized in Western Europe, we cannot but expect the
competition to continue elsewhere.

June 2, 1949

> *A former State Department official, Alger Hiss, had been
> indicted for denying under oath that he ever gave secret
> papers to Whittaker Chambers, who was a Communist cour-
> ier. Chambers produced microfilm evidence of such papers
> from a pumpkin on his Maryland farm. Now Hiss was on
> trial.*

I spent most of today in Judge Kaufman's court. That's where they
are trying Alger Hiss for perjury. It's a small courtroom—eight
hard oak benches, seating about ten people each, on both sides of a
five-foot aisle leading up to the rail. Inside the rail, the usual
assortment of stenographers, prosecution and defense staff, and
"friends of the court." Judge Kaufman, a small man with a thin
face and a light voice, teeters back and forth in his high-backed
leather chair. A few feet to his left sits Whittaker Chambers in a
gray suit, black tie, white shirt, completely relaxed. He has lost
some weight since his earlier appearances before the House Un-
American Activities Committee and Federal Grand Jury. Fourteen
citizens occupy the jury box—the jury and two alternates. One
woman wearing a blue hat and smoked glasses chewed gum most
of the day, the tempo of her chewing varying in direct relation to
the intensity of her interest.

This morning Assistant U.S. Attorney Murphy, a huge man wearing a British Guardsman moustache (looking sort of like a younger
and bigger edition of Charles Laughton), was questioning Chambers, the government's star witness. At times Chambers appeared
almost bored with the whole proceedings; he slouched to the right
in his chair, looked up at the ceiling to meditate, heaved a sort of
weary sigh before answering and closed his eyes when counsel approached the bench for conference. His voice was low, with a

147

tendency to swallow the ends of sentences. The judge and Lloyd Stryker, the defense counsel, kept asking Chambers to "speak up" (without noticeable effect). Murphy, in the quiet voice of a school-master, drew from Chambers the story of the books he had trans-lated from French and German, the various jobs he had held, where and how he first met Hiss. Chambers told his story, of how he came to New York and took Alger Hiss to Brooklyn, where, on the mezza-nine of a movie house, he introduced him to Colonel Bykov, a Russian agent. The three went for a walk in Prospect Park, re-turned to have dinner at the Port Arthur Restaurant in Chinatown, where Bykov—speaking German, with Chambers translating— asked Hiss if he would procure secret documents from the State Department; and, according to Chambers, Hiss agreed to do it. Chambers in answering questions has a tendency to become expan-sive, and Stryker repeatedly objected on the grounds that Chambers was drawing conclusions or introducing irrelevant testimony. Judge Kaufman sustained most of the objections.

Chambers told how, when he wanted a new car, Hiss gave, or loaned, him four hundred dollars. He told of seeing Mr. and Mrs. Hiss shortly before Christmas of 1938, when he said he pled with them to break from the Communist Party, and they refused. Cham-bers was handed forty-seven documents and two rolls of film. Asked whether he had received these documents from the hands of Alger Hiss, he went through them, taking an average of four seconds to a document, and said that that was true. He held the two rolls of film up to the light but couldn't read them. However, both defense and prosecution agreed that they could be placed in evidence. All this time Alger Hiss and his wife sat listening to the testimony with absolutely no change of expression. There was never a frown, a smile, a nervous gesture. Occasionally Hiss drew a folded piece of paper from his pocket and made a brief note. I think I have never seen anyone who had himself more completely under control— unless it was Whittaker Chambers.

Those three soft voices—Judge Kaufman, Murphy and Cham-bers—continued to unravel this fantastic tale, with an occasional objection by Lloyd Paul Stryker, attorney for Alger Hiss. When Murphy had finished questioning Chambers, Stryker, a short square-shouldered man, his white hair cropped short, took over the cross-examination. He barked at Chambers, "Do you know the meaning of an oath?" Chambers said, "Yes." Stryker hitched up his trousers, tightened his belt and went to work on Whittaker Chambers. He showed him an affidavit that he said Chambers had signed when he worked for the government (the WPA) in which Chambers swore to defend and uphold this government. "Is that signature yours?" snapped Stryker. "Yes," said Chambers. "Then you lied when you signed it," said Stryker. Again in that casual, almost bored voice Chambers said, "Certainly." Stryker wanted to know whether Chambers had ever used the name Crosley. Chambers said he wasn't sure, but he might have. Stryker had Chambers read a sentence from a letter which he had written saying that he had lied to the dean of Columbia University in order to gain readmission. Chambers said yes, that was right; he had written the letter. He was completely detached about the whole business, as though he were talking about someone else. The harder Stryker hammered at him the more casual and relaxed he seemed to become.

And during this whole time Mr. and Mrs. Hiss sat there as though they were watching a mildly interesting experiment, the outcome of which didn't concern them the least bit, one way or the other. There was something unreal about the whole scene—the impression of a flawless performance by everyone concerned. But at the same time there was the sense that there are forces and factors involved in this conflict that have not yet been placed upon the record.

Whatever the outcome of this trial, twelve of those people sitting in the jury box will have to decide which of these two men is telling the truth. And as I watched them file out of that jury box late this afternoon—just average-looking Americans, they were—I couldn't help thinking that there, so help me, in the whole system of trial by jury resides our greatest defense against tyranny.

> *Hiss's trial ended with a hung jury, and the case was set for retrial six months later.*

June 9, 1949

Now this is one reporter's comment upon the subject that has been assailing your eyes and your ears for the past several weeks—the whole area of espionage, treason and subversive activity.

Mr. Truman indicated at his news conference today, as he has done before, that a great deal of it is just "headline hunting." While it must be admitted that some of the headlines are so blown up that they appear to have been shot with a big telescopic sight, it seems to me that the situation that obtains in this country today merits careful and cool consideration. We are probably already well launched in a new era. We have abundant testimony from diplomats, military men, educators and statesmen that this "time of tension" will continue. It is no passing phase; it is not just the psychological and emotional turbulence in the wake of war.

This conflict with the Soviet Union presents us with a new dilemma. The present situation cannot fairly be compared to the one that existed after the First World War, because then the Communist concept was not supported and sustained by any considerable body of power. Now it is. The secretive, clandestine nature of Communist operations has induced both fear and suspicion. It is in the main stream of American tradition for us to differ with our neighbors, to suspect their motives, to denounce their policies or their political beliefs. But to suspect them of treason, of allegiance to a foreign power and ideology is probably more widespread now than at any time in our national history. That there is danger of Communist espionage and infiltration cannot be denied. That there is need for legal, constitutional methods of protection would seem to be equally obvious. But the current sensations which assail us on all sides shouldn't blind us to the fact that espionage, propaganda and infiltration have been employed by every tribe and state since the beginning of history. The Chinese, two centuries before Christ, spelled out techniques and methods of operation that are still valid today.

If this contest is to continue indefinitely we must, as in war, have a care for the morale of the home front. Fear of the unknown, fear of depression, should not blind us to the fact that this country represents the greatest conglomeration of power in the world today. It may be that it is a mechanistic, materialistic civilization; a nation of headline readers, as some of our critics claim. But the fact is that the climate for the development of Communism in this country is less salubrious than any other in the world. We have more material goods; we live in luxury compared with the rest of the world. And yet we are worried and apprehensive. We are also an impatient people, anxious for quick solutions, often intolerant, always desirous of action. I think that if we are going to sweat out successfully this continuing crisis, without losing our liberties while trying to defend them, we are going to have to do it in the old-fashioned way in spite of jet planes and television and all the wonders of science. We will have to remain conscious of our own good fortune as well as our strength.

The individual's independence of judgment must be protected. He can't be protected against sensational headlines or irresponsible broadcasters. But, so far as I know, nobody in this country ever lost his liberty through those instruments. We sometimes forget that the thing that makes this country what it is isn't our size or our racial mixture, or anything else, but the fact that this is a nation that lives under law; where we have the right to believe than any law is a bad law and agitate for its repeal; where with few exceptions a man cannot be convicted unless the rules of evidence are followed. This very fact makes it difficult to apprehend and convict Communist agents because a trial in open court may mean divulging information that would be damaging to the national security. I believe there have been cases where the government would have proceeded against individuals had it not been for this fact. It may be that we require new laws. I am not certain about that. It is deplorable that we have come to suspect each other more than we did before. It is regrettable that individuals and some organs of opinon are disposed to convict people by association or before they have been tried. If this tendency is accelerated, it may induce widespread fear and endanger the right of dissent. But so long as neither the state nor an individual can take punitive action against a citizen except through due processes of law, we shall have in our hands the weapons to defend our personal liberty and our national security.

During the darkest days of the war in England I remarked the frequent use of a simple word, one which is often effective with horses *and* with men. The word was "steady." In spite of the surface signs, hysteria and suspicion, it seems to me we aren't doing too badly. At least we haven't yet reached the point where we must follow, in fear, the advice once given by Will Rogers, who said, "So live that you wouldn't be ashamed to sell the family parrot to the town gossip."

September 23, 1949

> *President Truman announced, "We have evidence that*
> *within recent weeks an atomic explosion occurred in the*
> *U.S.S.R."*

The inevitable has happened. It happened rather sooner than most of our experts had predicted. This may well mean that the experts underestimated the industrial and technological potential of the Soviet Union—the same mistake Hitler made. Every statement by government officials, both here and in Western Europe, has been designed to prevent hysteria or excitement. In London, the British Broadcasting Corporation didn't even interrupt its regular program when the announcement came. They just waited till the next news broadcast was scheduled.

The Russians not only exploded an atomic weapon, they exploded an American myth—the belief widely held that we had, and could maintain, the secret of the bomb's construction. Almost two years ago Molotov stated that "the secret of the atom bomb has long since ceased to exist." Our responsible scientists kept warning us that there was in fact no secret. Now that the thing is out in the open, the basic elements in this world-wide conflict have not changed. It is probable that we shall see increased efforts to achieve some sort of international control of atomic energy. But there is no reason to think that that explosion in Russia increased the possibilities of success. In purely military terms we enjoy an advantage of an increasing stockpile, plus a five-year lead in research and development.

One result of today's announcement may be that the Atomic Energy Commission will be able to get on with its job without so much political sniping. A cable just received from Paris quotes the French scientist, Dr. Goldschmidt, who worked on the Canadian bomb project during the war and was the French government observer at Bikini, as saying, "Frankly we were stunned by the news; we didn't expect the Soviets to have the bomb before 1950 or '51." But he added, "This is, however, a complete victory for the scientists in our long-standing debate with the politicians about atomic secrets. The scientists always insisted there are no padlocks on the mind, and the tightest security could only slow up the inevitable."

Now that the inevitable has happened, it would appear that the President has acted promptly in divulging the information. And judging from the dispatches pouring into this newsroom, there is no trace of hysteria or undue excitement in the land. That in itself is a very considerable achievement. The fact that the Russians have the bomb cannot be regarded by any reasonable person as proof that war is either more or less likely. In all the volume of comment about today's announcement I rather prefer the one by French Foreign Minister Schuman, who said, "If the situation is not necessarily more peaceful, it is at least less nervous."

October 14, 1949

After one of the longest criminal trials in federal court history, eleven leaders of the Communist Party in the United States were convicted of conspiracy to teach and advocate the forcible overthrow of the government.

Let's examine some of the implications of the verdict. The men were indicted under the Smith Act, which was passed in 1940. It went through the Senate without a roll call, and only four votes were registered against it in the House. The verdict in Judge Medina's court will be tested before the Supreme Court, and that body will have to try to determine the constitutional limitations that may be placed upon advocacy of change through violence.

There are some things that can be concluded from the verdict: If you conspire, as these men were convicted of conspiring, then you face a prison sentence and possible fine. The verdict means that there will be a determined campaign by the Communists to try to sell to the country the issues that were lost in the trial. It means that the eleven Communist leaders aren't going to be available to direct the affairs of the party for some time. The question arises as to whether the men who replace them will also be guilty of breaking to whether the men who replace them will also be guilty of virtue of their membership or official position in the Communist Party. The government would have to produce evidence, witnesses, documents and bring them before a jury as they did in this case.

The verdict undoubtedly means Russian propaganda efforts to discredit our system of justice. But the verdict proves that under that system of justice, the accused can get a nine months' trial, plus a jury to hear the case—even if they are, as Prosecutor McGohey stated, "professional revolutionists."

But there are some things that this verdict does not mean. It does not mean that membership in the Communist Party as such is illegal. The party is not outlawed. The verdict does not mean that you must not read any specific books, talk as you will or peacefully assemble for any purpose other than to conspire to overthrow the government by force and violence. It does not mean that you are subject to legal action for saying things favorable to the Communist Party. Nothing in this verdict limits the citizen's right, by peaceful and lawful means, to advocate changes in the Constitution, to utter and publish praise of Russia, criticism of any of our political personalities or parties. You may, in short, engage in any action or agitation except that aimed at teaching or advocating the overthrow of the government by violence.

If this verdict is upheld by the Supreme Court, similar prosecutions may follow. But in each individual case it will be necessary for the government to prove, not only that the defendants were members of the Communist Party, but that they conspired to overthrow the government, and did so knowingly and willfully.

One result of the verdict may be to convince a number of people that the Communists are not just another political party. In view of the mass of evidence produced in Judge Medina's court, it will be pretty difficult in the future for anyone to maintain that he joined and worked for the Communist Party without really knowing that it advocated violent revolution. There have been many serious proposals to control, contain or outlaw the Communist Party in this country, efforts to hog-tie them without strangling our liberties with the loose end of the rope. It is both delicate and dangerous business. We can't legislate loyalty. But nevertheless the question of the control of subversion is one of the most important confronting this country.

Ten of the convicted Communist leaders were sentenced to five years in federal prison, the other to three years. The Supreme Court upheld the convictions in 1951.

154

January 25, 1950

This morning Alger Hiss was sentenced to five years in prison for perjury. This afternoon the drama moved to Washington, to Secretary of State Acheson's press conference. The question was: "Mr. Secretary, have you any comment on the Alger Hiss case?" Mr. Acheson replied in these words: "Mr. Hiss's case is before the courts, and I think it would be highly improper for me to discuss the legal aspects of the case, or the evidence, or anything to do with the case. I take it the purpose of your question was to bring something other than that out of me." And then Mr. Acheson said, "I should like to make it clear to you that whatever the outcome of any appeal which Mr. Hiss or his lawyers may take in this case, I do not intend to turn my back on Alger Hiss. I think every person who has known Alger Hiss, or has served with him at any time, has upon his conscience the very serious task of deciding what his attitude is, and what his conduct should be. That must be done by each person, in the light of his own standards and his own principles. For me," said Mr. Acheson, "there is very little doubt about those standards or those principles. I think they were stated for us a very long time ago. They were stated on the Mount of Olives, and if you are interested in seeing them, you will find them in the twenty-fifth chapter of the Gospel according to St. Matthew, beginning at Verse 34."

Here is the passage to which Mr. Acheson referred:

> Then shall the King say unto them on his right hand, come, ye blessed of my Father, inherit the kingdom prepared for you from the foundation of the world: For I was an hungred, and ye gave me meat; I was thirsty and ye gave me drink; I was a stranger, and ye took me in; naked, and ye clothed me; I was sick and ye visited me; I was in prison, and ye came unto me. Then shall the righteous answer him, saying, Lord, when saw we thee an hungred and fed thee, or thirsty and gave thee drink? When saw we thee a stranger, and took thee in? Or naked, and clothed thee? Or when saw we thee sick, or in prison, and came unto thee? And the King shall answer and say unto them, verily I say unto you, inasmuch as ye have done it unto one of the least of these, my brethren, ye have done it unto me.

We are reliably informed that Secretary Acheson knew the question was coming but had not discussed his answer with President Truman because he regarded it as a personal matter. When Mr. Acheson was up for confirmation before the Senate Foreign Relations Committee, he was questioned about Alger Hiss, said he was his friend and added, "My friendship is not easily given, and not easily withdrawn." He proved that today.

Republican Senator Capehart, of Indiana, renewed his demand that Secretary Acheson be fired. Republican Senator McCarthy, of Wisconsin, asked if Acheson is also telling the world that he won't turn his back on the other Communists in the State Department. Senator Knowland, Republican of California, wants the Appropriations Committee to tie up funds for the Executive Department until the Congress is told what influence Mr. Hiss had on "appointments and policy." Republican Senator Mundt, from South Dakota, wants to know the same thing and thinks this may be a greater scandal than Teapot Dome. Democratic Congressmen have apparently been reluctant to comment upon Secretary Acheson's statement. But a vicious controversy is just beginning.

March 8, 1950

Murrow began the broadcast by saying "This is some of the news" and explained in conclusion:

We are especially grateful for the friendly communication from an obviously learned gentleman who offers a sound suggestion. He writes, "Many people who like to listen to you are nettled by your announcement 'This is the news.' They think it is egotistical, smacks of pride and self-assumed omniscience." This gentleman is good enough to add, "It doesn't bother me. I have learned to be somewhat tolerant, after seventy-five years on this terrestrial spheroid. But," he continues, "I know it prejudices some people against you and your message. What would you think of graciously surprising us by saying once in a while, 'This is some of the news,' thereby suggesting that you do not know everything and are not reporting all the cosmic facts of the universe?"

This is certainly sound advice. This has been my effort to follow it, and this has been, as usual, *some* of the news.

March 10, 1950

Today's *New York Times,* in an unusually free-swinging lead editorial, thinks maybe we are not sufficiently grateful for people like Senator McCarthy; he may cause us to think about this matter of guilt by association. And anybody who does much thinking on the principle of the right to join things is likely to find that it is pretty closely tied up with ancient American traditions and liberties. Says *The Times:*

"An American citizen, as such, has the right to join any kind of society, club or organization he desires, provided he and his associates are not using, or advocating, unlawful means toward an objective. We each, and all of us, may get up an organization for the purpose of installing a single tax, for the purpose of denouncing or praising General Franco, for the promotion or extermination of wooden Indians, prairie dogs and various species of butterflies. We may peacefully advocate the coinage of money in denominations of seven and a half cents; we may get up fraternal societies and go parading around in red plush pants and with feathers in our hats, hoping thereby to improve things generally. . . . We may do all of these things, or any of them, and no grandma in the Department of Justice, no head constable anywhere and no committee of Congress has any right to say us no; nor is any such right created by the possible fact that some Communists may agree with us in some of the objectives we seek and may join with us in seeking them. It may be that we do not show good sense in such matters, but each of us will have to learn about that on his own responsibility. He cannot lawfully, or properly, be told by anyone in Washington with whom he is to associate."

The Times concludes its editorial in this fashion: "If these good old American principles are again generally accepted, some of us may feel like organizing an organization to raise money to set up a plaque, or something, in honor of Senator McCarthy. We will just have to hope that no Communists, or fellow-travelers, will join this organization. But if they should, we do not believe the other members of the organization can properly be denounced in Congress, or subjected to other cruel and unusual punishment."

I don't know about that suggestion of raising money to set up a plaque, or something, in honor of Senator McCarthy, but in my opinion *The New York Times* deserves a scroll, or something, for having used the Senator as the rather unsubstantial peg on which to hang an editorial with a good cutting edge, reminding us in these rather hysterical days that "guilt by association" is, in the true sense, an un-American doctrine.

May 5, 1950

Last year, feeling obliged to say something about horses on the eve of this great classic [the Kentucky Derby], we read you a small piece on how to harness a horse, continental fashion. It was written by Mark Twain who said he was not an expert on horses, didn't speak with assurance but could always tell which was the front end of a horse. Beyond that, his art was not above the ordinary. To-night, in response to public demand—maybe as many as a half-dozen letters—here again is Mark Twain's description of how to harness a horse, continental fashion:

"The man stands up the horses on each side of the thing that projects from the front end of the wagon and then throws the tangled mess of gear on top of the horse and passes the thing that goes forward through a ring and hauls it aft and passes the other thing through the other ring and hauls it aft on the other side of the other horse, opposite to the first one, after crossing them and bringing the loose end back and then buckles the other thing underneath the horse and takes another thing and wraps it around the thing I spoke of before and puts another thing over each horse's head, with broad flappers to it to keep the dust out of his eyes, and puts the iron thing in his mouth for him to grit his teeth on uphill and brings the ends of this thing aft over his back, after buckling another one around under his neck to hold his head up and hitching another thing on a thing that goes over his shoulders, to keep his head up when he is climbing a hill, and then takes the slack of the thing which I mentioned awhile ago and fetches it aft and makes it fast to the thing that pulls the wagon and hands the other things up to the driver to steer with. I have never buckled a horse myself," said Twain, "but I do not think we do it that way."

And if anyone should buckle a horse that way at the Derby tomorrow, it would make history.

June 7, 1950

This is the season of caps, gowns, diplomas and commencement speeches, a time for medieval ritual and Latin phrases (those who fail to understand the Latin may derive some comfort from Heinrich Heine's remark that "If the Romans had been obliged to learn Latin, they would never have found time to conquer the world."

This is the season when middle-aged or elderly men and women stand before graduating classes, and offer, with varying eloquence, congratulations and words of wisdom and guidance. These commencement speeches generally involve telling the youth of the speaker's hope that they will not make such a mess of things as did the speaker's generation. Graduates are informed that they are about to enter Life, with a capital L, that they will require courage and fortitude. They might also be reminded in the words of Channing Pollock that "no man in the world has more courage than the man who can stop after eating one peanut."

But it is the life ahead that concerns most commencement orators. Most of what they say has been said before, and with greater brevity. Wise men have disagreed as to what constitutes the full, complete and satisfying life. Josh Billings maintained that "life is short, but it is long enough to ruin any man who wants to be ruined." While Samuel Butler maintained that "life is the art of drawing sufficient conclusions from insufficient premises." Sydney Smith, on the other hand, took what might be called the clinical approach to this question when he said, "The great secret of life is digestion." The philosophical approach was perhaps best expressed by Susan Ertz, who remarked, "Millions who long for immortality do not know what to do with themselves on a rainy Sunday afternoon."

For the graduate who is an athlete, Wilson Mizner offered counsel in this fashion: "In the battle for existence, talent is the punch and tact is the clever footwork." And the athletes might also heed the warning of Margaret Halsey, for it may be applicable to them ten or fifteen years from now. She said, "He must have had a magnificent build before his stomach went in for a career of its own." That state of affairs is undoubtedly the result of accepting Alexander Woollcott's definition of life, which was this: "All the things that are really worth doing in life are either immoral, illegal or fattening."

The graduating students are of course being told that they emerge into a world that is dangerous and disordered, where everyone lives dangerously. The future is sombre and uncertain enough. But remember that Teddy Roosevelt concluded that "the poorest way to face life is with a sneer."

No commencement speaker, I suspect, can lay down valid rules—no matter how great his wisdom or wide his experience. For life is essentially a long lesson in humility, and only the man who lives it can sum it up. Mark Twain wrote: "It is not likely that any complete life has ever been lived which was not a failure in the secret judgment of the person who lived it."

When commencement speakers draw a grim but no doubt accurate picture of the road ahead, the new graduate may find comfort in the words of Samuel Butler, who said, "All of the animals, except man, know that the principal business of life is to enjoy it." Those of a more serious turn of mind will agree with William James that "the great use of life is to spend it for something that will outlast it."

We had thought on this day, when the news is light, to offer our salute to this year's graduating classes—a toast of some sort to the life ahead. I have an idea that an entire commencement speech could be made in a half-dozen lines. (And surely that would be a good thing.) These words were written by the great German poet and philosopher Goethe, and will, of course, like most commencement speeches, be forgotten. But just for the beauty of the language and the clarity of thought, I should like to read you the "complete" commencement speech in a half-dozen lines:

"There are nine requisites for contented living: Health enough to make work a pleasure; wealth enough to support your needs; strength to battle with difficulties and overcome them; grace enough to confess your sins and forsake them; patience enough to toil until some good is accomplished; charity enough to see some good in your neighbor; love enough to move you to be useful and helpful to others; faith enough to make real the things of God; hope enough to remove all anxious fears concerning the future."

June 27, 1950

On June 19, 1950, Murrow reported on the state of the American economy. Quoting experts, he said prospects for the coming year were pretty good. But, just before going on the air, he penciled in four words: "If nothing unexpected happens." Within a week, Communist North Korea invaded South Korea. The unexpected had happened.

For about three days this country faced a classic dilemma of saving peace, at least for a time, by condoning or accepting outright aggression, or of attempting to stop and throw back that aggression by employing means that in themselves endanger peace. Sometime yesterday the decision was taken, and at noon today President Truman announced that he had ordered United States air and sea forces to give the Korean government troops cover and support. Both naval and air units have been in action.

Mr. Truman also ordered the Seventh Fleet to prevent any attack on the island of Formosa, told Chiang Kai-shek to call off his war against the Communists on the mainland and left the whole question of the future of Formosa to be settled at some distant date. This pulls the political rug from under Chiang Kai-shek and is an effort to neutralize him while more pressing problems are taken care of. We have reversed our Far Eastern policy, drawn a line, risked a war and committed ourselves beyond the possibility of turning back. The support for this policy in Congress, and in the nations of the Western World, appears to be practically unanimous. This action, this new policy, commits us to much more than the defense of the southern half of the Korean peninsula. We have commitments quite as binding, obligations quite as great, to Indo-China, Iran and Turkey as we have to Korea. We have drawn a line, not across the peninsula, but across the world. We have concluded that Communism has passed beyond the use of subversion to conquer independent nations and will now use armed invasion and war. And we, for our part, have demonstrated that we are prepared to calculate the risks and face the prospect of war rather than let that happen.

A British correspondent said today, "For awhile I thought you were going to have your Munich, and now it looks as though it might be your finest hour."

June 30, 1950

American troops are now being flown into southern Korea. Brigadier General Church, our top commander on the peninsula, says the first battalion of the 24th Infantry is on its way to Pusan, on the southeastern coast. The decision to send troops to Korea was made by the President earlier today. He also announced that our naval forces will blockade the entire Korean coast. And he gave the Air Force authority to attack specific military targets north of the 38th Parallel. Heretofore, they've been restricted to attacks below the line that divides the north and south.

Many times during the last war the news from home made strange reading. If the GIs who are going ashore in Korea could read some of the statements made during the last couple of days, they might get a distorted picture of the climate of opinion that exists back home. Here are a few examples:

Republican Senator Taft demanding Acheson's resignation, saying the President has "usurped the powers of Congress."

On Monday, Republican Senators Knowland, Millikin, Kem, McCarthy, Bridges and Wherry—all playing party politics as usual during the gravest crisis this country has faced in the last five years.

Today Republican Senator Capehart, of Indiana, accused the Democrats of leading America into a shooting war for the third time in thirty-three years, said they ought to call themselves the War Party—"It would be a criminal disservice to America to support the Administration's foreign policy in the future." Representative Earl Wilson, of Indiana, was a little more extreme. He called the Korean situation "another crisis created for election purposes."

Today the leaders of both parties gave full support to the President's decision to permit United States ground forces in southern Korea.

My favorite quotation of the day came from Senator Cain, of the State of Washington. While he was making a speech, criticizing the military aid program, he was handed an announcement of the President's decision. The Senator said, "It means only that what we did not anticipate last week has come to pass. How far are we involved?" And he answered his own question by saying, "I don't know." I doubt that anyone does. We were caught in a position where we had to shoot or put down the gun. If we had put it down, our friends and allies would have done likewise, until in due course they would have been awakened in the dark of night by Communist gun butts hammering on the door. How far we are committed will eventually be answered by the Russians, for the decision is theirs to make. We have made ours. The Kremlin may well delay. The Communists from North Korea have moved with speed and handled their tanks well. And, in addition to Russian material, they have at least the possibility of drawing upon well-trained Chinese Communist divisions.

They may have struck this soft spot because Communism is held in check in Western Europe, and they may have moved in an effort to strengthen the Communist parties throughout Asia and to further damage American prestige in that area. If they succeed in this venture, it will severely shake the will to resist Communism, both in Asia and in parts of Western Europe.

If southern Korea falls, it is only reasonable to expect, on the basis of past Russian performance *and* Communist doctrine, that there will be other and bolder ventures. This one has at least exposed the utter and complete hypocrisy of the current Russian peace propaganda campaign.

There is room, and to spare, for recrimination. Syngman Rhee, prime minister of South Korea, who now complains bitterly that our aid is too little and too late, was loud in his insistence that American troops be withdrawn. Many of our military leaders were persuaded that the peninsula was just another Bataan and strategically unimportant. The combat potential of the South Korean troops was obviously overestimated. Our intelligence understandably failed to anticipate the blow. But before we undertake a search for those responsible for this state of affairs we might ponder Winston

Churchill's advice when he said, "If we engage in recriminations about the past, we may well lose the future."

August 1, 1950

Murrow went to Korea that summer, though, as he said, he "had thought to have seen enough of dead men and wounded buildings, of fear and high courage" during nine years in Europe.

This is Korea. It is clear that the decisive days are at hand. The whole business of coming out to this war in Korea is filled with familiar faces and memories. When we took off for Korea this morning, an elderly sergeant struggled into his parachute with the remark, "I have to pull this handle, and on this thing sawdust will fall out. Maybe a few moths, too."

There were five big canisters of blood aboard, all neatly sealed with red tops. Some of the boys had their feet resting on them. A lieutenant said, "Maybe that's some of my blood they're shipping over."

The pilot came in to land on a rough strip at Pusan. He bounced three times and couldn't make it. So he poured on the coal and took off for another try. He made it the second time. And when the crew chief came back he remarked, "Next week they're going to let that rugged pilot solo." When we took off again the crew chief went back to reading his magazine. It had to do with how to interpret dreams. It wasn't so different from the last war.

On the ground, this country seems only a few years ahead of the invention of the wheel. And the odors! The stench is as old as the world. Aside from the American military transports, the oxcart seems the modern means of transportation. Humans are pack animals, and even the packs are made of forked sticks tied together with handmade ropes. The big bulldozers, tankers, even the little jeeps and especially the aircraft, blasting great dust storms off the field, appear to have been sent down here from another planet.

This broadcast was written on a small child's desk in a former schoolhouse, and it's being made by candlelight while, about forty miles away, men who have finished with school are fighting in rough country that stands on edge. Outside the window, children too small for school, too young to know what it's all about, are squalling in the stinking evening heat. Their destiny, what they will learn at these little school desks, and a lot of other things, too, are being decided in those hills a little way to the west and south of here.

August 8, 1950

I spent most of the day with the 1st Cavalry. Going up, we stopped at a six-gun battery of 155s. They were firing about one round a minute at 16,000 yards. That's maximum. A plane was spotting for them and correcting fire. They didn't know what they were shooting at, but they thought it was enemy artillery. The spotting pilot kept calling in their directions but didn't tell them the exact target. I asked the captain of the battery when it had gone into action. He grinned and said he didn't know, but he remembered it was on a Sunday. We drove on up to the regimental CP, passed a burning village that had been set afire by our M.P.s as they pulled back. To the north, a force of Communists had crossed a river. South Koreans had surrounded them on a hilltop and had asked for an air strike. A young hot-shot jet pilot, attached to the ground forces, picked up his phone and literally grabbed off four aircraft outward bound on another mission. He described the hill, gave the map reading, and explained that the South Koreans would wave white flags when the fighters came in. The colonel said this would have to be a fairly tricky operation, sort of hair cutting on the hill. He hoped they wouldn't clobber the South Koreans by mistake.

In less than four minutes we heard the guns of the fighters working as they sprayed the hilltop. The jet pilot on the ground picked up four F-80s on the telephone and put them on the same target. After they had finished, word came through on the telephone from a Lieutenant Lee, commanding the South Koreans who were besieging the hill, and the message said, "The forces of the Republic of Korea wish to express their thanks to the Air Force for their timely intervention." The colonel of the 1st Cavalry said, "You know, the Air Force is doing a pretty good job out here." I never saw air and ground working in such close cooperation during the last war.

The enemy is across the Naktong at two places and in strength. We are still patrolling across the river, day and night, using mixed forces of South Koreans and Americans. We talked to a slow-talking sergeant from Texas who was over there yesterday on a patrol, part of a mixed force of about a hundred men. He said, "These patrols are supposed to be for information and prisoners, but they generally end up in a fire fight." That happened yesterday. The patrol lost one American and two South Koreans. Another sergeant carried the wounded GI for nearly 800 yards under fire. The boy had come back from the hospital only yesterday morning. He was twenty years of age. He'd been recovering in the hospital from a minor wound and had volunteered for the patrol. They brought him back to this side of the river and there he died. We asked the sergeant to describe him to us and his reply was, "He was a right good soldier." And he reckoned that the sergeant who carried him out ought to get a medal. Anyone who doubts the courage and tenacity of the South Koreans pushed back into this corner of their country should talk with the Americans who have fought alongside with them. They will tell you that they are very good fighting men.

Correspondents are not supposed to criticize command decisions, but there are responsible officers out here who doubt that we can afford the luxury of attacking in the south when we are so thin on the ground on the northern and central sectors of the front. In spite of our offensive at the bottom of the peninsula, we are still engaged in a desperate defensive action. If we lose the airfields in the north and the center, much of our power, offensive *and* defensive, will go with them.

August 14, 1950

> *On this date Murrow did a broadcast from Tokyo which was not heard by the American public, though short-wave reception was excellent. The broadcast was recorded for playback on the evening program. It was not used because, in the judgment of CBS, it might hurt the war effort. It was Murrow's conviction that reporting some unpleasant facts would help in this instance.*

166

This is a most difficult broadcast to do. I have never believed that correspondents who move in and out of the battle area, engage in privileged conversations with commanders and with troops, and who have access to public platform, should engage in criticism of command decisions or of commanders while the battle is in progress. However, it is now time to cast up an account of the past ten days. For the question now arises whether serious mistakes have been made.

Then Murrow, in short declarative sentences he hoped would be understood without a war map, set forth the disposition of the United Nations defense forces.

The Marine brigade arrived. We had the 5th Regimental Combat Team and the reinforced 35th Regiment. They were committed to that push along the southern end of the peninsula to secure the high ground east of Chinju. Experienced officers, some of them wearing stars, called it folly. They weren't going anywhere. This was not a decision that was forced upon us by the enemy. Our high command took it because, in the words of one officer who was in a position to know, "We decided we needed a victory."

Meanwhile, the battered and weary 24th Division was trying to hold better than thirty miles of the Naktong River line. And the 1st Cavalry, also under strength, was holding about the same distance. North of them came the 1st South Korean Division, and then the line was very thin from there to the east coast. For the first time we had power—could hold it in reserve, strengthen the river line, or plug the gaps in the north along the east coast.

The southern offensive was undertaken. On Thursday morning of last week the general commanding the right end of the line up on the east coast was asked if he needed help or reinforcements. He replied that the situation was well in hand. He didn't need any help. For days, there had been reports that the North Koreans were coming down on secondary roads behind the hills, safe from naval gunfire. About twelve hours after the general said all was well, we started a powerful relief column up to try to save the airfield at Pohang, the last operational airstrip we had left. It was being threatened. The column, moving at night, was ambushed, arrived too late to hold the high ground. And within less than twenty-four hours the field was evacuated. From that field between one third

167

and one fourth of our close support missions had been flown. We aren't flying anything from there now. One Air Force colonel remarked, "The enemy, even without air power, seems to place a higher value on this field than we do." That was one price we paid for the southern offensive.

Today, a spokesman at general headquarters denied that we had underestimated the enemy strength in the north.

Latest reports indicate that the enemy has at least one division across the Naktong River, about thirty miles south of Waegwan. Five more enemy divisions, plus one in reserve, have been identified on that central front. The pressure is building against the Waegwan-Taegu axis.

Our force to meet this threat is, or at least it was, down on that southern offensive. When our fresh forces arrived about ten days ago, we lay like a hand on the southeast part of Korea. The wrist and the arteries were at the port of Pusan, the fingers spread out from Yongdok on the east coast to Masan on the southern end of the peninsula. The end of each finger was being stepped on by the enemy. Our high command here chose to extend the thumb along the south coast, using our major strength to do it. One flank on the sea, the others opened to harassing attacks by the enemy. And he struck at our little finger, took Pohang and that vital airfield and began to mass against our middle finger on the Naktong River line. This means that the thumb will have to be pulled back, the little finger having been amputated. And the other fingers probably will have to be doubled back into one fist.

You will find battle-wise men out in Korea—some with stars and others with sergeant's stripes—who have fought Germans, Japanese, Italians, and North Koreans, who maintain that we gained nothing by this southern offensive and meanwhile have lost that vital airstrip and endangered the center of the line. They maintain that the fist must be bunched, providing a shorter perimeter that can be wired and mined—and held—from which refugees can be excluded, where fields of fire can be laid down for heavy machine guns, where the ground in front can be surveyed and plotted for artillery fire, and behind which we can build up for a real offensive later on.

While that is going on, we can kill North Koreans as fast as they decide to come onto that perimeter. I met no officer in South Korea

168

who believes we can mount an effective offensive with our present strength. The most reasoned and experienced opinion is that it will require eight divisions at full strength, and after that about six months of hard fighting to see this thing done, assuming that the Chinese Communist troops and Russian air do not join the battle. And yet correspondents here have received cables from their home offices indicating that air-conditioned sources in Washington think the thing can be wound up this fall. To paraphrase the GIs in Korea—that ain't the way it looks from here.

So far as this reporter is concerned, he doesn't see where or when this conflict will end. For this is not an isolated war, except in the purely geographic sense. It is isolated only for the men who are fighting it.

The other day I asked a captain what day it was, and he looked at his watch, instinctively, and then he laughed and said, "I haven't the least idea. Only minutes and hours count out here."

I am aware that some of the things I have said may have violated directives from general headquarters, particularly in quoting officers who believe that we paid too high a price for that southern offensive. I have not identified them because no reporter knowingly embarrasses generals or sergeants with their superiors. It is my personal opinion, for what it is worth, that we shall stay on that peninsula. The stuff is there, and the troops have the heart. But when we start moving up through dead valleys, through villages to which we have put the torch by retreating, what then of the people who live there? They have lived on the knife edge of despair and disaster for centuries. Their pitiful possessions have been consumed in the flames of war. Will our reoccupation of that flea-bitten land lessen, or increase, the attraction of Communism?

The other day in Korea I heard a psychological warfare officer tell how the Communists have made headway with their propaganda in southern Korea. He said, "One thing we must do is to write out our war aims. Tell them what they can look forward to when we have won the war. And then drop that statement in leaflet form on top of them." And a correspondent who shall be nameless said, "That will take quite a bit of writing and, when the pamphlet is done, maybe we should drop some on the American people, too."

September 6, 1950

It seems to me that this war in Korea is a testing ground, not only for weapons but for ideas. The Japanese, the Chinese, the whole mass of miserable millions in Asia are watching and listening. The Communist radio in North Korea and in China makes exaggerated claims of American losses and atrocities. Many of their claims are laughable when heard by Western ears, but there is a propaganda theme running through the whole output, and it is not designed either to frighten or impress us. The theme is this: Communism means change, change from the age-old oppression of the landlords. It means land for the peasant; it means lighter taxes. And Communism means both peace and plenty. The fact that Communism hasn't meant any of these things in practice in Asia is beside the point; the bright promise is there, and millions with little to lose have accepted it, are prepared to die for it.

The Communists have captured and channeled the surging desire for change, the resentment against foreign domination. They talk the language of Asia's aspirations. Their technique is always simple. For example, the North Korean radio hammers away on one refrain. It has nothing to do with justice, or the United Nations, or who started the war in Korea. What they say in essence is this: "Do you think it possible that the peaceful Korean peasant working in his rice field, who is shot down by American artillery or aircraft, do you *really* think he is the aggressor in this war? Or the humble worker in the factory whose life is cut short by American bombs, is *he* the aggressor? The women and children who live in shacks beside the railroad tracks. When death comes to them from the sky, are *they* the aggressors? Did *they* threaten the mighty United States?" And the theme continues. "Do you believe that the Americans who crossed thousands of miles of ocean with their modern war machines—tanks, flame throwers and bombers—can you really think that they are the *victims* of aggression? Did those peasants and workers threaten those Americans?"

That's the way it goes. The North Korean radio reports in considerable detail the factories that have been destroyed by American bombers. This information is highly important military information. It tells us how successful our air strikes have been. In the last war both sides did their best to conceal this sort of intelligence. The North Koreans broadcast it to their own people and to us. Why? Those who have spent many years in Asia have a simple and convincing explanation. They say that the people of Asia regard a factory, any kind of factory, as something which lightens their load just a little. Maybe it's soap or woven cloth or fertilizer. It has taken decades to build that factory; they feel a sort of part ownership, even though they may never have seen it or its products. In Asia there is no greater crime than to destroy a man's rice bowl, and the factory is regarded as a kind of big community rice bowl.

The Chinese radio makes much use of the fact that the great powers decided during the war to return Formosa to China, but they never mention that the same powers declared that Korea should be "united and independent." We are aware that we have no designs upon territory in Asia, that most of the free nations of the world have at least given moral support to our action in Korea, but there are millions in Asia who know nothing of these matters. One day we shall have enough men and firepower in Korea to start back through those valleys and towns, towns that *we* burned to the ground while pulling back. The bridges are blown, factories destroyed, the dikes of the rice paddies broken. There has been, and there will be, much slaughter. But there will be people left in Korea and in all of Asia. Most of us are convinced that our cause is just, that this United Nations action may well be one of the great pivots upon which the history of relations between nations turns. But do the peoples of Asia know all this? And how important is it that they should know?

With all our massive strength, speed of communication, productive capacity, high standard of living, we are not all-powerful. We checked the spread of Communism in Western Europe because the people who live there decided that with our economic help they *wanted* to stop it. We spoke their language, at least enough of us, and there was a common objective—the salvation of personal and national freedom. The problem of communicating ideas is vastly more difficult in Asia. The economic problems are appalling, but in the end of the day it's the people who will decide. It seems to me that few things are more important than that we learn to speak their language, that we use every device, and maybe invent some new ones, to tell them the truth about the world in which they live and whose future they will so powerfully influence. This would be a slow, costly and delicate business. We must accept the proposition that the *people* of Asia will decide their future, that we will not attempt to *dictate* it and that we will use armed strength, as we are in Korea, to prevent Russia from dominating them. If we accept that proposition, then it seems to me that an urgent obligation rests upon us to provide them with the information, and the example, upon which decision can be based.

October 12, 1950

This is Columbus Day. If that intrepid navigator and national hero should arrive upon our shores today, he couldn't get in. He couldn't get a visa—a permit to enter—because the State Department has suspended all entry visas for all foreigners, except displaced persons or those coming to this country at the expense of our government. We now have two or three hundred people on Ellis Island, and there will be more. That's where Columbus would find himself, for he came from a totalitarian state. And the queen who sponsored him did not permit her democratic principles to show.

This state of affairs arises as a result of the passage, over the President's veto, of what has come to be known as the Communist Control Bill. This bill provides, in part, for the exclusion of all aliens who in any shape, form or manner engage in activities prejudicial to our public interest, or endanger our welfare and safety. It excludes anarchists and all who have been members of any totalitarian party, either here or abroad, and all who advocate the economic, international or governmental doctrines of any other form of totalitarianism.

So far as is known, there is no legal definition of the word "totalitarianism." The wording of the legislation is so broad that the State Department has decided that nobody can come in, with a few exceptions, until the thing is untangled. They are trying to figure out what to do about admitting diplomats from Communist countries, as well as businessmen, doctors, students and others whom we have invited here in order to show them how democracy works.

172

The Attorney General can make an exception and allow a person to enter, but he must make a report to Congress in each case.

Yesterday we asked for permission to go to Ellis Island to interview some of the people held there. We were today informed by the office of the district director of the Immigration Service that this permission would not be granted, that things were too confused out there at this moment and that they didn't want any more publicity. Later on, in ten days or so, they would be glad to arrange for us to go out and interview some of the people there. This raises an interesting question, not regarding freedom of movement for aliens, but for American reporters.

This situation reminds me of something that happened in London in the fall of 1940. At that time, Britain was alone, the German bombers were through in the daylight over the heart of London; German troops were expected on the beaches the first foggy morning. And at that time the House of Commons, which might have been destroyed at any moment, devoted two days to the discussion of conditions under which enemy aliens were being held on the Isle of Man. For the House was determined that, though the island fell, there would be no concentration camp abuses of the rights to which interned enemy aliens were entitled.

Few citizens—and certainly not this one—would object to that part of the Communist Control Bill which is designed to exclude from this country Communists and those dedicated to the overthrow of our form of government. But it is now clear that the language of this particular section of the bill must be made more precise if it is to achieve its objective and if we are to avoid confusion at home, ridicule abroad and the issuance of orders by government departments which may or may not have been intended, or authorized, by the overwhelming majority of Congress which passed this bill in the closing days of the last session.

November 3, 1950

By mid-October, after four months of fighting, the Korean War appeared won. There was talk of getting most of the troops home for Christmas. Then Communist China intervened.

173

The war in Korea is definitely not going according to plan. From the very beginning it was our purpose to keep the Chinese Communists out of the war. They are now in it, in what strength we do not know. General MacArthur's headquarters and the Pentagon are both reticent, but correspondents with forward elements and officers commanding in the field are more outspoken.

General MacArthur said tonight that the situation would become serious if a foreign government intervened officially with all its strength. "But," he added, "I do not believe that will happen."

Tonight the Peiping Radio said for the first time that young peasants had decided to volunteer with the Korean Army. The voice of Communist China said that these volunteers were not limited to Manchuria, that some came from as far away as Tientsin. The Chinese Communist radio in the last couple of days has stepped up its propaganda against what it calls "American imperialism and aggression."

I am reliably informed that while we were debating about crossing the 38th Parallel into North Korea, the Chinese Communist foreign minister, Chou En-lai, summoned the Indian ambassador in Peiping on two occasions and informed him that the crossing of the parallel would cause the Chinese to intervene. The Indian government passed these messages on and appeared to believe that some basis for a peaceful settlement could be found. The subsequent Chinese invasion of Tibet may have caused the Indian government to change its mind.

November 28, 1950

On November 24, General MacArthur launched a new offensive toward the Yalu River. It was to be the last big drive of the war. "Tell the boys when they reach the Yalu they are going home," he advised his field commanders. Within twenty-four hours the Chinese counterattacked, necessitating "limited withdrawals." But it was soon obvious that Allied forces in Korea were in full retreat.

In Washington, General Marshall called for a sustained defense effort—permanent military preparedness. For his radio program, Murrow obtained a recording of Marshall's statement and wrote an introductory paragraph reflecting his own concern over the Korean situation.

This is a time when the citizen is obligated to stand steady in his shoes, when there is no clear, calm voice to tell us, "This is the way; these things we must do to be saved." Most of us are bewildered and flying blind, acutely aware that there are no easy or quick solutions. If there is an honorable and acceptable compromise for this crisis, no leader has voiced it. As a reporter I have had some experience in talking while nations meet their testing time. It isn't particularly difficult. For the next few minutes we could speculate about holding a line across the narrow waist of the peninsula, reminisce about battalion and regimental commanders we came to know in that terrible heat along the Naktong last summer, who are now trying to cut their way out in the cold dawn of tomorrow in North Korea. It would be possible to discuss for some time the utterances of those senators who are at least legally responsible and who have rushed into print with statements that we should drop some atom bombs. But I have the feeling that you would prefer to hear the cool, calm voice of a man who outranks any reporter, who is no stranger to crises and whose record is eloquent enough. For that reason we have recorded certain sentences spoken in Washington today by General George Catlett Marshall, our secretary of defense.

MARSHALL: I think everybody connected with the government is fully aware of how critical the situation is. The intense desire of all is to proceed in such a way that we can avoid a full world war. Yet we have this dangerous world situation, and we have to meet it. There's a unanimity of feeling that we must have immediately a very rapid buildup of strength; everybody's in agreement on that. But that is not sufficient. We must now figure out how we proceed from there and avoid the past, which is a succession of mountaintops and valleys, which is highly destructive if we get up on the heights and then it collapses and then the trouble comes. If we just build up great forces and don't have a system that can be carried on in some way which would be acceptable to our people, that will meet the reactions that come from the homes, the wives, the mothers—which is a tremendous reaction—if something exciting has not happened, if something terrible has not happened, the tension gets tiresome, and tensions do get tiresome, and we will make a very serious error, I think. I never can get away from the thought of the period of the World War, all Europe in the hands of the Nazis, and in August—I think at the end of August 1941—in that situation and at that date, we saved ourselves by one vote. It was the public; that was the public reaction. Now if our prayers are met, the best hope I can see at the present moment is a long period of tension during which we must maintain a posture of sufficient strength to make it increasingly improbable that that tension will be turned into a full-blown horrible war.

What we do must be very soberly thought out in the coolest, calmest, most calculating way we can meet the matter. To decide how we must meet the immediate increase, that's rather simple. If we're so cursed with misfortune that we get into a war, it's tragically simple. We go all out to full mobilization, which everybody will step into and do their level best. It's a very difficult situation, and we've got to be most sober-minded in our approach to it.

MURROW: That was the recorded voice of our secretary of defense, General George Marshall. You require no radio reporter to fashion words about the crisis that impends. The facts speak for themselves. For my own part I am able to rejoice that the nation is served by so considerable a man.

December 5, 1950

That word of evil ancestry *appeasement* is beginning to appear more frequently in print and in conversation. It is one of those words that has been somewhat distorted—a dictionary definition wouldn't help us to understand it as it is presently used because it is irrevocably tied to Neville Chamberlain's actions and pronouncements at the time of Munich. There is at least a possibility that we may come to confuse *appeasement* with *negotiation*. When Chamberlain agreed to talk with Hitler at Godesberg, that was negotiation. The whole process received the name of appeasement when, in order to avoid a war, Mr. Chamberlain agreed to sacrifice Czechoslovakia, thereby destroying an effective ally and increasing the

176

German appetite for conquest without gaining any commensurate advantage for the Western Powers. But this was only the beginning of appeasement. The British and the French governments then proceeded to try to persuade their own people that this action had produced a degree of security—relief from the threat of war. More than this, they failed to rearm, to take adequate measures to provide for a resort to force if their policies and their premises proved to be mistaken.

Negotiation turns into appeasement only when essential interests are sacrificed under duress, and when the appeasing government attempts to mislead its own people as to the character and consequences of that agreement or appeasement. It is possible to buy time, through diplomatic maneuver, just as it is possible to trade ground for time in a military action. But in warfare or diplomacy it may well be fatal to fail to use the time so gained to prepare for final collision.

It seems to me that there is at this time nothing in the negotiations between ourselves and our European allies, or between ourselves and the Chinese Communists, to warrant the charge of appeasement. This, for the excellent reason that we do not know what, if anything, has been agreed upon. These exchanges are taking place at a time when we are encountering military reverses, if not disaster. We may be forced off the Korean Peninsula; we may choose to evacuate it, or we may be able to form a line that will hold somewhere—I do not pretend to know. Our European allies may urge, and persuade us, to follow a policy that we ourselves would not freely choose. We may be forced, for a combination of diplomatic and military reasons, to abandon for the time being our stated objective in Korea. We must wait and see what happens.

But appeasement as I understand it, and witnessed it, consists of giving to your enemy an advantage, an increase in strength either actual or potential, without yourself receiving any commensurate advantage in terms of time, strength or freedom of action. In this situation our enemy's intention is perfectly clear. The Russians have written it as frankly as did Hitler in *Mein Kampf*, and they have demonstrated it on the maps of the countries on the borders of their great expanding empire. We have been warned, in ink and in blood. Our allies are frightened; our own strength is inadequate.

The current situation reminds this reporter, not of Munich and

177

appeasement, but rather of Britain in the winter of 1939. The war was phoney—no rationing, few controls, casual mobilization, little interference with the civilian economy. There was a war, but it was some distance away. The speeches of government leaders were resolute, as they are now in this country.

Even before the Chinese intervention in Korea we were committed, as a nation, to the proposition that our foreign policy must be based upon strength, ours and that of our allies. We had concluded that the Russians would not negotiate realistically until we had created sufficient "situations of strength." It is now revealed, on the maps and in the dispatches, that we do not have sufficient strength as of now to deal with the Communist threat in a situation where the Russians have not committed a single soldier. In this war, unlike the last two, we do not have a screen of friendly nations who can—in Winston Churchill's phrase—hold the line until those who are half asleep become half prepared.

Our leaders announced, and reannounced, a policy based upon strength. They have recently confessed the obvious, which is that we do not have adequate strength. And we do not appear to be acquiring it with any real sense of urgency. There is no evidence so far that we are paralleling the period of Munich appeasement but much that we are following the policies of Europe in 1939 and early 1940—policies that came very near to being fatal.

March 19, 1951

> *The Senate Crime Investigating Committee held a series of melodramatic hearings with former New York City Mayor William O'Dwyer and bigtime gambler Frank Costello as star witnesses. Costello established some kind of precedent by permitting only his hands to be televised.*

This program tries to avoid leaping at, or stumbling over, conclusions until all the evidence is in. Many of the disclosures in this investigation into organized crime are not new. Some of the information has been previously available, either in print or before grand juries. Many of the incidents recounted by worried witnesses occurred many years ago, and the memories of law enforcement officers and those of alleged gangsters are equally vague. It would

178

be well to remember that this Senate subcommittee was not established to catch crapshooters, or produce indictments of bigshots. The committee was created to investigate organized crime with a view to recommending new legislation.

In this reporter's opinion the hearings have amply demonstrated the need for such legislation. We have heard here in New York a former mayor, who now represents his country abroad, attempt to explain his visit to a notorious gambler, admit that he received political aid and comfort from a close personal friend of two notorious underworld characters named Costello and Adonis. Costello has recounted a veritable parade of political and judicial figures who came to his home seeking something or other, although Mr. Costello insists that he has never voted, never made a campaign contribution.

The committee has traveled more than a country mile in the direction of proving its charge that there is a "government within a government." The television performance has been fascinating, the audience fantastic—perhaps because the midgets in the box have been real. It may be that a few individuals may be indicted for contempt or perjury. But the real test of the usefulness of these hearings will come when Senator Kefauver's committee proposes new legislation. And that will be a test not alone for the statesmanship of the committee but also for the individual citizen, and for television, as well as the old-fashioned instruments of radio and print.

It seems to me that this committee has in effect been going about the country shouting the good old-fashioned American slogan: "There ought to be a law." They have been demonstrating in dramatic fashion why new law is required. If our interest, as individuals, is less in the law than it is in the shabby characters who have been parading before the television cameras, then in a few years we shall probably have a repeat performance—by which time, I am assured, the audience will be much bigger.

April 2, 1951

We are now in an argument about the draft deferment of college students. One thousand examination centers, at which college students will take tests for possible draft deferment, have been named. Scores on the tests, together with evidence of scholastic performance in college, will be used by local draft boards in considering the eligibility of students for deferment. We don't yet know what a "passing," or "deferring," score will be.

This action raises some fundamental questions of great importance. But first let's get the facts straight. The Selective Service law passed by Congress says "that adequate provision for national security requires maximum effort in the fields of scientific research and development, and the fullest possible utilization of the nation's technological, scientific and other critical manpower resources."

In order to carry out this directive, General Hershey, the director of Selective Service, appointed six committees representing various fields of scholarship. These committees made recommendations in 1948 and repeated them in 1950. These recommendations are the basis of the present college deferment order. The objective is to develop a corps of trained and specialized personnel that will be available for the nation's use. Those bright and promising students who pass the tests will be deferred. Their obligation to serve will not be canceled; if the student fails to live up to his promise, the deferment can be revoked. But remember, this deferment is possible for any student now in or preparing to enter college, regardless of how obscure or unimportant to the national welfare his field of study may be. What about the nineteen-year-old whose parents cannot afford to send him to college? There is no deferment for him. What about the student who has scrambled and worked his way through high school and whose intellectual equipment may have suffered as a result? Is deferment going to be possible only for those whose parents happen to have been intelligent or wealthy? Are those studying for medicine or physics to be deferred equally with those who purpose to study Sanskrit or French literature? Are the armed forces to get only the bottom half or the bottom third of the class? And can anyone, even the educational testing service of Princeton, devise a test that will tell whether a college freshman will make any contribution after four years of college "in the fields of scientific research and development and the fullest possible utilization of the nation's technological, scientific and other critical manpower resources"? These are questions left unanswered by the new directive.

It seems to assume that enrollment in college is proof positive of a man's future usefulness to the maintenance of the national health, safety or interest. If this rule had been applied in earlier days, people like the Wright brothers, Mark Twain, Phil Murray, Andrew Carnegie, Henry Ford, Thomas Edison and Harry S. Truman, among others, wouldn't have had a chance of being deferred because none of them went to college. We have never proceeded in this country on the basis of giving preference to an intellectual elite. We have deferred people on the basis of the usefulness to the state of their occupation or the profession for which they were trained. But we have never, I think, attempted to decide who should carry a musket on the basis of his intellectual horsepower.

It is, of course, necessary in crisis as in calm to nourish the minds of the youth of the nation and to fertilize research in all disciplines of learning, including the physical sciences and the humanities. But it is not less necessary to remember that in our history the word *equality* has been as important as test tubes, laboratories and research into the lower forms of animal life.

We are now concerned, in a time of crisis, to prevent the threat of war from drawing too heavily upon our future reservoir of intellectual power. Had we been equally vigilant about this in the days of peace, the present problem might not be so acute. But when we embark upon a policy which attempts to sort out, at an early age, those who at some future date may be so valuable to the State that they cannot be risked in combat—well, that will require quite a test, as well as quite a departure from our traditions.

April 3, 1951

It has been remarked before on this program, as a matter of personal opinion, that we as a nation seem to be searching for easy and quick solutions—some magic formula, some capsule that will cause our confusions and our difficulties to evaporate. We seem to be living in an age of disillusionment, a measure of disappointment, plus considerable frustration. Distinguished senators deplore the deterioration in public morals. Various individuals are accused of having their hand in the till of influence. Distinguished pundits who deal in the old-fashioned medium of print are moved to examine at length the social, political and ethical impact of television upon our bewildered and queasy society. Some of them appear almost in the role of the "machine-breakers" during the industrial revolution, being moved in this case to the use of double negatives in deploring the fact that this new gadget permits people to see and hear things that have only been seen and heard by the privileged heretofore.

We have perhaps become accustomed to "exaggerated" language. At the United Nations, and elsewhere, the disputes of diplomacy are carried on in language which would have caused the apprehensive citizen of earlier days to expect a declaration of war.

In the midst of all this oratory and exaggerated language many of us probably continue to search for that easy and elusive solution. The advertisements tell us of a radio that not only "looks smart and plays beautifully" but "automatically wakes you to music" and even has your coffee ready. At night it "lulls you to sleep, then turns itself off." Life can be as simple as all that! There is a set of books which guarantee to "take the guessing out of discussions." And there is something that absolutely promises to prevent your wife from being "a kitchen exile."

Meanwhile, politicians point out that down this path lies ultimate and absolute disaster; while others are equally sure that unless we follow the path charted by them, we shall encounter disaster and chaos, and richly deserve it for having failed to heed their advice.

The use of exaggeration is nothing new in our society; much of our humor and folklore is based upon it. From time to time the Federal Trade Commission has attempted to eliminate exaggeration from advertising. This I have no doubt is very difficult, for advertising men and adjectives are no strangers. For example, today the Federal Trade Commission told the people who make Carter's Little Liver Pills that they must stop saying, without qualification, that its pills are what you need "when you're down and out, blue, listless, fagged out, down in the dumps, irritable, bilious or sullen." The advertisements also state that "you'll jump out of bed in the morning, rarin' to go. Clear-eyed and steady-nerved, feeling just wonderful, alert and ready for work." The Federal Trade Commission said today that Carter's Little Liver Pills "were and are, as

182

the findings and facts show, nothing more than an irritative laxative compound." And the company was instructed to desist from advertising certain of its claims. Attorney for the company says the decision of the Federal Trade Commission will be tested in one of the U.S. Courts of Appeal.

Most of us these days would undoubtedly like, when we feel "sour, sunk and the world looks punk," to wake up clear-eyed and steady-nerved and feeling just wonderful. There are those peddling political and economic solutions guaranteed, so they say, to achieve just that. There is no Federal Commission of Ideas to say that their claims are exaggerated and no court in which the issue can be tested, except the one that each of us carries around with him in order to hand down a verdict at election time. Each has the opportunity to select his own medicine and to measure the claims against performances. No one political or diplomatic prescription, no national or international advertising slogan is likely to solve our difficulties.

This reporter has no knowledge of pills, or their making—is merely convinced that in the area of politics and policy our major obligation is not to mistake slogans for solutions.

April 9, 1951

> *For months, General MacArthur had publicly opposed Administration policy, which sought to contain the Korean fighting. His was a policy of all-out victory: bomb the Communist bases in Manchuria, use the idle forces of Nationalist China to open a second front. Public opinion in the United States became sharply divided as a result.*

The *affaire* MacArthur is rapidly replacing the Kefauver Committee, troops for Europe and mink coats as the subject of national conversation. Our allies in Europe are apprehensive, resentful and confused. The President has discussed the matter informally with his chief lieutenants. There are a few demands that the General should be dismissed, others that he be given more support. It has even been suggested that a bipartisan congressional committee be sent to Tokyo to solicit the General's views. MacArthur is accused of being a military genius with his hands tied, of open disregard for civilian authority, refusal to promote harmony with our allies, and so forth. That the General has been indiscreet, unorthodox, a source of embarrassment to his own government and its allies is not to be denied—it's all in the record. There is nothing in the record to show that General MacArthur has disobeyed any military order. He's been saying what he thinks our grand strategy ought to be.

There is nothing mysterious at all about this controversy. The Administration, the Joint Chiefs of Staff and, naturally enough, our European allies have concluded that in the event of war with Russia, top priority must be given to the defense of Western Europe, that the war must be fought and won there. General MacArthur has concluded that we are already at war with world Communism in Asia, and that's the place to fight and win it. And he has said that in a series of unprecedented public statements, and has been quoted to that effect by many politicians who have visited him. The General has shown a complete disregard for official and unofficial suggestions that he conduct the war and leave the talking on policy matters to the Administration. His views are supported by a vocal minority in Congress, and no one can be sure by how many people in the country.

How then is this controversy over Far Eastern policy to be resolved? The Senate has just spent three months making it clear to the President, the nation and our allies that Congress has a big voice in foreign policy and the distribution of troops in Europe. This is a slow and wearisome process, but the same technique might be employed in regard to Asia. There would seem to be nothing unreasonable in ordering General MacArthur home to express his views and conclusions before a Senate committee, as General Eisenhower did on the matter of troops for Europe. General MacArthur has not been reluctant to express those views at a great distance. Why not bring him home where he is close enough for all of us to see and hear him, instead of getting his views in distorted driblets from official and unofficial sources? The General hasn't been home in thirteen years, and it is possible *he* might gain something from the experience, too.

184

April 11, 1951

No words of any broadcaster will add to, or detract from, General MacArthur's military stature. When the President relieved him of his commands at one o'clock this morning, a sort of emotional chain reaction began. It might be useful to examine some of the issues raised by this decision, for they are rather more important than the fate of a general, or a president, or a group of politicians.

Did the President have the constitutional power to fire General MacArthur? He did, without question; even the severest critics of his action admit this. One of the basic principles of our society is that the military shall be subject to civilian control. At the present time when, as a result of our rearmament program, the military is exercising increasing influence and power in both domestic and international affairs, it is of some importance that that principle be maintained. It is a principle to which the overwhelming majority of professional soldiers subscribe.

There developed, over a period of months, a basic disagreement between General MacArthur on the one hand and the President, the Joint Chiefs of Staff, the State Department and our European allies on the other as to how the war in Korea should be conducted; and, more importantly, a disagreement as to how, and where, the forces of the free world should be deployed to meet the threat of world Communism. General MacArthur was sent certain instructions, and he ignored or failed to obey them. Those orders, wise or foolish, came from his superiors. We as private citizens are entitled to agree or disagree with the policy and the orders, but so far as military men are concerned, the Constitution is quite specific. It doesn't say that a President must be a Republican or a Democrat, or even that he must be wise. It says that he is the commander-in-chief. There occurred an open and public clash between civilian and military authority. It was dramatic, and it was prolonged over a period of almost four months. What hung in the balance was not MacArthur's reputation as a soldier, or Truman's as a statesman, but rather the principle of civilian control of the military men and forces of this country. The issue has now been resolved. It is, as many have remarked, a personal tragedy for General MacArthur at the climax of a brilliant military career. But these matters must be viewed in perspective. Tragedy has also overtaken about fifty-eight thousand young Americans in Korea, and for about ten thousand of them it was permanent—before their careers began.

That war is still going on. Is there any reason to believe that General MacArthur's removal will increase the prospects of ending it? Some diplomats are inclined to hope it will. They point to the fact that the Communists have labeled MacArthur the number one aggressor and warmonger. But there is nothing in Communist doctrine to indicate that their policies are determined by the personalities of opposing generals, nothing to hint that their objectives do not remain what they were. Probably the best that can be hoped for is that the diplomats attempting to reach a solution may now do so without interruption or obstruction from the military.

The European reaction to General MacArthur's removal has almost without exception been a mixture of praise for his military record, plus relief that he is gone. The fear that his independent action might involve us in a full-scale war in Asia has largely disappeared. Whether that fear was justified is beside the point. It did exist, and has now largely been dispelled as a result of this evidence that civilian control of the military has been reestablished, and that the policy of combatting the threat of world Communism agreed upon by our allies and ourselves will be pursued.

It does not seem to me that the dismissal of General MacArthur has altered substantially the situation that confronts us. True, it has reassured our European allies. It has deepened divisions within our own country. But it has hardly improved the chances either for victory of agreement in Korea. It has not diminished the danger of Communist aggression, nor has it reduced the urgent need for unity and preparedness in the free world.

General MacArthur is coming home in a matter of three weeks. It is to be hoped that he will have ample opportunity to present his point of view, although this is not a privilege normally accorded to those who are removed for insubordination. Whatever opinion we may hold about MacArthur, Truman or our grand strategy, it remains a fact that in a time of increasing militarism, the subordination of the military to civilian authority has been reestablished. That may appear to some to be an academic point, but not to people who have witnessed what happens when the civilian authority abdicates to the military.

April 12, 1951

Western Union has delivered about sixty thousand telegrams to Congress and the White House, most of them in favor of General MacArthur. Republican Senator McCarthy, of Wisconsin, says, "It was a victory for Communism and shows the midnight power of bourbon and Benedictine." In Los Angeles, a man smashed a radio over his wife's head in the course of an argument about MacArthur's removal. Reports say it was a table model.

June 6, 1951

Today, on the seventh anniversary of D day, General Eisenhower went back to have a look at the beaches he then commanded, the rusting hulks of ships and LSTs still lying offshore at Omaha and Utah. He looked at the huge cemetery above the shelving beach, drove again on the narrow roads between the Normandy hedgerows and said: "All the free world would rally here again if Western civilization is threatened by aggression. The soil of France is sacred; all others would do well to remember that. The free world is strong. Given the single ingredient of unity, there is nothing it cannot establish. Tragic experiences taught us that peace could never be the lot of those who were divided, fearful or wishing to remain spectators."

This might be an appropriate time to remember a few of the tragic milestones that marked the tragic route to those beaches. There was Japanese aggression in Manchuria; nothing was done about it. There was Italian aggression in Ethiopia and futile talk of sanctions. Hitler's legions went fearfully into the Rhineland—and got away with it. Austria fell in a weekend, and the rest of Europe was a spectator. Self-righteous but misguided men attempted to buy peace by crippling Czechoslovakia, which was later murdered. And

187

then finally there was war. Poland was destroyed. The Belgians and the Dutch wouldn't even have staff conferences with the British and the French, for fear of offending the Germans, and so they were overwhelmed in a week. France fell, and there was left a small island off the coast of Europe, outside the darkness that had overtaken the Continent. The British had lost most of their weapons and equipment at Dunkirk, but they fought as best they could with what they had for a year, and alone.

We were helping some, but we were still in a great national debate as to whether this highly successful aggression was really our business, threatened our tradition and our existence. The Japanese blasted us into the war at Pearl Harbor, and eventually—only seven years ago today—American and Allied troops bought at great price the Normandy beaches. They finally bought a great victory, and then we promptly decided to destroy the military machine that had made that victory possible. Now we are engaged in rebuilding it; we have had in the last five years much internal dissension; we have irritated our allies, and they have not always soothed us. We have had do-nothing Congresses and pettiness in high places; and we have slandered and libeled each other in public.

But have regard for a moment for what we have accomplished. Through the U.N. we caused the Russians to pull out of Azerbaijan. We stopped a war in Indonesia. We saved Greece from Communism. And before the grass had covered the scars of battle in Normandy, or the rubble had been cleared from the streets of German cities, we produced the Marshall Plan, which merely saved a continent from Communism. With the Berlin airlift we saved a symbol and a city of a couple of million people.

We fashioned the North Atlantic pact because we needed allies, and because they had no hope of survival without us. We agreed that an attack upon one should be regarded as an attack upon all. We reversed the whole course of our national policy and tradition. Then came overt and unprovoked aggression in Korea, a little country of which most of us knew nothing, and we chose to fight it. Our allies in varying degrees fought with us. We quarreled with our allies and with each other. There were times when the nation seemed without guidance or purpose, when accusation of disloyalty was mistaken for proof, and the level of public debate at the U.N. and in Washington became more and more vulgar and unrestrained. The tensions and the turmoil, both national and international, remained. They may well become worse.

But the argument basically is not whether but how to resist the new imperialism. Regard again the milestones that led up to the late war and compare them with those that this nation and its allies have erected in the five years since the end of that war. No one can see the end of the road; it may be another and more terrible war. But the record of American action, and the recognition of responsibility, cannot be equaled in such a short period of time by any nation whose record can be found in history.

Near where General Eisenhower spoke today there is Milestone Number One on the road that leads through the heart of Germany. The milestones that we have erected since the end of that war—all the way from Teheran to Taegu—may well convince future historians that we are a considerable people in peace as well as war. That was an opinion widely held by the boys who went ashore seven years ago today.

June 14, 1951

These are days when the reporter who gets paid for studying, trying to find and analyze the news may, I hope, be forgiven for becoming somewhat bewildered. The Senate committees were billed as investigating our Far Eastern policy and General MacArthur's dismissal. So Louis Johnson, a former Secretary of Defense, testifies that he doesn't know why he was dismissed—it just happened. Senator Brewster, of Maine, fails to pin down Secretary Acheson under questioning and goes forth to the floor of the Senate to denounce the Secretary as a liar.

Newspapers and magazines that have long attacked the Administration and its foreign policy confess that Acheson did a good job of testifying but say there he was, a sitting duck; the Republicans just didn't fire the right questions at him.

General MacArthur deplores the disunity in the country, to which he has made some considerable, though wholly legitimate, contribution. And the General suggests that we are too much dominated by our allies, by which he means the British for whom he has a built-in dislike. But Senator McCarthy today says, in effect, that

Defense Secretary George Marshall is a traitor, but his trouble is not accepting British advice but rather rejecting it in the last war. McCarthy says Marshall has been playing the Russian game all along. The senator from Wisconsin subedits history carefully and quotes from books where, if he had bothered to turn a page or two, he would have found the author engaged in high praise of General Marshall. There is probably no man in public life in this country who has been subjected to more interrogation by Congressional committees than General Marshall. His record is more fully exposed and at least as distinguished as that of Senator McCarthy. And Americans have a healthy habit of looking at the record.

The Administration, unwilling or unable to find competent civilians to take on difficult diplomatic and political tasks, chooses generals for the jobs and then appears outraged when the generals begin to act like diplomats or politicians.

Our official spokesmen denounce the Spanish government as an intolerable dictatorship and proceed to grant that government a thumping big loan. Everybody says we're fighting Communism, so we make another grant to Tito, who says he's a better Communist than Stalin.

Administration spokesmen say they'll settle for a cease-fire on the 38th Parallel. Responsible Republican leaders say that would be fatal appeasement.

This free-swinging, unrestrained debate chills our allies, for in the first place they don't understand us and in the second place they know that if we make a mistake, we may survive but they won't— no matter what the final outcome.

Still, with all the hypocrisy and vulgarity that is involved, all the confusion that results, it's our way of doing business and hammering out decisions. It's rough on the reputation of individuals, confusing and at times discouraging to the thoughtful citizen. Maybe it's a luxury we can't afford. But it's our method of making up our collective mind. I think probably General MacArthur has uttered no better sentence since he came home than the one in Austin yesterday when he said, "The march of events and the common sense of the American people cannot fail ultimately to reveal the full truth." And then, of course, when they think they've found the truth, there must be the indispensable minority trying to convince them that it isn't the truth at all but merely a myth.

190

June 29, 1951

The move for an armistice in Korea is developing with such speed that it might not be premature to examine the position that will confront us if the shooting stops. It is, of course, true that the Chinese have yet to be heard from and that the Russians say they haven't the "least idea" what the Chinese attitude is. The Russian statement is either the biggest lie or the biggest sellout of an ally in history, and it's probably safe to assume that the Russians knew the Chinese attitude before they made the move. Moscow's denial of any knowledge of Chinese policy or intention was probably calculated to strengthen the bargaining position of the Chinese Communists—the "volunteers," that is.

If an armistice is arranged, it merely means that the soldiers stop shooting and the diplomats start talking. It will mean that some American boys who otherwise would have died will live. But it is no guarantee that they will be home in weeks or months, for this would be essentially an armistice without military victory for either side, and the cease-fire would hang in delicate balance while diplomatic negotiations were in progress.

August 29, 1951

It seems to me that everyone should have the opportunity to tell one, or perhaps two, stories about his vacation. This is my opportunity to do so. I didn't meet any very famous people, or reach any profound conclusions, but there was a chance to listen instead of talk—to see something of this country from one coast to the other, as well as a bit of New Brunswick and Nova Scotia. There was an agreeable inn in Lyme, New Hampshire—a lot of books lying about, good ones, too. The innkeeper said, "If you find anything that interests you, just take it along and mail it back when you're finished reading it." I asked if this was his general practice and suggested it must result in a fairly high casualty rate amongst the books. He informed me that last year seventy-six guests had taken books away with them, seventy-five had been returned, and one lady kept writing him at intervals of about a month about the seventy-sixth book, saying that she had finished another chapter and would return it in due course.

I met some college students in various places. They seemed to me better informed than we were at their age—more curious but at the same time more reluctant to express unpopular or unorthodox views. There seemed to be fewer radical nonconformists than there used to be. Rebels seem rather to have gone out of fashion, which is perhaps only a reflection of the current hysteria which confuses unpopular or minority views with subversion or disloyalty.

No other country in modern times has housed or fed its people so well. And yet there seemed to me to be a climate of opinion which can only be described as fear and "feel sorry for ourselves"—fear of an uncertain future, sorrow about high taxes, political incompetence, inclement weather, the draft and foreigners who won't do what we think they ought to do.

There appears to be an increasing tendency, with individuals as with nations, to conclude that the dissenters—those who fail to agree with us—are evil, malicious and disloyal. We appear to have lost some of our belief in the power of persuasion and the right of the individual to be wrong.

I formed the impression from casual conversations that many of us are inclined to use Russia as the catchall for our troubles—disposed to overestimate Russian strength, cunning and planning, inclined to believe that no solution is available except through force.

I could detect no sign that we glory, or rejoice, in the world leadership that has been thrust upon us, and not very much recognition that it is our glorious and terrible responsibility to determine whether freedom shall survive on this planet.

Things are pretty tough. We have Russians, high taxes, Democrats, demogogues, overcrowded schools, allies and the boll weevil to deal with. But this attitude of "fear" and "feeling sorry for ourselves" does not seem to me to be warranted. We have power, and we can use it wisely. We have freedom, and we can defend it from internal or external threat. Compared to the rest of the world, we live in luxury. We have, as a nation, in the years since the end of the late war dealt with our friends and former enemies in a manner

192

more generous and magnanimous than any victorious nation in history. We have made mistakes and may make some more. We can afford them, can afford to argue about them. We may not be the wisest people in the world, but surely we are the most fortunate.

Once during my vacation I heard a broadcaster described as "one who thinks only with his vocal chords"—and I did not debate the point at any length—but I am privileged to be able to use mine to say that we have less reason to fear and feel sorry for ourselves than any people I know. Whatever means may be required, however long it may take, no matter what the sacrifice, we shall win this struggle for the world. But it seems to me that a lot of us could afford to believe a little harder that we can do it, and that it's worth doing.

September 3, 1951

There have been a lot of Labor Day speeches. We haven't read them all. But enough.

September 12, 1951

General Marshall, at the age of seventy, resigned as Secretary of Defense to retire to his farm in Leesburg, Virginia. His undersecretary, Robert Lovett, was named to take over the Defense Department.

The team of Marshall and Lovett has been broken up. This combination served the nation in the Army, the State Department and the Department of Defense.

General Marshall has probably been talked over and at more than any living American. He was eulogized when he retired as Chief of Staff, again when he resigned as Secretary of State and now when he resigns from Defense. Probably no man in the last ten years has spent more time before Congressional committees. His record is too well known to merit repetition; and it may be safely assumed that he will not now engage, in full uniform, in parades, posturing and political polemics. He has served in the spotlight for a long time. The public has had repeated opportunity to weigh and measure him, and historians may conclude that his greatest contributions were made in peacetime rather than in war. General Marshall is a man who held himself erect, but with a loose rein—the most completely self-controlled man I have ever known, capable of sitting through a long speech or a committee hearing without moving a muscle, but at the same time there was no tension about him. He can reprimand the wandering and verbose informant by saying in a mild voice, "Would you mind repeating what you have just tried to say?" And he can now cultivate his garden in Leesburg, warmed in the autumn of his life by the respect and admiration of most of his fellow countrymen and the gratitude of millions of Europeans who were, by his vision and drive to action, saved from slavery.

Mr. Robert Lovett, his successor, has much of the General's quiet equanimity. He is an old hand at serving his government, with a built-in urge to get things done, having served as Assistant Secretary of War for Air, Undersecretary of State and Undersecretary of Defense. There is no doubt that his appointment will be confirmed by the Senate, and the small-caliber minds in Washington which delight in sniping at everyone who works for his country may well find Lovett as tough a target to hit as was Marshall.

September 27, 1951

How simple it would be if our national and international affairs could be conducted under established rules, in language we could all understand. Then Mr. Acheson, at San Francisco, would have thumbed the Polish delegate out of the auditorium when he refused to surrender the microphone. When Gromyko protested, Acheson could have cleared the whole satellite bench. In baseball when the umpire says, "Out" or "Safe," we know what he means. But in diplomacy if a nation says, "We take a serious view of this," we aren't quite sure what is meant; the issue is still in doubt. In the Iranian oil dispute, the British wanted to refer it to an umpire, the World Court. The Iranians said, "We don't trust the umpire and

194

won't accept his decision." There is no method of declaring that the Iranians have thereby lost the game.

If we understood public service as well as we understand baseball, we might conclude that Secretary of Defense Bob Lovett is one of the best pinch hitters of the last decade, that General MacArthur was sent back to the minors because he wouldn't accept orders from his manager. Think what would happen if Vice President Barkley were an umpire! Today he might send Senator Joe McCarthy to the showers and tomorrow eject Senator Bill Benton from the floor.

We are a baseball-loving people, fond of action and quick decision. The umpire provides that. There is no appeal, no arbitration, no prolonged discussion. Under the rules the player gives up most of his freedom of speech and action to the control of the umpire. That keeps the game moving and finally produces a decision. I am not suggesting changing the rules or the umpires.

What I *am* trying to say is that the application of the umpire principle to political and diplomatic decisions is highly dangerous. The same thing is true in the field of news. It was reported the other night, on this program, that President Truman had issued an executive order establishing security officers in all government departments and agencies, that these security officers would label documents "top secret," "secret" or "confidential." The purpose of this directive was stated to be the denial of information that might be useful to a potential enemy. No effort was made to define what that information was. What the President did, in effect, was to direct the appointment of a flock of umpires, even for those departments and agencies whose activities have no direct relation to national security or defense.

Tonight the Office of Price Stabilization has directed its employees throughout the country "to prohibit the disclosure of material, or the release of any other internal information, that might cause embarrassment to the Office of Price Stabilization." Presumably anything that might embarrass the O.P.S. would give aid and comfort to the Russians. This is the type of umpiring, or censorship, that we have never before tolerated in this country. A considerable section of the American press and radio has accepted the appointment of these umpires—who are empowered to make up their rules as they go along—without much criticism. (Senators threatened to cut off funds for O.P.S. unless this secrecy order was revoked; the President revoked it a few minutes ago). Mr. Truman's original order sets up umpire censors where reporters and the umpires are both playing in the dark without established rules. Umpires are practically dictators on the baseball field. But let's keep them there.

October 4, 1951

At today's news conference, President Truman defended his recent executive order directing government departments and agencies to appoint security officers, these officers to have the power to classify or mark "secret" any documents which, in their opinion, might be useful to a potential enemy. This order has been attacked by considerable sections of radio and press, and by a number of Congressmen. Mr. Truman said the order has been misinterpreted and misrepresented. It was an honest effort to keep secrets from falling into enemy hands. The President had no desire to suppress freedom of speech or press. The nature of our defense system requires that military secrets be made available to nonmilitary agencies; these secrets must be protected. Mr. Truman said another purpose of the order was to make sure no information would be withheld from the public unless it does, in fact, involve national security.

The President said that "newspapers and slick magazines" have made public 95 per cent of our secret information. He said a study made by Yale University showed this. We checked with Yale and were told that all details are confidential by order of the government. They couldn't say what professors participated in the project. It was undertaken for the Division of External Research. We finally located the Division of External Research, which isn't listed in the government directory, and were told that they had made the deal with Yale to undertake the study, that they hadn't actually seen the results as they went to the Central Intelligence Agency. The Central Intelligence Agency had no comment. This raises a nice question: If the Yale professors arrived at that figure of exactly 95 per cent revelation of our secrets, did they know all of the secrets—that is, a hundred per cent? Otherwise, how and by whom was that 95 per cent figure reached?

Mr. Truman contended that responsibility for not publishing security information is in the hands of the press and radio, regardless of the source. Reporters wanted to know if that meant maybe they shouldn't use official information released by the Defense Department. Mr. Truman said that's what he meant. The President complained about a map that appeared in *Fortune* magazine showing the location of atomic energy plants. *Fortune* says the article was prepared with the consent and cooperation of the Atomic Energy Commission. Pictures and text were cleared for security. (There was no information in the map not available in any good library in the country.)

Mr. Truman said he had heard broadcasters express their views on future strategy after coming back from Korea. Wars can't be fought on that basis. Mr. Truman complained about aerial maps showing our principal cities, with an arrow pointing to key targets. When told this map was given out to make people aware of the danger of A-bombs, the President said he didn't care who put it out—it shouldn't have been published.

Mr. Truman said pictures and information about the pilotless bomber, the Matador, should not have been made public. (This information was cleared and made public by the Defense Department.) Mr. Truman himself had told a news conference that the Matador was one of the "fantastic new weapons" he had mentioned in a public political speech. The President didn't remember saying anything about it.

Some time after this confusing and contradictory news conference, the White House issued a statement attempting to "clarify" the President's views on security. It said, "Every citizen, including officials and publishers, has a duty to protect our country; people who get military information from responsible officials may assume that it's safe to publish it." (That contradicts what the President said at his conference.) If reporters get military information from sources not qualified, they should exercise most careful judgment before publishing it. This clarifying statement says, "The President's executive order does not in any way alter the right of citizens to publish anything." That is correct; it doesn't. It merely sets up the machinery which may well deny access to information which is in no way related to military affairs or national security.

The President's specific examples indicate that his complaint is against existing security officers, rather than against newspapers and slick magazines, and radio. Mr. Truman implies that his executive order applies only to military and security information originating in the Pentagon and passing from there to some civilian agency such as the F.B.I. or the Central Intelligence Agency. But that is not what the order states. It authorizes every government department and agency to name a security officer who can, on his own responsibility, mark documents *secret* or release them for publication. And there is no appeal.

Mr. Truman "hopes for more rather than less information," has no desire to suppress freedom of speech or press, is proud of his record of defending civil liberties. But that's what the order states. Precisely 95 per cent of our secret information has been made available through newspapers and slick magazines. Enemy agents now have only 5 per cent to go, without even having to read a book. This startling statistic was dug up by a group of Yale professors whose names we are not allowed to know. Operation Clamming-Up in the campaign for sealed lips appears to be progressing very well.

October 11, 1951

Occasionally a reporter reads a speech with the feeling that here is one we shall hear again many times in different forms. Senator Lyndon Johnson of Texas made one of those speeches today. He said, "I can foresee a time when we will decide we have had enough of indecisive fighting, of battles without victories." He believes the American people will become impatient and demand a showdown. The senator said, "Unless those who plot the destruction of our civilization change their ways, it will come, and the time may not be too far distant." Lyndon Johnson thinks we can go on fighting in Korea, probably handle another war in Indo-China, take on a bout in Iran or Yugoslavia, but "somewhere, sometime, someplace something will snap." What we are doing now in Korea is, as Johnson sees it, "the business of battling the slave and letting his master go scot free." The Senator thinks the time will come when we will say to the Russians, in some sort of proclamation, "We are tired of fighting your stooges. We will no longer waste our substance battling your slaves. We will no longer sacrifice our young men on the altar of your conspiracies. The next aggression will be the last, for we will recognize, and the world will recognize, that you yourself and not your puppets are the real aggressor. We will strike back—not just at your satellites—but at you. We will strike back with all the dreaded might that is within our control, and it will be a crushing blow."

That possibility is one thing that paralyzes our allies in Europe. They don't doubt that we can deliver the blow—most of them share our feeling of frustration and outrage—but they know that if we deliver that blow, the Russians will be moving [to retaliate]. And even if we win the war, they and their countries will be utterly destroyed.

October 24, 1951

Murrow flew to London to cover the British elections and Churchill's bid, at the age of seventy-six, to depose Attlee as the king's first minister.

It is unlikely that two more dissimilar men ever contested for high office than Mr. Winston Churchill and Mr. Clement Attlee. Mr. Churchill is a highly visible man; Mr. Attlee is scarcely noticeable. Nothing in his manner or dress distinguishes him from the thousands of bank clerks or underpaid civil servants who come into London on morning trains. Everything about Mr. Attlee seems to be neutral, even the color of his hair—what's left of it. His public speeches resemble the lectures of the tolerant professor to a class that is not too bright but for which he has hopes. I don't believe the records show that Mr. Attlee ever coined a phrase or produced a brilliant ad-lib reply in parliamentary debate. Mr. Attlee is a moderate, temperate, self-effacing little man who for six years has presided over the government that produced a great social revolution by consent, and yet no man ever looked or acted less like a revolutionary or fanatic than does Clement Attlee. During the war, when he was deputy prime minister under Winston Churchill, he was completely overshadowed by his chief and didn't seem to mind it a bit.

Mr. Attlee is the son of what we in this country would call a Wall Street lawyer. Went to all the right schools, including Oxford, served with considerable distinction in the First World War, came out of it a major—twice wounded. Most of the efforts to write a profile of Mr. Attlee have failed. He is too modest to talk about himself. (Mr. Churchill is supposed to have remarked that he has a great deal to be modest about.) Some students of Mr. Attlee's career and personality have concluded that he has always been the middle-man, the compromise choice between the two really powerful men in his party—Herbert Morrison and the late Ernest Bevin. There is, or at least there was, some truth in this, but it does not explain the fact that for the past several years, according to all the public opinion polls, Mr. Attlee's personal popularity and following has been considerably greater than that of his party. Part of his success may be due to the fact that he is an excellent listener and appears able to compromise conflicting views, to judge nicely the point where further discussion is useless and decision is required. At times he has done the work of half his cabinet but never appears to show any physical strain, perhaps because he has the ability to make a decision and then forget it. He manages, even in the course of a bitter political campaign, to appear the reasonable, reasoning little man who is just a little bit above the battle.

There is nothing brilliant, heroic or dramatic about Mr. Attlee. He is just a modest, steady little man doing his job. If he is returned to power, it will be done in large measure by the women of Britain, for there are about two and a half million more women than men voting here, and if he is flung out of office, his policies reversed, he will continue to enjoy, even from his political opponents, the respect that is due to a modest man of great integrity.

This reporter had a half-hour's private conversation with Winston Churchill this morning. He had traveled back by train from Plymouth after his final speech of the campaign last night. I am not privileged to report this interview in the usual way, for it was far-ranging, informal and not for quotation. However, I am entitled to reach certain personal conclusions about the health, spirit and demeanor of one of the most considerable men of our age. I had been told that he was enfeebled, and becoming deaf. If this is true, this reporter is one of the least observant of our age. For at the age of seventy-six, at the end of a campaign that has left candidates half his age exhausted and nervous, Mr. Churchill continues to resemble the indestructible juvenile. He said he couldn't walk quite as far as he used to but could still work just as hard. While other and younger candidates are resting and recuperating, he displayed certain signs of impatience at the two days of enforced idleness before the results can be known.

As on previous occasions, Mr. Churchill's restless and well-stocked mind roved the world and its problems, giving the impression that this island is too small a stage for him to play upon. His voice has perhaps lost a little bit of its resonance, but his mind retains its cutting edge. He is aware that in this election both parties are in a sense contesting for the crown of thorns. But he has less reluctance than some of his colleagues to wear it. I formed the impression that if Mr. Churchill is returned to power, those who predict that he will, after a few months, lay down the heavy burdens of office and retire, will be proved wrong. More than any man I have talked to over here, Mr. Churchill appreciates the enormous significance of America's acquisition of power. As the history of the late war unfolds, it becomes clear how much his eloquence, persuasion and persistence influenced the application of our power then. Unlike some British politicians in both parties, he is persuaded that Americans can be persuaded and reasoned with, though not always successfully from the British point of view.

This has been one of the most frustrating reports I have ever attempted. My mind is still filled with those brilliant Churchillian improvisations and his analysis of the world situation. But I agreed to do no more than to inform his not inconsiderable number of friends in America of his health and well-being.

> *The Conservatives won, returning Churchill to power. The people, Murrow reported, voted "their apprehensions of the future and their memories of the past."*

November 2, 1951

> *Murrow went from London to NATO headquarters in Paris, where he called on General Eisenhower.*

It would appear that everyone who comes to Paris sees the General. This reporter is no exception. The rules for these interviews state that there will be no quotation and no attribution. And yet many people who have talked with the General have drawn conclusions, have emerged from that modest office persuaded that he will be available for the presidential nomination. I am not going to disagree with them, but at the same time I cannot confirm their unquotable, nonconfirmed conclusions. I have known few people in high position who would not entertain the idea of becoming President of the United States. It may be that General Eisenhower seeks that position and will actively attempt to secure it. I do not know. He did not say. I would guess that he is somewhat reluctant to enter into the type of vicious and personal politics that precede the selection of a President. There would exist the possibility that his armor might be tarnished or dented and that he would risk the respect and admiration of his former troops, which he values above everything else. I do not pretend to know what his final decision will be or when he will announce it, and I have some doubt that the General himself knows the answer to those questions. He can afford to wait.

General Eisenhower at the moment is confronted with problems as difficult, complex and pressing as those encountered by a President. If he is looking for a soft berth, he might as well try to become President as to achieve his aims in Europe. He has produced a major miracle in restoring confidence, self-respect and the will to resist to the peoples of Western Europe. I would suggest—and I'm quoting only myself—that for the next months it would be healthful to promote and develop a campaign that might be labeled "Let Ike Alone." I have no hope that this will attract any considerable number of faithful followers. But the fact is that in the next three or four months his mission over here will either succeed or fail. If at the end of that time he decides to become a candidate for the presidency, there will be ample opportunity for the individual voter to scrutinize his record. Meanwhile, he has got the most difficult and delicate job that has ever been given an American commander in war or peace; indeed, a responsibility that no single man has assumed in some two thousand years of European history.

November 14, 1951

> *The Korean truce talks began on July 10. After four*
> *months, when it seemed the negotiations were getting no-*
> *where, Murrow explained why, in his opinion, so little prog-*
> *ress had been made.*

About an hour from now, the negotiators attempting to arrange an armistice in Korea will be meeting again. Yesterday's session, which lasted for five hours, found the Communist spokesmen challenging the U.N. forces to break off the talks if they insist upon continuing the battle. The U.N. communique says it is now "unmistakably clear" that the Communists want to end the fighting on land, sea and air. The Chinese general said the negotiators must reach a decision now as to where to stop the fighting. And he said that if we wanted to use our military strength to try to change the present battleline, we could stay away from future talks and go ahead and try to change it.

The real issues involved in these delicate negotiations have become confused because both sides have changed their ground. For example, on June 26th Secretary Acheson said our objective would be achieved if the Communists withdrew behind the 38th Parallel and gave satisfactory assurances that they wouldn't start fighting again. On August 1st, Mr. Acheson said the 38th Parallel was no good as a defensible line. A few weeks ago the Communists gave up their contention that the 38th should be the line of demarcation. Then last week, in Paris, Russian Foreign Minister Vishinsky said it *should* be the 38th Parallel. The Communists have been saying one thing in the tent at Panmunjom and another thing in their press and radio. The policy of our negotiators in briefing correspondents has varied between great secrecy and full disclosure. But as near as we can figure it out the position at the moment is this: Both sides have agreed that the cease-fire line should be the current battleline. Both sides have agreed on a buffer zone about two and a half miles deep.

The question is when this line shall be drawn. The Communists say right now; let's stop all the shooting. The U.N. command says not yet. And our reason for delay is that before we agree to stop shooting, before we discard our constant threat of military action, we want the Communists to agree about the method of exchanging prisoners of war, the supervision and inspection of rear areas to prevent a build-up for a new offensive by either side, and we want them to agree about recommendations for the ultimate withdrawal of all foreign troops from Korea. We appear to feel that if we agreed now to a cease-fire, the Communists would probably not subsequently agree to anything else and we would have denied ourselves the constant threat of military pressure to make them agree. If we were to accept the cease-fire on the present line, without any agreement as to exchange of prisoners or inspection of rear areas, then if the Communists continued to refuse to exchange prisoners or agree to inspection, we would either have to break the truce and start the war again, or just sit there and do nothing.

December 31, 1951

The New Year approaches, and one of the first casualties will be that old familiar friend the penny postcard—a victim of inflation. In future, it will cost you two cents to post the epistle saying, "Having wonderful time; wish you were here." The Post Office figures this will raise an extra 120 million a year. If you've got any old penny postcards lying about, and mail them before midnight tonight, they'll go through all right. After that, they'll either be returned to you or delivered marked "postage due."

We deplore the passing of the penny postcard. This event set us to riffling through some postcards recently received in the hope of retaining some of the flavor of an era that is passing. We found, somewhat to our surprise, that we would willingly have paid the additional penny had they arrived marked "postage due."

Now, here is one that says, "Your pontification this evening was a classic." Another says I exist solely on the canned propaganda of the Truman-Acheson gang. Another postcard informs me that an individual, whose signature I cannot decipher, has decided to run for President. I am sure only that the name at the bottom isn't Eisenhower. Here's one which says, "Lately it seems you have joined the Red-hating, truth-distorting crowd." And, right under that, here is another penny postcard reading, "I used to enjoy your news broadcasts, but lately you sound so much like that ——— Taft that I am inclined not to listen to you any more." And another communication, which cost only a penny, which says in part—and only the milder part—"You are a Fair Deal, socialist hypocrite."

But then there turned up someone else, with a penny, to comment upon my "wide understanding, freedom from prejudice and open-mindedness." I cherish particularly the card which begs my pardon for a card mailed the day before saying the first card was intended for Elmer Davis, and adding, "If you ever see that clown, give it to him." I will. Although I might not recognize him in a clown's costume, I am aware of him as a right smart news analyst.

Hereafter, postcard praise and abuse will cost twice as much. This state of affairs led us to contemplate whether we might usefully address a few oral postcards in order to beat the midnight deadline. We thought to send one to Senator Taft saying merely: "Is it true what they say about Ike?" And we could, of course, send one to General Eisenhower with the inscription, "Waiting to hear from you." That one could be signed "Anxious." We were tempted to send a final penny postcard to President Truman, knowing full well it wouldn't get past the clerks in the mailroom. That one would read, "Hope you find a new broom."

We gave up the idea of sending a penny postcard to Brooklyn's pitcher, Ralph Branca, expressing the hope that next year no baseball could be hit for more than two bases. We may yet send a postcard to the Alsop brothers, those intelligent merchants of gloom, reading, "It hasn't happened yet, has it, fellows?" And we do indeed address a card—a very special one—to the engineers and telephone operators around this network saying, "Our best thanks."

We think seriously to send a postcard to our colleague and partner Fred Friendly, reading merely, "Watch the budget!" And another one to Senator McCarthy, reading, "Look before you leap; the pool may be empty."

If we were permitted a communication with the troops in Korea we would write only what they already know: "It is the waiting time that is hard, my brothers." If obliged to write to the parents and friends of many who will not return from Korea, I would feel compelled to quote that classic communication originally written by

Napier to the family of a subaltern killed storming Badajoz, "None died that night with greater glory. And there were many died, and there was much glory."

New Year's Day, 1952

> *In his first broadcast of 1952, Murrow listed the good news he would like to be able to report in the new year. "I suppose," he said, "reporters are entitled to hope, too, in a modest sort of way."*

I would hope to report an end to the killing; but with the world in its present state, I would suspect that the cessation would be only temporary. I should like to be able to report that no one on this minor planet was hungry, that everyone was free to read and write and speak as his conscience commanded; like to report a cure for cancer, the beginnings of disarmament, a notable increase in racial tolerance and a real reduction in the fear that imprisons the minds of so many people. (This sort of reporting is not likely to be more possible in the new year than it was in the old.)

I should like not to report any more casualty figures, lynchings or tragedies in the air, on land or the sea. I should like not to report any more reckless, irresponsible assaults upon the character, integrity and loyalty of public servants, when not accompanied by real evidence or proof. These hopes, likewise, are vain.

But there is an area where a reporter may hope to record some real progress in the course of the coming year. It is possible that our manners—and, who knows, perhaps even our morals—will improve. That we shall be more tolerant one of another, less disposed to label those who disagree with us as either Fascist or Communist. We may come increasingly to understand that our allies have deep and rich culture and history behind them, and we may develop more patience and understanding in dealing with them.

As individuals, and as a nation, we are a year older. And time changes nations as well as human beings. Often the changes are almost imperceptible. For the past five years this nation has been living at a furious pace. No nation in history has ever affected so vitally the affairs and the fate of so many other nations. Slowly but

206

perceptibly we have gained maturity and steadiness. Our new responsibilities have neither frightened us nor caused us to develop undue arrogance. We have made mistakes in the use of our strength, but by and large it seems to me that we have used it as our heritage demands. We have, as Disraeli once said—and he was laughed at for saying it—"generally chosen the side of the angels."

Pretending no knowledge of the future, and having only an imperfect one of the past, it seems to me that our national record over the recent past might cause our ancestors to conclude that the courage, sweat and sacrifice required to create the nation was worth the effort. As a nation we may say of our recent history that we have lived a life and not an apology.

February 6, 1952

The British have a new queen. King George VI died in his sleep last night at the age of fifty-six. His daughter, Queen Elizabeth, is due in London tomorrow, flying back from Kenya.

Throughout most of the world the flags are at half-mast. Even King Farouk of Egypt has ordered his so-called court to go into mourning for fourteen days. General Eisenhower canceled a cocktail party for the press. At Sandringham a notice was posted saying the day's shoot had been canceled. President Truman said this of the sad-eyed, suffering man who never wanted to be king: "His heroic endurance of pain and suffering during these past few years is a true reflection of the bravery of the British people in adversity."

In Britain the monarch occupies a position that is difficult to describe. He is a symbol, as the Great Seal of the United States is a symbol. A monarch is essential to the British system of government—they couldn't pass laws or run the country without one. But a British king or queen is much more than a focal point for allegiance, or a mere figurehead for ceremonial occasions. The king or queen is in a sense merely the instrument of the government in power. But there have been times in recent history when a discreet suggestion from the throne has powerfully influenced history.

It is true that the royal family enjoys the unamimous support of the British press and radio. But it is likewise true that the affections

207

of the British people must be earned slowly, for they neither give or withdraw their allegiance lightly. When King George VI came to the throne, after the abdication of Edward VIII, he was a painfully shy but determined man. He was good at knitting and at playing golf. He sat a horse well and was one of the finest wing shots in his empire. He did most of the things that royalty is supposed to do, never displayed any signs of brillance, as a student was generally near the bottom of his class. He undoubtedly saw more of his subjects than any previous British monarch. During the war he was to be found in Coventry and Plymouth immediately after the big raids. During the winters of 1940 and 1941 there was a third-rate song sung in the music halls of London called *The King Is Still in London.* It seldom failed to bring the audience to its feet. When a German dive-bomber hit Buckingham Palace, I overheard a pedestrian in Regent Street say, "Now the silly Germans have gone and done it. This will upset people no end."

King George VI had a rare kind of courage, and it had to do with a microphone. He suffered from a serious speech defect. It was suggested to him that his broadcasts to the empire, and the world, be recorded in advance so that the engineers might eliminate the hesitations, the stammering, before his message was broadcast. The king refused on the grounds that his message should be delivered directly. A live microphone produces a certain terror in most people who have normal speech. The courage to face one, handicapped by a serious speech impediment, knowing that much of the English-speaking world was listening, required the sort of four o'clock in the morning courage that is not often demanded of soldiers.

King George VI violated no traditions, showed no signs of eccentricity, was a reliable family man—a quality highly regarded by the British. Gradually he developed a certain ease of manner in his public appearances but never managed to convey the impression that he enjoyed them. That fact further endeared him to his subjects because most of them had the same difficulty. This king lacked glamor and brillance. He was predictable. And he had that quality that the British admire in horses, bird dogs and monarchs—he was steady.

The new queen is twenty-five. After a decent interval there will be a coronation. Queen Elizabeth's father presided over the liquidation of a considerable portion of the British empire. The new queen now becomes a prisoner of circumstances. She cannot greatly influence the course of world events—there will be no change in British policy, domestic or foreign. But her throne is steadier than any other.

February 27, 1952

Our High Commissioner in Germany, John J. McCloy, today made his quarterly report to the State Department. I should like to make a personal comment on this report. Not very many people familiar with German affairs will challenge its accuracy. It is the sharpest warning Mr. McCloy has yet given about the revival of German nationalism. This should surprise no one. A smashing defeat and the passage of seven years in time do not alter the mentality or the aspirations of a nation. Of course, the Germans, to quote Mr. McCloy, "vilify the Allies and seek to distort their policy." We have still got armies of occupation there. If you can imagine that we had lost the last war and were now occupied by German troops, we would be engaging in some vilification and distortion.

German nationalism, despite Mr. McCloy's warning, will continue to increase. Few, if any, German politicians will be elected who do not demand the return of their eastern provinces and the unification of Germany. We have done everything possible—frequently against the advice of our Allies—to convince the Germans that they are indispensable for the defense of the West. They are aware of their bargaining position and are using it as any other nation similarly situated would use it. The Germans are the most industrious, hard-working, inventive and determined people in Europe. They are already, so soon after utter defeat, with their country still divided, formidable trade rivals of both Britain and France. Germany's natural and traditional markets lie to the east, behind the Iron Curtain. And in due course, as their power and independence increase, they will trade through the Curtain, whether we like it or not.

There are some portions of Allied policy that the German nationalists don't need to distort very much. For example, a considerable

209

number of war criminals who were proved on evidence to have committed almost indescribable crimes were sentenced to death or long terms of imprisonment. Many of the sentences have not been carried out; other sentences have been reduced. Many have been set free, and most of those who are still in jail will be let out soon. Is this because they are less guilty now than when they were convicted? Not at all. This has been a progressive "deal" to win German support. They have insisted upon it and are in a fair way of getting it. Are they to be blamed if they conclude that Western justice is rather "flexible" and will respond to pressure?

There is no reason in history to assume that defeated Germans, occupied and divided, will not continue to act like Germans when the opportunity affords and seek traditional German objectives as their power increases. The combination of geography, economics, folklore and tradition, plus other intangible considerations, determines a nation's policies. Communist Russia now seeks many of the same objectives sought by czarist Russia, although with more different and deadly techniques. General MacArthur may have democratized Japan, but that country—barring a general war—will in due course trade again with Manchuria and the Chinese mainland, or its economy will collapse.

We have too long deluded ourselves that a military victory, occupation, the signing of a treaty will alter permanently national aspirations or objectives. It just doesn't work out that way—at least it never has.

April 17, 1952

> *The flooding Missouri River poured out over a million acres, routing a hundred thousand persons from their homes in seven states. Murrow flew to Omaha, where the river was still rising. The fight against the river reminded Murrow of war.*

There is being waged on both sides of the Missouri River a grim and grinding battle. There is great strain on the dikes and levees, and fatigue and determination mark the faces of men and women. Man

210

crowded the river too closely but is determined not to retreat. Flying up the river this morning, there were grain elevators sticking up out of a sullen brown sea. It seemed that they should have had lights revolving on top of them, like lighthouses. A double line of cottonwoods led up to just the roof of a house. As we approached Omaha the pilot said, "Where's the city? There should be a river there somewhere." We were flying over a brown ocean that seemed to bend up to meet a grey, dripping sky.

In this battle, as in war, it's the people who lift your heart—accountants and bank clerks wrestling sandbags, the mechanic acting as traffic cop who has stood at that intersection for twenty-two hours. You ask him how much longer he can stand it, and he says, "Just as long as I have to." No bravado, no heroics—just a job to do. The boy driving a big bulldozer who admits under questioning that he has been home, off that big cat, once since last Saturday. Questioning also reveals that he isn't sure which day of the week this is.

This is a business of men and machines against the river. It's rained all day. Over on the other side of the river about six hundred blocks have been evacuated in Council Bluffs. There are no children in the playgrounds; the roller coaster stands like a monument to a past age. You can look straight through the houses. They even took the window curtains, as well as furniture, ice boxes and all the rest, when they moved out. There is no traffic except for an occasional official car. GIs with carbines huddle around fires built in garbage cans. They look like all the other soldiers you have seen trying to keep warm. They're there to prevent looting, and there has been very little of that. The garage doors stand open and the cars are gone. That part of Council Bluffs is a ghost town that hasn't had time to fall down. There is a sign outside one house saying, I SHALL RETURN! There are trucks that were delivering fur coats and fancy dresses only last week; they're now delivering sandbags. A delivery wagon with the name of a sewing machine firm painted on its side opens its doors and dispenses hot coffee. This is a motley army if ever I saw one.

Fishing boots, galoshes, tennis shoes, golf shoes, sports jackets, business suits. They fight the river face to face, and then it seems that the river attacks from the rear. Out here they call it sandboils. The water crawls under the dikes and erupts like a geyser behind them. The only thing to do in that situation is to build a ring of sandbags around the erupting water and then to just keep on building it, higher and higher and higher, until the water in that circle of sandbags reaches practically the level that obtains in the river itself. Last night, there was sandboil. It took seven hundred men to corral it, but they did it all right.

There is nothing frantic or excited about this effort. The people who were doing a job don't seem to hate the river. They're too busy trying to control it. They may win or they may lose. The big test will probably come some time tonight. The men are wet and cold and hungry. Their eyes are the eyes of men just out of combat, the eyes of the men who fought the big fires in London during the blitz. Tonight in Council Bluffs the troops will be sleeping in their clothes. Men with lanterns and flashlights will be patrolling the levees. Many of them are veterans. They have fought the river before. They can anticipate its tactics. Whatever the outcome may be, these people have already met the big test. There has been speculation as to how those of us who live in this nation would stand up to the disasters that march with modern war. The answer is here. There is a community of effort, there is a great deal of improvisation, but, above all, there is a steadiness and a willingness to work.

May 19, 1952

It is my inclination, if not my duty, to report certain recent events which in combination affect everyone interested in what's going on in this country or the world. Last September, by an executive order, the President authorized, and directed, every government department and agency to create its own security officer, that officer to be empowered to classify and declassify information— that is, to label it "secret" or release it for publication. This was an unprecedented move in our peacetime history. Newspaper publishers protested vigorously; broadcasters were less vehement in their objections.

Speaker of the House Sam Rayburn, on his own authority, banned all microphones and cameras from open, public hearings held by House committees. He refused to discuss, elaborate upon or defend his decision.

About a week ago, the House of Representatives, by a voice vote, with only 31 of the total membership of 435 present, voted a new investigation to examine the extent to which radio and television programs contained immoral or otherwise offensive matter, or place improper emphasis upon crime, violence and corruption. And, further, the committee is to make recommendations about laws that may be required to eliminate offensive and undesirable radio and television programs. That resolution was introduced by Representative Gathings, Democrat of Arkansas.

That brings us up to today. Senator Pat McCarran, chairman of the Senate Judiciary Committee, introduced a bill to bar from all Senate committees radio microphones, television cameras and still photographers. This would apply to open, public hearings to which the general public and newspaper reporters with pencil and paper are admitted. Senator McCarran said his resolution follows a recommendation of the American Bar Association.

What follows is one reporter's comment upon these recent developments.

In combination, they represent both a threat of censorship and a denial of the right of television and of radio to employ the tools of their trade—the microphone and the camera—to disseminate information. And let it be said right here that the newspapers have protested rather more vigorously than either radio or television against these prohibitions. So far as the opinion of the lawyers of the American Bar Association is concerned, I would suggest that their opinion on this subject carries, or should carry, precisely as much weight as a group of doctors, plumbers or steelworkers. In the absence of any specific law, their credentials on the matter of news and information are as good but no better than those of any other organized group in the community.

Remember, this ban against cameras and microphones in House committee hearings, and the proposed one against Senate hearings, applies to open, public meetings. I don't care whether it's McCarthy attacking, Owen Lattimore defending, Acheson explaining foreign policy, Lovett defending a defense appropriation—I would rather hear the relevant excerpts of their testimony in their own voices than to read it or hear it after it has filtered through the minds of

213

reporters and editors, whether in newspapers or on radio. (No politician or witness has yet claimed that his own voice misquoted him.)

Whenever the government of the day, or the opposition, desires to advocate or urge legislation or action upon the country, they request and receive radio and television time, although there is nothing in the law requiring the networks to provide that time. But when broadcasters desire to show Congressional committees in action, the freeze is on so far as the House is concerned, and the McCarran Bill will do the same thing for public hearings by Senate committees. If the McCarran Bill is passed, and is not fought through to the Supreme Court, the radio and television companies will be negligent—derelict in their duty both to themselves and those who depend upon them for information. There was a time when the widespread use of print was regarded as a danger to the established order of the day. But it couldn't be suppressed. The same will be true of these newfangled gadgets, radio and television. It's only a question of time.

As for the House investigation into the effect of radio and television on juvenile deliquency, loose morals and crime, and also a study of books, magazines and pamphlets to be followed by recommendations for legislation, this personal comment is offered. There is material on radio, television and in print that is an offense to both the eye and the ear. There are great opportunities and an urgent need for improved content and maturity. But there exists no compulsion to read, look or listen. When Congress attempts to legislate on matters of taste, improper emphasis—what is offensive and undesirable—then it is only another short step to increasing controls over what the individual may say and how he may act.

As one who has had some experience with government-controlled radio and press, I should prefer to take my chances with the sometimes raucous, too frequently sensational method of disseminating news and information that we now have. For under this system, as a citizen, I can take it or leave it alone, have a wide variety to choose from and can complain or agitate for change with some hope of success. It is, I believe, in the national interest necessary for us to turn over a substantial amount of what we earn to the government. But it is not necessary, and it is not safe, to turn over to the government increased control over what we may read, see and hear. What is required is more information, more widely spread, regarding what our government is doing, and that is the thing that is in danger.

The bill to bar radio and television from Senate committee hearings was not passed. However, the Rayburn ruling, banning such coverage in the House, remained in effect.

June 4, 1952

General Eisenhower announced in January that he was a Republican and would accept "a clear-cut call to political duty." The "call" came from the liberal wing of the Republican Party, and now, accepting it, he had gone home to Abilene, Kansas, to make the first speech in his campaign for the presidency.

General Eisenhower finished speaking here in Abilene about 15 minutes ago. We are talking from a small truck near the stadium where he spoke. Before he arrived, it rained. They call it a Kansas shower. In other parts of the country they would probably call it a minor cloudburst. The mud was literally ankle deep, but the rain stopped just before the General, dressed in a raincoat, arrived to start his speech.

General Eisenhower's train arrived on schedule from Kansas City shortly after noon. There were dark clouds building up in the west. As the General stepped off the train, followed by his traveling companions and Mrs. Eisenhower, it was clear that there was to be no Eastern influence on this occasion. Lodge, Duff, Dewey, Hoffman, the Eastern advisors, were all absent.

The General walked to the small platform where the Eisenhower Memorial was to be dedicated. He spoke without notes and with considerable eloquence about his parents, their honesty, thrift, courage and integrity. The fact that the Bible "lived" for them; they were frugal. Eisenhower said, "I have found in later years that we were very poor, but the glory of America is that we didn't know it then."

The crowd of two or three thousand stood in what was a cornfield last year. It was not a demonstrative crowd. Later came the parade depicting Eisenhower's life practically from the time his parents arrived here, until—as people hope—he goes to the White House.

In the course of the speech, General Eisenhower concerned himself primarily with the need for unity, the danger of inflation, high taxation and the dangers of bureaucracy and big government. The speech was rather bland. Those who wanted Ike to come out swinging, as they put it, will be disappointed. It was more a declaration of faith than a political document. Many of the things the General said would be subscribed to by Harry Truman and Robert Taft. There was no criticism of Administration foreign policy, except a casual reference to Yalta, and that had to do with secrecy rather than substance. He did not attempt to assign partisan blame for the collapse of China. He did not lash out at corruption in high places in government but pointed out that it sort of seeps up from the bottom.

Those who have accused the General of "me-tooism" will find support for their contention in this speech. Those who have urged the General to conduct a dignified, high-level campaign will be pleased by today's effort. I doubt that this speech will set the prairies afire or start any great stampede. But it cleared some ground as to where the General stands in terms of the dangers that confront us. Just what he would do about them is somewhat less clear.

The hallmark of this speech was restraint, coupled with a belief that the traditional virtues—thrift, honesty and belief in God—are as essential to the country as they were when Eisenhower was a boy here.

July 11, 1952

Eisenhower won the presidential nomination on the first ballot. The convention action constituted, in Murrow's view, a revolt.

It is too early to measure the degree, the seriousness, of the damage that has been done to the Republican Party here in Chicago. In spite of Eisenhower's statements of unity, it will take a long time for this bitterness to evaporate. The convention overruled two of its

216

most important committees and then refused on the first ballot to give the nomination to Senator Taft. The official, recognized and established machinery of the Republican Party was overthrown. A lot of personal hopes and ambitions were shattered in the process. The Republican Party experienced a revolution by ballot. But the revolutionists have not yet decided what to do with their victory, or who shall get the major spoils.

The coalition that brought General Eisenhower the nomination was made up of a wide variety of men with varying ambitions and objectives. The conduct of the campaign on his behalf, until he reached Chicago, reflected the conflicting advice to which he was being subjected. During that period the General could take refuge in generalities, statements that he was in the hands of his friends and that he really knew nothing about politics. But now he is the Party's candidate, and decisions will have to be made as to who is going to run his campaign. There will be hot competition for the place nearest the throne. The coalition supporting Eisenhower was formed in a desperate attempt to seize control of the party from what is generally called the Old Guard. It has succeeded. But the young guardsmen are ambitious, by no means unanimous as to what they want to do, and the Old Guard sulk in their tents. General Eisenhower will need a substantial number of the Old Guard if he is to win. Much of the General's reputation is based not upon prowess in battle but rather upon his extraordinary ability to reconcile and compromise divergent views and opinions that were honestly held. In this area of conciliation he will have need to call upon his full talents during the coming months. At least a few of those who worked most vigorously for his nomination now have varying ideas as to the kind of campaign he should conduct. The brutal and bitter battle of Chicago has ended, but the battle to control and influence the candidate is just beginning. The General will have to pronounce upon issues with which he is but slightly acquainted. There is no time for him to inform himself thoroughly on the details of all the complex issues that confront the country. He must of necessity rely upon a political chief of staff and good staff work.

Political parties change course slowly. The Republican Party is now trying to chart a new course in waters with which the skipper is not altogether familiar. The result may be some confusion on the bridge in the early days of the campaign. It would be reasonable to assume that on the basis of reward for effort, Governor Dewey will be one of the select few standing on the bridge. If this happens, some of those who labored with him to nominate Eisenhower will not be happy. And so it would seem that this new "young guard" Republican organization must try to figure out a way to heal some of the wounds they inflicted on the old-timers; they must select and organize their own high command, while at the same time figuring out a way to beat the Democrats.

Those who were hoping for a knock-down, drag-out fight between traditional, conservative Republican principles and those of the Fair Deal will be disappointed. Time after time in the last week the Taft supporters said in one fashion or another, "Don't change anything." The Eisenhower men said in effect, "We've got to change to win." The convention applauded the Old Guard, but they voted for the young one. The young ones appear to this reporter to be taking serious rather than hilarious satisfaction in their victory. They appreciate that they must pick up many pieces of broken fences inside their own party before they can get down to the serious business of trying to fence in the Democrats in November.

July 22, 1952

> *Twenty-four hours after the start of the wide-open Democratic National Convention in Chicago, Governor Stevenson of Illinois had become the odds-on favorite to win the nomination.*

Whatever happens here tonight, and in tomorrow's fight over the civil rights plank of the platform, one man stands to lose nothing, no matter how acrimonious the debate may be. That man is Governor Adlai Stevenson, who remains above the battle, is not required to make decisions or attempt to influence delegations. The more bitter the battle becomes, the more indispensable is Stevenson as the ultimate peacemaker. The governor of Illinois has now reached the point of no return; he cannot now disavow his supporters without having his whole public career blow up in one great burst of cynical laughter. Governor Stevenson has not been seeing reporters today, but we are told that he has not received any formal or informal word from the White House. The absence of such a message should not displease him, because one of his primary concerns has been to disassociate himself from any deals, agreements or inheritance from the Truman Administration.

Governor Stevenson had planned to come out to the amphitheater tonight to listen to Mrs. Roosevelt's speech, but the latest word is that he is not coming for fear of touching off a premature demonstration. Some of the Governor's more enthusiastic backers are now predicting his nomination on the first ballot, but this would require major desertions from favorite sons—the collapse of Senator Russell or the abdication of Mr. Harriman and Senator Kefauver.

We are told that Stevenson has now made peace with his own conscience, believes that what's happening is an honest and legitimate draft, is prepared to go through with it but has given no thought to his acceptance speech or his running mate. It remains at least remarkable that most of the delegates now beating the drums for Stevenson have not bothered to inform themselves of his stand on controversial issues. In this sense his nomination, if it comes (and only a major miracle can prevent it), will be similar to that of General Eisenhower. Most delegates to conventions have a personal and political interest, not in states' rights, or in platforms, or in rules, but in a winner. And the collective judgment of these delegates appears to be that they've got a better chance to win with Stevenson than with anyone else.

Stevenson won nomination on the third ballot, after running second to Kefauver on the first and second ballots. Harriman withdrew in Stevenson's favor.

July 29, 1952

Tonight, for probably the last time, I should like to make reference to the conduct of the conventions, specifically in relation to the political exploitation of religion. This is a delicate subject, but it is a fact that certain of the prayers sounded more like keynote speeches than appeals for divine guidance. The current issue of a nondenominational Protestant weekly, *The Christian Century*, comments upon this aspect of the conventions. It suggests that true faith in God ought not to be worn once every four years "like a campaign button." And the editorial continues, "Men not known previously for piety had suddenly become polite and profuse in their public references to God. Others who seldom darken the door of a church openly identified themselves and their causes with religion. Scriptural references crop up unexpectedly in addresses, and sometimes the holy name of God is mentioned in the body of a political speech."

But *The Christian Century* has not only hard words for politicians. There is criticism of some religious leaders who offered prayers at the conventions. The question is asked, "Were these petitions really addressed to God, who judges the heart and is not impressed by windy intercessions, or were they tailored as if they were political speeches to the television audience. The length, and especially the substance, of many of the prayers indicate they were designed for human, not divine, ears."

I think it was my friend Bob Trout who said that the conventions were disposed to argue about everything except the invocation and *The Star-Spangled Banner*. Now there is argument about the invocations. Candor impels the confession that that editorial is quoted here in part, not just because there isn't much news today, or because it is rather well written, but because this reporter agrees with it. There were some exceptions, as mentioned in the editorial, but they were not numerous. There is even a question that could be raised about the playing of the *The Star-Spangled Banner*, not perhaps at political conventions but elsewhere. The national anthem played and sung before a couple of second-rate fighters belabor each other about the head, before horses run or the ball players try to earn their pay does not necessarily add dignity to the song or the event. Symbols of belief in nations, or faith in a supreme being, probably ought to be used sparingly and in suitable circumstances, lest both suffer from collision with commercial or partisan interests. It would seem reasonable to request and expect, as *The Christian Century* does, that a speaker's platform temporarily turned into a pulpit should be regarded as a privileged place unsuited for partisan pleading. There was enough of that from the laymen present.

July 30, 1952

In the British House of Commons there is a procedure known as a vote of confidence. This means that the House makes up its mind whether it continues to repose confidence in the Prime Minister and his government. When the government loses a vote of confidence on a matter of major importance, it must resign.

It seems to this reporter that the forthcoming presidential campaign will be essentially a test of confidence. It will not be a test between the Truman Administration and Senator Taft as it might have been. Neither candidate is beholden to the traditional machinery of the party he represents. Whichever man is elected will have unique opportunities for freedom of action in determining both policy and personnel of his administration. It will be a contest between an officer and a gentleman and a politician and a gentleman. Each must try to win the vote of confidence, not on the basis of his party's platform and not really on the basis of his party's record. For neither man can swallow many of the things for which his party has stood during the past few years. And there will be skirmishing about the Taft-Hartley law, rumblings of revolt over civil rights, promises of reduced expenditures and integrity and honesty in public office. The second-string Democratic speakers will say in effect, "Did you ever have it so good?" The Republicans will say, "Twenty years in office leads to corruption, inefficiency, and a general weakening of the moral fiber."

The New Deal has been played out. The Democratic Party confirmed that at Chicago. The Taft wing of the Republican Party also was dealt out at Chicago. There is no demand from either of the candidates for a basic or drastic reversal of national policy. Even as controversial a matter as the Korean War was dealt with formally only twice—once by General MacArthur and again by Senator Paul Douglas.

It is uniquely in the character of both candidates to inspire confidence. It is impossible to talk with either man privately without becoming aware that they share, to a remarkable degree, the realization of the tragedy that may impend—the internal and external threats to our civilization and our existence. Both are aware that these massive and complex issues, and the methods by which they may be resolved, are beyond the comprehension of the average

221

man. There is honest and prayerful humility in both candidates. There are considerable areas of public policy where both are uncertain and confused, for both have said as much. It seems to me, therefore, that both candidates must of necessity concentrate upon building a body of confidence, rather than upon belaboring each other with secondary issues. Each must attempt to persuade the voter that the chances of peace are improved if he is elected in November; each must attempt to persuade that he can and will inaugurate an era of responsible, respectable and incorruptible administration of the nation's affairs. Both candidates must attempt to convey the impression that they are surrounded by able men of integrity and character who will form the nucleus of the new government. Neither man is likely to promise easy, quick or painless solutions to the nation's problems, for if he does, he will not be believed. Both candidates may have some difficulty in restraining some of their more ardent and irrational supporters.

I do not suggest that there are not issues of substance dividing the two parties, or that the positions of Stevenson and Eisenhower are so similar they might as well draw straws and save us the trouble of a long campaign. But I do believe that in the absence of some unexpected development this campaign more than any in our recent history will hinge upon which man can inspire the greatest degree of confidence in his own person and his own judgment. There has been so much loss of confidence in basketball scores, in tax collectors, ambassadors, in politicians, in our allies, and perhaps even in ourselves, that there exists, I think, a real desire to repose confidence in an individual and what he stands for. In spite of party platforms, regional differences, party strategy and traditional loyalties, the vote is likely to go to the more believable man.

It would be astonishing to this reporter if either man engages in personalities, and yet this will be one of the most personal campaigns in our history. Essentially it will be a vote of confidence not on the Fair Deal (that is finished), not on the Republican platform, not on Eisenhower's military record or on Stevenson's political record; it will be a vote of confidence as between the two men—the character, credibility and believability that they can establish between now and November. Senator Lodge said the other day it was going to be a horse race. It seems to be more likely to be a thoroughly human race.

September 9, 1952

Today General Eisenhower made a big decision, and it was in the tradition of the political game. He spent most of the day with Indiana's Senator William Jenner, who will introduce him when he speaks tonight in Indianapolis. Senator Jenner, in his speeches and voting record, is about as far from General Eisenhower as he could possibly be. He has called General George Marshall "a living lie" and "a front man for traitors." Eisenhower has defended General Marshall, and Eisenhower calls for Jenner's reelection. Yesterday, Eisenhower's national chairman endorsed Senator McCarthy, another vigorous critic of Marshall whose voting record does not conform to the statements made by Eisenhower. But the issue is not personal friendship, not agreement as to policies to be pursued, but who's going to win. What happened today was that General Eisenhower tried to make a tent big enough to cover all Republicans. He and his advisors beat that wing of the Republican Party represented by Taft, Jenner, McCarthy, Kem and others at the convention. Now the General and his advisors have decided to join them.

Senator Taft raised the question repeatedly as to whether Eisenhower, if nominated, would attack the Administration with sufficient vigor. The General's speech tonight ought to reassure Senator Taft on that score. The Administration is made up, according to the General, of quack doctors, barefaced looters, fear-mongers, vandals and a gang of robbers. He is sure that Senator Jenner and other Republicans will support his policies when he is elected. (This will require considerable change, either in the Senator or in General Eisenhower's policy.)

Tonight's speech will be the roughest and most hard hitting that the General has yet delivered. It is also his major bid to those forces in the Republican Party that he defeated for the nomination. He needs their support if he is to win. And if in order to win he must take the Jenners and the McCarthys with him, that is quite all right. Eisenhower's contention is that the people in each state are best equipped to know, to choose the kind of man they want to represent them in Washington. And so long as the men selected are Republicans, he'll support them. Whether they have in the past supported

223

the General's policies, or whether they can be counted upon to do so in the future, are both beside the point. The effort is to do what can be done to heal the bitter breach in the party created in Chicago. There is nothing new or unprecedented in this situation. In politics, as in war, there is no substitute for victory.

September 23, 1952

> *In the midst of the campaign came what Richard Nixon later described as the most scarring personal crisis of his life. The* New York Post *reported that a group of California businessmen had contributed to a secret Nixon fund. Nixon confirmed receiving eighteen thousand dollars in contributions while serving as senator from California but said the money was for political expenses, not for his personal use. Nevertheless, Eisenhower was under pressure to dump Nixon as a running mate.*

About an hour and a half from now, Senator Richard Nixon will explain his actions and his ethics on radio and television. There are very subtle issues, both legal and moral, involved. This reporter is unable to adopt the unrestrained language either of defense or condemnation applied to Senator Nixon's actions. Whatever happens to him, the nation is likely to survive. Other young men of his age have faced greater tests, though not with such attendant instruments of publicity. Perhaps a "symbol" of this sort is required to remind us that we do not run the nation's business very well and that something should be done about it.

This question bulks rather larger than the "keeping or casting away" of Senator Nixon. In recent days there has developed quite a line of volunteers in Washington willing to testify that they can't live on their salaries as senators or representatives. The answer to this question would seem to be obvious: raise their pay. They're running the biggest business in the world, and being a senator shouldn't be a part-time job. Independence from financial worries will not guarantee independence of mind and action, but it ought to help. It's a big company we're running, and there's no reason why senators shouldn't draw twenty-five or even fifty thousand dollars a year. But a raise in pay wouldn't solve the problem, wouldn't take care of the men whose votes consistently just happen to coincide with the interests of those who contributed to their campaign funds. Campaigning has become a very expensive business, and the persuasive power of the contributor is inevitably much greater than that of the man who didn't contribute.

In theory there is no reason why all campaign contributions in a national election should not be abolished, made illegal. Let the federal government appropriate a given sum on a per capita basis—so many cents a head for each voter—and limit party expenditures so that amount under a rigid system of inspection. There are obvious dangers in this plan, but it would prevent the party with the biggest war chest from buying the most newspaper space or the greatest amount of radio and television time. More importantly, it would eliminate the present system where a candidate is likely to mortgage his future vote, knowingly or unknowingly, in return for financial contributions to his campaign fund. Under this system men in the House and the Senate would be free to intervene with government agencies on behalf of their constituents without being accused of "paying off" for past contributions. The rich men running for public office would have no advantage over the man of modest means. And once the successful candidate reached Washington, he would be paid enough to live on and discharge his official duties. You couldn't staff a moderate-sized corporation with moderately competent officers for the salaries paid to either elected or appointed government officials. No legislator can be insulated from either prejudice or pressure by money. But the present low level of pay is not likely to attract ability or contribute toward integrity.

In addition to higher pay, and no private contributions to campaign funds, we might consider a really adequate pension plan under which a senator, for example, would receive an adequate lifetime pension upon the completion of his duties, no matter whether he served six years or thirty. The amount of money involved would not be considerable, and the independence of mind and action—particularly in an election year—might be substantial.

I would contend that men of great ability, or of none at all, who have been elected should not be penalized because they are working for the taxpayers, and the taxpayers ought to pay them adequately.

(And, of course, watch them carefully.) It could be contended that this would set up a sort of welfare state for politicians. Maybe it would. Certainly it would be no guarantee that the individuals would consult the national rather than the party interests. But it might serve to create a little more independence, both financial and otherwise, on the part of politicians.

There are subtle and ill-defined issues in the Nixon affair, and there is precedent for what he did. It is no part of a reporter's function to defend him or denounce him. I am merely suggesting that the issue should not be either so subtle or ill-defined. The rules ought to be spelled out, and then enforced.

> *With his wife beside him, and his political life at stake, Nixon argued his case before sixty million Americans, the largest audience in radio-television history up to that time. Twenty-four hours later, in Wheeling, West Virginia, Eisenhower embraced Nixon and said, "You're my boy!" As far as the Republican Party and a majority of the electorate were concerned, the incident was closed.*

November 5, 1952

Our wise friend Carl Sandburg once said, "The people, yes the people, have eternally the element of surprise." Yesterday the people surprised the pollsters, the prophets and many politicians. They demonstrated, as they did in 1948, that they are mysterious and their motives are not to be measured by mechanical means. The result contributed something to the demechanization of our society. It restored to the individual, I suspect, some sense of his own sovereignty. Those who believe that we are predictable, who believe in sampling and then reducing the whole thing to a simple graph or chart have been undone again. (They were as wrong as they were four years ago.) And we are in a measure released from the petty tyranny of those who assert that they can tell us what we think, what we believe, what we will do, what we hope and what we fear without consulting us—*all* of us.

In a real sense, General Eisenhower's election was an overwhelming personal tribute. It must be credited to the man rather than to any section, group or bloc of the country. Taft didn't win it for him, neither did Dewey. The victory did not stem from labor, or the farmer, or the South. He did not attract this measure of allegiance from the big cities or the rural areas. It came from the entire country. The voters did not give him a comfortable majority in either House. He ran ahead of his party in most sections of the country. He will have great freedom and great power, if he chooses to use it, because he is beholden to no single section of the national community. He can unite and lead, or he can be captured. There will be not only the opposition but members of his own party ready to ambush him. Only time will tell whether he can read the political maps of this unfamiliar terrain sufficiently well to avoid them.

The Democrats, led by a man who spoke often in the accents of greatness, were defeated because too many people liked Ike. The three pillars that have supported the Democratic Party for twenty years gave way at the same time—the big-city vote, labor, and the South. And nobody pulled them down but the people.

December 16, 1952

Murrow decided to return to Korea for Christmas. He wanted, in his phrase, "to try to do a little firsthand reporting from out there." Flying across America on a night flight at twenty thousand feet, he made these notes for broadcast the next day.

For this reporter there will always be something remarkable about flying in safety and comfort at night. There is no tension, the food is good, the passengers doze. The crew up on the flight deck do all the work. The red exhaust flames lick back along the leading edge of the wing. That's Scranton, Pennsylvania, down there, all lit up. No one calls "fighters!" from the tail-gun position; there are no searchlights reaching for us, no flak that bursts red and white and rocks the big ship. There is none of the old talk of a big bomber on a night mission. All the intercom says is, "That's Pittsburgh just below us." The blast furnaces look as though a leading flight had put down a nice cluster of incendiaries. And the stewardess asks if you would like another cup of coffee or perhaps a pillow. The man sitting alongside you calls for a Scotch and soda. You fasten seat belts and let down for Detroit. You wonder if the lake is frozen over.

Airborne again, you overfly Chicago, but the flaps come down again and you're on the snow-covered field at Minneapolis. No time to visit your favorite Scandinavian restaurant. Gasoline for the steady motors. Heading west again, you know you're over the country once held by the Sioux and the Chippewa. If you could see through twenty thousand feet of darkness, you might find the faint scars left by the covered wagons. Now it's rolling country and the wheat fields of North Dakota. The Red River is down there somewhere and the Badlands.

Now it's Montana. One out of every twenty-five square miles in this country is in that state. Somewhere down there is the Yellowstone and Billings and Butte and the Little Big Horn, where an officer named Custer lost his whole command. Down there is copper and silver and country where a man must look at the sky. And the rocks of the Rockies are punching up through the clouds below. The inland empire. There will be great rolling oceans of snow-covered land down there, wheat country, and soon we should be over Grand Coulee, then Mount Rainier. And we start letting down for Seattle. Is that salt water or clams that you smell? You know that there will be no snow and there will be that warm, wet wind that blows from the west.

Flying across this generous and capacious land, even at night, gives a reporter a little time to think, to think of the courage and determination of the men and women who made it in wagons, of the disgraceful fashion in which we treat the remaining Indians from whom we took the land by force of arms. Time to think of the boys who have gone forth from those small towns and isolated farms to fight two wars and those who are now fighting another one in Korea. From the air, this continent of ours is a big, straggling island off the coast of Kamchatka, but it is the pivot of freedom's power.

December 24, 1952

This is Korea—Christmas Eve—and I should like to make this brief report for Casey, our seven-year-old son. This may be an abuse of privilege, but I hope not. There are a lot of fathers out here and when you talk to them about this time of year, ask them what they would like to be doing at Christmas, they say they'd like to see their sons or daughters around the Christmas tree and, of course, their wives. The other day one of those fathers was showing me pictures of his son—they all carry pictures and will show them to you without any urging—and he said, "Why don't you do a broadcast for Casey and for other little boys whose fathers are out here? Tell 'em what it's like." I said I'd try but probably wouldn't do it very well because I haven't been out here very long, certainly not as long as the other dads, and I'd be going home pretty soon and maybe I'd get it all wrong, never tried anything like it before. But here goes, and if you're listening, Case, don't go to sleep in the middle of this one the way you usually do.

I'm talking from a place called Seoul. When the war started the North Koreans captured it because they surprised the South Koreans and they had more soldiers and more tanks. The city was bombed and shelled, and most of the houses were knocked down. Finally, our soldiers and the soldiers of the other nations that had decided they would fight rather than have the Communists capture this country, we took the city. They landed from boats at a place called Inchon, not far from here, and the people of Seoul were glad to see them because the Communists ran away and they were free again. A lot of our soldiers were killed, fighting their way back up here, because Korea is mostly mountains and the Communists would sit up on the high hills and shoot at our boys with rifles and cannons and our boys had to climb up the hills, but they were brave and the Air Force helped a lot, dropping bombs on the enemy, and the Navy helped by firing big guns from the warships and putting soldiers and Marines ashore behind the enemy lines. They used landing barges, just like that toy one you have, Case, only much bigger, of course. But the Communists were brave, too, and they fought very well, but our boys were helped by the South Koreans and also by soldiers from England and Turkey and France and all the countries that had agreed to fight alongside us, and now our General Van Fleet has his headquarters here in Seoul and the soldiers have put up a big Merry Christmas sign with cardboard reindeer on it, also a Christmas tree with colored lights. Today, Santa Claus arrived there in a helicopter and the general gave out presents.

The Korean children are very quiet and well behaved. Their eyes are black, their skin a sort of golden brown, and when it's cold their cheeks shine like the red side of a well-polished apple. A lot of them have no mother or father to give them presents at Christmas time because their parents were killed during the fighting, so the American soldiers give them presents and parties. The Korean kids remind them of their own kids back home and, if you could see the big smile on a little Korean boy's face when he gets just one little toy costing maybe ten cents, you would realize what a lucky fellow you are. The Korean children don't have much warm clothing, but then they can stand the cold better than we can—they're used to it—and they don't skate the way we do, standing up. They squat down and push themselves along with two little sticks. They raise a lot of rice in Korea and they work very hard and the people are terribly poor, but they're proud and friendly and they love their country as much as we do ours. They work way up on the side of mountains, building little terraces for the rice, and right now there's a little snow in the bottom of the furrows. But the brown edges are bare. Looks like someone had scattered flour in the furrows or traced with white chalk on a brown blackboard.

The Koreans don't have many automobiles and they carry huge loads on their backs. A Korean half my size can carry twice what I could. Their legs are strong from climbing those mountains. These people are fighting for their country just like we once did. Ask Mom to show you that picture of Valley Forge again and you'll get the idea. It's pretty cold out here, Casey boy, but not much colder than when we were putting those lights on the outdoor tree last Christmas. Our soldiers have lots of warm clothing and all the food they can eat. The presents from home have been pouring in. There must be more fruit cake in Korea than you could put in the Empire State Building. Our soldiers are up there in the mountains north of Seoul. Mostly they live in tents or holes dug in the ground and lined with logs. They keep warm by burning oil in little round stoves. There isn't any electricity up there and they use candles or lanterns, and right at the front they daren't show any kind of light or the Communists will shoot at them. Right now some boy's dad, lots of them in fact, will be looking, straining his eyes, to see if the Communists are trying to sneak up the hill and kill him.

The war doesn't stop for Christmas, you know, and then, when that father can get back to his tent, he'll have some hot coffee and relax and there will be a picture, maybe on the wall of his tent, probably in his pocketbook, and he'll take that picture out and look at it, picture of his wife and a little guy about your size—who forgot to comb his hair!—and that soldier will be so lonesome that he won't want to talk to anyone, just sit there and think of home. He remembers the first time he took his boy fishing, just as I remember that two-pound heavy bass you caught, and maybe he'll smoke that new pipe his son sent him. Maybe he'll decide to write his son a letter, but it probably won't be a very good letter, just as this isn't a very good report to you, because loneliness on Christmas Eve must be felt, not written about, and that dad up near the front won't be waked early tomorrow morning by the shouts of his son who found that new train under the tree. He will be waked by a sergeant, or he may be waked by a Communist artillery shell exploding. But if it's a quiet night with no fighting, he may dream that he's home and when he wakes there will be that second when he thinks maybe he is home and then he will have to go back to the fighting. He will probably pick up his gun, put on his helmet, tap the pocket that holds the pictures, and go out to his tank or his gun and he will still be lonely.

I can't quite figure out how to tell you how lonely that father will be, Casey boy. I suppose it's as though you went away, thousands of miles away, to a strange school and you wouldn't see Mom or Dad for maybe a couple of years and the boys in the next school were always trying to kill you. You'd be mighty lonely on Christmas Eve. Maybe you'd have trouble keeping from crying just a little when you talked with the other fellows about home. Well, there are a lot of dads out here in Korea who feel sort of that way tonight and I think it would be all right with them if I said, for them, to all the little boys and girls who have dads out here: God bless you, Merry Christmas! Do what Mom tells you, or I'll wallop you when I get home.

1953

1961

February 5, 1953

So long as this nation is threatened by external foes and internal subversion we shall have with us the problem of the loyalty and reliability of people who work for the government. In the past, efforts have been made to determine loyalty and reliability by committees, review boards and by Congressional committees. In the process the public mind has been confused, and personal reputations have been destroyed. The policing of the loyalty and reliability of federal employees cannot be adequately done by committees without endangering the reputation and the careers of people who may be wholly innocent of any subversive intent or action. We were reaching the point where anyone fired from government service was liable to be suspected of disloyalty, or worse. Many of us were inclined to forget that an individual can be fired because he is incompetent, fails repeatedly to do his job, doesn't show up for work on time, fails to follow directions, or is just plain not able to do the job he's been assigned.

In his State of the Union message, President Eisenhower laid down a basic principle which, if it is applied, may prevent in some measure this process of "suspicion unlimited" whenever anyone is fired from government service. He said, "The primary responsibility for loyalty, efficiency, reliability on the part of government employees rests with the executive branch of the government." In other words, with the head of the department that hires the employee.

The President admitted that the application of this principle would be difficult, but he believes that he has sufficient powers under existing laws to carry it out.

It seems to this reporter that what the President has done is to restate a principle—business principle—familiar and long practiced by the members of his cabinet; that is the right of department heads to hire people, within the limitations of the budget, and their right to fire them. The department head, or his subordinates, may fire people for frivolous or capricious reasons—because they drink too much, or talk too much, put their feet on the desk, are not properly respectful, or just because the department head doesn't think they're pulling their weight in the boat or doesn't like the way they comb their hair. This will be unfortunate for the people who are fired from government service, just as it is for people who are fired from the service of big corporations. But under this new "basic principle"—if it works—any individual who is dismissed, while he may have been dismissed without adequate cause, will not automatically fall under suspicion as being disloyal or a poor security risk.

February 13, 1953

Murrow was vacationing in Europe when Julius Rosenberg and his wife, Ethel, were executed in Sing Sing Prison on June 19, 1953. However, he did comment on the case four months earlier, after President Eisenhower turned down the Rosenbergs' clemency appeal.

The execution date for the condemned atom spies, Julius and Ethel Rosenberg, will be set on Monday. Federal Judge Irving Kaufman said today he didn't believe anything can be accomplished in too long a delay, "except bringing upon the prisoners mental anguish by instilling false hopes in them." Counsel for the Rosenbergs asked that the executions be delayed for a month or two. The judge said he had been harassed more than ever by various groups since the President denied the Rosenbergs' appeal for clemency. He said, "It is as if a signal had been given. I have received many telephone calls and telegrams and letters."

Alexander Kendrick cables from Vienna that today the whole Communist world opened an unbridled attack on the Eisenhower Administration in connection with the Rosenberg case. All Communist newspapers and radio stations called for world-wide agitation from what they called "democratic forces." All satellite newspapers and all Communist papers in West Europe led their front pages with the President's rejection of the clemency plea. The Communist line was that the Eisenhower Administration had started its term with a "cold-blooded double murder." One Vienna Communist paper said that the Jelke vice trial here in New York was being deliberately staged by the Administration in order to detract attention from the Rosenberg case. All stories reported as a matter of fact that the Rosenbergs are innocent and were convicted on framed testimony.

In France, the Communist papers, of course, followed suit, but the conservative and non-Communist papers were also highly critical. One said, "The correctness of Eisenhower's decision may not be questioned, but its wisdom is something else again. We had all hoped for clemency that would demonstrate democratic justice tempered by mercy." Another highly influential non-Communist French paper, *Le Monde,* front-pages an editorial saying, "A measure of clemency would not have endangered American security. The execution will not frighten Communist fanatics, who consider they have a holy mission to perform. It will only give them an extra theme of propaganda to exploit."

Judge Kaufman was obviously correct; a signal *has* been given. Totalitarian states, whether Communist or Fascist, know how to create and make use of martyrs. The Russians are using the Rosenbergs as expendable weapons of political warfare. And the Rosenbergs, who have refused to talk, are apparently still willing instruments of the conspiracy they once served. There has been no responsible claim here that the two defendants have not received every consideration and every opportunity provided under American law. No new evidence has been produced since their conviction.

Most people familiar with Communist tactics of political warfare would probably agree that the Rosenbergs dead will be of more use to the Russians than they would be alive. Dead they can be made a symbol; alive they might one day talk. But it seems to this reporter that there is here involved something more important than a small skirmish in propaganda warfare. There is a law—it provides certain penalties. There was a trial, complete and open, conducted under the law. A verdict was reached by a jury. A sentence was imposed. And, as President Eisenhower concluded in one of the best written statements to come from the White House in a long time, he "feels it his duty in the interests of the people of the United States not to set aside the verdict of their representatives." This case will—already has—damaged us abroad. But a departure from that principle might damage us fatally.

February 20, 1953

Senator McCarthy's committee is investigating alleged waste and mismanagement in the Voice of America. Probably few citizens will doubt that this is a legitimate area for inquiry by a Senate committee, for the Voice of America is the principal instrument through which we tell our side of the story to the rest of the world. It speaks not only for senators but for all citizens. And it would undoubtedly be useful if more of us knew more of what the Voice is saying, and how it is being run. The evidence produced so far is not very illuminating, and certainly not conclusive. One employee asserts that his scripts were "watered down" by three employees whom he "believed to be friendly to the Communist cause." Another employee of the Voice of America who was dismissed says that in her opinion the anti-Communist broadcasts aimed at France were as detrimental as could be to the welfare of our country. Another employee in the French section says, "It should be called the Voice of Moscow." Many broadcasts tended to discredit the United States and to favor the Communist cause. One employee alleged that her boss had asked her to join some sort of "free love, collectivist, Marxist group."

The Voice of America speaks on behalf of all of us. Like any big organization it probably has its share of dismissed or disgruntled employees. Moreover, there are no listener ratings behind the Iron Curtain, or in friendly nations to which the Voice broadcasts. The result is that it is difficult, if not impossible, to tell how effective the broadcasts are, or how many people listen to them. But if the committee is interested in content, in what is said, the evidence is readily available. The scripts are there in the files; in many cases recordings are available and can be listened to. The record of what has been said—how the news and information has been handled—is all there. It would seem to this reporter that the important thing about any broadcasting operation is what comes out of the loudspeaker. If that reflects disloyalty, or subversive intent, then it should be relatively easy to identify the individuals responsible for that content.

I am not suggesting that there are, or are not, disloyal persons either now or in the past employed by the Voice of America. I do not know, and the evidence produced by the committee so far is insufficient to warrant any conclusions on this score. And the evidence, by its very nature, may in the end leave the individual citizen confused and in doubt as to the reliability and effectiveness of the Voice of America. The important thing is the end product. The arguments, the personal jealousies, the differences in news judgment that are inevitably involved in the preparation of any broadcast are of secondary importance.

This administration is making wide and apparently intelligent use of committees and study groups. It would be possible for a group of professional newsmen and information specialists to study the output of the Voice of America over a period of weeks or months and to make an informed report regarding the accuracy and reliability of the reports being broadcast. Evidence of distortion or of broadcasts prejudicial to the interests of this country could be uncovered, if it exists. Such a study of contents of the Voice of America programs would either revalidate the credentials of the people who are now running this important operation, or it would result in producing sufficient evidence to warrant their replacement. In any event, we are all entitled to know more than we now know about what is being said in our name to the rest of the world.

March 6, 1953

Stalin died, reportedly of a brain hemorrhage, and was succeeded by Georgi Malenkov, the Party Secretary. Molotov returned as Foreign Minister, replacing Vishinsky, who became Russia's permanent representative at the United Nations.

So far as we can judge, the Russians have managed an orderly transfer of power, and there is nothing in the composition of the new government to indicate any substantial change of policy. The Russian leaders were confronted with a unique problem. Stalin had been made into a god. Every instrument of propaganda was bent to make him even more important than Communism. It took almost thirty years, this effort to deify this man. There was no provision for a successor; a new Communist god could not be created overnight. That takes time, even when all instruments of information are used for the purpose. So they chose Malenkov, Stalin's principal and ruthless disciple, presumably on the assumption that he could rule in the shadow, and with some of the authority, of the departed leader. It will take time and ingenuity to legitimize the succession. But while this is going on, Malenkov can act as an echo of Stalin.

Amongst the Communists in the satellite countries Stalin's name has been magic. It was the psychological cement which held the satellite Communist parties together. Stalin was the leader, the connecting link between Magyars, Czechs, Rumanians and other non-Russian peoples. He was the symbol that made Russianism palatable to people who have a deep historical hatred for all things Russian. In the satellite countries the Communists have been in control for only five or six years. Their governments and economic systems have not hardened as in the Soviet Union. The satellite governments do not have thirty-five years of Communist power and mythology behind them to cushion the shock of change. They haven't completed the process of liquidation and butchery which establishes the party as the sole, unassailable, monolithic power in the state. These satellite countries are only now passing through the political and economic stage that the Soviet Union passed through twenty years ago. There are too many men who remember freedom. The satellites are plagued by sabotage and absenteeism. There have been purges, but nothing like the ones which liquidated opposition in the Soviet Union. Many of the satellite leaders were kept in power by Stalin, rather than by their own party organizations or their own people.

Nothing may happen on this Russian fringe as a result of Stalin's death, at least for some time. But empires always begin to crumble away at their edges. And if there are to be changes in Stalin's empire as a result of this death, the signs will first be seen in Prague, Budapest and Warsaw, rather than in Moscow. The change may well be only bloodier and more brutal oppression, but the new rulers of the Russian Empire—like all rulers of all empires in history—must worry about their outposts.

March 27, 1953

> *Eisenhower nominated Charles E. Bohlen, an expert on Russia, to be ambassador to Moscow. McCarthy fought the appointment, claiming that information in the FBI files indicated Bohlen was a security risk. Confirmation did not come until after a month of rancorous Senate debate.*

The Administration won its fight for the confirmation of Charles Bohlen as ambassador to Moscow as it had to do. Today the charges of possible disloyalty evaporated, and the principal complaint was that Bohlen had served Democratic administrations, as indeed had President Eisenhower and Secretary of State Dulles. When Senator Taft was asked whether he thought the argument over Mr. Bohlen signaled a break between the Senate Republican leadership and the President, Taft replied no, and then repeated it three times. However, the nature and the size of the opposition would seem to indicate that if President Eisenhower is to carry out a foreign policy in accordance with the Republican platform and campaign promises, he can probably do so only with the help of Democrats.

The Bohlen affair was in the nature of a preliminary skirmish, unrestrained and at times ridiculous. But it served to illustrate the President's method of dealing with Congress. He stayed with Bohlen all the way but at the same time refused to criticize or condemn those senators who opposed his confirmation. The President contends that he is not the keeper of the conscience or the conduct of the Congress. In this case, he achieved his objective without openly attacking those who opposed him. Mr. Eisenhower, during his military career, particularly during the late war and at SHAPE, talked much of the team and team spirit. And he was more likely to chastise an officer for criticizing another nationality on the military team than for criticizing another officer in the same uniform. The

President believes that the White House and the Republican Congress can work as a team, even though some of the members engage in dirty tactics or even run away with the ball. This is especially true when he is confident he is going to win the game anyway, as he was in the Bohlen affair. The testing time will come when members of his own party endanger a piece of legislation the President considers vital to the national interest. If the time should come (under those circumstances) when he chose to make an appeal to the country, some of the men who voted against him today may discover that his influence is considerably greater than theirs.

Mr. Bohlen's task has not been made easier by this debate, for the seeds of doubt have been planted, and if our affairs with Russia should go awry, blame will attach to him whether he deserves it or not. The conduct of the Senate will not have increased our prestige abroad. But perhaps the most serious aspect of this incident was the precedent established in connection with the FBI's report on its Bohlen file. The senators, being unwilling to accept the assurances of the President, the Secretary of State and the Attorney General, sent two of their number to have a look at the documents— Senators Taft and Sparkman. They were satisfied. They did not choose to divulge any of the hearsay, rumor or gossip that clutters the files of many people investigated by the FBI. But the precedent was set.

September 14, 1953

This is Berlin—at the end of the corridor, one hundred miles deep in Russian-held territory. Here you can walk and ride and look behind the Iron Curtain. This is a window where we can look into the Communist world and where they can look at us. In the western sector there are a few American, British and French troops. They couldn't hold this city for more than a few hours if the Russians should decide to move. They are part of the window, for, if it is broken, then the third world war has started.

I have known this city since 1930, was here during the airlift, saw it when Hitler came to power and when he moved into Austria, saw it one night from a Lancaster bomber when six hundred of them unloaded fourteen thousand pounds apiece on this city as it writhed in smoke and fire far below. In the days just after the war there were bodies in the canals and in the lakes, broken tanks and guns, and the remains of houses choked the streets. In the last seven years millions of words have been written trying to describe what's left of this city. This reporter has written a few from time to time and always with a sense of futility, and it is so tonight. So let's try to compare it with two years ago.

Now the shops are full of goods. People are wearing better clothes and better shoes. One or two streets blaze with lights at night. The ballet and the opera are flourishing. There is even television for a few hours at night. In the western sector the people on the street have a calm cast of countenance. No more strain in their faces, perhaps less than you see on the faces of New Yorkers who are getting ulcers hurrying on their way to something that is of no importance. The western sector of this city is very steady, but there are huge piles of coal to be seen, a reserve against a new blockage, for the Russians can tighten the noose again whenever they choose. Yesterday the bells of the remaining churches rang out over the city, and the sound bounced off the wreckage of homes and synagogues and banks and office buildings and finally wandered off across the brick-dust desert that used to be a great city. Occasionally the sun bored its way through a black cloud and lit up a ruin like a huge searchlight on an abandoned Hollywood set. At night, American, British and French jeeps prowl the sector frontier, and the West German police, some of them with police dogs, wander through the dark streets. A couple of blocks away the Communists are doing the same thing while music drifts up out of cellar cabarets. And when the wind is blowing, that brick dust cuts keenly at the eyes and fills the nostrils.

In the dim light you can see small shrubs growing on mounds of rubble where humans used to live. They look like trees on a mountain top. A few blocks away there are bright lights and automobiles and well-dressed Germans. Only seven years and a war separate the bright lights and the rubble. The rebuilding in the West Zone, as well as the East, has been enormous in these last two years. On both sides of the line people are better dressed. In the Communist sector yesterday people strolled at apparent ease along the streets, or they worked in their little gardens in the suburbs. There were no obvious signs of tension on either side.

This is the eye and the ear of the West, deep inside Communist territory. People, ideas and information flow easily across the frontier, and there is a belief, widely held here, as to what the Russians are going to do. It is this. They are going to play for a period of what Mr. Harding once called "normalcy." They will ease the tension in the West, reduce the terror in the satellite countries and wait to see what turns up. Whether that estimate is correct or not, the Berliners in the West appear well content to stand steady and wait. They have been doing that for a long time. And that is one of the most remarkable facts about this city. There are men and women here writing and broadcasting some of the most effective anti-Communist propaganda in the world. They know that if a war comes they and their families will be dead in a matter of hours, for this place is not defensible, but they don't flinch and they don't become hysterical. They know that here in Berlin this contest is not one of invective and accusation, but, rather, one of example. What the western sector does in the way of food, information, reconstruction and personal freedom may well be more important than what it says to the Communist sector. Here, the contest between freedom and Communism is divided by half the width of a street.

This is a city without a country. Even Hitler said it was not, and never would be, an artistic city, and in that at least he was right. But for six years it has built a history of restrained and reasoned resistance to Communism, has become a magnet that has attracted hundrds of thousands to leave their homes and make the desperate gamble for freedom, leaving all but hope behind. There is an example here that even great nations, in all their security and luxury, might follow.

November 26, 1953

I would suppose it to be true that most of us have personal and private reasons for giving thanks—reasons which we would not publish or utter before a microphone. But I should like to suggest a few perhaps unorthodox reasons for national thanksgiving. We

242

should give thanks for the burdens we bear; they are part of the price of power. As a nation we are in a position to influence, and indeed determine, the course of history. Other nations have been created and then crushed without ever having such an opportunity, or such an awesome responsibility.

We should give thanks that we have allies—great and proud nations whose history and culture are thicker and longer than ours, and who have joined with us, not as satellites seeking survival but because we and they desire to live in the same kind of world. Troublesome as allies often are, we should give thanks that they do not follow us blindly, that they argue and contend and are frequently disposed to counterbalance our impatience with their experience.

We should give thanks that in a period in the history of this minor planet when humans have devised a method of destroying humanity we, as a nation, are not a spectator. The decisions we have been called upon to make in the last few years have been hard and harsh, and we may again be forced to bite upon the iron. But the power of decision is ours and we cannot abdicate.

We should be thankful that we are not isolated—that our inheritance, received almost before we reached maturity, includes the hope of survival, freedom and the dignity of the individual.

We should be grateful for the knowledge, possessed by most of us, that if we fail, there will be no interest, anywhere, in apologies for that failure.

We should be thankful that we can still argue, that most of us can still distinguish between dissent and disloyalty, and that there is, slowly but perceptibly, occurring in this country an increase in racial tolerance. We are confronted with internal and external threats. We are required to be vigilant lest we lose our liberties in the process of preparing to defend them.

We might give thanks that however well or ill we discharge our duties or face our responsibilities, it will be done by what Will Rogers used to call the "big, normal majority" through the laborious process—slow and painful—of the people who live in this country making up their collective mind.

We should give thanks for the burdens we bear, because we must believe that we can bear them—must believe that all the blood, and all the history, which brought us, however reluctantly, to this position of leadership was not merely a series of accidents. When Mr. Roosevelt said this nation had a rendezvous with destiny he stated no time limit. It seems to me that we have not yet reached the rendezvous point.

And who among us would cast off these burdens, responsibilities and demands for decision? Who would willingly become a spectator, leaving the power of decision—however terrible or hopeful the consequences may be—to other men and other nations? Ernst Reuter, the late mayor of Berlin, used to say during the airlift, "We have to be heroes, whether we like it or not." For our part, we have to be leaders with all the dangers and obligations that that word implies, whether we like it or not.

February 3, 1954

The proper way to make coffee is in a five-pound lard pail over an open fire at least twenty miles from the nearest highway or railroad. You let it boil over three times, then hit with a dash of cold water to settle the grounds—and you have coffee. That's about all this reporter knows firsthand about coffee, but it seems the price is too high, for the Senate Agriculture Committee has voted to put the coffee exchange under federal regulations.

February 23, 1954

Murrow analyzed the Zwicker case. It was his first heavy attack on McCarthy's tactics.

When the transcript of a sensational attack by Senator McCarthy on a witness is published, it is natural to expect it to supply the reason for the attack. Senator McCarthy last night read passages from the transcript of his examination of General Ralph Zwicker, commandant of Fort Kilmer. That was in a speech accepting a gold medal from the Sons of the American Revolution. Now the whole transcript of the General's examination has been published. It fails to answer the question that needs clarification if the public is to judge whether Senator McCarthy was justified in denouncing the General.

The Senator at the hearing was trying to show that General Zwicker should have delayed the honorable discharge of Major Irving Peress, a dental officer, which he had been ordered to give. The Senator thought he should have done it because of evidence about Peress heard by his subcommittee. This evidence had been heard after the General had received orders to give the honorable discharge. The Senator passionately denied General Zwicker's fitness for command on the ground that he did not postpone the action.

What needs to be made clear, if possible, is why the General did not act. He said it was because the evidence of the McCarthy subcommittee on Peress was about matters already known to those who ordered the honorable discharge. Senator McCarthy at the hearing presented the General with this analogy. Suppose a major was about to be honorably discharged, and someone brought him evidence the day before that he had committed a fifty-dollar theft. Would the General delay the honorable discharge? The General said he would, so as to check the facts. Then why not do it if the allegation was membership in a Communist conspiracy, Senator McCarthy asked. The way the question was put made it sound as though the General did not think that membership in a Communist conspiracy was as bad as a fifty-dollar theft. But the General patiently explained that he did not postpone the discharge on his own initiative because he knew of no evidence before the McCarthy committee which had not been known to those who ordered the discharge. That is, without new evidence, he couldn't interfere. He had not heard of any new evidence. And even the statement of an undercover agent that Major Peress had been the liaison between his [the agent's] Communist cell and the American Labor Party was not, he said, substantially new.

Surely the issue insofar as General Zwicker is concerned is whether the McCarthy subcommittee had produced evidence the Army had not known, so that the General would be justified in postponing the discharge. The transcript does not show that Senator McCarthy tried to establish that the evidence it had produced was of this kind. New or not, he used it as a basis to attack the fitness of General Zwicker for command.

Last night Senator McCarthy told his audience that he had been too temperate in the attack, and if he had it to do over again he would be even more vigorous. But he did not attempt to show that the General had been given the new facts he needs for action. All he did was to strengthen his attack. It is a familiar strategem to strengthen an accusation without strengthening the evidence. In present-day America, charges are easily mistaken for evidence, something Senator McCarthy well knows.

People who have read only of the abuse heaped on General Zwicker may not realize what Army Secretary Stevens last week wrote Senator McCarthy about the Peress case. He told the Senator new procedures had been ordered so that another Peress case would not occur. He also told the Senator that he did not believe a man should be given a commission who refused to answer properly asked questions about his loyalty. This is what Dr. Peress had done in pleading the Fifth Amendment at the McCarthy hearing. It can't happen again, Mr. Stevens assured the Senator. But he also told him that what had been done could not well be undone. "The separation of an officer under circumstances such as this," he wrote, "is a final action, and there is no means of which I am aware by which the action could be successfully reversed." He said the only new fact available to the Army on which charges could be based was the refusal to answer questions before the committee. A previous case based on a similar charge, he told the Senator, had failed in courts-martial. All this General Zwicker knew before he testified. And so did Senator McCarthy. So what the Senator was trying to do was to maneuver the General into criticizing his orders and those who issued them. The General did say that he thought Communists should not receive commissions or honorable discharges. But he was under Presidential orders not to testify on security matters, and when pressed to violate the order, he refused. When he refused, he was abused.

There may not be any permanent harm in this abuse, but more is at stake than a scolding by Senator McCarthy. What is at issue is whether a senator is to delve into departmental matters, goad subordinates into criticism of their superiors, taint them with insinuations of Communist sympathies and impugn their judgment and integrity to the demoralization of the department. This is not the way Senate investigations are supposed—or entitled—to function.

They do have a proper and important role in our system of government. This is not the role.

March 9, 1954

> *The half-hour "See It Now" broadcast of this date was devoted to a report on Senator McCarthy told mainly in the words of the Senator while campaigning and sitting as chairman of his investigating committee. The purpose, and achievement, of the CBS television program produced by Murrow and Fred W. Friendly was to document publicly McCarthy's methods. Viewers heard Murrow say in conclusion:*

No one familiar with the history of this country can deny that congressional committees are useful. It is necessary to investigate before legislating. But the line between investigation and persecuting is a very fine one, and the junior senator from Wisconsin has stepped over it repeatedly. His primary achievement has been in confusing the public mind as between the internal and the external threat of Communism. We must not confuse dissent with disloyalty. We must remember always that accusation is not proof and that conviction depends upon evidence and due process of law. We will not walk in fear, one of another. We will not be driven by fear into an age of unreason if we dig deep in our history and our doctrine and remember that we are not descended from fearful men, not from men who feared to write, to speak, to associate and to defend causes which were for the moment unpopular.

This is no time for men who oppose Senator McCarthy's methods to keep silent, *or* for those who approve. We can deny our heritage and our history, but we cannot escape responsibility for the result. As a nation we have come into our full inheritance at a tender age. We proclaim ourselves, as indeed we are, the defenders of freedom—what's left of it—but we cannot defend freedom abroad by deserting it at home. The actions of the junior senator from Wisconsin have caused alarm and dismay amongst our allies abroad and given considerable comfort to our enemies. And whose fault is that? Not really his; he didn't create this situation of fear, he

247

merely exploited it and rather successfully. Cassius was right. "The fault, dear Brutus, is not in our stars but in ourselves."

The New York Herald Tribune, a Republican newspaper, said Murrow had presented "a sober and realistic appraisal of McCarthyism and the climate in which it flourishes." Jack Gould, television critic for The New York Times, *called the broadcast "crusading journalism of high responsibility and genuine courage," an "incisive visual autopsy of the Senator's record." Jack O'Brian, radio-TV columnist for Hearst's* New York Journal-American, *labeled the broadcast a "smear."*

March 11, 1954

Murrow saw in the allegations publicly leveled against Annie Lee Moss, a Negro employee of the government, a case of McCarthyism at its worst.

Mrs. Annie Lee Moss was suspended from her job with the Army Signal Corps in Washington because she was accused of being a "dues-paying, card-carrying Communist" in 1943. The charge was made by Mrs. Mary Markward, a former FBI counterspy who testified before the McCarthy committee that she had seen Mrs. Moss's name on a list of dues-paying Communists. Today, Senator McCarthy, who left the hearing early, told Mrs. Moss, "We had testimony that you are a Communist, and we are rather curious to know how people like yourself were shifted from waitress to the code room." Mrs. Moss then testified she did not work in the Signal Corps code room, had never been in a code room in her life. She said, "At no time have I ever been a member of the Communist Party, and I never saw a Communist card." She said she never subscribed to *The Daily Worker* and didn't know what Communism meant until 1948, five years after she was supposed to be a party member.

Committee Counsel Roy Cohn told the senators that the committee has evidence to corroborate that of Mrs. Mary Markward from another witness he did not name. At this point Democratic Senator McClellan, of Arkansas, objected. And Acting Chairman Mundt ordered Counsel Cohn's statement stricken from the record. Mundt explained that the "other witness" was now in contact with the FBI, and the committee would have to consider whether to release the name. McClellan objected again. He said, "That testimony shouldn't be revealed to the public until we have a chance to weigh it. If you cannot call a witness, you should not mention it." McClellan charged that Mrs. Moss was being tried by hearsay evidence, rumor and innuendo. And Democratic Senator Symington told her, "I believe you are telling the truth." Mrs. Moss replied, "I certainly am." And the Senator went on to say, "I believe in this country a person is innocent until proved guilty. I think it very important that evidence be presented along with the implication of additional evidence." And he told the suspended Army Signal Corps employee, "If you are not taken back by the Army, come around and see me and I'll get you a job."

It was established that Mrs. Moss told the truth, and the Army rehired her.

April 20, 1954

The agitation has subsided somewhat that followed Vice-President Nixon's remarks favoring American troops being sent to Indo-China if the French pull out. It has been stressed that the Vice-President spoke hypothetically. He was giving his personal views. He was not sending up a trial balloon. Even so, what he said has not been put into clear perspective. It is significant that someone who listens to the discussions of the National Security Council should have such strong views on keeping Indo-China from falling to the Communists. Obviously no decision has been made to send American troops to Indo-China. But neither has a decision been made *not* to send troops under any circumstances. And the second statement may prove to be even more important than the first.

The Nixon incident has set off a lot of discussion that is beside the point now. For at this moment the issue is not, and cannot be, whether the United States will intervene in Indo-China. If ultimately it comes down to the bare choice of losing Indo-China to the Communists or saving it, some form of intervention may appear inescapable. But any talk about intervention prior to a fully informed consideration of how to keep Indo-China in the free world is premature and even unrealistic. For one thing, intervention by itself might not save Indo-China. It might be countered by full-scale Chinese intervention with unforeseeable consequences. And advocates of intervention are unrealistic if they assume that the problem in Indo-China is primarily military. Actually it is much more political. The victory in Indo-China is not to be won by more foreign ground troops or guns, be they French or American, at this stage of the struggle. It is not to be won by the capture of strongpoints. The Vietminh have no strongpoints. It is to be won first of all in the realm of convictions. Only if the people of Indo-China believe that the fight against Communists is the fight for their own freedom will they turn the present tide of the conflict. At present the Communists are succeeding in Indo-China largely because they have convinced villagers and peasants that they are liberators, and that the battle is to break the rule of French colonialism. This is the situation despite the promise of independence within the French Union made by France to Bao Dai.

Observers looking only at Indo-China may be tempted to scold the French for dragging their feet in this matter of Indo-Chinese freedom. They may think that Paris should have seen long ago that it was not able to win a political battle by military means, if backed by only halfway political concessions. Observers may even recognize that France has been so cautious because it felt that the future of the French Union was at stake. The French know full well that North Africa is boiling up with extreme and hostile nationalism. Every concession made in Indo-China will have to be duplicated in Africa. Some observers may say, very well, even liberalized French colonialism is out of date and had better be sacrificed. But the French can be forgiven if they do not see their problem in these extreme terms. To many of them the choice is not between colonialism and surrender to hostile nationalism. For a liberalized colonialism they would substitute the voluntary association of politically free peoples. But to achieve this takes both time and wisdom. And one of the questions of the hour is whether enough of these elements is available, both in Indo-China and Paris.

May 18, 1954

The unanimous ruling against racial segregation in the public schools by the Supreme Court yesterday will have an impact which cannot at this time be calculated. It not only goes to the heart of one of the acutest of domestic problems, it counts substantially in the great conflict of ideas which now divides and dominates the world. The court, intentionally or unintentionally, has met—and gone far to dispose of—one of the most persuasive arguments used against the United States abroad. This has been that the practice of democracy in this country has been tainted by undeniable racial inequality. The argument has been losing some of its validity. The progress in Negro education in the last decade has been notable. The armed services, when they banned segregation, demonstrated equality in a new and vivid way. Now the Supreme Court has swept aside its finding in 1896 that constitutional requirements were satisfied when Negroes received a "separate but equal" education. It recognized that if segregation is legally sanctioned the education is not truly equal, and hence the segregation is unconstitutional. Students of world opinion can testify that this decision will add power to United States influence in the world. How much is naturally hard to say. The ethical pieces in the armor of American defense aren't comparable with the other pieces, but they are no less essential, and they may be even more important. Now American democracy has been made more convincing to the very persons whose understanding we need and seek.

Since the Supreme Court was breaking with the past—its own past in the ruling of 1896 and the past of segregated education in the South—it can be called fortunate that this could be done unanimously. It is sure to make the transition to new practices quieter. It also can be classed as judicial statesmanship that the ruling is not to be applied immediately. Even the arguments about how the ruling is to become operative will not be heard till the autumn term. This will give the South time to catch its breath and examine plans for the future. It is reasonable to assume that some years will be needed before segregation has wholly disappeared from our public schools.

251

Though the difficulties ahead are not to be minimized, they do not appear to be as dangerous as would have been predicted a while back. For one thing, Negro education in the South has improved remarkably in recent years, and this has been due quite as truly to the idealism of white educators as of Negroes. It is even conceivable that the end of segregation can be accomplished with good management and sense. Only five southern states still close the doors of their state universities and colleges to Negro postgraduate students. In the other states, integration has already been achieved, on the whole not unsatisfactorily. In Arizona and New Mexico, where local conditions have a certain similarity to the South, integrated schools have been established with little confusion or turmoil. Where the community could think through the changes in advance there was little trouble. The Ford Foundation has reports on two or three dozen communities in all parts of the country where integrated schools have been established, and the only one where there was real trouble was in the Middle West. And that one community was an admittedly "sick community," not at all typical of conditions in the South.

One of the big obstacles to integration in the South is finance. Northerners may not realize it, but the southern states devote a much larger part of their income to public schools than those in the North. Even so, they are only now in sight of having schoolrooms and teachers enough to accommodate all their children. They have spent more on white children than on Negroes, on a ratio of $165 to $115. Now if education becomes equal, the standard may actually decline, at least temporarily, as a result of the ruling. For some communities will find it next to impossible to increase taxes enough to give the Negro children the education now provided the whites.

It is this economic problem that accounts for much of the vociferousness of the southern outcry against integration. The economic problem is all the harder because of the drift in the South from the farm to the city. It costs considerably more to educate a child in the city than in the country. The gap between the difference in cost has been widening and now is twice as much as a few years ago. And as the southern population is rising steadily, the states are rightly troubled to know where the school money is to come from. The Supreme Court's requirement of equal education is sure to add to the attractiveness of the idea of federal contribution to the nation's school bills.

The court itself was not thinking in these terms. "Today," it said, "education is perhaps the most important function of state and local government." But it was not stressing who paid the bills. It was holding forth on the value of education. And the passage on this theme as written by Chief Justice Warren is among the most noteworthy statements of social objectives ever to have come from that august body, or any organism of democracy.

May 20, 1954

Thirteen days after the fall of Dienbienphu, a nineteen-nation Geneva conference began drafting terms for a cease-fire in the Indo-China war.

Dispatches from Geneva are in general agreement that things are not going well for the Western powers there. The Russians and Chinese are clearly stalling, while the Communists in Indo-China mount a new attack against the Red River delta. The French are suing for peace at Geneva without any trump cards to play, either there or in Indo-China. At the outset of this Geneva conference, the Russians and Chinese were frankly alarmed at the prospect of American intervention. They, too, have to calculate the risk that Indo-China might touch off the third world war. The American threat of toughness slowed the attack against Dienbienphu, and produced caution on the political front at Geneva. Then it became clear that there was to be no American intervention. At that point the Communists launched their all-out attack against Dienbienphu. President Eisenhower's statement about reaching some method whereby the two sides could live together in Indo-China was widely regarded in that country as an American withdrawal. Then came Mr. Dulles's statement that all Southeast Asia is not necessarily lost if Indo-China should be lost. That was regarded as final proof that we had written off Indo-China. So the Communists started mounting their attack against the delta.

One of our basic difficulties is that as of now we do not have a firm, determined and cohesive Vietnam government to support. That government has not yet asked for our aid. We are backing an emperor who has left his country, with his wife and children, and who receives five thousand dollars a month as a subsidy from the secret funds of the French government. The entire Vietnam cabinet, with the exception of the defense minister, has left the country, many taking their wives and children with them. David Schoenbrun, who spent a month in Indo-China and is now in Geneva, cables me tonight that the Western democracies are fighting against the Communists without the support of the Vietnamese people or a representative regime. Vietnam still doesn't have a genuine treaty of independence, nor a democratic assembly nor a national front. Unless Emperor Bao Dai goes home and takes over the active leadership of his people, unless an independence treaty is signed and sealed, we face the alternative of writing off Indo-China, or undertaking a war without coherent and effective Vietnamese support. The free world must decide to make war or make peace.

The British apparently feel that there is still the possibility of making peace. That is basically what the argument is about. There is a plan being discussed in Geneva which involves an armistice and elections that would be guaranteed and supervised by the five big powers, including Communist China. These five powers would guarantee the continuation of peace in the area. This plan is based upon the assumption that there can be no peace without Chinese participation and responsibility for it. Those who have produced this plan believe that such an agreement would cause the Communists to realize that a renewal of the war in Indo-China, or active subversion on its borders, would mean war without limit. This in a sense is a return to an earlier doctrine enunciated by Mr. Dulles.

In all this speculation, confusion and contention, one fact emerges: there is in prospect no diplomatic victory at Geneva, no military victory in Indo-China, unless or until American policy is clarified and agreed to, not only by the Western powers but by Indo-China's neighbors.

A truce was signed in Geneva on July 21, ending the Indo-China war. The French agreed to withdraw, and the Communists were ceded control of North Vietnam, pending elections within two years to reunite the country. The United

States did not sign the armistice agreement but warned that any aggression in violation of it would be viewed with "grave concern." The scheduled elections were never held.

May 28, 1954

I should like to read the text of the statement issued by the White House today, for it is likely to be a considerable footnote in the history of our turbulent time. Jim Hagerty, the President's news secretary, told reporters:

I talked this morning with the President and the attorney general, and at the direction of the attorney general I should like to issue the following statement in his name, with the approval of the President: "The obligations and duties of the executive, judicial and legislative branches of our government are defined by the Constitution. The executive branch of the government has the sole and fundamental responsibility under the Constitution for the enforcement of our laws and presidential orders. They include those to protect the security of our nation, which were carefully drawn for this purpose."

The statement continues:

"That responsibility cannot be usurped by any individual who may seek to set himself above the laws of our land, or to override orders of the President of the United States to federal employees of the executive branch of the government."

This was an obvious and direct reference to Senator McCarthy's statement of yesterday when he said publicly, "I would like to notify those two million federal employees that I feel it is their duty to give us any information which they have about graft, corruption, Communists, treason, and that there is no loyalty to a superior which can tower above and beyond their loyalty to their country." Today Senator McCarthy's reply to the White House statement was that he hoped to remain in the Senate, see many Presidents come and go; said he was going to continue to get information from within the government whenever he can and to protect his informants.

In this reporter's opinion the issue between the Eisenhower Administration and Senator McCarthy has finally been joined. It is constitutional, and therefore fundamental. The President and the

Attorney General have labeled the Senator as one who "seeks to set himself above the laws of our land and to override orders of the President of the United States." This is not a dispute between the Attorney General and the Senator about a document or a ruling by the Justice Department. It is a head-on collision between the President and the Senator. In due course it will cause senators and citizens to be counted on whether or not there is to be an elaborate system of informers inside the government violating the law and their oath by providing to a senator documents and information which can only properly be described as stolen. There arises also the question, at least in theory, about the legal status of those who knowingly receive stolen goods. For many months supporters of the President have been saying that in due course, and on ground of his own choosing, the President would deal with Senator McCarthy. The ground has been chosen. The President, even before he was elected, did everything possible to appease the Senator, to make him a "member of the team." It didn't work. And once more the result of appeasement is conflict.

Both sides are fully committed, and there would seem to be no possibility of compromise or withdrawal. On the investigating committee the Republicans have supported, or at least not opposed, Senator McCarthy's position. Now they and the other members of the Senate must choose on a fundamental issue between the position taken up and clearly defined by the President of the United States on the one hand and the Junior Senator from Wisconsin on the other.

A great deal has been spoken and written about the waste of time, the circus atmosphere, the need to expedite and the unimportance of the current investigation. But out of it has emerged, in outlines so clear that all can understand, a basic constitutional issue. It can be simply stated. Who is going to run the government of this country, protect its security, direct its affairs and manage the nation's business? There have been times in our history when the executive branch of the government has attempted to dominate the legislature, and even the judicial. There have been times when the Congress has made inroads on the prerogative of the executive. What is here involved is whether a single senator shall publicly recruit and legalize what might be called a private Gestapo within the ranks of those employed by the federal government. The contribution to public enlightenment that has been made by the President and by the Senator is to delineate and define the issue so that reasoning men and women may debate it.

June 1, 1954

Disloyalty charges against Dr. J. Robert Oppenheimer, the nuclear physicist, were investigated by a special review board of the Atomic Energy Commission. After lengthy hearings, it issued its report.

The board reviewing the case of Dr. Oppenheimer was made up of Gordon Gray, president of the University of North Carolina; Thomas Morgan, former president of the Sperry Corporation, and Ward Evans, professor at Loyola University, Chicago. The board agreed that Dr. Oppenheimer had been loyal and discreet, but it decided by a vote of two to one—Professor Evans dissenting—that he should not be cleared as a consultant to the Atomic Energy Commission. The board heard forty witnesses, listened to over three thousand pages of testimony. The meetings were secret; Dr. Oppenheimer was represented by counsel, usually four in number.

The report of the board acknowledges that this case puts the security system of the United States on trial. It recognizes two points of view: "There are those who apprehend that our program for security at this point in history consists of an uneasy mixture of fear, prejudice and arbitrary judgment. They feel that reason and fairness and justice have abdicated, and their places have been taken by hysteria and depression. On the other hand, there is a strong belief that in recent times our government has been less than unyielding towards the problem of Communism, and that loose and pliable attitudes regarding loyalty and security have prevailed to the danger of our society and its institutions."

The board found itself in agreement with much that underlies both points of view. The majority of the board found that Dr. Oppenheimer had been "less than candid" in some of his testimony, that he had in the thirties and forties associated with a considerable number of Communist-front organizations, that he had made contributions to these organizations. The majority also found that he had associated with known Communists. On the subject of the hydrogen bomb, that Dr. Oppenheimer, during the latter part of the war, had no misgivings about its development, after the war urged continuing research in the field; but that in the autumn of 1949 he opposed the development of the H-bomb on moral and political grounds. His views became known among scientists, but the board did not find that Dr. Oppenheimer urged other scientists not to work on the H-bomb program. However, the majority thought that his enthusiastic support would have encouraged other scientists to work on it. The board made no categorical finding as to whether Oppenheimer's opposition to the big bomb definitely slowed down its development. The board was impressed by the fact that "even those who were critical of Dr. Oppenheimer's judgment and activities testified as to their belief in his loyalty." The board believed that had Oppenheimer given his enthusiastic support to the H-bomb program, a concerted effort would have been made at an earlier date.

Professor Evans, in his minority report, contends that much of the derogatory information about Oppenheimer was in the hands of the commission when he was cleared in 1947. He says of Oppenheimer: "His judgment was bad in some cases and most excellent in others, but in my estimation it is better now than it was in 1947 and to damn him now and ruin his career and his service—I cannot do it." Professor Evans says, "Oppenheimer did not hinder the development of the H-bomb, and there is absolutely nothing in the testimony to show that he did." Professor Evans contends that the failure to clear Oppenheimer will be a black mark on the escutcheon of our country. "His witnesses are a considerable segment of the scientific backbone of our nation, and they endorse him. I am worried about the effect an improper decision may have on the scientific development in our country."

Under the rules and regulations, Dr. Oppenheimer is entitled to request a review of his case by the personnel security board. He has waived this right of review and requested immediate consideration of his case by the whole Atomic Energy Commission. His lawyers are preparing a brief, and have asked to make oral argument before the commission. Oppenheimer's lawyers take issue with four conclusions reached by the majority. The first two conclusions alleged serious disregard for the requirements of the security system and susceptibility to influence. Oppenheimer's lawyers contend that the facts do not support the conclusions. They contend that the injection into a security case of a scientist's alleged lack of enthusiasm for a particular program is "fraught with grave consequences to this country." And they ask, "How can a scientist risk advising the government if he is told that at some later day a security board may weigh in the balance the degree of his enthusiasm for some official program?"

Both the majority and minority reports on the Oppenheimer case will repay careful reading, for they go to the heart of one of the most difficult problems of this scientific age—the relationship between scientists and the government and the conduct of the nation's security program. This hearing was conducted with decorum, in secrecy. The board's findings and the minority report have been published. Professor Oppenheimer was represented by counsel with the right of cross-examination. And Professor Oppenheimer has the right of appeal.

On June 29, the Atomic Energy Commission—by a vote of four to one—upheld the denial of Oppenheimer's security clearance. In 1963 a new Atomic Energy Commission under President Kennedy honored Oppenheimer by awarding him the $50,000 Enrico Fermi Prize for his contributions to nuclear science.

June 10, 1954

The climax of the Army-McCarthy hearings came when McCarthy attacked Frederick G. Fisher, Jr., a young Boston attorney, for having once belonged to the National Lawyers Guild.

Yesterday, after Senator McCarthy had named Mr. Fisher as a member of an organization which he termed "the legal arm of the Communist Party," Army Counsel [Joseph N.] Welch, of whose law firm Fisher is a member, became highly emotional. He said, "Until this moment, Senator, I think I never really gauged your cruelty or your recklessness." He begged that "this lad be not assassinated further." He asked if the Senator had "no sense of decency."

Mr. Welch, a veteran of the courtroom, was near to tears because a young man whom he liked, knew, trusted and worked with had been attacked. It is safe to assume, I think, that had Mr. Welch never heard of Mr. Fisher, his emotion—his anger—would have been considerably less. It seems to this reporter that there is a widespread tendency on the part of all human beings to believe that because a thing happens to a stranger, or to someone far away, it doesn't happen at all. Someone once said something to the effect, "Do you consider it strange that I regard a cut upon my finger as more important than the death of thousands, if I be separated from those thousands by oceans and continents?" For most of us reality attaches only to those things that strike near home, and that is as true of a bomb as of an accusation. The human conscience becomes calloused. The muscles of moral indignation become flabby when those who are being damaged, either in their bodies or their reputations, are remote and unknown. Despite modern communications it is difficult to communicate over any considerable distance, unless there be some common denominator of experience. You cannot describe adequately the destruction of a city, or a reputation, to those who have never witnessed either. You cannot describe adequately aerial combat to a man who has never had his feet off the ground. We can read with considerable equanimity of the death of thousands by war, flood or famine in a far land, and that intelligence jars us rather less than a messy automobile accident on the corner before our house. Distance cushions the shock. This is the way humans behave and react. Their emotions are not involved, their anger or their fear not aroused until they approach near to danger, doubt, deceit or dishonesty. If these manifestations do not affect us personally, we seem to feel that they do not exist.

Perhaps this is selfishness, perhaps it is lack of imagination—I don't know. I do remember discussing this aspect of human behavior with many friends in London during the V-1 period, when those lethal machines, sounding like a slow-speed washing machine, would cut out directly overhead and nose down to explode several blocks away. The individual reaction was one of relief, and very little consciousness of, or compassion for, the individuals who were destroyed only a few blocks away, unless they happened to be personal friends. It must be presumed, I think, that Counsel Welch is familiar, very familiar, with Senator McCarthy's record and tactics. He had, up to yesterday, maintained an almost affable, avuncular relationship with the Senator. He was pressing Mr. Cohn—but by Mr. Cohn's admission doing him no personal injury—when Senator McCarthy delivered his attack upon Mr. Fisher, at which point Counsel Welch reacted like a human being.

September 6, 1954

Since the beginning of the atomic age, it seems to this reporter that some kind of giant has stood astride this planet, holding in one hand the threat of devastation, destruction and death beyond the power of men's minds to grasp; in the other hand there is the promise of plenty, of revolutionary advances in power, in medicine, in agriculture—even the possibility that one day there would be no more hungry people on this planet.

President Eisenhower today chose to speak of the promise—"a historic step forward," he called it, "opening for all of us new avenues to constructive employment, to prosperity, to respite from burdensome toil." He spoke of our first atomic power plant of commercial size at Shippingport, Pennsylvania. But then he ranged out and beyond that single plant, which after all will produce only enough electricity for a hundred thousand people. He said, "We do not stop with this plant, nor indeed with our own country's hopes and dreams. Our many proposals for peaceful use of the atom have so far been cynically blocked in the councils of the world. But we shall proceed onward. We shall proceed now, under safeguards set forth in our law, to share atomic technology with others of good will." And the President said, "We have just agreed with a number of other nations to go ahead now with the formation of an international agency which will foster the growth and spread of the new atomic technology for peaceful use. We will set up a school to train people from friendly nations for their own atomic programs."

The President did not name the nations participating in this international agency. But a White House aide, who did not want his name used, said that Britain, Canada, Australia, South Africa and France were among the nations participating, and that other nations will be joining in the program. Mr. Eisenhower left the door open for the Russians when he said, "We hope that no nation will long stand aloof from the work of this agency."

Today the President took up where he left off last December 8th, when he made the original proposal for peaceful use of atomic energy in a speech to the United Nations. After many months of private negotiation the Russians decided they wanted no part of it, so now the free world is going ahead on its own.

It seems to this reporter that there are at least two conclusions to be drawn from this announcement. The first is that the free world now has enough fissionable material to devote some part of it to peaceful research and experimentation, and we are prepared to share our knowledge and know-how with our friends. The second conclusion is rather less obvious. This new agency, if it be pressed forward with vigor, will do more than months of propaganda to persuade millions of non-Communists that our purpose is peace. It is at times difficult for us to understand that there are, in fact, millions of non-Communists in Europe and Asia who regard our country as being a threat to the peace. They speak of our lack of maturity, our lack of firsthand experience of what even an old-fashioned war was like; they are unduly impressed by some of our belligerent oratory, and the ill-concealed talk of preventive war. They are impressed with our power and our production, but they are likewise aware that if war comes—and even if we should win it—the outcome would have no interest for them because in the process they would have been expunged from the map.

The construction of a commercial atomic power plant in Pennsylvania does certainly mean, as the President said, that "mankind comes closer to fulfillment of the ancient dream of a new and better earth." This would likewise be true of an atomic power plant in India or Pakistan, in a valley in South Wales, or in any of the power-starved areas of the world. Here are the beginnings of the promise to counterbalance the threat.

September 10, 1954

Yesterday this reporter had the privilege of looking into the eye of Hurricane Edna. We took off from Bermuda at 11:30 a.m. in a specially equipped B-29. For about an hour and a half there was nothing to do except remember that flying is made up of many hours of boredom, interspersed with a few minutes of stark terror. There were a few whitecaps, but no cloud. Then the whitecaps grew in size—surface wind about thirty miles an hour, a few scattered cumulus clouds ahead. A big cloud seemed to summon its neighbors, and they built castles and lakes and cities on hillsides, all white against the blue of the sky. We bored through a few and skirted others. Then there was a big mountain of clouds ahead, and we went in. A few rain squalls but little turbulence. The texture of the cloud changed, became a ghostly grey; we couldn't see the wing-tips of the aircraft. Twenty minutes later there was a little blue-grey light, but it seemed to come from all around us. Suddenly blue water again, no whitecaps, but the ocean was heaving about below as though a giant were shaking a rug.

Into another cloud, out on the other side, and the ocean had changed its face. Long irregular furrows, like a drunken ploughman had been ploughing a field of blue velvet and turning up snow. We went down to seventy-five hundred—surface winds now estimated at sixty miles an hour—flew right along the top of a flat cloud with the feeling that if the pilot let his wheels down he'd leave a track in it. The next time we saw water the wind was cutting the top off the whitecaps, and there was a thin gauze of spray as far as we could see. Then into the cloud again, and that ghostly gray light that seemed to rub off on the faces of the crew members and cause them all too look as though they were ill and hadn't slept.

Radar kept reaching out, looking for Edna's eye. It showed a high bank of clouds to the right and to the left—we were flying blind in that gray stuff in the valley between. Suddenly there was a hole in the cloud, maybe a quarter-mile across, and at the bottom there was foam, like looking down a deep well with a huge eggbeater churning up milk at the bottom. We flew on and began the real search for the eye of the hurricane. There were sudden changes in temperature, more rain. Radar reported; the engineer reported. The navigator wanted to know if anybody could see surface wind. The radar-scope didn't show anything. We were bounced around a little. The skipper said, "There's a storm around here somewhere, let's find it."

The navigator asked for a turn to the left, and in a couple of minutes the B-29 began to shudder. It was a twisting, tortured motion. The co-pilot said, "I think we're in it." The pilot said, "We're going up," although every control was set to take us down. Something lifted us about three hundred feet. Then the pilot said, "We're going down," although he was doing everything humanly possible to take us up. Edna was in control of the aircraft. We were on an even keel but being staggered by short, sharp blows. Then we hit something with a bang that was audible above the roar of the motors; it was a solid sheet of water. Seconds later, brilliant sunlight hit us like a hammer; a little rainbow spun off the starboard outboard propeller. Someone shouted, "There she is!" and we were in the eye. Calm air, flat, calm sea below; a great amphitheater, round as a dollar, with white clouds sloping up to twenty-five or thirty thousand feet. The water looked like a blue alpine lake with snow-clad mountains coming right down to the water's edge. A great bowl of sunshine. Someone, I think it was the right scanner, shouted, "So help me, there's a ship down there!" And there was— right in the center of the eye. We guessed her to be a ten-thousand-ton merchant ship, moving very slowly in that calm water with only a thin feather of wake behind her. She appeared to be in no trouble, but trouble was inevitable sometime because she was surrounded by those cloud mountains and raging water.

The eye was twenty miles in diameter. We went down to fifteen hundred feet and flew back and forth across it, making shallow penetrations of the storm area. The temperature went up fourteen degrees; the altimeter said four thousand feet, but we were actually at fifteen hundred. The civilian weather officer aboard looked at Edna with a clinical eye and said, "She's a copybook hurricane— beautifully formed." We took her temperature, measured her speed, threw overboard scientific gear which might help to chart her future movements. We continued to fly around in the calm at the bottom of that funnel of white clouds. The eye of a hurricane is an excellent place to reflect upon the puniness of man and his works. If an adequate definition of humility is ever written, it's likely to be done in the eye of a hurricane.

The engineer reported some trouble with the number three engine; we climbed to ten thousand feet and bored into the wall of white cloud that surrounded the eye. It was not as rough going out as coming in because the navigator had picked his exit well.

Going back to Bermuda, we talked of hurricanes. One of the pilots said, "We were certainly disappointed in Carol; we just didn't think she would do what she did." He had flown through Carol so often that he regarded her as a friend who had committed a major misdemeanor.

These young men who fly the Air Weather Service are doing all that can be humanly done to provide information upon which adequate warning can be based. After all, the only thing you can do about a hurricane is to watch it and get ready for it. After flying only nine hours with those young men of the Air Force yesterday, on a routine mission, I think they deserve combat pay.

Like Carol the month before, Hurricane Edna was a killer. Sweeping across the northeastern United States and Canada, it took 23 lives. When Hazel struck thirty days later in one of the worst hurricane seasons, 347 persons died.

September 17, 1954

Somewhere in the Bible there is a phrase that says, in effect, "The eyes of a fool are on the ends of the earth." We are concerned about Indo-China, European unity—or lack of it—Formosa, Trieste, the disposition of the Russian air force. There is no shortage of distant matters giving rise to deep concern. But there is a situation near at hand which merits concern and attention. This week and next the public schools of this country will admit more than thirty and one half million students. That's a million and a half more than last year. More than four and a half million will be entering the first grade.

The position, unlike diplomatic negotiations relative to atomic strength and all the rest, can be simply stated. There are too few teachers, too many teachers who are not fully qualified to teach. Classrooms are too crowded. Some schools will be working three shifts, holding classes in cafeterias, churches, synagogues and, in at least one case, a converted chicken coop. There is a shortage of almost 125,000 teachers, and this shortage must be made up for in "emergency" teachers. Children are being cheated. Overcrowding is worse than it has been before. This year there will be about 6.5 per cent fewer teachers than last year. Also last year something like 75,000 teachers quit their jobs for better pay and further opportunity. And the peak in students attending public schools will not come until 1960. The figures are not to be disputed. We require more teachers and more classrooms, which in turn means more money.

Probably no country in the world pays more unanimous lip service to universal education than we do. It seems at times that we will do anything except pay for it. Teachers, like the rest of us, work for a living, but generally more is expected of teachers than is required of the ordinary workman. There is a tendency on the part of parents to assign their duties and responsibilities to the teacher. The teacher is expected to lead a more exemplary existence than is required of the rest of us. In ethics, morals and example the teacher must be a first-class citizen. But when it comes to income, the teacher occupies a second-class position.

It seems to this reporter that the average citizen can do but little to influence or control directly most of the major issues that confront the nation. He can't advise Mr. Dulles in Bonn or London. He can't directly influence what the Russians are going to do. He can't measure the importance of a bililon dollars more or less in the military budget. But he can recognize that we haven't got enough good schools with enough competent and well-paid teachers. About that, he can do something in the hope that his investment will pay dividends in terms of human beings better able to cope with the problems that will still be there when they grow up. There could be a new definition of S.O.S., and it could be Save Our Schools.

September 27, 1954

The Watkins Committee today unanimously recommended that the Senate censure Senator McCarthy.

Here is a summary of the charges considered by the committee and the findings reached by it:

It was charged that Senator McCarthy refused repeated invitations to appear before a Senate subcommittee, that he contemptuously refused to comply with its requests for information about some of his financial dealings and that he ridiculed and defamed Senator Hendrickson in vulgar and base language, calling him a "living miracle without brains or guts." The committee concluded that Senator McCarthy's conduct toward the subcommittee and his statement about Senator Hendrickson was contemptuous, contumacious, and denunciatory without reason or justification. For this conduct it was recommended that he be censured by the Senate.

The second charge was that Senator McCarthy incited government workers to violate the law and executive orders by handing him secret documents. The committee concluded that such action "tends to create a disruption of the orderly and constitutional functioning of the executive and legislative branches of the government, which tends to bring both into disrepute." It said, "Such conduct cannot be condoned and is deemed improper." However, the committee gave Senator McCarthy the benefit of the doubt and felt that this charge did not, under all the evidence, justify a resolution of censure.

The next charge had to do with the famous two-and-a-quarter page FBI letter which the Senator attempted to introduce in the Army-McCarthy hearings; that it was a spurious document, and that he was in possible violation of the Espionage Act. The committee found that in offering to make public the contents of this classified document, Senator McCarthy "committed grave error," manifested a high degree of irresponsibility. But the committee recognized that, at the time, Senator McCarthy was under the stress and strain of being tried or investigated, and under the circumstances it does not recommend censure by the Senate on this charge.

The next allegation against Senator McCarthy was that he had ridiculed his colleagues in the Senate, defaming them publicly in vulgar and base language. Specifically Senator Flanders, who had been called senile and of whom Senator McCarthy had said, "They should get a man with a net and take him to a good quiet place." The committee branded these remarks concerning Flanders as highly improper but found that they were induced by Senator Flanders's conduct and concluded that the remarks about Flanders do not constitute a basis for censure.

The final category of charges was whether Senator McCarthy should be censured for his treatment of General Zwicker. It was claimed that the Senator had impugned the loyalty, patriotism and character of the General, and that he resorted to abusive conduct in his interrogation of Zwicker. The committee found that the conduct of the Senator toward the General was reprehensible, that he disclosed the proceedings of an executive session in violation of the rules of his own committee, and this was inexcusable. So the committee recommends that for this conduct Senator McCarthy be censured by the Senate.

The committee dropped certain charges against Senator McCarthy because it was concluded they were legally insufficient for Senate censure. But the report added, "We do not want to be understood as saying that this committee approves of the conduct alleged."

The Select Committee also had something to say on the question of revising the rules for Senate committees. It proposes that, except in special circumstances, not less than two members of the committee be present to hear any witness, that witnesses are to be questioned only by committee members and authorized staff personnel, and no one shall be employed or assigned to an investigation until approved by the committee. Testimony taken in executive sessions is not to be published in part or in summary, unless authorized by a majority vote of the committee.

This was a bipartisan select committee—three Republicans and three Democrats. The investigation was conducted in a judicial atmosphere. The report was unanimous. In opening the hearings, the chairman, Senator Watkins, said, "We realize that the United States Senate in a sense is on trial, and we hope that our conduct will be such as to maintain the American sense of fair play and the high tradition and dignity of the United States Senate under the authority given it by the Constitution."

When the Senate reconvenes on November 8, the entire body will decide whether or not the select committee has properly fulfilled that assignment.

> *Two months later—on December 2—the Senate censured McCarthy for obstructing Constitutional processes and tending to bring the Senate into disrepute. The fourth U.S. senator in history to be so disciplined, McCarthy lost none of his senatorial rights. But, in fact, as a political force he was finished.*

October 5, 1954

Murrow cared about many people; he reserved his affection for a few. Carl Sandburg was one of the chosen few, and Murrow interviewed him at his North Carolina goat farm for "See It Now." The broadcast was called simply "A Visit to Flat Rock—Carl Sandburg."

MURROW: —Good evening. There are men who can point to a skyscraper, to a railroad, to a billion-dollar corporation, and say, "That's mine. I did that. That's my life work." These twenty-eight volumes represent the life work of Carl Sandburg, who is seventy-six. It starts back in 1916 with *Chicago Poems,* and extends through to the single volume of *Lincoln,* to be published the day after tomorrow. Mr. Sandburg spends much of his life writing. Six volumes on Lincoln—a million and a half words. He has spent much of the last three years condensing, compressing that into one volume. Recently we had an opportunity to spend three days with Carl Sandburg at his goat farm in Flat Rock, North Carolina. Charlie Mack was the cameraman. Carl, I know that you do a lot of your work here in the house, but you also do some of it up on this rock, don't you?

CARL SANDBURG: —Once in a while. There's some five months out of the year here that you can sit outside, if it isn't raining, and I have a chair up there and a bench down here, and I have written thousands of words with a lead pencil. I have not bothered to drag a typewriter up.

MURROW: —Carl, why did you come to Flat Rock to settle, anyway?

SANDBURG: —Well, we had no pasture for the goats in Michigan. The Missus says if we could go where the winters are not so long and not so cold, we will live longer, and then we came up here. And out of several places, we thought we liked this one for scenery and for some air and some good pasture; and you can raise most anything on some of the ground here.

MURROW: —How old were you when you scored your first literary success?

SANDBURG: —I was thirty-eight when *Chicago Poems* was

269

published. That was my first book by a regular publishing house.

MURROW:—And when did you really begin to be seriously interested in Mr. Lincoln?

SANDBURG:—Well, I have been nearly all of my life. Heard men talk about him when I was a boy—politicians and preachers—and I knew sometime I would do at least a small book on Lincoln, to be titled *The Life of Abraham Lincoln for Young People.* And as I went through the basic Lincoln research books, why, it came over me there was something else I was started on—and I ended up with six volumes and a million-and-a-half words on Lincoln. And I don't know yet what to make of it.

MURROW:—A million-and-a-half words and then *Always the Young Strangers.* You sat in that chair with a pencil, a pad, and that fabulous memory of yours, and wrote it here on this rock under the trees. Is that right?

SANDBURG:—Trying to recollect with a memory that I think is imperfect, very—no one knows better how imperfect it is than I. But people say I have got total recall. I deny it.

MURROW:—Well, let's sit in this chair where you wrote *Always the Young Strangers* and talk about Mr. Lincoln. I have got an advance copy here of this one-volume Lincoln, and in the preface you have got some of, I think, the noblest language I ever read. Will you read a little bit of it for us?

SANDBURG:—Well, there are some good lines at the end of that preface. I did not write them. I chose them from thousands of commentaries on Lincoln that I have met in my life. These are among the most significant, about why Lincoln lasts:

"There is no new thing to be said about Lincoln. There is no new thing to be said of the mountains or of the sea or of the stars. The years go their way, but the same old mountains lift their granite shoulders above the drifting clouds. The same mysterious sea beats upon the shore. The same silent stars keep holy vigil above a tired world. But to the mountains and sea and stars, men turn forever in unwearied homage. And thus with Lincoln, for he was a mountain in grandeur of soul. He was a sea in deep undervoice of mystic loneliness. He was a star in steadfast purity of purpose and service. And he abides."

270

MURROW:—Carl, why did you spend so much time with Mr. Lincoln?

SANDBURG:—Oh, the straight-off simplest answer to that is because he was such good company. I have been through all the basic research material about him, and I have sort of lived with him off and on for forty years and more, and he still is good to brood about. He still has laughter and tears that are good for a fellow. Well, he was also the first humorist to occupy the White House, the first man of humor. He was pre-eminently a laughing man, and he used to say that a good story was medicine.

MURROW:—Carl, tell me, why do you dislike adjectives?

SANDBURG:—I am not sure it didn't come out of an experience I had at West Point.

MURROW:—What was that?

SANDBURG:—At West Point, for two—for a while there, I was a classmate of Douglas MacArthur and Ulysses S. Grant the Third. I was a classmate of theirs for two weeks. I was notified by the superintendent that I had failed in arithmetic. I might have expected that; but grammar—grammar—I probably failed to remember the definition I had read of a verb. And, I don't know, I might have gotten a hate of adjectives then.

MURROW:—What do you think is the worst word in the English language?

SANDBURG:—The one word more detestable than any other in the English language is the word *exclusive*. Exclusive—when you're exclusive, you shut out a more or less large range of humanity from your mind and heart—from your understanding them.

MURROW:—What do you answer when people ask you how you write? How do you go about the business of writing?

SANDBURG:—Much depends on who is asking the question. Sweet young things that will ask that question, "How do you write?"—and I say, "Simple. It's easy. You just sit up to the type-writer and put down one word after another. If you try to put down two or three words, you are sunk." And they take that as very valuable advice. And then there are some nice, earnest, serious college boys, and I try to reduce it to the formula of, say, Ty Cobb. There were some baseball writers got around him at the end of one season and they asked him, they told him: "You have eleven different ways of sliding to second. Now, we would like to know at what point between first and second base do you decide on which one of those eleven ways you are going to use?" And Ty said, "I don't think about it. I just slide, that's all."

MURROW:—I think you said once that an author must write what he thinks, and a poet must write what he must. Is that right?

SANDBURG:—That will go for different kinds of writers. It will go for, oh, a good many of the best poets. There is being written today a lot of cerebral poetry—poetry right out of the brain, with nothing of the blood in it, and it's rather pathetic. You need footnotes, and you need diagrams. Oh there are readers of it that say, "Well, I understand it. I understand it." And then there are those who are honest enough to say they don't understand such poems. And then there are still others that have had it explained to them, and they say—they say to those who told them, those who explained it, "I understood it, until you explained it to me."

MURROW:—Carl, would you rather be known as a poet, a biographer, a historian—or what?

SANDBURG:—I'd rather be known as a man who says, "What I need mainly is three things in life, possibly four: To be out of jail, to eat regular, to get what I write printed, and then a little love at home and a little outside." Those four things, and I don't need to be called either poet, historian, biographer, guitar player, folk singer, minnesinger, and what—there was one more—novelist.

MURROW:—Now, Carl, you have got all four of those things. Right?

SANDBURG:—In a way of speaking. What was it you told me one time about your return to North Carolina after many years?

MURROW:—Oh, that was when I went to see an uncle and he gave me an almost Elizabethan greeting. I hadn't seen him for a long time, and I met him out near the barn and he said, "Ed, if you had come as often as I thought of you, you wouldn't be such a stranger as you are."

SANDBURG:—That's nice. That's nice. The Elizabethan things that stick along—I don't know—it isn't Elizabethan, but they tell it to you in North Carolina, about a witness on the stand. He was asked to—his name and age and the rest of it—and the first question put to him, "Can you read and write?" And he said, "Well, I can't write, but I can read some." "What do you mean you can read

272

some?" "Well, I'm going along the road and I come to one of these crossroads where the sign—where there is a sign, and I can—I can always read how fur, but not where to."

MURROW:—Maybe that's part of the trouble with the world now. They can read how fur but it's very difficult to tell where to, isn't it?

SANDBURG:—That's right. That will go for this time of ours. Most inscrutable world scene that there ever was.

MURROW:—Do you think the people still have it? You know more of our past than, I think, anyone I know. Do you feel that we are in danger of tearing ourselves apart?

SANDBURG:—There never has been a time—there never has been a time that there were not clouds upon the horizon in this country, and there was one crisis after another that could be named: in the Colonial times, in the American Revolution and that Civil War, the like of which almost no other country has ever had. And then the two world wars. Over and over again it has looked as though we were sunk as a nation. And always—it's the point I try to make in that novel, *Remembrance Rock*—always there has been a saving remnant. Always there has been enough of a small, faithful minority—faithful to the death.

Every generation in American history has had its demagogues. Sometimes they rose to high influence, came near to having very high power. George Washington—he had his caluminators. Over and over again, in the speeches and letters of George Washington, you will find that word *calumny*. They were lying about him—liars, creating this calumny that fell on him. And there was Major General Benjamin F. Butler, a Massachusetts lawyer and politician; over and over again he was Lincoln's problem, and again he was Grant's problem. He commanded an army and got no results with it. He lied and lied about political affairs. And the time came, though, when his blunders had reached the point where Grant and Lincoln threw him out of the Army and sent him home to Massachusetts. A very curious entry in John Hay's diary: One time in 1861 he was saying to Lincoln that Butler was the one man in the Army that he feared could become dangerous if he had power. And Lincoln answered—as Hay wrote it in his diary—"Yes. Yes. Butler is like Jim Jett's brother. Jim used to say that his brother was the damnedest scoundrel that ever lived, but in the infinite mercy of Providence he was also the damnedest fool." And that will go for the demagogues of nearly every generation in American history. And that's that.

October 12, 1954

According to the dictionary, the "dog days" come in July and August—hot and uncomfortable—so called because the Dog Star rises and sets with the sun at that time. The political dog days came late this year, yesterday to be exact, ushered in by a casual comment made in Detroit by Defense Secretary Charles Wilson.

Mr. Wilson was asked a question about unemployment. He said that about a year ago a group had complained to him that unemployment would be increased in a certain area because draft requirements had been reduced and a number of young men wouldn't have to go to Korea and fight. Mr. Wilson said he told the group, "The idea that a nineteen-year-old boy could be drafted and sent to Korea to be shot at, and he didn't have enough gumption to go a hundred miles and get himself a job—I don't go for that." And then Mr. Wilson added, "I've got a lot of sympathy for people where a sudden change—unemployment—catches them. But I've always liked bird dogs better than kennel-fed dogs myself. You know, one who'll get out and hunt for food rather than sit on his fanny and yell."

Mr. Walter Reuther, head of the C.I.O., immediately yelled to the President in a five-page telegram, saying Mr. Wilson should either apologize or quit the cabinet. George Meany, the president of the A.F. of L., said Mr. Wilson "showed a complete ignorance of what it means to be unemployed." Reporters made it clear that Mr. Wilson smiled when he made the comment, but the words carried farther than the smile. The President issued a statement in Denver, saying he had "never found Wilson in the slightest degree indifferent to human misfortunes."

Late this afternoon, Mr. Wilson issued a statement. He thought he was in no danger in his own home town of having anything he said taken out of context and misinterpreted. He has always had the greatest sympathy and understanding for men and women who needed work and were ready and willing to work. He intended no invidious comparisons or insinuations likening people to dogs in any sense. Mr. Wilson thinks a distorted version is being used by Democrats to misinterpret the full meaning of what he actually said. What he actually said is now clear, as just recounted. He wasn't comparing auto workers to dogs. But his phraseology, the smile notwithstanding, will bring no aid and comfort to Republican candidates where the labor vote is heavy.

It is not easy to tell exactly what Mr. Wilson meant by his reference to the nineteen-year-old boy, and his explanation throws little light on this point. He appeared to assume that a draft-age boy would find work if he had the gumption to travel a hundred miles. Enemies of unemployment insurance in all lands have argued that way, as though in this complex mass-production, mass-employment world, every worker is sure to find work simply by going out and looking for it. It is difficult to tell whether Mr. Wilson was employing rather homely and blunt phraseology in a careless fashion, as he has done before, or whether he was expressing a social philosophy, as he either did or he didn't when he said, "What's good for General Motors is good for America."

Mr. Wilson's remarks of yesterday, in context and without distortion, have delighted Democrats and distressed a considerable number of Republicans. So it is perhaps accurate to describe the remainder of the political campaign as the dog days, sure to be "hot and uncomfortable."

November 30, 1954

The British are an emotional, sentimental people with a great fondness for antiquity. The sentiment and the emotion are seldom displayed, but it happened in London today. The occasion was the eightieth birthday of Sir Winston Churchill—a flood of gifts, a joint session of Parliament, nonpartisan oratory, a portrait, a fund that may go to three million dollars—all in honor of perhaps the most considerable man to walk the stage of history in our time. His own island, wrapped in the Atlantic mists, was never a large enough stage for him to play upon. He has served six sovereigns; his experience of war extends from the last full-dress cavalry charge to the hydrogen bomb. For fifty-two years he has sat in the House of

Commons. He has not always been right, but never has he been ambiguous.

Today was the most memorable public occasion of his life. Today, in recalling the war years, he said, "The people's will was resolute and remorseless. I only expressed it. They had the lion's heart. I had the luck to be called upon to give it the roar."

This ancient aristocrat, born in the tranquil, serene Victorian era, has spent much of his life as a man of war. His recognition of the enemies of freedom was sure and certain. His faith in Constitutional procedure was never shaken. During the late war Sir Winston Churchill presided over a coalition government equipped with dictatorial powers and was scrupulous in his regard for the authority of the House of Commons.

His political obituary was being written when he had scarcely passed forty. He sat for years in the House, warning of the menace of Nazism, while the big clock above the speaker's chair ticked off the wasted hours. He was a lonely but not a bitter man, always enjoying the cut and thrust of parliamentary debate, where no man was his match. When he came to power in the spring of 1940, he brooked no recrimination about the past, lest the future thereby be lost. He mobilized the English language and sent it into battle to steady his fellow countrymen and hearten those Europeans upon whom the long dark night of tyranny had descended. He understood the first principle of war, which is to recognize the enemy, and had Hitler invaded Hell, Mr. Churchill would have found opportunity in the House of Commons to make passing and not altogether unfavorable reference to the Devil.

I am sure that if he could pluck one year from the incredible eighty and print it indelibly in the pages of history, he would choose that one year when Britain stood alone, while those who were half asleep became half prepared. He would choose it, not because of his rhetoric, not because of the Battle of Britain or the steadiness of the civilian population, but rather because democratic processes, the rights of the individual, did not shrivel or shrink even when held so near the fire of total war.

The British Prime Minister is both a gambler and a crying man—Mr. Lincoln did considerable crying, too. One of the greatest gambles in the history of warfare occurred in the autumn of 1940, when he stripped the island of its pitiful remnants of armor—most of it had been lost at Dunkirk—and shipped it around the Cape to Egypt. When the German beam was on London, guiding their bombers in, he would drive up from the country for no other reason than to be there with the other subjects of the king. There was a grim gaiety about the man, a certain fascination with physical danger, a restless, roving mind which caused him to be concerned about minute details, memoranda showering right and left reading, "Pray inform me on this matter within twenty-four hours," telephone calls to cabinet ministers in the middle of the night. And always the ability to savor and taste a well-turned phrase, to polish it until it would come out in the House of Commons in a fashion described by a friend as a "thunderous and well-rehearsed improvisation."

When victory had been achieved, his fellow countrymen turned him out to grass. With one brilliant exception he did not complain. His mind had changed on very few subjects, and it was a time of change. He wrote and he painted, and sought power again. Finally it was his. Scarred and toughened as he was by political wars, the charge that hurt most in that last campaign was that he was a man of war not to be trusted with power. He remains the man of war seeking peace. Younger men, waiting for him to lay down the heavy burdens of office, grow old and impatient while waiting.

He moves with uncertain steps. Some of the fire has gone from his voice, but his language continues to illuminate the political scene in England and abroad. He said today, "I am now nearing the end of my journey, but I hope I still have some services to render." His services to date have not been inconsiderable, for men who love freedom, and indeed those who now enjoy it, are considerably in his debt. He has enriched our language and fortified our heritage.

January 31, 1955

> *Communist China was vowing to "liberate" Formosa and, this time, appeared moving to carry out its pledge. President Eisenhower requested, and received, from Congress a declaration of U.S. readiness to fight to keep Formosa free. Peking and Moscow accused Eisenhower of raising the threat of a new war.*

277

It has often been said that the presidency of the United States is the most powerful, most lonely job in the world. Both the power and the loneliness have been considerably increased. The congressional action giving President Eisenhower a free hand in dealing with Formosa and related matters is a massive vote of confidence. It could be called an act of faith which few presidents in our history would have received in such full measure under similar circumstances. Moreover, the President has said that he will discharge this fearful responsibility himself, that he will not delegate authority to commanders in the field.

The decision General Eisenhower had to make in those weary, windy hours before he gave the signal for D day may well have been a minor one compared to the decisions he will have to make in the course of coming weeks and months. The consequences of a mistake, or a miscalculation, may involve not merely the success or failure of an amphibious operation but the survival of much of civilization.

The President does not lack for advisors, both public and private. The advice conflicts—allies must be considered—and the final fateful decision must be made by one man. He has his mandate, clear-cut and unequivocal, expressed by the elected representatives of the people. No test, no burden of this magnitude has before been placed upon the shoulders of the leader of a free state. In 1939 Neville Chamberlain was required only to consult Britain's treaty with Poland and his cabinet; he had no choice but to declare war. Pearl Harbor struck choice and decision from President Roosevelt's hands. President Truman regarded the entry into Korea as a police action undertaken in common with other free nations.

In this present situation the grim alternatives confronting the President may continue for a long time. If he adopts what appears to be a bold and belligerent attitude, that could cost us our principal ally. For in Britain the Labor Party is united against American policy, and some time within the year there must be a general election in Britain, which Labor is capable of winning. We in this country are familiar with the impact of domestic politics on foreign policy, and the same thing happens in Britain. If the President pursues a cautious policy, there will be cries of "appeasement" and "a display of fatal weakness." If he finds an ominous build-up of Communist forces on the mainland which he believes threatens

Formosa and gives orders to bomb it out, there may be a wave of revulsion against the United States throughout Asia.

Juridically and militarily our right to help defend Formosa cannot be questioned. Our right to fight in defense of the offshore islands will be widely questioned in the non-Communist world.

April 12, 1955

The sun was warm, the earth coming alive; there was hope and promise in the air. The occasion called for banners in the breeze and trumpets in the distance. Instead, the scene was Rackham Auditorium, here at the University of Michigan. About six hundred scientists and reporters. The atmosphere combined that of a clinic and a church. The camera lights were hot. The family of Dr. Jonas Salk sat well down in the front, the tall, serene Mrs. Salk and the three boys. The little six-year-old mopped his brow with a clean white handkerchief and then tucked it carefully back in his breast pocket. There were the usual speeches of welcome. Then came Dr. Thomas Francis, Jr., director of the Polio Vaccine Evaluation Center, the man who made the measurements and the checks on all the field tests. No oratory, no rhetoric. He was spelling out this unprecedented experiment step by step. His was no effort to persuade— merely to expound. Chart followed chart, graph followed graph on the big screen behind him while he talked on in the dark.

The Salk vaccine works. It is effective, and it is safe. It is not perfect, but the speculation has been ended. One set of figures followed another. Adverse reactions to the inoculations were nearly negligible. Four children who received placeba—that is, the so-called "blank shots"—died. No child who received the vaccine died. The figure of 80 to 90 per cent effectiveness in preventing paralytic polio has been used in describing the Salk vaccine.

Here are the words used by Dr. Francis: "If the results from the observed study areas are employed, the vaccine could be considered to have been 60 to 80 per cent effective against paralytic polio; 60 per cent against type 1, and 70 to 80 per cent effective against disease caused by types 2 and 3. On this basis it may be suggested that vaccination was 80 to 90 per cent effective against paralytic polio, that it was 60 to 70 per cent effective against disease caused

279

by type 1 virus, and 90 per cent or more effective against that of type 2 and type 3 virus."

The report by Dr. Jonas Salk, of the University of Pittsburgh, based on his own studies, closely paralleled the findings of Dr. Francis and his group. There was no vanity, no complacency in this small man who looks like an unusually serious graduate student and whose name now becomes part of the medical and social history of this country.

Almost every speaker referred to the number of people involved in this massive experiment. Basil O'Connor, president of the National Foundation for Infantile Paralysis, said, "Each man needs to feel that he belongs, that he has an expressible relation to others, that he is part of a community in which he can live not only within himself but outside himself, contributing to the welfare of his fellow man."

Those of you who have contributed to the fight against polio would have received your dividend in full measure had you been here today. And yet it was a quiet sort of victory. Perhaps because most of the people present were professionals and realized that this was only a step, although a gigantic one, in the field of preventive medicine. Some of the wisest words of the day were spoken by Dr. Alan Gregg, vice-president of the Rockefeller Foundation, who said, "It has been the wise policy of the National Foundation for Infantile Paralysis to avoid making promises it cannot be sure of keeping, to refrain from letting dreams pass for deed and wishes for thinking." At a time when the media of modern communications are overly inclined to persuade, astonish, frighten, or amuse, and are tempted to exaggeration and prematurity in each of these gainful activities, there can be a lasting advantage in sobriety of statement.

Dr. Gregg spoke of the parents and children who took part in last year's unprecedented mass experiment. One could not imagine a more phenomenal or heartening example of reasonableness and courage than these volunteers have given. They were not conscripts; there was no certainty of personal advantage; in fact, the uncertainty of it was explicit. There was no deception from above and no defection in the ranks. They willingly took part in a huge unselfish experiment, a loyal, steadfast and intelligent part in an enterprise that called for exactly those qualities: loyalty, steadfastness and intelligence.

280

In speaking of today's announcement, Dr. Gregg said, "It is as though music that began in a minor key, befitting bewildered suffering and dogged patience, now strikes the major chords of relief and exultation."

May 4, 1955

The crisis in South Vietnam is getting worse. Some seven hundred local and regional officials from all parts of the country came to Saigon today, trying to decide whether to oust Emperor Bao Dai, or whether just to oblige him to yield his powers to Premier Diem. They could decide to set up a constitutional monarchy with Bao Dai as merely a figurehead ruler. Bao Dai, who is still on the French Riviera, today asked Diem to disavow all action taken by what he termed "a seditious minority which is far from representing our people and risks being carried away by the Communists." By which he apparently means the meeting in Saigon today.

In this confused situation a spokesman for our State Department said it's not true that we favor the establishment of a constitutional monarchy in Free Vietnam. He said it's up to the Vietnamese to resolve their own problems and decide their own form of government. Nevertheless, Secretary of State Dulles is apparently still determined to keep Diem in office.

The French and Bao Dai claim that Premier Diem's so-called "revolutionary committee" has been infiltrated by the Communists. American authorities say privately that this is not true. So we have a four-cornered situation: Premier Diem and his supporters, Emperor Bao Dai, the French and the Americans. Apparently no two of the four can agree as to what should be done.

Today, on the Riviera, Bao Dai conferred with Diem's brother in an effort to find a way out of the crisis, but nothing was settled. It is reasonably clear that the forces that want freedom in South Vietnam are disorganized and that the only well-organized revolutionary apparatus in the country is the Communist-led Viet Minh. Premier Diem may fear that the Communists will take over from the inside, for he continues to plead for Bao Dai's support.

My colleague David Schoenbrun has spent an hour and a half with Bao Dai on the Riviera during the last two days. He reports that Bao Dai is hoping for something like a high Council of State, limited to five or six top Vietnamese personalities, including Premier Diem. These men would then try to order the revolutionary committee to disband, offering amnesty and positions of power to those members who would rally to the new council. The council would then call on Bao Dai to come home, telling him he must transfer his absolute powers to the council in order to create a constitutional monarchy. As Bao Dai sees it, this would be a fine solution for all concerned. The United States wouldn't have to choose between Diem and Bao Dai. Diem's face would be saved, since he would remain as premier until the change had been effected. His opponents would be satisfied; Diem would no longer be a one-man ruler with supreme powers. Bao Dai would remain as the figurehead emperor, but he would be relieved of running his country's affairs, which he hasn't been doing anyway.

If Diem should proclaim a republic and ask for recognition, the French have threatened to pull out their troops and wash their hands of the whole mess. If this happens, *we* will inherit the mess.

September 27, 1955

> *President Eisenhower's heart attack lent new urgency to the question of succession in case of presidential disability. Murrow was wary of any unconstitutional assumptions of power.*

Vice-President Nixon's office said today that the National Security Council meeting for Thursday and the cabinet meeting for Friday, which have been announced, were called by the Vice-President. Neither meeting had been scheduled before President Eisenhower's illness. The next regular meeting of the Security Council is not due till next month. The cabinet does not normally meet if the President is out of Washington, though if it meets, it usually does so every Friday. When President Eisenhower went to Geneva he arranged for the cabinet to meet in his absence with Mr. Nixon presiding. But no one was saying today that President Eisenhower had issued instructions for the two meetings which Mr. Nixon called.

The meetings were announced after a luncheon yesterday where Mr. Nixon consulted with Acting Attorney General [William P.] Rogers, Presidential Counsel [Gerald D.] Morgan and Presidential Assistants [Sherman] Adams and [Wilton B.] Persons. It also is possible that Mr. Nixon at some time had discussed with President Eisenhower what to do in an emergency such as this. If so, he may have been acting as the President asked him to do. Certainly neither Mr. Nixon nor the officials at yesterday's luncheon have said anything to suggest that calling these meetings was a formal action taken under the Vice-President's constitutional obligation to act as President in case of the disability of the President.

Attorney General Brownell, now back from Spain, may issue a ruling on whether to delegate any of the President's powers. Officials were saying in Washington that since no urgent papers await presidential signature, and he might recover very soon, it may be wholly unnecessary to delegate any powers. They said they hope that the problems raised by the President's illness could be solved by informal action. Obviously they considered the meetings of the Security Council and cabinet as informal actions. And the statement about the meetings stresses that the subjects on both agendas are of a normal, routine nature.

But these are matters that lie just short of one of the most controversial areas in our constitutional experience. When President Wilson suffered a stroke in October 1919, Secretary of State [Robert] Lansing on the next day called an extraordinary meeting of the cabinet and about the same time tried to have Vice-President [Thomas] Marshall step in as acting president. Dr. [Cary T.] Grayson, who was Wilson's personal physician, was called before the cabinet. He refused to be specific about the President's illness. The cabinet did nothing, since no machinery existed by which the President's disability could be certified. Both Secretary [Joseph] Tumulty and Dr. Grayson refused to certify it. Later, Mr. Tumulty said that if anyone else tried to certify it, both he and Dr. Grayson would stand together and repudiate it. Mr. Lansing continued to hold cabinet meetings until President Wilson wrote him and bitterly chided him for committing a serious breach in the constitutional system. Thereupon, Lansing resigned.

For months, Mrs. Wilson, Secretary Tumulty and Dr. Grayson decided what to lay before the President and so, in a limited sense, they were acting presidents. But at the beginning of the illness, the specialist Mrs. Wilson called in advised against resignation, which Mrs. Wilson earnestly wished. "If he resigns," said the physician, "the greatest incentive to recovery is gone, and as his mind is clear as crystal, he still can do more even with a maimed body than anyone else." Two months after the stroke, two senators called on the President to size up his condition and reported back that "his mind is vigorous and active." So the question of his disability was not completely answered either way. Under the circumstances, Vice-President Marshall refused to act. He said he would assume the presidency only on a resolution of Congress and with the approval in writing of Mrs. Wilson and Dr. Grayson. "I am not going to seize the place," he said, "and then have Wilson—recovered—come around and say, 'Get off, you usurper.' "

The problem of a president's disability also arose after President Garfield was shot. That happened in July, 1881, and he did not die until October. Vice-President [Chester A.] Arthur did not budge, even though the President was incapable of performing his duties. He was not going to take it upon himself to decide something that the Constitution and Congress had not seen fit to decide. So he set a precedent which Marshall subsequently followed. Arthur pleaded with Congress to define the procedure for certifying the President's disability and his fitness to resume his duties. Again and again Congress had been urged to do so. It never has acted. Today the vagueness of the Constitution creates a very urgent problem and contributes nothing to its solution. And Congress has not understood the need for its own action.

Mr. Nixon, in calling the two meetings for this week, may have gone a tiny step further than either Arthur or Marshall. But any more steps without waiting for legislation run right into a constitutional hornet's nest.

It was ten years before Congress approved the Twenty-Fifth Amendment dealing with succession in case of presidential disability. The Amendment became law when it was ratified by the thirty-eighth state legislature on February 10, 1967.

November 28, 1955

Murrow could not fly in the European sky without reliving his experience with men who fought the air battles over Europe during the Second World War. This is a piece he did from Paris, where he had gone to cover a French government crisis.

About twelve hours out of New York you step out of a Super Constellation, walk across a hundred yards of concrete and climb into a two-engined chartered aircraft bound for Villacoublay. There are seats in the aircraft for eight persons, but you're alone. A winter sun is losing its fight against the mist that shrouds the island. As you taxi to the end of the runway, memory takes you back to other take-offs when the air was filled with the thunder of motors and when the bellies of the aircraft were filled with bombs. The take-off is routine. At about six thousand feet you break out of the clouds. The sun is just off your right wing. There's a full bomber's moon off the left wing. At 3 o'clock high there are contrails of a jet. He comes out of the eye of the sun, close enough so you can see he's wearing a yellow scarf. The bold markings of the Royal Air Force show on the wing as he rolls away. The boy flying it was probably only ten years old—in knee pants—when the sky was torn and shaken by Spitfires and Messerschmitts during the Battle of Britain. The clouds below are ragged and broken, like a field of snow plowed by a drunken farmer.

Somewhere down there is Dover, and you wonder what's happened to that grey old seagull who used to sound the warning of approaching German aircraft before the sirens screamed. You notice that the seats in this chartered job are covered with plaid. And, for no reason, that reminds you of Bob Sherwood over the Bay of Biscay in 1942, flying to Algiers in an unarmed plane. The pilot came back and said to Sherwood, "Keep an eye out for enemy aircraft." And Sherwood said, "If I see one, what do I do? Ask for a prayerbook?" All voices of all the men you have ever flown with seem to come pounding into your ears. The pilot ought to be Colonel Joe Kelly, smoking that big cigar, flying level and straight in a bomb

285

run with all the B-26s strung out behind him. You wait for that sensual shudder that goes through the aircraft when the guns are tested. You remember the big sergeant from New Jersey, with his legs dangling out of the door of a C-47, going in for the Arnhem-Nijmegen drop, how he looked down and saw English girls harvesting potatoes. "Look at those tomatoes," he said, "digging potatoes!" And you remember the drop across the Rhine, riding in a Halifax, pulling a glider, and you hear again the glider pilot just before he cut loose saying in a casual fashion, "I'll be leaving you now. Thanks for the ride."

At about this point you're over the Channel, although you can't see it, but you remember what it looked like on D day—all the ships like matchsticks in a bowl of soup. You look at the moon off your left wing and it seems to be the same moon you saw over Berlin in 1943, but then it was tinged with red from the fires below. Your chartered aircraft seems slow, as though the air were tired and thin from being beaten by so many propellers so many years ago. It's a little difficult to breathe, although you're only at seven thousand feet. And that reminds you of the time you left the waistgun position in a B-17 to go forward, forgot to pick up your oxygen bottle and almost passed out.

Now there is a glimpse of the French countryside, and you remember flying as observer in an old P-6 in Korea at a hundred feet or less, and you're ashamed you can't remember the pilot's name. You can hear his voice, remember that he was blond and that he could follow tank tracks like an Indian scout. But the name is gone. You remember how a bomber crew used to tighten up when they crossed the enemy coast. The distance between tail gunner and pilot did not exist. Every man's shoulder was against the other. You see a railroad switching yard below you, and you remember the time when a B-26 outfit lanced down through a hole in the clouds and took a similar switching yard as a target of opportunity, and left the rails looking like tortured spaghetti. At about this time the young pilot in the chartered job takes up the horn and calls the tower of Villacoublay. This is something you do remember: There was a fighter pilot—his name was Curley Rogers. He came from Selma, Alabama, and he flew you piggy-back in a P-47 over the Remagen Bridge.

All during this chartered flight from London to Villacoublay the voices of flying men who are now dead kept pounding through the intercom which didn't exist. You looked upstairs for your flight cover—and it wasn't there. You looked back to see whether the other aircraft were in formation, and you saw only the emptiness upon which the plush chartered job had not left a mark. You were up there all alone. And you wondered whether the scars cut by Spitfires and Messerschmitts on the green ground below had healed. And then your aircraft touched down at Villacoublay. The motors were cut and the ghosts were gone. And you decided that middle-aged reporters with about forty combat missions as parasites should not fly alone.

February 1, 1956

There was an activity, an excitement of creation, in Israel which reminded Murrow of the building of the American West. He flew to Tel Aviv and left immediately for a frontier settlement close by the Gaza Strip.

We came down here, down the winding road through a desolate area of huge gray boulders lying in brick-red soil. Off to the right, the Wadi Sherish where Samson courted Delilah. On the left, the Arab village of Abrugot. On the other side of the road, on top of the hill, a prosperous-looking rural village founded by German-Jewish immigrants who came here to escape Hitler. On down through the rolling hills of Judea is the place where David met Goliath. A little farther on is the remnant of a road built by Hadrian. And, finally, down to the flat, rich land heavy with winter green reaching from the northern edge of the Negev Desert, a country that reminds you of Wisconsin in the early spring.

As dusk came gently down, men with rifles were walking toward the bridges, the night guard against infiltration and sabotage. About twelve miles from this kibbutz we picked up an escort of two jeeps loaded with Israeli soldiers. We were approaching the Egyptian frontier. When we arrived at Nahras it was almost time to turn on the lights, the floodlights that surround this community of fifty-five families, seven thousand chickens, fifty-five head of cattle, seven tractors and other modern equipment. Outside the flood-lit area is barbed wire, slit trenches and concrete bunkers. Watch towers about forty feet high command the entire perimeter. This kibbutz covers about twenty-four hundred acres. The boundary between Israel and Egypt is only about five hundred yards from the main buildings, which are surrounded by the barbed wire and floodlights. The watch towers are manned every night, each man spending two nights a week on guard duty. And some of the outposts are modern and complete, even to field telephones. Outside some of the wooden buildings, extra concrete walls—about eight inches thick—go up to the second floor windows. That's to prevent sniper fire.

This is a young kibbutz, only about two and a half years old. It is manned and worked by Israelis. Most of them young; all of them ex-soldiers and rifles as much in evidence as pitch forks. The frontier here lies in a lovely green rolling valley. It is marked only by a deep furrow down the middle. Youngsters cultivate right down to the demarkation line. When they get near to the line, frequently one man drives the tractor while two others with rifles ride along just in case. There is mud ankle deep everywhere. You remove your knee boots before entering the house.

Right now there are four relatively new babies squalling or yawning on a porch in the winter sunshine. The trees are beginning to grow. Some of them are a good fifteen feet tall. The food is adequate but plain. The milk, produced by the Holstein herd, is excellent. The clothing worn is nondescript, including a number of army castoffs, and rubber boots at this time of year are required wearing for men and women. They sing in the cowsheds and in the showers in the evening, and I'm assured this is not an act put on for a visiting fireman.

In this kibbutz, I have heard the word *we* more often than in any other community of comparable size. They will tell you that *we* have brought in an oil well not far from here, that *we* are developing a long-staple cotton of excellent quality. They deplore the fact that in the limited area that they're able to irrigate they must bring the pipes inside the barbed wire at night. Most of the youngsters here came out from the cities. They can leave if they want to. They get no pay. But their clothing and their basic needs are provided. The farm belongs to no one but to all of them. One youngster told me last night that he went to Europe last summer to study cattle breeding. I asked him who sent him, and he said, "The farm, who else?" This isn't free enterprise, but it is enterprising. A curious combination of defense and agricultural production.

February 10, 1956

There is no doubt that a crisis is building up in the Middle East. The flash point could be almost anywhere. It might well be on the Jordan River between Syria and Israel. The Israelis contend that they have the right to tap the waters of the Jordan for power and irrigation. Syria claims that if this is done, they may be an explosion. The Americans, British and French are trying to agree what to do in the event of renewed fighting. They are talking about appealing to the United Nations to order the fighting to stop and, if this fails, the application of an economic embargo and a naval blockade.

The military balance between Israel and her neighbors is shifting. The Egyptians, in particular, are getting stronger. The Israeli leaders deny any aggressive intentions, but they recognize that their relative strength is declining. The danger lies, not in an isolated border incident, but rather in uncertainty as to what Western policy, and particularly American policy, is. It seems to me unlikely that either platitudes or promises will prevent an explosion. The Israelis are determined that their new nation will not die without battle. If they fail to secure the defensive weapons they require, the so-called activists may decide that they must strike now before the weight of men and metal against them becomes overwhelming. The Jews in Israel have a fierce sense of belonging to their tiny state. There is a quiet but fervent determination to survive fully equal to that in Britain during the year when Britain stood alone.

Two things appear to be certain: the Israelis are not going to sit there forever watching the Arab cliff that surrounds them grow higher and more menacing. If fighting comes, it will be necessary to go back to biblical terms to describe its ferocity. And if the United States has a policy for this area, it should be stated—and soon. If we have a policy, no one in Israel knows what it is. There is a surface calm in the country, but there is also a degree of desperation and a sense that time is running out.

April 30, 1956

News of the death of Alben Barkley, for whom Murrow had special affection, came late in the day. Murrow composed this tribute against the deadline for his evening broadcast:

In the woods, when a great and ancient tree that has weathered many storms suddenly comes crashing down, there is the noise of smaller trees snapping back into position, the rustle and the cries of small creatures, and the descending noise of twigs, branches and bits of moss falling to the ground. And then there is silence, more complete and oppressive than any silence that went before. Frequently this happens on a dead calm day for no apparent reason. So it was today with Senator Alben Barkley of Kentucky. He was making the keynote speech at Washington and Lee University. The occasion was their mock Democratic convention. The Senator had just said, "I would rather be a servant in the house of the Lord than sit in the seat of the mighty." He collapsed and was pronounced dead ten minutes later.

It was altogether typical of the man that he devoted his last hour to politics and to youth. He was a man without cant, without rancor—a politician respected and admired, even by his opponents. In defeat he was resolute, and in victory indeed magnanimous. Few men have ever so endeared themselves in the hearts of their fellow-men. He had humor, but seldom used it to hurt. He was a man who wore both power and popularity loosely, almost carelessly, like an old cloak. He was tolerant of most things, except intolerance. He had been in politics since 1905. He was helpful to young men. He was a tireless political campaigner. And he was an orator of what is generally called "the old school." Anyone who heard his keynote speech at Philadelphia in 1948, or his brilliant performance at Chicago in 1952, heard political oratory at its best. At Chicago he had thought the presidential nomination to be within his grasp. He lost it—knew he had lost it—and then went before the convention, shrugged his broad shoulders and proceeded to demonstrate how a good politician, and a good loser, should act and speak.

He served as vice-president under Mr. Truman, became known

as The Veep and was always the Gentleman from Paducah. He loved the cut and thrust of parliamentary debate. He was known during his years in the Senate as The Ready Man, ready at the drop of a gavel to deliver a brilliant and lengthy speech, without benefit of notes or ghost writers. While he was vice-president he refused to have a bodyguard, saying, "I'm a big boy now, and who would want to harm a young man like me, anyway?" He was loyal to his party, but did not hesitate to break with Roosevelt in 1944 when the President vetoed a tax bill.

He was a man with manners, who liked people, who enjoyed good stories; some of them were old, but they were reinvigorated by the Barkley telling. After he finished his term as vice-president, he spent a couple of years in Kentucky and then went back to politics. He was elected the state's junior senator for the term beginning in January of last year. So he went back to Congress where he had first arrived as a representative in 1913. He once said he hoped to keep on politicking to the end—and he did. To this reporter, Senator Barkley was always a man who took his duties and his responsibilities seriously, but who was always able to laugh, both at himself and his opposition. There will be many tributes to his ability, his loyalty and his humor. Some of them will be eloquent. But mostly they will resemble the sound of smaller trees snapping upright, branches, twigs and moss falling to the ground after a giant tree has come crashing down.

August 10, 1956

> *On July 26, Nasser seized the Suez Canal. Murrow commented on the Canal seizure in his first broadcast upon returning from vacation. The broadcast originated in Chicago, where he had gone to cover the Democratic National Convention.*

Chicago, which once counted as a capital of isolationism, found itself today situated, in a sense, on the Suez Canal. The Suez crisis has been felt to be too immediate to permit handy treatment in the Democratic platform now being drafted here. But the Democrats were startled, first by the stock market break on Monday and then by the summons to the White House conference called for Sunday. This will send key Congressional leaders back to Washington. Mention that the Administration may examine a request for standby powers in the Mediterranean has suddenly made Democrats realize that more is going on in the world than next week's national convention.

The Suez crisis might be called different from most choices between force and negotiation. For this time either alternative is dangerous for the West. This can hardly be a story with a happy ending, no matter which way it is written. Nor is it unrealistic to speak of the dangers of negotiation. It looks highly doubtful that Nasser can be prevailed upon to restore international control over the Canal or its traffic. That is, he seems even likelier to win a victory if force is not used than if it is.

If force were used, and even if it were restricted to a blockade without occupation of Egyptian territory, Nasser could be brought down fairly soon. But the cost of such action to the British and French and to Americans, too—even if this country did not take direct part in a blockade—is considered very high indeed. Too many people would refuse to accept it as a Simon-pure defense of international rights established by treaty. It would be seen as an attempt to bring Nasser down, as indeed it would be, and not without provocation. Nasser, having Suez in his hands, would be in a position to shut off much of the Middle East's oil and so paralyze British and French economy. If his Canal policy paid off, all foreign investments in oil throughout the whole area would be in danger of nationalization. In a very real way Nasser would have his hands at the jugular vein of Western prosperity.

The violent reactions in London and Paris reflect genuine fear. Thirty years ago the use of force against Nasser would have been the most natural thing in the world. But today the world is different. Free nations are emerging from past subjugation, and world sympathies—generally in the West, too—are with the free nations rather than with the declining empires, even when the young nations are headstrong and impulsive.

What remains unexplained about the crisis is how the State Department came to set it off. Which it did. Nasser decided, belatedly it is true, to accept the United States offer of aid in building the Aswan Dam. And then when he called in the United States ambassador to say so, he was told that the offer had been withdrawn. This was a rather melodramatic slap in the face, and the public has never been adequately told the reason for it. The public knew that Nasser had been something of a disappointment. He had played very closely with the Kremlin. He had recognized Red China. He had broken his promise to keep hands off the Algerian conflict. He seemed to be ambitious for supreme power in the Arab world, so as to use it chiefly against the West. But if Mr. Dulles thought the time had come to get rid of Nasser, he would have gone along with the British and French military plans after the Canal was seized.

Mr. Dulles has called the withdrawal of the Aswan Dam offer a calculated risk. This word "calculated" is a little odd, for the State Department hardly calculated that Nasser would answer by nationalizing the Suez Canal. It looks as though Mr. Dulles thought it safe. And he started a course of events of which the end is not yet in sight. And which, as things now look, are going to bring Nasser unexpected rewards. And the West very serious losses.

August 16, 1956

Adlai Stevenson has reached what seems his inevitable nomination tonight a free man without limiting commitments to anyone. And he did so after overcoming difficulties that sometimes appeared insurmountable. A candidate often has to buy his way out of difficulties, getting support wherever he can pick it up. That is normal in politics. In 1952, Stevenson also was nominated without owing political debts, but that year he was a reluctant candidate who had been drafted, so his freedom was not surprising. Now he has come to his renomination after four years of front running, and for him still to be free is something of a phenomenon.

Nobody is so vulnerable as the front runner in a long political campaign. To win he not only has to be stronger than his nearest rival; he has to be politically stronger than the combined opposition. It isn't really like a foot race. In a foot race, the slower runners don't unite first of all to push the fast man off the track. But in a political campaign all the competing candidates have the common need of getting rid of the front man, and the longer the campaign the greater the chance of doing so.

Stevenson was the first candidate in the field, and as soon as he announced himself he was exposed to all the hazards of a front runner. One of the greatest was that he had to go into the primaries against Senator Kefauver, who had a special knack for primary fighting. This nearly proved Stevenson's undoing in Minnesota, and precedents were enough to convince anyone that he had lost the nomination then and there. But he made himself master it, and in the end he outcampaigned Kefauver. He didn't make so many of his superb speeches, but he wooed and won voters.

With his California victory, his dangers actually mounted. He had to come to the convention and produce more power than all the opposition combined. This meant not only Kefauver and Harriman—and as it turned out, Harry Truman, too—it meant Lyndon Johnson and then the galaxy of the favorite sons who between them might quite easily produce a fatal deadlock. This was the perfect setting for a deal. If Stevenson had been a normal politician, he would have seen just how he could buy his way out, do his own combining and get nominated. It would cost a price, but in politics victory normally costs prices. But Stevenson did not buy his way out. He didn't have to pay a price. He felt he was strong enough to get the nomination without tying his hands. And so he was. That he should do so in 1956 is more to his credit than in 1952. It showed astuteness, first of all. It showed quiet self-confidence. And it also showed character.

Stevenson went into the long campaign with several drawbacks. One was that he had lost the 1952 election. And in a sense he was handicapped in being the kind of man he is. He is not a back-slapper and a spellbinder. He is genial and cordial, but he also is aloof and, in a very real way, solitary. He cannot promise glibly. He thinks and he weighs; he studies both sides of questions and seeks the right answers, which are not always the popular answers. Such characteristics don't make a man unpopular, but they certainly don't build him up—except perhaps in the perspective of history. In 1952, Stevenson had come upon the scene as something unusual and fresh, a man with a gift for making eloquent, lucid and often humorous speeches, who had behind these talents a hard core of intellectual integrity. Part of his strength four years ago was the surprise of the country in discovering such a man. But after four years the surprise was gone. His dedication to the New Deal and the

Fair Deal—in a time when the Republicans had pretty well accepted both—could be taken for granted. But Stevenson was more interested in the present and the immediate future. He regularly sought, and studied, advice from some of the ablest experts in the country. They have not always convinced him. He has to make up his own mind.

Just how much of this will be dramatized in the coming campaign remains to be seen. Stevenson has a supreme gift of communicating ideas. The difficulty of defining the changing world needs this talent, no matter who wins the election.

October 16, 1956

At a time when mankind is able to destroy itself with nuclear weapons, no subject would seem more appropriate for discussion in an election campaign than the prevention of atomic warfare. Certainly Mr. Stevenson intends to go on talking about the hydrogen bomb, and to press his proposal to end all tests of it. Since this is the only topic thus far introduced in the campaign that bears even remotely on disarmament and its controls, no exception need be taken to its being raised in the opinion of this reporter. Mr. Stevenson's address last night was a sober discussion of the unprecedented dangers that come with the H-bomb.

In raising the subject, Mr. Stevenson was asking for room with Mr. Eisenhower on the platform for peace. It does not disparage Mr. Stevenson's dedication to peace to point out that banning the H-bomb tests actually has no direct connection with peace. We and the Russians already have the H-bomb and could use it in a war whether we went on with the tests or not. Mr. Stevenson did not propose to ban the weapons or the development of other weapons. His chief argument against the H-bomb tests was the danger to people from the increased radiation that would result if the tests continue.

This argument has an imposing weight of scientific opinion behind it. We do not yet know how much radiation the human race can safely stand. The perils may well be greater than we suppose. The amount of radiation present in the atmosphere today may be well below the level of tolerance. But that would not justify adding to it.

The H-bomb, however, is by no means an ideal subject for public debate. To start with, the general public has not been allowed to know much about it for reasons of security. The public doesn't know how big a hydrogen bomb can be. It doesn't know to what extent it can be used to spread death-bringing poison over vast stretches of the earth. It doesn't know whether the H-bomb could be made still more horrible without further testing. Debate about a subject so carefully wrapped in secrecy can't be very convincing. There is another angle. Scientists hope one day to control the fusion of the hydrogen atom, and so to harness this power for peacetime uses. If this is achieved, the human race would have unlimited power for the rest of its existence. To what extent this research can go on if H-bomb tests are banned also is not clear.

Mr. Stevenson last night was careful not to propose anything that entailed one-sided risks. He was for full preparedness and the maintenance of adequate power for deterrence. He wanted to develop long-range ballistic missiles. What he was against was nuclear war, just as Mr. Eisenhower repeatedly has been against it.

It is fair to suggest there are more fruitful ways to approach the problem of preventing war than banning the H-bomb, even though starting with that would make for good will. The policy of the United States in the disarmament discussions has been a bewildering zigzag. It would be highly instructive to hear it criticized and defended. True, disarmament is a complex subject, but not more so than nuclear physics. And controlled disarmament, of course, is the key to permanent peace.

It may be that the control of disarmament can't be solved at present, and for this reason disarmament is now unattainable. For example, there is no way to detect the existence of secreted nuclear weapons. But if total disarmament is impossible now, how much disarmament would be safe? That is a big question, but surely not too big for an election campaign and not bigger than the H-bomb. Americans who are able to face the facts of life presumably are adult enough to face the facts of death.

October 19, 1956

There are increasing signs of discontent throughout Russia's satellite empire. There is confusion and dissension. One of our most eminent experts on Russian affairs, Mr. George Kennan, says there is an extensive disintegration of Moscow's authority within the Soviet orbit.

Recently, dissenters in the Communist parties of Poland, Czechoslovakia and Hungary have been restored to good standing. Some who were anti-Stalinist and were killed for it have now been declared innocent of any crimes against the state. The Communist parties, particularly in Italy, are demonstrating greater independence from Moscow control. And then today the mountain really came to Mahomet. Khrushchev and three top-ranking Russian army officers arrived unexpectedly in Warsaw. They didn't summon the increasingly restless and rebellious Poles to Moscow. The Central Committee of the Polish Communist Party was meeting when they arrived. One order of business was to restore to influence and power those Polish leaders who had wanted to follow an independent line like Tito.

What has been happening in Poland is not a revolt against the philosophy of Communism, although no one who knows that country can believe that more than a small percentage of its people are Communists. What has happened is a revolt against dictation and domination by Moscow. The leaders, even those recently returned to power, continue to contend, as Marshal Tito has for years, that they are faithful Communists, merely unwilling to rubberstamp whatever is decided by the big bosses in Moscow. Whatever happens during these critical and indeed astonishing talks in Warsaw, it does not mean that the satellite nations are about to become free and independent countries. But it does mean that even the independence that Tito has enjoyed is a contagious thing.

It seems possible that our investment in Tito is paying substantial dividends. And it is certainly true that the forces of freedom—limited freedom—are stirring inside the vast Soviet empire. This in turn means that the forces of real freedom have an opportunity to seize the initiative if their leaders choose to do so.

October 24, 1956

The revolt in Hungary is continuing. The new Titoist government of Premier Nagy, less than twenty-four hours old, admits that heavy fighting is still in progress in Budapest. According to the Budapest radio, the action is centered about a barracks, which is besieged by revolutionary forces, and a party headquarters in the city's 13th District. The Budapest radio says that government troops, supported by tanks, are fighting for the second day to keep the headquarters from falling into rebel hands. And a state of emergency has been proclaimed throughout Hungary.

Train travel between Austria and Hungary is prohibited. My colleague, Ernest Leiser, reports from Vienna that telephone communications are also out and that the Hungarian government refuses to grant him a visa at this time. No one is being granted a visa to enter the country. Travelers in Hungary, and who have tried to reach Budapest, have found their way blocked by Russian tanks. One of these travelers estimated that 350 persons have been killed so far, but this can only be a guess. The Budapest radio itself admits that the casualties have been high. Throughout the day, the Budapest radio called on the rebels to lay down their arms, promising them amnesty if they would comply.

The action began late yesterday as a struggle for an independent Hungarian brand of Communism. The Stalinist premier was kicked out and the Titoist Imre Nagy put in his place. When violence continued, Nagy promised government reforms and a higher standard of living for workers. When this had no effect, he imposed martial law, then called for the support of Russian troops. The Russian people were informed of none of this until tonight. The news agency Tass said "underground revolutionary organizations" had attempted an uprising in Budapest "against the people's regime."

The breakup of empires—British, French and now perhaps the Soviet Union's—has made up a big share of the political news of this generation. It is possible to include all three of them in a single generalization, because their chief undoing has been nationalism. We still don't know where the process of disintegration will end with any of them. Indeed, it may be much too soon to speak of the breakup of the Soviet empire, though it hardly will again be what it was under Stalin.

All three empires have dealt with nationalism in different ways. The British made part of their empire into a commonwealth of purely voluntary membership. But the Commonwealth has been too diverse to continue a commanding role in world affairs. At the same time, British power in the Middle East and part of Africa has been sinking fast. The decline of British power is one of the sensational chapters of history.

The French tried to go modern by making the most advanced segments of the empire a part of France with full French citizenship. They bypassed the commonwealth idea and tried to hold their colonies by promising ultimate promotion to full citizenship. The program failed. France has lost Morocco and Tangiers outright and now is losing Algeria itself, despite its having been part of France for a century.

The Soviet Union under Stalin produced an empire at the close of the war that outweighed all other existing empires in military might and cohesion. It was a novelty; it was held together by Communist ideology and merciless party discipline. For a time it seemed that a new cement had been found that could hold even nationalist states together under a single dictator. One crack developed in Stalin's time—the rift with Tito. But the free world will not soon forget how frightening Soviet power became and how trivial the defection of Tito seemed for a time.

But Stalin died without leaving an heir to dictate ruthlessly in his stead. And now the Soviet empire, like the British and French, must cope with that solvent of empires, nationalism. There is not a little irony in this. Communist propaganda, in trying to wreck other colonial empires, lit and fanned the fires of nationalism in every colonial corner. Now these flames are lighting the skies over Warsaw and Budapest.

Some observers are saying that Khrushchev himself lit these fires inside the Soviet empire when he made his pilgrimage of repentance to Tito. Perhaps Khrushchev's head will fall. But probably only if someone unexpectedly becomes another Stalin. It is important to bear in mind that Moscow still holds the satellites by strong bonds. A few changes in satellite personnel and a few days of rioting will not much loosen them. One of these bonds is the continuance of Communist governments in Warsaw and Budapest. The Poles and Hungarians are not rebelling for the right to join the West, or for the blessings of Western civil liberties. They are rebelling for independence. They are nationalists. In the long run the majority may be able to put nationalists and non-Communists in the government. If they do, the Soviet empire would become un-recognizable. But that is not what is happening now.

November 2, 1956

> *The Israeli Army invaded Egypt, Israel said, to put a stop to Egyptian raids on its territory. Britain and France moved in with air, sea, and land forces to deal Nasser the death blow.*

It is only a slight oversimplification to say that what has happened in the last few days went something like this: Israel, Britain and France reappraised, with what agony we do not know, American leadership of the free world. They decided it was not good enough —did not serve their national self-interests—so they decided to use force. President Eisenhower decided to let them stew in their own juice.

The difference in attitude about the Suez Canal can be easily summarized. For us it is a convenience; for the British and French it is a condition of economic and national survival.

The primary intention of Russian policy for ten years has been to split the Western alliance, and now, for the time being at least, it has at last been split. And without any substantial help from the Russians. Our policy in the Middle East has been bewildering. We justified the contradictions by saying we were trying to preserve the peace. We did more than any other nation to persuade the British to get out of Suez. That meant the abandonment of a position of power. We refused to sell arms to Egypt. The Egyptians told us they would buy them from Russia. We apparently thought the Egyptians were bluffing, but they weren't. The deal was made, and Russia for the first time had a firm foothold in the Middle East.

The Israelis wanted to buy defensive arms to offset the threat of the Communist weapons bought by Egypt. We delayed and discussed. We encouraged the French, the Canadians and the British to sell a few obsolete aircraft and weapons to Israel. Either it was right or it was wrong; either it was in our national self-interest or it wasn't to see to it that Israel was not driven to desperation by the lack of defensive weapons. We did not make up our mind, but rather tried to arrange for Israel to get a few weapons under the counter.

We tried to bribe the Egyptians not to join the Soviet camp by promising to help build the Aswan Dam. Presumably we had figured the odds as to whether Nasser could carry out his end of the deal. Then we abruptly withdrew the offer. Both the offer and the withdrawal were political. Nasser's answer was to seize the Suez Canal. Nasser's stature increased in the Arab world. We rejected the use of force and insisted that the British and French renounce it, too. That meant that in the negotiations that followed Nasser knew that force would not be used, that he was safe in rejecting any attempt to restore international control of the canal. Mr. Dulles created the Users' Association, which is already forgotten. The matter came to the Security Council. We voted with the British and French for international control, but the Russians vetoed it. It was stalemate. We had gained no friends in the Middle East and had lost the friends we already had.

Now a word about what the British and French intend. They have announced that they want only a temporary occupation of the canal zone. Sir Anthony Eden stressed the word *temporary* in his statement in Parliament. They do not want to go all the way back to the time of permanent occupation. They want international control, as advocated in the resolution the Soviet Union vetoed in the council. They want a guarantee that Egypt will not be able to strangle their economies. They failed to get it following our lead; now they are going their own way. Many Americans consider their methods and devices reprehensible, but we already have agreed to their objective.

Russia threatened the invaders of Egypt with atomic retaliation. The United States, condemning its allies' action, pressured Britain and France to pull out. The Israeli forces also withdrew. Nasser not only kept the Suez Canal but surprised the West by running it successfully.

November 6, 1956

The Egyptian invasion, to Murrow, was too big a story to sit out in a broadcasting studio in New York. He flew to Israel and made this short-wave report.

301

This particular phase of this war is over. The Israelis control everything on this side of the Suez Canal. They aren't going anywhere else. At least not yet. The end came on a shirt-sleeve day, when people were bathing in the Mediterranean here at seven o'clock this morning. And this afternoon a few Israeli troops were bathing in the Gulf of Aqaba, way down at the end of the Sinai Peninsula.

They were mostly farmers and farmers' sons called up under the reserve. In forty-eight hours they had started moving, one brigade—about eighteen hundred men—across the desert to the Negev, which is no bargain for track vehicles, and then they moved into the Sinai Desert. They had five days' supply of water. They had no armor at all—just jeeps, four-by-fours and six-by-sixes. A few mortars. And the maps didn't tell them very much. That country is the most rugged I have ever seen. There was nothing like it in Korea. It all stands up on edge. There are no roads. They traveled the wadis, the dry beds of streams cut by flash floods.

The colonel commanding had been a driver for the British 8th Army in the western desert in the late war. He cut the loads on the six-by-sixes to two tons per vehicle. They hit sand dunes. And for twenty miles they had to push and pull the trucks by hand. They had one small fire fight, lost four men killed. At one time a C-47 dropped them some gasoline. They ran short of water. They had been civilians a week before, but they had all had their two and a half years of military service.

When they reached the dip of the peninsula, where the Egyptians had six-inch naval guns covering the entrance to the Gulf of Aqaba, they had to come out of a narrow wadi. The Egyptians were just starting to dig in, trying to put a stopper in the mouth of that narrow valley. The Israelis called for their air—it could operate unopposed because of the British and French destruction of Egyptian airfields. An Israeli pilot flying a Mystere Mark Four was hit by flak. He bailed out, started to run. The Egyptians were chasing him. Other Israeli fighters drove them off. And then a Piper Cub came in and picked him up at last light.

This afternoon, a brigade was formed on three sides of a hollow square. It was dusty, and the flies were busy. On the fourth side of the square stood a weapons' carrier, a nine-foot bamboo pole lashed to the bumper. The blue-and-white Israeli flag was broken from that little pole. Moshe Dayan, Israel's chief of staff, made a little speech standing on some ammunition boxes. He read a letter from Prime Minister Ben Gurion giving the Israeli casualty figures: 150 killed, 700 wounded and 20 taken prisoner by the Egyptians. Down there at the tip of the Sinai Peninsula there were no cheers, no demonstrations. The Israelis had been killed in this fantastic operation. There were about 700 Egyptian prisoners behind barbed wire and more coming in—those who had taken to the hills and came in when they were cold and thirsty.

That Israeli formation had traversed about 300 miles of desert. They were equipped with Bren guns, Sten guns, Italian machine guns, carbines, 45s. Some of them had tin helmets; some didn't. Some had stout leather boots; some wore sandals. Some were driving captured Egyptian vehicles, which are a lighter brown than the Israelis'. Someone from the quartermaster corps suggested that it would save tanks and money to paint all the Israeli vehicles the same color as the Egyptians'. There were no overt signs of emotion down there at the rim of the peninsula today. The Gulf of Aqaba is now open to Israeli shipping. The six-inch naval guns which controlled the entrance are silent. The farmers and their sons did it, a reserve outfit.

February 4, 1957

If the epitaph of the United Nations is ever written—assuming there is anyone about to write it—it will have to read: "Moral force was not enough." Not enough to prevent a planet from going over the brink into complete disaster. It was not moral force that stopped Communist aggression in Korea; it was the blood and metal of the free world, especially the United States.

It is easy enough for us to deplore the ineffectiveness of moral force when we are not directly involved. In order to get the thing in perspective we might look forward a few years to the time when a vast majority of the United Nations will ask us to get out of Okinawa, which we occupy by right of conquest. We are not likely to do so.

It was not the moral force of the United Nations that brought about the cease-fire in Egypt and the withdrawal of British, French

303

and Israeli troops. It was primarily the Russian threat of military action and the American threat of economic sanctions. In the case of Hungary, moral force of the United Nations was not strong enough to open the borders so that a few neutral observers could watch the slaughter. The degree of independence that has been won by Poland from Moscow's domination was not the result of a U.N. resolution but rather the bold, stubborn pride of the Poles who would be master in their own house, even though for the time being it remains a Communist house.

The value of the United Nations, other than being a public forum, is moral. And when national self-interest is involved, the moral power and persuasiveness evaporate. That is why the French say to the U.N., "Hands off Algeria," and the British say, "Cyprus is no concern of a world organization." That is why the Israelis say they will stand at the mouth of the Gulf of Aqaba and in the Gaza Strip, until firm and fast guarantees are forthcoming. That is why Nehru says there will be no U.N. forces in Kashmir. And it is for the same reason that this country would in all likelihood refuse to turn over to the U.N. any area regarded as vital to our national interest.

The United Nations has no automatic legal authority. It is not a government, and it can only hope to get what it wants by exerting moral power. In the Middle East crisis, the United States has been greatly concerned that the U.N. should exercise this moral power. But when it comes to trying to prevent the area from falling into the hands of the Communists, it is King Saud with whom we deal, who is not exactly to be equated with moral power. It has been proposed that the Israeli troops in the Gaza Strip and along the Gulf of Aqaba be replaced by U.N. forces. This could be done if both Egypt and Israel agree. They don't. And so long as they both refuse, the moral power of the U.N. is frustrated.

The world, even the small nations in it, remains more willing to put its trust in weapons in hand than in the moral power of the U.N. All nations seem to say: "Let all nations be upright, moral, responsive to world opinion—but at a distance."

March 5, 1957

A new nation came into existence tonight, the state of Ghana, formerly the African Gold Coast. This not only is a rare event; it is

304

happening in a rare way. Ghana is not raising its national flag amid the graves of a prolonged and bitter guerrilla war. One might almost say it is graduating with honors after a collegiate course in law and self-government. It has fulfilled the conditions set for membership in the British Commonwealth and now has achieved that status, including the full right of secession. This is true independence.

But it must not be made to sound too easy. Prime Minister Kwame Nkrumah, the first head of the new state, was sitting in a prison cell when his party won a sweeping majority in the election of 1951. He had been sentenced to two years for calling an illegal general strike. The British governor general wisely pardoned him so that he could take his place as prime minister. Then he went on working for full independence.

Ghana is a small territory, not much larger than England, and has a population just under five million. But it is the second largest earner of dollars in the British Empire, ranking next to Malaya. It produces half the world's supply of cocoa and has vast resources of bauxite, which may make it a big producer of aluminium once the great Volta Dam is built. It also has gold and diamonds. It may be small, but one day it may be very rich. Certainly it is no colony the British found troublesome and were glad to be rid of. They trained it for freedom and then recognized that the time for freedom had arrived.

So it becomes the first all-Negro colony of Africa to win its independence, the eighth member of the British Commonwealth—its first all-Negro member—and the ninth sovereign state in Africa. If Ghana makes a go of democratic independence, the other colonies may in time blossom in the same way. On the other hand, if Ghana does not live up to its promise, the future of Africa may be different. The present empires are sure to pass, but the nations shaped from their colonies would hardly be democracies. They would be dictatorships and would gravitate to the center of dictatorships in Moscow.

April 5, 1957

One of the puzzling phenomena in American life is the complacency of the public with a third-rate postal service. This comment is in order today because of the battle between the House Appropriations Committee and Postmaster General Summerfield over the restoration of thirty million dollars in the postal budget. Mr. Summerfield is threatening to stop rural and city mail deliveries on Saturdays altogether, along with other curtailments, if he doesn't get his money. The impoverishment of the postal service has been going on for a long time, and what is hard to explain is that the public doesn't mind. If it minded, the House committee wouldn't dream of crippling the postal services still further.

It would be hard to find a country that called itself modern that has as few mail deliveries as we do. In Tokyo, mail deliveries number six a day, and no large European capital is without at least four to five deliveries. New York City, which boasts of having the busiest post office in the world—one that carries one tenth of the nation's postal load—has one residential delivery a day. And now Postmaster General Summerfield talks of reducing deliveries to five a week.

Foreign postal deliveries are better, not only in number but in speed. Mail goes overnight almost from any part of England or France to any other part. It crosses London and Paris in a few hours. In New York, mail may take two days or longer to get from one side of Central Park to the other. Two days is the usual time for delivery between relatively close cities like New York and Washington, almost as though trains and planes didn't exist.

Because the United States Post Office is one of the biggest public utilities in the world, with a budget of around three billion dollars, its inadequacy is often put down to bureaucracy. But it is nearer the truth to say that the public can get what it wants if it is willing to pay for it, and it no longer is willing to pay for first-class postal service. The three-cent rate for first-class letters has been in effect since the depression year of 1932, without regard to the doubling of costs.

This raises some interesting speculations. One is that we are less dependent on personal mail than we used to be. More communication between businessmen, members of a family and friends is done by telephone, even though it costs more. One must think so, or the outcry against exasperating slowness of mail would shake the walls of Congress. Once upon a time the American community was knit together by its postal services. That was in the time when

Benjamin Franklin was proud to be at the head of the colonial posts. Today, the country is knit together by other media—by television, radio and telephone, as well as by the letters and periodicals that come through the mail.

May 2, 1957

Senator Joseph R. McCarthy died tonight at Bethesda Naval Hospital at the age of forty-seven. The hospital announced that he succumbed to acute hepatitis, a disease of the liver, at 6:02 p.m., Washington time. The Senator was admitted to the hospital last Sunday, when his condition was reported "serious." He is survived by his wife and an infant daughter they adopted early this year. McCarthy had been a Republican senator from Wisconsin since 1946.

May 30, 1957

Mao Tse-tung, the boss of Chinese Communism, has made two secret speeches that may prove to be as historic as the one secretly made by Khrushchev on the evils of Stalinism. They were speeches on doctrine and advocated a milder approach to domestic problems inside China. That suggests at once that the head of the Chinese regime realized that the brutal and oppressive tactics of the Communists no longer pay dividends.

And that, in a sense, was what Khrushchev was saying in his famous speech on Stalin. But Mao Tse-tung also criticized the Soviet conduct of the Hungarian crisis as though he wanted, above everything, to make sure that the same mistake will not be made in his own country. In doing so, he laid down a doctrine that in some particulars is miles apart from the Communism preached and practiced by the Kremlin.

This is important not only for its effect on six hundred million Chinese. It affects Communists everywhere. Already it has served to give strength and direction to the independent Communism of

Gomulka in Poland. But what may be still more significant, it sets up a second center of Communist orthodoxy, and so puts Peiping into potential rivalry with Moscow for control of the Communist world. That could have most far-reaching consequences.

The principle Mao stressed was that a Communist regime must not use the same power against its own people that it uses against an enemy. In China, he said, the class struggle is over. Divergences still remain, even between the bourgeoisie and the proletariat, but these are only an internal conflict among the people and must be dealt with by so-called "democratic" means; that is, by persuasion and free discussion. He said that if the Kremlin had dealt with the Hungarian crisis in this way, the violent outbreak of last autumn would have been avoided. The events in Hungary, he said, were due to the dissatisfaction of working people with the Communist leadership, not to the antagonism of the old bourgeoisie. And he added that Russia could expect more large-scale uprisings in Eastern Europe unless it changed its policy.

These statements certainly are irreconcilable with the official Peiping line on Hungary, which is one of complete approval of the suppression of the Hungarian uprising. One can only conjecture that Mao, as the sage of the party, said in privacy what was on his mind, while Chou En-lai, as foreign minister, said what seemed to be expedient.

The Mao speech is remarkable for more than the criticism of the Kremlin's handling of the Hungarians. He declared that strikes are a form of protest against the bureaucracy and must not be suppressed, or the strike leaders punished. He reaffirmed last year's slogan: "Let all flowers bloom together, let diverse schools of thought contend." Capitalists and intellectuals, he said, must be re-educated by mild, persuasive methods to combat bourgeois mentality. The same treatment should be given national minorities and religion. And he said that broadcasts of the British Broadcasting Corporation would be carried over the Chinese radio, together with some material from the Voice of America.

One effect of these speeches has been a new campaign in China, known as the "Change the Wind" campaign. Small discussion groups are meeting for heart-to-heart talks with non-party members attending. In this campaign the party is finding out who is dissatisfied with the regime, and if the winds change again, it will know on whom to crack down. For the present, more discussion is being allowed inside China, and the right to opposition is being recognized at least in theory. But this does not mean that anybody in the Communist party, from Mao down, dreams of allowing the opposition to win out or take over. It does appear that the harsh wind has been tempered, at least temporarily.

September 10, 1957

Token integration of Central High School in Little Rock, Arkansas, was scheduled for September 3. Governor Faubus surrounded the school with National Guardsmen in order, he said, to prevent violence. However the Guardsmen barred Negro students from entering, and the Justice Department asked U.S. District Judge Ronald Davies to restrain Faubus from obstructing desegregation of the school. It was the first major test between the federal government and a state government on the issue of public school desegregation since the Supreme Court decision of 1954.

If Governor Faubus should surprise everybody, and prove his case, either in Judge Davies's court or the higher courts, the South would have the formula for nullifying the Supreme Court ruling on integration. But if he fails to convince Judge Davies to begin with, a long delay is to be expected. He would appeal to the United States Court of Appeals, and if he loses again, to the Supreme Court. In the meantime integration in Little Rock would be suspended, and a breathing space would be provided.

No one will deny that the danger of violence in Little Rock and in other Southern cities at this moment is acute. But this is not the issue before Judge Davies. He is not ruling on conditions *today.* What he must decide is what they were before Governor Faubus called out the National Guard.

It is very much to the point to say that Little Rock, and the other Southern communities that are obstructing integration, are costing the country dearly in world prestige. The United States today was fighting in the United Nations Assembly for its resolution condemning the Soviet subjugation of Hungary. Today, also, we were trying to bolster up opposition in the Middle East to the extension of Communist domination. The Communists could not have asked for more timely and effective anti-American propaganda than our own dispatches about Governor Faubus, the dynamiting of a Nashville school and the use of troops to keep children from entering their schoolhouse. The damage is not only in the countries we are exhorting not to submit to Communist tyranny. We are losing the respect of our most dependable friends.

When the civil rights bill passed Congress it could be said that it would do us more good abroad perhaps than any measure since the Marshall Plan. But the benefit of the law has been snuffed out like a candle. And that is quite an achievement to attribute to a single person. And it does not lessen its consequences to every American for him to say he was doing what he believed to be right.

> *Judge Davies ordered Faubus not to interfere with the desegregation program. When violence broke out, President Eisenhower dispatched federal troops to enforce the court order.*

October 7, 1957

> *The Soviet Union orbited the first man-made satellite on October 4, 1957. Sputnik I weighed 184 pounds and circled the earth at 18,000 miles an hour.*

It is to be hoped that the explosion which flung the Russian satellite into outer space also shattered a myth. That was the belief that scientific achievement is not possible under a despotic form of government. Most of us have been taught to believe that scientists, if they are to be productive, must be free to follow the truth wherever it may lead them. We failed to recognize that a totalitarian state can establish its priorities, define its objectives, allocate its money, deny its people automobiles, television sets and all kinds of comforting gadgets in order to achieve a national goal. The Russians have done this with the intercontinental ballistic missile, and now with the earth satellite. Their emphasis has been on the development of weapons, rather than the creation of comfort. They have mobilized their scientific skills in the service of the state. And they have won a very considerable technical and psychological victory.

We in this country have been proud of our scientific achievement—our "know-how." We have brushed aside the fact that the original work in nuclear physics was done more in British and German laboratories than in our own, that our final success was in considerable measure due to the creative work of scientists from abroad. The atom bomb wasn't part of the cargo of the *Mayflower*. It was a cooperative international venture.

We should have learned from the Nazis that an unfree science can be productive. Their scientists came within months of winning the war for them. Had their jet fighters, their V-1s and V-2s been operational six months earlier, the outcome of the war might have been altered. The Germans were consistently ahead of us in the field of rockets and jet propulsion. General Eisenhower wrote in *Crusade for Europe*, "It seemed likely that if the German had succeeded in perfecting and using these new weapons six months earlier than he did, our invasion of Europe would have proved exceedingly difficult, perhaps impossible." So even the late war gave us no reason for complacency as to what a captive science can do. If the Nazis had had their extra six months, or a year, and had won the war, the freedom or lack of freedom of science would have had nothing to do with it.

Now the Russians have carried the rocket and jet propulsion to their logical conclusion. They have made both the A-bomb and the H-bomb. They have proved that they can turn out as perfect instruments of destruction as our own, and in some cases do it quicker. They are ahead of us in ballistic missiles. They are flying their satellite. The White House, in the person of Mr. Hagerty, may not be surprised or impressed, but the rest of the world certainly is.

I am not suggesting that our freedom is not our strength. We have the freedom and the power to make ourselves invincible by our conscious effort and by adequate sacrifices. This is surely a better way than the Russian way, wherein a few men at the top can deprive a herded nation of freedom, decent living standards and the dignity of the individual in order that all effort can go into military and industrial power. But in recent years we have put our security and our survival second to our desire for luxuries and gadgets—a sound economy is no substitute for a solid defense. There is no reason to think that we are less capable than the Russians when it comes to making weapons. We cannot and would not bend all of our scientific endeavor to the will of the state and for purposes of defense, unless it be done by persuasion, by leadership which the majority believes to be in the interests of the nation. The contest is not between scientists free and non-free, but rather between political capabilities. Under our system, we must be persuaded, our representatives must vote the money, the scientists must be recruited, the objective defined, and criticism must be permitted. The citizen and his representatives must agree to whatever sacrifices are required. So far, we haven't been asked to make very many.

There are men high in the defense establishment who contend that we are busily engaged in turning out weapons that will be obsolete before they are operational. We have failed to effectively pool the scientific talents of our allies. But the real question is not the relative capabilities of free and non-free scientists in the matter of making weapons of destruction. It is whether we, as a free people, care more for our own security than the dictators care for theirs. It rather looks as though the price for that security may be rather higher than has been advertised.

November 8, 1957

In a nationwide broadcast, President Eisenhower announced a program for overcoming the "science gap" separating Russia and the United States.

Two basic facts can be said to have moved President Eisenhower to go to the people in last night's broadcast. One is that the Russians have passed us in one vital respect, overtaken us in others and are catching up in many areas. The second fact is that we had not been prepared for this—we knew it, but failed to take it in—and now we must act if we are to restore our lead and redeem our leadership. The crisis called for a talk that showed concern in terms of the gravity of the situation. It called for a program of action on two levels—immediate action to push our weapons program and long-term action to enable us to outdistance the Russians in science and education and to stay ahead. And because the situation is alarming it called for reassurance, since we and our allies need a shot in the arm.

All three elements made up the President's broadcast last night: concern, reassurance and a program of action. But Mr. Eisenhower gave reassurance first place, action a close second and a show of concern third. His action program was limited to immediate steps. The long-term steps needed to establish the necessary educational program in science and technology are to be the subject of the next broadcast.

Because it dealt mostly with short-term solutions, the broadcast did not light up the full magnitude of the crisis. But the President devoted a few sentences to it. They are worth repeating. "It is entirely possible," he said, "that we could fall behind. I repeat, we could fall behind unless we now face up to certain pressing requirements and set out to meet them at once. According to my scientific friends," he continued, "one of the greatest and most glaring deficiencies is the failure of us in this country to give enough priority to scientific education and to the place of science in our national life. And no amount of money spent now on weapons can meet a future danger as the scientists see it," the President said, "because education requires time, incentive and skilled teachers."

The appointment of Dr. James Killian as the President's right-hand advisor was the big item in the action part of the talk. Dr. Killian has the confidence of scientists and commands respect as an administrator. Surprise was expressed today that he was not given cabinet rank. In a sense, his appointment is a repudiation of the policies of Defense Secretary Wilson, and he may need status equal to the Defense Secretary's to put through the new policy. It also was pointed out that President Eisenhower's treatment of the crisis seemed to add up to finding that what had been wrong was a defect in organization in the government. Obviously it was due to weak leadership, insufficient money and too little attention to science. But this is the way Washington reacts. The truth about the crisis was blurted out by Assistant Defense Secretary Foote to a Congressional committee yesterday. "The real reason we're behind the Russians," he said, "is because they started in 1945—that is, with rocketry. We didn't start until 1951 or 1952 because the sentiment after the war was against scientific and military development, and we slowed down."

What the President said about scientific cooperation with our allies had been anticipated. But it contained a word that no doubt is being studied uneasily in Europe today. Mr. Eisenhower spoke of sharing "appropriate" scientific information. The word *appropriate* implies a limitation, exercised at our discretion. He also seemed to limit sharing to information the Russians already have. Since our hope to equalize the Soviet intercontinental missile lies in using our medium-range missiles from Allied bases, the Allies are acutely aware of being in the front rank of danger. It may be doubted whether President Eisenhower convinced them that they are to become full partners in the projected rebuilding of NATO.

Perhaps the outstanding omission from the talk last night was a candid appraisal of the extent and nature of the sacrifices this country must make. The Russians have accepted sacrifices, however unwillingly, to be where they are. It will be harder for us to sacrifice, perhaps, because we must do it voluntarily. We must ask for it, as well as be asked.

February 25, 1958

It may have come as something of a shock to this country that the first genuinely free election in Argentina in thirty years has produced a regime that is expected to be neutralist and mildly anti-American. Arturo Frondizi, who won a landslide victory, does not admit that he is anti-American and says he hopes to improve relations with Washington. But a large number of his followers are Fascists or Communists, and he told Joseph Newman of the New York *Herald Tribune* that the recognition of Red China, while not decided, will be taken under consideration. And during the election campaign he promised that the lives of Argentinians would not be compromised by any regional pact—meaning an agreement with the United States.

Argentina is a special case, and the result of an election there is not typical of all Latin America. But the result is startling, and it raises a legitimate question whether Washington's somewhat studied indifference to democratic liberalism in Latin America has not been carried dangerously far. The basic conditions that determine political results are changing in Latin America, and it may be that truly free elections will produce more governments that shy away from the leadership of the United States. The good-neighbor policy, which brought Latin American countries into close accord, no longer appears as paramount. The near unanimity of all the Americas in great international issues no longer exists.

One reason for this is the United States preoccupation with the needs of European, Middle Eastern and Asian countries, which has led to a rising disinterest in the welfare of Latin America. Our influence has been waning for another reason, which is the too rigid insistence of Washington on keeping hands off domestic affairs below the border. We do not cultivate and encourage the personalities who hope to be the heirs of the reactionary or dictatorial regimes. This is a sound political principle if not carried too far. But we can have correct and even close relations with dictatorships, without throwing away our mass appeal as the great sponsor of political freedom and democracy. We should be making Latin Americans acutely aware that every step to extend democracy is sure of the sympathy of the United States. We have to be polite to the dictators, but we do not have to ignore their opponents.

If we get absorbed in conducting the Cold War on the other side of the globe, we may find the Cold War is being brought to our own backyard, and that we are strangely incapable of dealing with it.

March 18, 1958

Premier Gaillard won his vote of confidence in Paris today, but in Paris it is being said that even the starlings know that he will fall. All that is uncertain is when it will happen. And what everyone in Paris twitters about—presumably the starlings, too—is Gaillard's successor. Most of them are saying it will be General De Gaulle, who, if he is not the next premier, will be premier after the next premier. So General De Gaulle is on the verge of becoming an inevitability.

This is a promotion for De Gaulle. Until recently he has been a man in the background being used as a threat. Politicians treated him as a kind of shotgun to point at other politicians to force them

315

to do what they didn't want to do. Thus the Independent Party which, though conservative, doesn't want De Gaulle, threatens to pull out of the government if Gaillard makes concessions to Tunis in the Algerian crisis. That would bring De Gaulle in.

The shotgun is also pointed at outsiders, like the United States and Britain. Both governments are trying to promote a settlement between France and the Algerian nationalists. That would be a retreat for France and, in the eyes of ultra-patriots, a defeat. So France's allies are told that if they don't back up France in Algeria, they will get De Gaulle. And to the United States in particular that is meant to sound dreadful. Experience has taught Americans that De Gaulle has the amiability of a cactus. And his views are likewise forbidding. He was against European union. He is capable of taking France out of NATO.

What is remarkable about De Gaulle is that simply by standing silently in the wings of the French stage for a few years, events are now pushing him toward the stage. Maybe he is like the recession in America; nothing has made it so inevitable as just the talk that it is inevitable.

March 28, 1958

> *Khrushchev forced the "resignation" of Premier Bulganin and assumed power.*

One fiction in Soviet life has now come to an end—the myth of collective leadership. It was a convenient name to call the interim period in which contending leaders tested their strength against their rivals. It was clear from the outset that collective leadership in a dictatorship was a contradiction in terms. Sooner or later, by a kind of natural law, power would gravitate to fewer and fewer men, and ultimately to a single man.

Khrushchev must now proceed to consolidate his power. He has become fully and officially responsible for his radical industrial and agricultural reforms. He is now the commander of the satellites, the commander of Soviet scientific progress, responsible for improving living conditions at home, maintaining the peace and negotiating with the free world. He now is committed; he has to go all the way and take all the power. He cannot compromise. That, in a dictatorship, is the nature of things. He must deal with the disappointed followers of such men as Malenkov, Molotov, Zhukov and Kaganovich. He must placate the members of the industrial bureaucracy who have been downgraded through decentralization.

For the time being, Khrushchevism looks like Stalinism with a smile, a kind of semi-enlightened totalitarianism. Khrushchev is a realist, a product of the most brutal and cynical school in political history. He, better than anyone, knows the price of failure in that system. He is a gambling man and is now gambling on his ability to wield total power. Even if Khrushchev strives to be an enlightened despot, despotism is perpetually insecure. One reason is that the despot is mortal, and when he passes the walls shake and the ground quakes, and nobody knows whether the whole structure will collapse. He probably does not know whether this process of bloodless execution can continue, or whether he must resort to the strong-arm techniques of Stalin.

Already his vanity—never in short supply—must have been considerably inflated. Over the last two months, the Soviet press has carried on a hidden-persuader kind of campaign aimed at convincing the Russian people that Khrushchev is the world's outstanding authority on agriculture, housing, art, politics, ballistic missiles and international negotiations. His name is in the headlines every day; so is his picture, touched up so that he looks as though he's balding, not bald. He is hailed as "the leading theoretician of Communism"—that puts him in line with Marx, Engels, Lenin and Stalin. The Khrushchev personality cult is in full flower. If a summit conference is called, he wants to be the Russian leader who will talk with Mr. Eisenhower, not sit in the shadow of a figurehead premier. And Khrushchev, a devoted Communist, has an immense faith in the vitality and expansion possibilities of the Soviet economic system. He is convinced it can do any job, even catch up to the United States and surpass us, which would make Khrushchev, in the eyes of Communist history, a greater Communist than even Lenin.

Khrushchev feels that given ten years of peace, he personally can lead Russia to its final victory over capitalism, and not fire a shot. He believes he can bring Russia the unchallenged economic mastery of the world; then, by its example, the underdeveloped areas of the world will be brought into the Communist camp and the Western world will be isolated. That is his dream. At home he must continue to train scientists and technicians in increasing numbers, but like the enlightened despots of the eighteenth century, Khrushchev in this century may discover that enlightenment is a two-edged sword, that a literate population may turn against the despot.

No one knows what this elevation will do to Khrushchev the man, but Lord Acton was certainly right when he said, "All power corrupts, and absolute power corrupts absolutely." Khrushchev has made no secret of his intentions; we have been adequately warned.

April 7, 1958

It is by now possible to strike a kind of propaganda balance sheet on the subject of the suspension of nuclear tests. The Soviet announcement that it is giving up the tests has echoed around the world and it has met wide approval, much of it uncritical approval. It has not been recognized that the Soviet Union timed its offer to come at the conclusion of its own tests that contaminated the atmosphere more than any nuclear tests ever made. Nor was it widely noted that the Kremlin can resume testing any time it chooses and that its recess carries no provision for international inspection.

But the United States reply, which also has echoed around the world, has not won this wide approval. Our dismissal of the Soviet announcement as meaningless, and President Eisenhower's description of it as a "gimmick" have not been endorsed abroad. Mr. Dulles had a success with his argument that because we have a free press and an opposition party in this country, we are forbidden from winning propaganda victories in the Soviet way. This was a plea to the jury, but the jury was the American public. And winning over American support is only part of the objective of such propaganda; one might say a minor part. It is Allied opinion and world opinion beyond that has to be convinced if American prestige is to be maintained.

The American case was probably made less effective by Mr.

Dulles's revelation that President Eisenhower and his advisors had actually considered stealing a march on the Russians and announcing a suspension of nuclear tests first. They decided not to, and Mr. Dulles told why. It was not because such a course would be unworthy of us. It was for another reason, and on this reason we now have staked our prestige. Mr. Dulles explained that we do want to eliminate nuclear weapons from world arsenals altogether. But, he went on, if that is not going to be done, we wish to develop clean weapons that can be used effectively without mass destruction of humanity. It is a duty to the American people and to humanity, he said, to develop small, clean bombs for tactical use.

Had Mr. Dulles promised that we will use only the small, clean, tactical weapons and were foregoing strategic bombing and the concept of massive retaliation, that would have been revolutionary and much more sensational than any recess in tests. But that is not what Mr. Dulles meant. And what he said in effect was that we are determined to add to our present nuclear arsenal. It may well be in our national interest to do so. But many people who do not understand the complexities of disarmament negotiations or the rivalry in power believe that humanity would be better served by suspending tests than by adding new weapons, even clean ones.

What makes our case hard to explain is that there has been a kind of surge in Washington to modify our disarmament program and to start with an offer to suspend tests under adequate international controls. We had been linking this with a cut-off in manufacturing nuclear weapons, which the Russians opposed. But we have been on the verge of separating the issues so as to get disarmament negotiations going again. So what stands between us and the Russians on the test issue may be only international inspection. And Khrushchev in Budapest said that if that is so, the Russians are willing to negotiate international inspection. With that assurance we have a chance to restore our prestige. We can offer to call a recess in testing just as soon as our currect program is over, which is just what the Russians have done. Further, we can publish what we know about the record-breaking contamination from the Russian tests and point out again that we shall be testing relatively clean weapons. And we can offer to start negotiating the terms of international inspection immediately.

It is reliably reported that such an offer is under active consideration in Washington. If it is made, the world may recognize that a first step in disarmament is at last possible. If it is not made, some other proposal of equal persuasiveness had better be made quickly. Our prestige needs it.

September 10, 1958

> *During the summer, Communist China began shelling the offshore islands of Quemoy and Matsu on a massive scale. The United States warned that American forces would defend the islands if a Communist attack on them was deemed a threat to Formosa. Khrushchev warned that an attack on China would be regarded as an attack on the Soviet Union.*

Since the United States still stands close to the brink of war over the offshore islands in the Formosa Strait, the ordinary citizen is entitled to all the help he can get to understand why. What he is getting from Secretary Dulles does not go the whole way. Mr. Dulles himself admits this. In his news conference yesterday he said: "I am aware of the fact that the elements that go into making final decisions are so delicate, oftentimes not subject to public appraisal, that there lies a responsibility upon the President and his principal advisors that cannot be shared with the general public."

Mr. Dulles said that the elements in the situation are essentially the same as they were four years ago. But in 1955 the Chinese Nationalists evacuated the Tachen Islands, and Mr. Dulles was asked why that action did not threaten our position in the Pacific as he considers the loss of Quemoy and Matsu would do today. He replied, "The facts speak for themselves that our analysis of that situation was correct. I believe," he said, "that our analysis of the present situation also is correct." This hardly qualifies as an explanation. And if the parallel between the Tachen Islands and Quemoy and Matsu is examined further, the difference between them grows smaller. Four years ago, Quemoy and Matsu were not considered strategically vital to the defense of Formosa. Their value was not defensive; it was offensive. They would be stepping stones for a Nationalist invasion of the mainland. But today the value of Quemoy and Matsu has become defensive. The President himself has said so. The reason is not geographic. It is simply that Chiang Kai-shek has put a third of the Nationalist Army on them. If these men are lost, the defense of Formosa obviously is jeopardized.

Four years ago, we would not have gone to war over Quemoy and Matsu as such, and Congress did not include the offshore islands in the American guarantee. Today we might go to war over them. And the huge difference in American policy is the result of Chiang's decision to weaken his defense of Formosa by putting so many of his best troops on the islands. In other words, Nationalist China increased the obligation of the United States. It may be that Chiang was encouraged to do so by elements in this country. But it is certain he was not dissuaded from doing it, as surely he might have been. Now Mr. Dulles feels entitled to say that the threat of aggression against Quemoy and Matsu is a threat to the whole Western world, comparable to the threat in Korea and the Berlin blockade. Mr. Dulles spoke with so much conviction about this that one can be sure it is crystal clear to him. But the public would benefit from further clarification.

It is only fair to Mr. Dulles to point out that if he has presented an obscure case for United States policy, it may be due in part to his inability to talk freely about a Nationalist withdrawal from Quemoy and Matsu at this juncture. One is entitled to assume that he wants it, if it can be linked with a Communist pledge not to use force to regain Formosa. But that must come as the fruit of negotiation. Bargaining with Communists is sure to be tedious, tough and exasperating. However, to get to the bargaining table must be the basic United States policy, as Mr. Dulles himself stresses. And everything that Mr. Dulles and the President have to say about it can only be crystal clear if it explains that we really are doing our utmost to get there.

September 23, 1958

A House investigation disclosed that presidential assistant Sherman Adams had accepted gifts from Boston industrialist Bernard Goldfine and interceded on his behalf with agencies of the federal government. Three months after the disclosures, Adams resigned.

The retirement of Sherman Adams puts the American people on notice once more that something needs to be done to modernize the office of the President. It is one of the two most powerful offices in the world in its impact on world affairs. Its power over the affairs of this country is stupendous. The presidency shares all the duties and responsibilities of the federal government with Congress and the Judiciary. The other two branches are far-flung institutions numbering hundreds of picked men. The presidency is filled by a single individual. He alone is responsible for his office. Many Americans assume that he personally wields all his power, but this he does not and cannot do. The government has become too big and too complex. Even if the President had unbounded vitality, he could not do it. President Eisenhower, whose vitality is strictly limited, is able to exercise still less of it. But the rest of the power must be wielded by someone, and until last night that someone was Sherman Adams. Officially he was assistant to the President. In fact, he was assistant president, or to use another title, the general manager of an institutionalized presidency. As such he worked silently and invisibly; he was a powerful but not a public figure.

The problem of Mr. Adams's retirement is much less his relation with Bernard Goldfine and its ethical ramification than the simple one of filling his place. As presidential assistant he had done an exceptionally important work extremely well, and it will be hard to find someone as capable. No one who succeeds him will have had his five years experience of daily contact with President Eisenhower. No one will know as well how to mesh with the President's ideas, principles and attitudes. When a person of so much power bows out, a vacuum of power has to be filled. And now one of the most interesting tasks in Washington is how to fill it.

It can be done in one of two ways. One is simply to look for another but less experienced Sherman Adams and limp along with him till 1960. The other way is to take this opportunity to complete the modernization of the Office of the President. Mr. Adams had begun it, but did not go as far as he thought necessary. At one time he advocated a division of the presidential functions into three sections, with a chief of staff for each. One would have charge of the ceremonial duties of the office, one would deal with foreign affairs and the third with domestic affairs. He even played with the idea that these three staff heads should be vice-presidents, duly elected to their offices and responsible to the people.

Now the thinking has changed, and two assistants to the President are favored—one as chief of staff on foreign affairs, the other in charge of domestic affairs. The idea of a foreign affairs chief of staff came up at the time of Secretary Dulles's operation. General Walter Bedell Smith was about to be given the post when Acting Secretary Herbert Hoover, Jr., objected. Mr. Dulles is now well, but the idea persists. For many in Washington are under the impression that foreign policy, which is a function of the presidency, is now being made by Mr. Dulles with less than sufficient opportunity for the White House to study it.

A chief of staff for domestic affairs might do much to bring the President into close touch with individuals in Congress and public life, and keep him informed about what is being written and said throughout the country. This would avoid the effects of Mr. Adams's astringent regime, which has isolated the President in trying to conserve his strength.

One of the interesting suggestions heard in Washington is that Vice-President Nixon now be given an active role in the White House. He is reported to want it, so as to get administrative experience, and it might work in his case. But it could set a dangerous precedent. In future times the vice-president, even though a member of the president's party, could be a bitter rival of his and at odds with him on policy.

In view of the importance to everyone of the presidency, the modernization of the office deserves the widest discussion and the best possible solution. No appointment Mr. Eisenhower makes through the rest of his term can hardly have greater significance or usefulness.

October 12, 1958

Another Murrow-Friendly production on CBS television was "Small World," a half-hour program in which prominent persons in various countries exchanged views by short-

wave. Since communications satellites did not exist, partici-
pants in these international discussions were filmed sep-
arately. Later the segments—recorded voice and film—
were combined and broadcast from New York.

The dramatis personae of the first broadcast in this weekly
series, besides Murrow, were Prime Minister Nehru of India,
Governor Dewey of New York and Aldous Huxley.

MURROW: Good evening. "Small World" is a four-way intercontinental conversation dedicated to the proposition that talking over
each other's back fences is a good idea, electronic or otherwise. We
have linked together three continents with some twenty-four thousand miles of short-wave circuits and telephone links, and have
recorded the conversation at those points. From New Delhi, India,
Prime Minister Jawaharlal Nehru. Prime Minister Nehru has just
returned from some of the world's most inaccessible areas—Bhutan
and Tibet. How were those fifteen-thousand-foot passes on a pony,
Mr. Prime Minister?

NEHRU: I am afraid my voice is not very sweet, because I
brought back a sore throat from Bhutan.

MURROW: Well, we read you loud and clear from New Delhi.
There's a little carrier signal in the background, but I'm sure if Mr.
Dewey or Mr. Huxley have difficulty in hearing you, they'll let us
know. Mr. Prime Minister, I'm sure you've met our governor,
Thomas E. Dewey.

NEHRU: Yes, he was good enough to come to India.

DEWEY: I hope that Mrs. Dewey and I will have the pleasure of
seeing you again in New Delhi and enjoying your gracious hospitality.

MURROW: Mr. Dewey is in Portland, Maine. And from Turin,
Italy, Britain's illustrious man of letters, Aldous Huxley, whose
shocking predictions in *Brave New World* some twenty-three years
ago have turned out to be, in so many ways, prophetic understate-
ments. Good evening, Mr. Huxley.

HUXLEY: Good evening.

MURROW: Well, what about this modern communication in both
time and space. Is it a good thing that a whisper from New Delhi
can be heard in a matter of seconds in Formosa or in Washington?

NEHRU: That surely depends on what the whisper contains. It

may have a peaceful effect, or it may have the opposite effect if something wrong is said.

HUXLEY: After all, there is a phrase in the Gospel, "Sufficient unto the day is the evil thereof." May it not be also true, "Sufficient unto the place is the evil thereof"? Communications are so good that a relatively small evil anywhere is immediately propagated like the waves in a pond, when you throw a stone, to the utmost ends of the earth and causes very often excitements quite beyond what the immediate, small crisis warrants. I mean . . .

DEWEY: The trouble is that people forget the background against which other people speak, and we get irritated with what somebody says, and then they get irritated with what we say. For example, if I were sitting in New Delhi, I would be pretty careful about what I said about nations who had four or five million men under arms and a thousand miles of common border with them, as India has with Russia and China. They are there; they are very real. They are an aggressive threat, and I think I'd be both polite to them, and I would try to get along with them.

MURROW: Prime Minister Nehru, arising out of what Governor Dewey just said, I wonder if we might talk for a moment about neutralism and non-alignment. It will come as no surprise to you that you are frequently criticized in this country for that policy.

NEHRU: Yes. Well, Governor Dewey just said something which is partly an answer. That is, the world looks different from different standpoints. If we look at it from the North Pole, it will look very different. If you look at it from Washington, it will not be quite the same as from Paris or Peking. Or Delhi. Not only does the world look different, but the problems look different—and *are* different, in fact. Now I don't like the word *neutralism,* and I don't like it being said that India is neutral, but I do say that India is not aligned because we have no military alliance, and we do not wish to be associated with any military grouping. We think that thereby [as member of an alliance] we do not serve the cause of peace or, indeed, any cause. Thereby we merely add to the tensions, and that does not mean, of course, that we want to remain helpless and invite an invader to come to our country. Naturally, we have to take our own precautions. But we do feel that military alliances have added to tension—added to fears, added to armaments and not led to any real security anywhere. In fact, it rather lessened security.

HUXLEY: I sympathize very much with the Prime Minister's point of view. I feel that it's very valuable to have a great country like India outside the system of alliances, standing for a position of mediation. It seems to me that the more there is in the world which can exercise a mediating influence, the better for all concerned.

DEWEY: What would happen if the United States took that position?

HUXLEY: Well, I mean, the United States after all is trying, doing its best to negotiate. I mean, I think . . .

DEWEY: The reason I asked the question, of course, is supposing we went neutralist, too, who would protect the rest of the world from immediate conquest by the Soviet? They say they are going to do it, and the trouble is they might be speaking the truth, and probably are. They intend to take the rest of the world.

NEHRU: Well, I don't think they are quite as inflexible as all that except in the language of statesmen, which appears inflexible often enough. I think it is realized on both sides that rigidity doesn't take one very far, but statesmen have got a habit of speaking in rather rigid terms. I don't think, if I may say so, that a military alliance adds to security.

DEWEY: Well, if there is no alliance . . .

NEHRU: Where does it lead to? If it leads to a world war, it's all wrong. If it leads to constant tension, it's also wrong. So, by protecting oneself and what one holds dear, if we can reduce tensions by various processes, it's all to the good.

DEWEY: South Korea couldn't protect herself when the Communists launched their attack, and it took a whale of a lot of help from other people to keep them from being engulfed and murdered—and enslaved. That's the simple meaning of alliance. If the Communists attack you, we will come to your defense. If we don't do that, they'll take us one piece at a time, as they did at the end of World War II when they took Estonia, Latvia, Lithuania, Hungary and all the way down to Albania, and a hundred million people. We wouldn't like to see that continue and . . .

NEHRU: Well, you wouldn't like me to contradict Governor Dewey, would you?

MURROW: I am sure he would. I would.

DEWEY: I would. I certainly would.

NEHRU: I do not think history points that way at all. Modern history, if I may say so, has seen the failure of this military alliance system in Western Asia—the complete failure, in fact. The very thing that was sought to be avoided has happened there because of those military alliances. If in Western Asia you deal with the ruling authority, and that ruling authority is not thoroughly representative of the people, then the alliance is not much good, as happened in the recent case.

MURROW: That brings us to the question of Formosa. One of the principal points in your foreign policy, Mr. Prime Minister, has been non-interference in the internal affairs of other countries. In the Formosa Strait, who is interfering with whom?

NEHRU: Well, you have put me a question about which I have no doubt. We have recognized only one government in China, and that is the People's Government of China. We do not recognize the other government which may exist in Formosa. Apart from that, I cannot understand insofar as these islands of Matsu and Quemoy are concerned, which are about ten or twelve miles from off the mainland, how any government can tolerate having a hostile force ten miles from its mainland, and be bombarbed by it. It is a position which no government would like to face.

DEWEY: I think the World Court is the proper place to determine whose real estate those little islands are, and if the Communists won't agree to the World Court, then the United Nations could ask for an advisory opinion. I am sure that the United States would abide by the World Court, and I can't imagine that the Nationalists on Formosa would refuse to abide by it. It may well be that those islands are properly part of the mainland, and if so, the World Court, I am sure, would say so.

NEHRU: It's a very odd situation. The People's Government of China on the mainland is not recognized by the United Nations. If it is not recognized, how can you ask them to recognize any organ of the United Nations? One can't have it both ways. Either they must have a place in the United Nations, or else they will simply ignore the United Nations, as they have been doing.

MURROW: Of course, Britain and India recognize Communist China, and we do not. Winston Churchill once said that diplomatic recognition was not the conferring of a compliment but the acquiring of a convenience. Would you agree with that, Mr. Prime Minister?

327

NEHRU: Well, this is a phrase with which one may agree, but it doesn't, of course, give the whole truth. The point is, normally diplomatic recognition goes by the factual state of affairs, not by agreement of the country.

DEWEY: Perhaps it is an admission of the fact.

NEHRU: Yes?

MURROW: An admission of the fact and nothing more.

NEHRU: It's admission of a fact, yes, which, of course, may lead to other types of contact. That depends on the two countries—how far they wish to go.

DEWEY: Also, there is just another little problem as to what you do then with two Chinas, and the two-China concept is one that some people who want Red China in the United Nations are opposed to. So it's a very delicate and difficult negotiation. In due course, I think it will be solved. I just hope it isn't going to be solved by guns.

MURROW: Prime Minister Nehru, I remember your saying to me once, oh, a couple of years ago, that all politicians would be the better for having spent a few years in jail.

NEHRU: Yes.

MURROW: Do you still feel that way?

NEHRU: Oh yes. I think it's a very good discipline.

MURROW: Well, certainly some of your best writing was done in jail. Governor Dewey, you wrote a book. Do you think it would have been a better book had you written it in jail?

DEWEY: Well, it's not for me to say it could have been much better, but I—I am sure it would have been a whole lot worse if I were in jail, and this business of jail raises a question in my mind. I believe Hitler wrote *Mein Kampf* in jail. Didn't he?

NEHRU: In the British Museum.

MURROW: I think it was Karl Marx who did most of his writing in the British Museum. But, Mr. Prime Minister, speaking of Karl Marx, I gather from your writings that you have considerable respect for what Marxism has accomplished in the Soviet Union in the field of education and the social services, that your primary objection to Communism is that it is based upon violence—the threat of violence against the individual and the threat of violence against neighboring states. Is that correct?

NEHRU: My objection is to any suppression of the individual. I believe in individual freedom, in the development of creativeness in

328

individuals, and anything that suppresses that, therefore, I think is ultimately harmful. Secondly, that there is a background of violence in regard to other states. Partly, of course, this background has been created by the fear complex, because when the new Soviet state came into existence for years and years it had to defend itself against attacks, but it's a thinking that is too much involved in violence. But one thing about the Soviet which has struck me very much is their educational system. Apart, for a moment, apart from the particular color they give it—its ideological color—it's a good system for the child, and as for the scientists and others, they have a very great deal of freedom in it. I have a notion that if education is fairly good all around, it is bound to lessen the restrictions that are placed on individual freedom. The individual normally likes freedom. He may be duped into not liking it—that I don't know—but he normally likes it. He resists any pressure on his freedom, and therefore I thought that one of the hopeful signs in the Soviet Union was the great growth of education at all levels.

DEWEY: Well, my own feeling would be that—and I am sure as to this point that both the Prime Minister and Mr. Huxley would disagree—that where you put the instruments of production into the hands of the state, there being only two kinds of capitalism—state capitalism and private capitalism, where you do that, you have to, therefore, deliver such control over peoples' lives that you have a dictatorship, and dictatorship can basically be maintained only by force. So when you have what is known as socialism on a total national basis, where no one can work without the consent of the politicians of the moment, you have thereby created, automatically, totalitarianism, and I do not believe that the history of the world has ever shown any society where you had totalitarianism where it was not accompanied by brutality—force and all of the things that we regard as the most serious evils.

MURROW: I take it that the Prime Minister's hope is based in part at least upon the belief that if you cannot educate part of a man, that if you give him free and complete education in science, then his curiosity will carry him over into the field of human freedom and political freedom.

NEHRU: May I suggest to Governor Dewey that perhaps a way out of this difficulty of centralization of power should be decentralization, not only of the state power to a large extent but of economic

329

power, because those dangers come of centralization; I mean, whether it is a socialist structure or a capitalist structure. Also, Governor Dewey may perhaps know that while we talk in India about aiming at a socialist structure of society, we have far less socialism in India—social controls, rather—than the United States of America. The social controls become inevitable in a complex society, and they grow in spite of its economic structure. So there needn't be any fight about names, as far as I can see—or words—but I do believe certainly in decentralization, both insofar as it is possible of the political power and economic power. Further, I should like to mention that one can't lay down one simple rule for every country. The United States of America has developed in the last, well, two hundred years or more, into a tremendous power—great wealth, productive capacity and all that. Now, when I have to deal with my country, India, I have to start from scratch and do my job fairly rapidly. I can't leave it to normal processes which might take a hundred, two hundred years. That would be fatal for my—for me.

MURROW: Governor Dewey, for a moment there I thought Prime Minister Nehru was beginning to sound like a Republican, didn't you?

DEWEY: If you could always be assured that there was such great dedication to the peoples' liberties and to their welfare at the head of the state, I would have no fears at all of the concentration of economic power in the hands of the elected political leaders. But most of our history, and that of the rest of the world, is that, basically, people ultimately do rebel against concentrated—either political or economic power, and, therefore, I personally don't like to see both things combined in the same hands. Political power can always control economic power. When you give all power to one group, I doubt if you can maintain freedom over a period of time. At some time, the wrong fellow or the wrong type of group will get in and they will never give up the power. That's the fear that Mr. Huxley has so beautifully articulated.

HUXLEY: Well, those seem to me the two impersonal forces pushing in the direction of totalitarianism. Then there are the various technological advances, particularly in the field of psychology and physiology which can be consciously used, but I would certainly say that the pressure of population upon resources, and what may be called over-organization, are great impersonal forces pushing in the direction of more and more control. The problem, of course, of any underdeveloped country is the problem of capital. What the governor was saying just now about private and public ownership is really, in a sense, irrelevant. I mean, the real problem is where you are going to get the capital from. The private capital doesn't exist, and the public capital is extremely small. This is the immediate, practical problem now of where you are going to find the capital, and can you find it in other ways than by forced labor in one means or another, which has been the method used in totalitarian countries in the past. This is the most agonizing question, and I don't know, in the least, how it's to be solved.

MURROW: Well, Mr. Huxley, if it is true that there is a direct relationship between capital and freedom, is it not true that there is also a relationship between hunger and freedom?

HUXLEY: Suppose you have a population in which 5 per cent of the people are getting three thousand calories a day, and the remainder are getting under twelve hundred. Who is going to rule whom? It is pretty obvious that the people with three thousand are going to have the energy and the drive to dominate the remainder. I mean, this is one of the tragedies. We can talk about human rights, but to what extent does the word *right* have meaning to those who just don't ever have enough to eat.

MURROW: Governor Dewey, would you say that the best-fed people in this country are the most concerned about the preservation of our freedom?

DEWEY: I would think they probably were when they bothered to think about it, because they don't regard their freedoms as in any danger. In this particular country we have the embarrassing problem of worrying about too many calories, and it makes you feel that there is a pretty bad maldistribution of food in the world.

NEHRU: It is obvious that hunger—the satisfaction of hunger—is one of the primary needs. It's not much good talking about freedom to a person who is starving or is hungry. Of course, he wants freedom, but it is not a primary issue for him because he is suffering from another lack of freedom, which is terrible. That is lack of food.

MURROW: This was one half-hour of a two-hour conversation between Prime Minister Nehru in India, Governor Thomas E.

Dewey in the United States and Aldous Huxley in Italy. From "Small World," goodnight and good luck.

December 5, 1958

Secretary Dulles's speech yesterday on Far Eastern policy was notable for the crucial importance he attached to the non-recognition of Communist China and his vehemence in saying so. "If we were to grant political recognition to the Chinese Communist regime," he said, "it would be a well-nigh mortal blow to the survival of the non-Communist governments in the Far East." He also said, "It is certain that the diplomatic recognition of the Chinese Communist regime would gravely jeopardize the political, the economic and the security interests of the United States. The Pacific, instead of being a friendly body of water, would in great part be dominated by hostile forces and our own defense be driven back to or about our continental frontier." That adds up to saying that the maintenance of the free governments in Asia is of utmost importance to this country and that the non-recognition of Red China is essential to save them.

But this speech was also notable for something it did not say. It omitted any reference whatever to India, which is the largest non-Communist country in Asia and, indeed, the world, and which is now in dire need of economic aid. India finds itself under great pressure from Red China, a land of impoverished peasants like itself which is using the most drastic and despotic methods to raise its standard of living. The methods are repulsive, but if China succeeds by them, and India's own efforts in freedom should fail, it appears inevitable that India will fall to the Communists. That would seem to be more decisive for the rest of free Asia—and to the United States—than Mr. Dulles's policy of not recognizing Red China.

Mr. Dulles did not omit India from his speech because he is not concerned about helping that country. The State Department has worked hard to induce the Administration to broaden its program of aid to India. But Mr. Dulles was making a speech about Far Eastern policy, and India may have been overlooked because it is not a Far

Eastern country. But it is significant that what Mr. Dulles said about saving the free countries of Asia did not emphasize the rivalry between them and Red China in achieving prompt economic success. Right now the Red Chinese are getting some striking economic results, as Mr. Dulles admitted. The increase of their agricultural output this year is at least 30 per cent. They are spawning small industries all over the country. And they are exploiting their huge labor reserves to create public works on a large scale, thus turning this labor into immediate capital investments.

The contrast with India is striking. The second Five Year Plan has until April 1st, 1960, to run. By next April there will be a shortage of 350 million dollars in foreign exchange. The sum must be borrowed or begged. India is getting this amount from the United States, Britain, West Germany, Canada, Japan and the International Bank. But by April the following year the foreign exchange gap will be another 600 million, and the same crisis recurs. The cost of putting India on its feet is high, nearly a billion dollars just to close the foreign exchange gaps, and perhaps another billion or two billions to make the third Five Year Plan a success. But if the free countries in Asia are not to choose the Communist short cut, this seems to be part of the price.

The nature of the Asian struggle has changed. An old friend of the United States, Ambassador Romulo of the Philippines, spoke out frankly last night. Asians, he warned us, are not interested in our own way of life, or our political and economic doctrines. "The struggle which interests Asians," he said, "is the bitter struggle for life itself, the struggle against hunger, poverty, disease and ignorance." And he added, "The once ingrained belief in the Asian mind of the invincibility, superiority and invulnerability of the West is gone—finished, forgotten. And what is happening in Asia, when Asia looks at the United States, springs from this fact."

January 2, 1959

The astonishment caused by Fidel Castro's rise in Cuba is a reminder that people still do not properly evaluate the power of guerrilla warfare. If skillfully used, it can be the greatest material force in the modern world, next to nuclear energy. Perhaps it has changed things even more than atomic energy. For guerrilla warfare won China and thus was able to commit a nation of six hundred million to Communism. It smashed the French empire— first in Southeast Asia, then in North Africa. It won its first great modern victory in Yugoslavia under Tito, and it has since revolutionized the basic concepts of military power. The up-to-date army of planes, tanks and highly drilled infantrymen is helpless before guerrilla fighting, if the guerrillas have support of the local population and the will to win. As Batista, the fallen Cuban dictator, put it, an army needs a hundred men for every single guerrilla fighter. The most significant thing about Fidel Castro may be that he grasped the potential power of guerrilla warfare while in his early phase.

February 3, 1959

> *An ailing Senator Green, of Rhode Island, relinquished the chairmanship of the Foreign Relations Committee and was succeeded by Senator Fulbright, of Arkansas.*

In our system of government the President makes foreign policy with the advice of the Senate, which gives the Senate Committee on Foreign Relations special scope and influence. It can examine and question pretty much what it pleases in the field of foreign affairs. The Secretary of State, through whom the President conducts his foreign policy, can be under no illusion that he is immune from criticism by the committee or can hold back information from it. His success to some extent is mortgaged to the committee. So in foreign affairs three men play the greatest role—the President, the Secretary of State and the chairman of the Senate committee.

Normally the committee does not cause much trouble to an administration. Usually the party in power in the White House is also in power in the Senate, and party regularity smooths things out in the committee for the Secretary of State. Normally, too, the seniority system does not put an exceptionally strong man at the head of the committee. But these are not normal times. The Administration forces are a minority in the Senate, and the new chairman of the Foreign Relations Committee is a strong man who for some years has been outstanding for his criticism of Secretary Dulles.

"Bipartisanship in foreign policy" has been a saving phrase for secretaries of state since the days of Senator Vandenberg. It could be evoked to shut off unpleasant debates. But it is a little hard to fit Secretary Dulles and Senator Fulbright into the old pattern bipartisanship. Both are too positive for that. Who is going to dominate the other? Mr. Dulles conducts foreign policy with more independence from anyone save the President, and certainly from the State Department, than anyone in modern times. He is not going to junk what he has so carefully built up for the sake of Senator Fulbright. And the Senator, who has been unhappy over the way Mr. Dulles runs things, is not going to keep his mouth shut to suit the Secretary. So it is suggested that we are now entering an area of what the British call a "loyal opposition" in foreign affairs. In Britain, that means unfettered debate but no obstruction. Presumably Senator Fulbright would subscribe to the doctrine of no obstruction. There is no question about his belief in unfettered debate.

Senator Fulbright is interested in finding a new approach to the issues between us and the Russians. That is, he wants to settle them. It is significant that last night, after the first conference with the Secretary since becoming chairman, he could report that Mr. Dulles is looking for counterproposals to put to the Russians in the present crisis. This was not the result of the Senator's persuasiveness, but it was what he was delighted to hear. He and the Secretary will be happy together only if the search goes on for new proposals to make to the Russians; that is, the Senator wants a positive policy.

Mr. Fulbright has waited a long time for the power and distinction he now will enjoy. As long ago as 1943, when a member of the House, he wrote the Fulbright resolution which authorized the United States to enter the United Nations. Later he authored the plan for the exchange of students and teachers with foreign countries which has made the name Fulbright better known in school circles around the world than that of Cecil Rhodes.

At fifty-three he is a world figure and chairman of one of the most powerful of Congressional committees. With an unusually able complement of senators on the committee, he can genuinely "advise" the Administration as the Constitution prescribes. And he also can serve the public here and abroad with constructive discussion of foreign policy.

February 10, 1959

> *The White House announced that Secretary of State*
> *Dulles was entering Walter Reed Hospital for correction of*
> *a hernia condition. It was his last illness.*

Those who disagree with Secretary Dulles's foreign policy do not on that account lack admiration for his character, devotion and ability. And they join his strongest admirers in deploring his absence from his desk just as the German crisis [over Berlin] comes to a head. He had grasp of the situation as no one else in this country. He had had the privilege of consulting, in turn, Mr. Macmillan, General De Gaulle and Dr. Adenauer, after being the guiding figure at the last NATO foreign ministers' meeting. For him to take leave at this moment introduces an element of uncertainty into the conduct of Western policy toward Russia. President Eisenhower cannot take his place either in running the coalition or shaping American policy. He begged off from spending more time than he does on foreign affairs when questioned at his news conference today. Undersecretary Herter may have the stature to fill Dulles's place, but he doesn't have the essential prestige. And he, too, is not a well man, being handicapped by arthritis. Undersecretary Dillon, now acting during Mr. Herter's absence, has knowledge, realism and ability, but hardly qualifies as both a national and international pilot at this juncture.

Mr. Dulles obviously feels quite keenly that he is well-nigh irreplaceable at this moment in the East-West conflict, and indeed he seems to be. No doubt it was this sense that led him to write as he did to the President. For he said he would continue to be available for consultation with him and with the acting secretary of state, and added that he welcomes the opportunity to have some time free from routine cares so as to concentrate on the problems of the coming East-West negotiations. But this letter tends to advertise the serious effect of Mr. Dulles's illness on the conduct of foreign affairs. For though he has kept a long-standing promise to take leave the moment he is unable to do his work, he has not really made room for anyone to take his place. He will go on being the President's chief advisor from his hospital bed and will keep on guiding his subordinates. And so long as he says he intends to do this, no one else can gracefully undertake the planning job.

So the wise guidance of American and Western foreign affairs depends on the Secretary's ability to go through another surgical operation and regain his fullest vitality in a few weeks. This is a gamble. It may turn out all right. Mr. Dulles sincerely believes that it will; so does the President. But it is no disparagement of Mr. Dulles's almost fabulous capacity to surmount his disabilities to say that the odds of the gamble are not overwhelmingly in his favor.

June 26, 1959

On his evening radio broadcast, Murrow announced that he was taking a leave of absence.

Tonight this reporter departs this microphone for a year's leave of absence—a departure which has been rather overpublicized. Permit me a few words of personal explanation. I haven't been fired, haven't quit, my health is all right. For many years there has been a clause in my long-term contract with CBS permitting me to take a year off. I asked for the year off, and the corporation granted it. For twelve of the more than twenty years that I have been broadcasting, reports have been made at this time. They have represented the work of many people, here and abroad. We have tried not to abuse this privileged opportunity to communicate and have not knowingly done violence to the truth. I would speak my gratitude to my colleagues and critics, both too numerous to mention by name.

The next year will be spent in traveling, reading, listening, keeping silent—in the language of radio, receiving instead of transmitting, trying to fill in some of the enormous gaps in my knowledge of this fascinating world. Unless curiosity curdles, I shall return to face this frightening microphone with a little more knowledge and assurance, at least the illusion that I know what I am talking about, being fully aware that some of you are of the opinion that this reporter has suffered from an acute sense of that illusion for many years. My thanks to those of you who have reminded me that an amplified voice does not increase the wisdom or understanding of the speaker. At the end of the year I shall hope to have learned a little. The hope may be vain, but the prospect of trying is most pleasing.

It was the last daily newscast he did. On his return, Murrow continued his work with "CBS Reports" and undertook a weekly radio program, "Background," featuring reports by CBS News correspondents and his own analysis of the news.

July 3, 1960

Murrow's first report after his sabbatical was made on the program "Background."

This reporter has spent most of the past year looking at his own country from the outside, wandering about the world, and would offer a few personal observations.

Vast areas of the world, including much of Western Europe, would like to contract out of the current power struggle between the United States and the Soviet Union. They reason this way: If these two great giants decide to destroy each other at extreme range, we, too, may perish—but not earlier than if we tie ourselves to the tail of this rather erratic American kite. Western Europe is relatively prosperous and would like to remain that way, and is unwilling to make major sacrifice in preparing its own defense.

For the time being, the West Europeans have no alternative but to maintain solidarity with the United States. Official statements of agreement and common purpose abound and will continue. But there is discernable, and not far beneath the surface, the desire to become a spectator. Bellicose statements by American generals and admirals may impress the Russians; they certainly depress and at times frighten our allies. We should talk more quietly about our big stick, which doesn't appear to be as big as it did a few years ago.

In the so-called "backward" or "emerging" countries, we encounter a special problem. We appear to expect them either to imitate us or to obey. They are going to do neither, and no amount of economic aid will change that. They can't imitate us because ours is to a large extent a society built upon business, and they don't have any businessmen. Moreover, they're not terribly attracted by consumer goods which rapidly become obsolete. There is here not a competition for men's minds but for their bellies. Or, if you prefer a more elegant word, the competition is in the area of expectancy. Below a certain caloric intake, the words we cherish—freedom, independence, human dignity, the right of dissent—are quite simply without meaning. We ought to draw the obvious conclusion from the fact that nations to which we acted as midwife and fairy godmother have decided that our way is not their way. We cannot expect gratitude for our generosity. We should give over the idea that anyone who criticizes our country or its policies is automatically a Communist.

As viewed from the outside we are running a luxury establishment. True, we have given money, but it has come from our fat, not our muscle. We have not sacrificed in order that others might achieve.

There is a widespread suspicion that in our country things are in the saddle and ride mankind, and that we have lost our appetite for change.

We in this country can't be deposed, and we are unlikely to resign, from the position of leadership that has been thrust upon us. Since the late war we have saved Western Europe from going Communist. We have learned for the first time the irritation that comes from having allies. We have learned that although we are the paymaster for new nations, they will not imitate us. But we have forgotten that we, and not the Russians, hold the patent rights on revolution, forgotten that those who strive to be free deserve our aid and assistance, even though they be not public or proclaimed friends of ours. Our power, our wisdom, our generosity cannot be limited to those who agree in advance that they will slavishly imitate us.

After a year of wandering about the world, this reporter would suggest that on our national birthday we remember that we are only 184 years old. In the saga of nations, that brings us to the edge of maturity. We are young, but we are not bold. We are troubled about our neighbors on this shrinking planet. We can no longer give the old excuse of our youth for our indecision. My own feeling is that what we do in this country in the field of human freedom, expanding educational opportunities, the right to dissent without being accused of disloyalty, the right of the citizen to question the rightness of his rulers is now being conducted in full light of the mass

339

media. Our best hope of survival, to say nothing of leadership, is that we in this country can demonstrate—in action and in terms of our friends and those who are searching for new allegiances—that righteousness exalteth a nation.

Our example may be more important than our dollars.

August 7, 1960

> *The presidential candidates—Kennedy and Nixon—seemed*
> *preoccupied with foreign policy.*

There will be ample time later to examine the record and performance of the two young men who are engaged in such a relentless pursuit of the presidency. Right now I am uncertain—somewhat bewildered—and therefore speak with the utmost restraint when I suggest that, as of now, both parties are in some danger of perpetrating a fraud upon the American people. The solution to the problems that press in upon us simply cannot be as simple or as painless as they have been made to appear. There is not the slightest chance that any government can supply security from womb to tomb, solve the problem of civil rights, expand our economy, compete with the Russians economically and militarily, nourish the underprivileged nations and continue with business as usual. It is doubtful that we as a people can stand in line for a second helping of automobiles, refrigerators, television sets and all the rest while more than half the world goes to bed hungry at night.

Both parties are running against Khrushchev. Both agree that the outcome of the election may be determined by the voter's opinion as to which man is most capable of dealing with Khrushchev in the kitchen, at the U.N., or elsewhere. They may further inflate Mr. Khrushchev's already high opinion of himself, but it contributes little to the solution of the problems that confront us. We are not in the process of choosing a champion who can do battle with Khrushchev. Foreign policy is not either words or dollars. It is power—stability. It is tolerance. It is example. It is the sum total of what we are. It is not traveling salesmanship; it is not proposing worldwide free elections for people to choose between Communism and our way of life. It is steady, implacable, persistent pursuit of aims that are shared by men who are, or desire to be, free. When we support governments abroad that do not enjoy the support of the people they govern we create the impression that we have no real or abiding interest in liberty, decency or justice, and that we have departed from our own doctrine and our own heritage.

Our split personality is apparent to our friends and enemies alike. In the Mediterranean area we stand firmly with one foot planted in Fascist Spain and another in Communist Yugoslavia. One day last winter I lunched with the editors of the *Züricher Zeitung*, one of the great newspapers of Middle Europe—or of the world, for that matter—and one of them said to me, "It has just been announced that your great President is going to stop in Madrid to cuddle up to Franco, while he has also appointed a committee to examine into the reasons for anti-American sentiment in Latin America." He suggested that one step or the other was not necessary. Our enemies and our friends were looking when the President went to Formosa, accompanied by the Seventh Fleet with five hundred jets flying cover about a hundred miles off the mainland of China. The visit perpetuated the myth that Chiang Kai-shek's government represents six hundred million Chinese, when there is no assurance that it represents the majority of the Formosans. It is a fair question to ask what our reaction would be if Khrushchev should arrive in Cuba accompanied by such a display of military might.

Spokesmen for both parties have welcomed economic competition with the Soviet Union, but they have not gone on to ask the basic question: whether a free enterprise system can compete effectively with a government trade monopoly which can operate at a loss for political purposes, whether it is necessary to grant huge tax concessions to American corporations operating overseas, new guarantees against expropriation or even relaxation of the antitrust laws to deal with foreign trade. I do not know the answer, but we are unlikely to find it until we begin asking the right questions. Senator Kennedy is fond of quoting Winston Churchill. Our attitude ought to be, instead of arguing about who can best stand up to or deal with Khrushchev, we might say to him what Churchill once said to Hitler: "You do your worst. We shall do our best." But candor would compel either candidate to add to that the doing of our best will not only be expensive in terms of dollars; it may.

require sacrifices, sacrifices made in cold blood going far beyond anything we encountered in the last two wars.

I am not sure about the missile gap, but there is developing between us and our allies and the neutrals a confidence gap. It can probably be bridged by the new President, but not merely with words or dollars or goodwill business. It will have to be done to a large extent by the example that we as a nation set. We will, I suggest, have to get over the idea that all criticism of our policies, both at home and abroad, stems from Communists. We will have to abandon the juvenile notion that those who are not unquestionably with us are automatically against us and that neutralism is a nasty word. Present developments in the Congo illustrate the importance of neutrals. Had every nation been lined up firmly on one side or the other, collision would have been inevitable. The neutrals give the big powers elbow room to maneuver. Under the forced draught of events, and the cool judgment of men such as Hammarskjold and Bunche, the world has taken two staggering steps in a direction of sanity—the U.N. Emergency Force in the Gaza Strip, separating Egypt from Israel, and now the operation in the Congo.

If the two presidential candidates meet in debate, we may discover not only whether a man's face can hide what is in his heart but what the two men propose to do other than stand up to Khrushchev. Two proposals already made in the field of foreign policy merit attention. The Democratic proposal that a National Peace Agency be established, committed to a sustained effort and study of disarmament. In short, to determine a basis, if any, upon which we are prepared to settle with the Russians. The second was Mr. Nixon's promise that if elected he would bring all the nonmilitary agencies operating abroad into one group. There is no question that our overseas representation is bloated, that we send too many people abroad for too short a time with too little training, with too little knowledge of languages and too little curiosity about the history and culture of the countries where they are stationed. There are some shining and, indeed, inspiring exceptions, some people of ability of a very high order. Our Foreign Service and the U.S. Information Service are both improving. But they can do no more than reflect or report what is happening here.

The big story in terms of news—and, I suspect, in history—is right here in this country. There is an obvious danger in this political preoccupation with foreign policy. That is that in the heat of the competition things may be said which will mislead grievously either our allies or the Russians. That is a danger that is inherent in our system. But our political campaigns are fortunately not confined to serious, somber issues. There is still room for the political story. And we'll hope to tell you one from time to time.

October 2, 1960

The electorate witnessed a major political experiment on September 26, when Kennedy and Nixon confronted each other for the first of four nationally televised debates.

I shall try to say a few words about the great debate that wasn't. It has been the subject of public comment, ranging from sports writers to Arthur Krock. Much of the comment has had to do with manner and appearance, rather than with content.

It seemed to this reporter that both candidates had adopted the attitude of most sponsors—do not under any circumstances offend anyone. They extended this doctrine to the point of not offending or directly challenging each other. It was a demure and superficial affair, created widespread discussion, may have made some dent in the apathy of voters but contributed very little to the illumination of the basic issues of domestic policy.

It should be clearly understood that the format—the method of presentation, the division of time, the presence of the interrogators—was recommended by the candidates and accepted by the networks. Members of Vice-President Nixon's staff insisted upon special lights, which did not operate to the advantage of their candidate. His make-up would have brought no joy to the heart of a professional in that exacting art. There has been considerable comment upon the obvious fact that Mr. Nixon perspired. It so happens that some people sweat mightily under those lights, and others don't. It is no proof of either nervousness or uncertainty. Maybe in the future two managers will have to negotiate the temperature to be created in the studio.

It was also the candidates' demand that the encounter be broadcast simultaneously on all three networks. No reasonable man could have expected that the subject of domestic policy would be exhausted in one hour. It might have been more statesmanlike, more of a service to the public—certainly less monopolistic—to have presented three one-hour programs at different times on different networks. There would seem to be no compelling reason why, in a competitive society, two politicians should be relieved of competition.

This was the test flight of a new technique, and consideration is now being given to certain changes in the rules. The first effort was rather like a widely advertised confrontation between Matt Dillon and Bat Masterson, where neither drew his gun or even talked tough. I am not suggesting that it would be useful, or desirable, to have political dialogues resemble a barroom brawl, but one of the arts of politicking on television is to avoid a question without appearing to do so. If this practice is to continue, it might be more revealing if the two candidates were required to dodge each other's questions, with only a third man in the ring to hold a watch and maintain order. In this week's encounter it seemed to this reporter that neither man entered the ring. Nevertheless, it represented progress of a kind, and the double political act is undoubtedly here to stay.

January 22, 1961

> *This was Murrow's last newscast. By the following Sunday, when he was scheduled to be heard again, President Kennedy had appointed him director of the United States Information Agency.*

During the past week, we have heard two major speeches, one by the oldest President in our history, the other by the youngest. Both speeches were prepared during the period of transition which has been carried out with unprecedented cooperation and good will, and in the hope that the words spoken might find a dignified resting place in history.

Eight years ago, in his first inaugural, President Eisenhower said that we were living in "a time of tempest." His speech was devoted almost exclusively to foreign policy. But in his farewell message he devoted much time to domestic affairs, or rather to the impact of the world situation upon our society. The Eisenhower concern, as I read it, was a fear that we may lose our liberties while preparing to defend them. He reminded us that our military organization is unprecedented. We have created a permanent armaments industry of vast proportions. Three-and-a-half million men and women are directly engaged in the defense establishment. Each year we spend more money on military security than the net income of all the United States corporations. He counseled us to guard against the unwarranted influence of the "military-industrial complex." He was, in fact, suggesting that the machine may get beyond human or political control, that we could reach a point where, in fact, "things would be in the saddle and ride mankind."

And then the retiring President went on to issue another solemn warning. In speaking of the technological revolution, he said, "Research has become central; it also becomes more formalized, complex and costly. A steadily increasing share is conducted for, by or at the direction of the federal government." He indicated that our free universities have experienced a revolution in the conduct of research; because of the huge costs involved, a government contract becomes virtually a substitute for intellectual curiosity. Mr. Eisenhower regarded with gravity the prospect that the nation's scholars might come more and more to be dominated by the federal government because the government puts up the money for the research. In short, he warned that our limited supply of scholars might come to spend their time looking for what the government asks them to look for and is willing to pay for, rather than pursuing the truth wherever that pursuit might lead them.

President Eisenhower issued another warning when he spoke of the danger that public policy could itself become the captive of a scientific, technological elite. In that phrase, he appeared to be warning of the real danger that as our technology and our weaponry become more complex, more sophisticated, more difficult to understand, more baffling and bewildering to the layman, the individual citizen may abdicate his responsibility, come to believe that he is not wise enough to exercise the power of choice, and that he had best leave the whole matter of running the country to the experts who do understand, or at least claim to understand.

President Kennedy's inaugural speech was brief, confident without being arrogant, firm but not belligerent, somber in tone but resolute withal. Mr. Kennedy did not refer to the recession, but he has said that a situation in which more than five million Americans are unemployed is a condition that must be remedied without delay. A depressed areas bill may be the first legislation to reach the new President's desk.

In the new President we are seeing the operation of traditional forces. For whatever qualities or qualifications past Presidents have brought to the office, the interesting and important development has been what the office has done to the man. It surrounds him with a certain indefinable aura, and there is no escape. His actual power is less than it is generally believed to be, and most of that power rests on his ability to persuade.

The impact of the office upon the man was evidenced not only by President Kennedy's inaugural speech; it was perhaps even more clearly in evidence in his speech to the Massachusetts Legislature. It was a speech tinged with a sense of awe. Success or failure would be determined by the answers to four questions. The first was courage—courage to stand up not only to enemies but to one's own associates, courage to resist public pressure as well as private greed. The second question was judgment, of the future as well as the past, wisdom enough to know what we did not know and enough candor to admit it. Third, integrity. Never run out on the principles in which you believe or the people who believe in them. Neither financial gain nor political ambition should ever divert from the fulfillment of our sacred trust. And, finally, Mr. Kennedy was willing to be judged on the matter of dedication, with an honor mortgaged to no single individual or group and compromised by no private obligation or aim, but devoted solely to serving the public good and the national interest.

Those are high standards by which to judge any man or group of men. As of today, that speech and the inaugural address must be regarded as rhetoric, though rhetoric of a high order. For the record of courage, judgment, integrity and dedication is just beginning to be written.

President Kennedy's inaugural address could be summed up by the quotation: "Difficulty is an excuse history never accepts." He did not minimize the seriousness of the times. He promised that we shall pay any price, bear any burden, meet any hardship, support any friend or oppose any foe in order to ensure the survival and success of liberty. He promised that he would cherish old allies, and he promised new nations that they would not pass from one form of colonial control into a far more iron tyranny. By implication, he welcomed the neutral states into the society of the free, so long as they are truly neutral. There was a special pledge for Latin America, to help cast off the chains of poverty and to see to it that the Western Hemisphere remains the master of its own house.

The new President asked that both sides begin anew the quest for peace, remembering that civility is not a sign of weakness and that sincerity is always subject to proof. "Let us never negotiate out of fear; but let us never fear to negotiate."

There was a word of warning for those who expect great speed. "All these things will not be done in a hundred or a thousand days, perhaps not in our lifetime. But," said the President, "let us begin."

TWO SPEECHES

On June 28, 1954, Murrow received the annual Freedom House Award with the citation: "Free men were heartened by his courage in exposing those who would divide us by exploiting our fears."

Appropriate response to this generous and gracious citation would appear to require the eloquence of the ancients on some aspect of freedom. But there is little new to be said; the words have been better said by others; the challenge we face today has been faced before. Freedom is not to be bought in the bargain basement—nor for a lump sum—it must be paid for and argued about by each succeeding generation. Weapons may change, maps may be altered, alliances falter; but freedom remains the continuing concern of men and women who are conscious of their heritage and who would remain free. Freedom may be hammered to death on the anvil of war; or it may be nibbled away, or wither from neglect; or come to be regarded as a luxury we can't afford. With your permission I shall talk briefly about how much freedom we can afford, in the context of the fearsome, frightened time in which we live.

One of the pitfalls into which freedom can fall is in our thinking that any national or world emergency justifies putting curbs on freedom. We all recognize that in wartime, when national survival is at stake, it could be dangerous to take chances with extreme activities in the opposition. We do not know how great a peril the dissenters may prove to be. They could weaken the war effort; they might by themselves destroy security. It would take time to give

349

them the benefit of the doubt, or search their motives in lengthy legal procedures. Time is short in a war, and it is the general feeling that it is better to suspend some individual rights for a while than to endanger the whole community. But it is generally understood that this can only be tolerated while survival is at stake. When the emergency is over, a democracy expects to return to its normal practices and to the full protection of minorities and individuals. That is, when danger is sufficiently acute—when victory means survival—a democracy can decide not to be completely democratic but does so in the assurance that when the emergency ends it will promptly return to its true character.

It doesn't always turn out that way. After the First World War the drive for conformity persisted in this country and some time was needed for the advocates of democracy to take over from impatient and headstrong enemies of dissent. There was an ugly time when individual rights were being cut down without national survival serving as a justification.

The test of the validity of reducing freedom in a democracy is not simply danger; it is the immediacy of the danger. It takes time to practice democracy, and in an acute danger there just may not be time for slow democratic ways. So the question we need to answer today is whether the danger we now face is so near that we no longer have time to be democratic. During the hot war we felt we did not have it. Do we have it in a cold war?

You will recognize that all the curbs on freedom advocated or imposed today are justified or excused on the ground that we are in a cold war and that our survival is just as much at stake as in a hot war. That may well be so. But it isn't so that we have no time in the cold war. We have plenty of it. The cold war isn't being decided soon; it may not be for a lifetime.

Just let your mind run over the recent instances when individual freedom has been curtailed or overridden and ask yourselves whether there has not been plenty of time to enforce the laws in normal democratic ways, without in any way threatening national survival. There has been no pressing need for self-appointed crusaders to replace the courts and to prosecute and condemn dissenters in committees, or in the newspapers, or on television or radio. Many individuals have been cruelly punished. I am thinking of those who have not been placed behind prison bars after a trial but of those who have been stigmatized as though branded for life with a hot iron. More than a few have been rendered permanently unemployable and have been relegated to a condition of social inferiority like India's untouchables. I am not saying that none of these was guilty. How should I know? I only say it was not democratic to punish them without a fair trial.

In a hot war it may be unsafe to try to maintain the military effort and all the democratic principles at the same time. In a cold war it not only is safe, it seems to me imperative to do so. For one of the elements of our power in the cold war is our democracy and the sincerity with which we live it. For our democracy is the chief remaining guarantee of the safety of freedom anywhere. I say it actually endangers our national security and reduces our chances of survival as a democracy if we throw this asset away or impair it.

If an atmosphere is created in which dissent and independent individual thinking are penalized, the tendency of the citizen will be to avoid trouble. He can be safe on his job, enjoy the approval of his neighbors and be immune from misinterpretation and persecution simply by saying nothing. And if enough citizens say nothing, the result is nationwide conformity. That may be pleasing to those who don't understand democracy or value it, but nationwide conformity means a static society, one that has lost the initiative to change itself. The only way such a static society changes is by the examples set or by the pronouncements made by those who have become the self-appointed, fear-breeding arbiters of what is right and what is wrong.

If we become a static society, we lose one of the basic functions of democracy, the freedom to change. It is a truism that democracy is a means of dealing with the human imperfections of society. It recognizes that no form of government is perfect, no administration can be faultless, no legal system beyond improvement, no economic order as good as it might be. Where there is imperfection there must be change. And to produce change, unless it is imposed by tyranny, there must be difference of opinion; there must be opposition; there must be pioneer thinking; there must be freedom to criticize; there must be the unremitting conflict and testing of ideas. This undoubtedly involves a great deal of confusion. But the liveliness of a democracy can be measured by the activity of the minds of its citizens. Security and serenity in a democracy are not

351

IN SEARCH OF LIGHT

at all the same thing. They may even be opposites. Those who think that since we are in a cold war we are committed to conformity may not realize that they are asking to make democracy dormant, and that a dormant democracy is really on the way to becoming a tyranny. If our democracy is kept dormant for as long as the cold war continues, the end will be a world in which two tyrannies confront each other. The test of military power between them may not have been risked, but the ideological struggle will be over. The free world will have ceased to be free.

So one of our troubles is knowing how to appraise and measure the emergency. I yield to no one in my desire to root out subversion. But I insist on a broad definition for subversion. I call subversion anything that subverts our political order, whether it be giving active aid to an enemy or curtailing the freedom of the democracy to deal with its own imperfections. We must know that democracy cannot be kept alive by putting it to sleep. We have to be just as much engrossed with promoting its vigor and liveliness as its military security. One freedom that does not make sense, even in a cold war, is the freedom to reduce freedom. And I am not thinking of the inherent necessity for restraints if freedom is to thrive. Obviously, freedom that is not responsible is mere willfulness, and it is not what I am talking about. But when freedom takes it upon itself to reduce itself permanently, or for as long as a cold war lasts, it is in the initial stages of self-destruction.

There is a false formula for personal security being peddled in our market place. It is this, although not so labeled: Don't join anything; don't associate; don't write; don't take a chance on being wrong; don't espouse unpopular causes; button your lip and drift with the tide; seek the ease and luxury of complete equanimity by refusing to make up your minds about issues that wiser heads will one day decide. This product, if it be bought by enough people, leads to paralysis.

We must, I think, for our very lives remember that freedom will reside and flourish here in this generous and capacious land, or it will survive nowhere on this minor planet. Our strength in this continuing conflict with the forces of evil lies not alone in bombs and planes and physical courage. We must have stable ground upon which to stand and fight, if fight we must. Nations have been known to destroy their freedom while preparing to defend it. We are the head of a grand alliance of freedom-loving people. They have joined with us because they believe it to be in their own self-interest, and because we are strong. But there is another reason for their joining their fate with ours. We are free, and whatever we do to limit or foreshorten that freedom will reduce by that much our reservoir of goodwill abroad. There is no such thing as a Voice of America. That voice is made up of senators, and admirals, and clergymen, the Supreme Court, the price of wheat on the big board in Chicago, trade policies, race relations. There is no longer such a thing as a purely domestic news story; each is part of the voice of this country abroad. And if that collective voice tells the story of reduced freedom, of a tyranny of silence, of a fear of change, then within measurable time we shall find ourselves a great, powerful continental island off the coast of Kamchatka, with the rest of the world either united against us or indifferent to our fate. Our example, our demonstration of freedom in action, may be more powerful than our dollars, more persuasive than the threat of our bombs. We must continue to provide ourselves and our allies with that most dangerous and explosive force known to mankind—knowledge. And no man and no group may be permitted to chart in advance the course or the books to be followed in pursuit of that knowledge.

We live in a time of fear and prejudice, and freedom is hard-pressed both at home and abroad. But freedom will survive and flourish unless it be destroyed by the consent of the free. I say consent, for acquiescence or silence is a form of consent. I believe there has been more acquiescence than is healthy because too many people have mistakenly thought it was necessary to be undemocratic to deal with the emergency. They have thought there wasn't time to be both safe and free. No more fateful mistake can be made. For in the cold war there is no safety whatever unless we remain free. Democracy is our one chance of survival. For if we emerge from the long crisis undevastated by total war but no longer free, we have but chosen the cheapest and least heroic way to give tyranny the victory.

Murrow was invited to address a convention of radio and television news directors in Chicago on October 15, 1958. He accepted and challenged the broadcasting industry to live up to its responsibilities. It was perhaps the major speech of his career.

This just might do nobody any good. At the end of this discourse a few people may accuse this reporter of fouling his own comfortable nest, and your organization may be accused of having given hospitality to heretical and even dangerous thoughts. But the elaborate structure of networks, advertising agencies and sponsors will not be shaken or altered. It is my desire, if not my duty, to try to talk to you journeymen with some candor about what is happening to radio and television.

I have no technical advice or counsel to offer those of you who labor in this vineyard that produces words and pictures. You will forgive me for not telling you that the instruments with which you work are miraculous, that your responsibility is unprecedented or that your aspirations are frequently frustrated. It is not necessary to remind you that the fact that your voice is amplified to the degree where it reaches from one end of the country to the other does not confer upon you greater wisdom or understanding than you possessed when your voice reached only from one end of the bar to the other. All of these things you know.

You should also know at the outset that, in the manner of witnesses before Congressional committees, I appear here voluntarily—by invitation—that I am an employee of the Columbia Broadcasting System, that I am neither an officer nor a director of that corporation and that these remarks are of a "do-it-yourself" nature. If what I have to say is responsible, then I alone am responsible for the saying of it. Seeking neither approbation from my employers, nor new sponsors, nor acclaim from the critics of radio and television, I cannot well be disappointed. Believing that potentially the commercial system of broadcasting as practiced in this country is the best and freest yet devised, I have decided to express my concern about what I believe to be happening to radio and television. These instruments have been good to me beyond my due. There exists in my mind no reasonable grounds for personal complaint. I have no feud, either with my employers, any sponsors, or

354

with the professional critics of radio and television. But I am seized with an abiding fear regarding what these two instruments are doing to our society, our culture and our heritage.

Our history will be what we make it. And if there are any historians about fifty or a hundred years from now, and there should be preserved the kinescopes for one week of all three networks, they will there find recorded in black and white, or color, evidence of decadence, escapism and insulation from the realities of the world in which we live. I invite your attention to the television schedules of all networks between the hours of 8 and 11 p.m., Eastern Time. Here you will find only fleeting and spasmodic reference to the fact that this nation is in mortal danger. There are, it is true, occasional informative programs presented in that intellectual ghetto on Sunday afternoons. But during the daily peak viewing periods, television in the main insulates us from the realities of the world in which we live. If this state of affairs continues, we may alter an advertising slogan to read: LOOK NOW, PAY LATER. For surely we shall pay for using this most powerful instrument of communication to insulate the citizenry from the hard and demanding realities which must be faced if we are to survive. I mean the word *survive* literally. If there were to be a competition in indifference, or perhaps in insulation from reality, then Nero and his fiddle, Chamberlain and his umbrella, could not find a place on an early afternoon sustaining show. If Hollywood were to run out of Indians, the program schedules would be mangled beyond all recognition. Then some courageous soul with a small budget might be able to do a documentary telling what, in fact, we have done—and are still doing—to the Indians in this country. But that would be unpleasant. And we must at all costs shield the sensitive citizens from anything that is unpleasant.

I am entirely persuaded that the American public is more reasonable, restrained and more mature than most of our industry's program planners believe. Their fear of controversy is not warranted by the evidence. I have reason to know, as do many of you, that when the evidence on a controversial subject is fairly and calmly presented, the public recognizes it for what it is—an effort to illuminate rather than to agitate.

Several years ago, when we undertook to do a program on Egypt and Israel, well-meaning, experienced and intelligent friends shook their heads and said, "This you cannot do—you will be handed your head. It is an emotion-packed controversy, and there is no room for reason in it." We did the program. Zionists, anti-Zionists, the friends of the Middle East, Egyptian and Israeli officials said, with a faint note of surprise, "It was a fair count. The information was there. We have no complaints."

Our experience was similar with two half-hour programs dealing with cigarette smoking and lung cancer. Both the medical profession and the tobacco industry cooperated in a rather wary fashion. But in the end of the day they were both reasonably content. The subject of radioactive fall-out and the banning of nuclear tests was, and is, highly controversial. But according to what little evidence there is, viewers were prepared to listen to both sides with reason and restraint. This is not said to claim any special or unusual competence in the presentation of controversial subjects, but rather to indicate that timidity in these areas is not warranted by the evidence.

Recently, network spokesmen have been disposed to complain that the professional critics of television have been "rather beastly." There have been hints that somehow competition for the advertising dollar has caused the critics of print to gang up on television and radio. This reporter has no desire to defend the critics. They have space in which to do that on their own behalf. But it remains a fact that the newspapers and magazines are the only instruments of mass communication which remain free from sustained and regular critical comment. If the network spokesmen are so anguished about what appears in print, let them come forth and engage in a little sustained and regular comment regarding newspapers and magazines. It is an ancient and sad fact that most people in network television, and radio, have an exaggerated regard for what appears in print. And there have been cases where executives have refused to make even private comment on a program for which they were responsible until they had read the reviews in print. This is hardly an exhibition of confidence.

The oldest excuse of the networks for their timidity is their youth. Their spokesmen say, "We are young; we have not developed the traditions nor acquired the experience of the older media." If they but knew it, they are building those traditions, creating those precedents every day. Each time they yield to a voice from Washington or any political pressure, each time they eliminate something that might offend some section of the community, they are creating their own body of precedent and tradition. They are, in fact, not content to be "half safe."

Nowhere is this better illustrated than by the fact that the chairman of the Federal Communications Commission publicly prods broadcasters to engage in their legal right to editorialize. Of course, to undertake an editorial policy, overt and clearly labeled, and obviously unsponsored, requires a station or a network to be responsible. Most stations today probably do not have the manpower to assume this responsibility, but the manpower could be recruited. Editorials would not be profitable; if they had a cutting edge, they might even offend. It is much easier, much less troublesome, to use the money-making machine of television and radio merely as a conduit through which to channel anything that is not libelous, obscene or defamatory. In that way one has the illusion of power without responsibility.

So far as radio—that most satisfying and rewarding instrument—is concerned, the diagnosis of its difficulties is rather easy. And obviously I speak only of news and information. In order to progress, it need only go backward. To the time when singing commercials were not allowed on news reports, when there was no middle commercial in a 15-minute news report, when radio was rather proud, alert and fast. I recently asked a network official, "Why this great rash of five-minute news reports (including three commercials) on weekends?" He replied, "Because that seems to be the only thing we can sell."

In this kind of complex and confusing world, you can't tell very much about the why of the news in broadcasts where only three minutes is available for news. The only man who could do that was Elmer Davis, and his kind aren't about any more. If radio news is to be regarded as a commodity, only acceptable when saleable, then I don't care what you call it—I say it isn't news.

My memory also goes back to the time when the fear of a slight reduction in business did not result in an immediate cutback in bodies in the news and public affairs department, at a time when network profits had just reached an all-time high. We would all

357

agree, I think, that whether on a station or a network, the stapling machine is a poor substitute for a newsroom typewriter.

One of the minor tragedies of television news and information is that the networks will not even defend their vital interests. When my employer, CBS, through a combination of enterprise and good luck, did an interview with Nikita Khrushchev, the President uttered a few ill-chosen, uninformed words on the subject, and the network practically apologized. This produced a rarity. Many newspapers defended the CBS right to produce the program and commended it for initiative. But the other networks remained silent.

Likewise, when John Foster Dulles, by personal decree, banned American journalists from going to Communist China, and subsequently offered contradictory explanations, for his fiat the networks entered only a mild protest. Then they apparently forgot the unpleasantness. Can it be that this national industry is content to serve the public interest only with the trickle of news that comes out of Hong Kong, to leave its viewers in ignorance of the cataclysmic changes that are occurring in a nation of six hundred million people? I have no illusions about the difficulties of reporting from a dictatorship, but our British and French allies have been better served—in their public interest—with some very useful information from their reporters in Communist China.

One of the basic troubles with radio and television news is that both instruments have grown up as an incompatible combination of show business, advertising and news. Each of the three is a rather bizarre and demanding profession. And when you get all three under one roof, the dust never settles. The top management of the networks, with a few notable exceptions, has been trained in advertising, research, sales or show business. But by the nature of the corporate structure, they also make the final and crucial decisions having to do with news and public affairs. Frequently they have neither the time nor the competence to do this. It is not easy for the same small group of men to decide whether to buy a new station for millions of dollars, build a new building, alter the rate card, buy a new Western, sell a soap opera, decide what defensive line to take in connection with the latest Congressional inquiry, how much money to spend on promoting a new program, what additions or deletions should be made in the existing covey or clutch of vice-presidents, and at the same time—frequently on the same long day —to give mature, thoughtful consideration to the manifold problems that confront those who are charged with the responsibility for news and public affairs.

Sometimes there is a clash between the public interest and the corporate interest. A telephone call or a letter from the proper quarter in Washington is treated rather more seriously than a communication from an irate but not politically potent viewer. It is tempting enough to give away a little air time for frequently irresponsible and unwarranted utterances in an effort to temper the wind of criticism.

Upon occasion, economics and editorial judgment are in conflict. And there is no law which says that dollars will be defeated by duty. Not so long ago the President of the United States delivered a television address to the nation. He was discoursing on the possibility or probability of war between this nation and the Soviet Union and Communist China—a reasonably compelling subject. Two networks, CBS and NBC, delayed that broadcast for an hour and fifteen minutes. If this decision was dictated by anything other than financial reasons, the networks didn't deign to explain those reasons. That hour-and-fifteen-minute delay, by the way, is about twice the time required for an ICBM to travel from the Soviet Union to major targets in the United States. It is difficult to believe that this decision was made by men who love, respect and understand news.

So far, I have been dealing largely with the deficit side of the ledger, and the items could be expanded. But I have said, and I believe, that potentially we have in this country a free enterprise system of radio and television which is superior to any other. But to achieve its promise, it must be both free and enterprising. There is no suggestion here that networks or individual stations should operate as philanthropies. But I can find nothing in the Bill of Rights or the Communications Act which says that they must increase their net profits each year, lest the Republic collapse. I do not suggest that news and information should be subsidized by foundations or private subscriptions. I am aware that the networks have expended, and are expending, very considerable sums of money on public affairs programs from which they cannot hope to receive any financial reward. I have had the privilege at CBS of presiding over a considerable number of such programs. I testify, and am able to stand here and say, that I have never had a program turned down by my superiors because of the money it would cost.

But we all know that you cannot reach the potential maximum audience in marginal time with a sustaining program. This is so because so many stations on the network—any network—will decline to carry it. Every licensee who applies for a grant to operate in the public interest, convenience and necessity makes certain promises as to what he will do in terms of program content. Many recipients of licenses have, in blunt language, welshed on those promises. The money-making machine somehow blunts their memories. The only remedy for this is closer inspection and punitive action by the F.C.C. But in the view of many this would come perilously close to supervision of program content by a federal agency.

So it seems that we cannot rely on philanthropic support or foundation subsidies; we cannot follow the "sustaining route"—the networks cannot pay all the freight—and the F.C.C. cannot or will not discipline those who abuse the facilities that belong to the public. What, then, is the answer? Do we merely stay in our comfortable nests, concluding that the obligation of these instruments has been discharged when we work at the job of informing the public for a minimum of time? Or do we believe that the preservation of the Republic is a seven-day-a-week job, demanding more awareness, better skills and more perseverance than we have yet contemplated.

I am frightened by the imbalance, the constant striving to reach the largest possible audience for everything; by the absence of a sustained study of the state of the nation. Heywood Broun once said, "No body politic is healthy until it begins to itch." I would like television to produce some itching pills, rather than this endless outpouring of tranquilizers. It can be done. Maybe it won't be, but it could. Let us not shoot the wrong piano player. Do not be deluded into believing that the titular heads of the networks control what appears on their networks. They all have better taste. All are responsible to stockholders, and in my experience all are honorable men. But they must schedule what they can sell in the public market.

And this brings us to the nub of the question. In one sense it rather revolves around the phrase heard frequently along Madison Avenue: The Corporate Image. I am not precisely sure what this phrase means, but I would imagine that it reflects a desire on the part of the corporations who pay the advertising bills to have the public imagine, or believe, that they are not merely bodies with no souls, panting in pursuit of elusive dollars. They would like us to believe that they can distinguish between the public good and the private or corporate gain. So the question is this: Are the big corporations who pay the freight for radio and television programs wise to use that time exclusively for the sale of goods and services? Is it in their own interest and that of the stockholders so to do? The sponsor of an hour's television program is not buying merely the six minutes devoted to his commercial message. He is determining, within broad limits, the sum total of the impact of the entire hour. If he always, invariably, reaches for the largest possible audience, then this process of insulation, of escape from reality, will continue to be massively financed, and its apologists will continue to make winsome speeches about giving the public what it wants, or "letting the public decide."

I refuse to believe that the presidents and chairmen of the boards of these big corporations want their corporate image to consist exclusively of a solemn voice in an echo chamber, or a pretty girl opening the door of a refrigerator, or a horse that talks. They want something better, and on occasion some of them have demonstrated it. But most of the men whose legal and moral responsibility it is to spend the stockholders' money for advertising are removed from the realities of the mass media by five, six, or a dozen contraceptive layers of vice-presidents, public relations counsel and advertising agencies. Their business is to sell goods, and the competition is pretty tough.

But this nation is now in competition with malignant forces of evil who are using every instrument at their command to empty the minds of their subjects and fill those minds with slogans, determination and faith in the future. If we go on as we are, we are protecting the mind of the American public from any real contact with the menacing world that squeezes in upon us. We are engaged in a great experiment to discover whether a free public opinion can devise and direct methods of managing the affairs of the nation. We may fail. But we are handicapping ourselves needlessly.

Let us have a little competition. Not only in selling soap, cigarettes and automobiles, but in informing a troubled, apprehensive but receptive public. Why should not each of the 20 or 30 big corporations which dominate radio and television decide that they will give up one or two of their regularly scheduled programs each year, turn the time over to the networks and say in effect: "This is a tiny tithe, just a little bit of our profits. On this particular night we aren't going to try to sell cigarettes or automobiles; this is merely a gesture to indicate our belief in the importance of ideas." The networks should, and I think would, pay for the cost of producing the program. The advertiser, the sponsor, would get name credit but would have nothing to do with the content of the program. Would this blemish the corporate image? Would the stockholders object? I think not. For if the premise upon which our pluralistic society rests, which as I understand it is that if the people are given sufficient undiluted information, they will then somehow, even after long, sober second thoughts, reach the right decision—if that premise is wrong, then not only the corporate image but the corporations are done for.

There used to be an old phrase in this country, employed when someone talked too much. It was: "Go hire a hall." Under this proposal the sponsor would have hired the hall; he has bought the time; the local station operator, no matter how indifferent, is going to carry the program—he has to. Then it's up to the networks to fill the hall. I am not here talking about editorializing but about straightaway exposition as direct, unadorned and impartial as fallible human beings can make it. Just once in a while let us exalt the importance of ideas and information. Let us dream to the extent of saying that on a given Sunday night the time normally occupied by Ed Sullivan is given over to a clinical survey of the state of American education, and a week or two later the time normally used by Steve Allen is devoted to a thoroughgoing study of American policy in the Middle East. Would the corporate image of their respective sponsors be damaged? Would the stockholders rise up in their wrath and complain? Would anything happen other than that a few million people would have received a little illumination on subjects that may well determine the future of this country, and therefore the future of the corporations? This method would also provide real competition between the networks as to which could outdo the others in the palatable presentation of information. It would provide an outlet for the young men of skill, and there are some even of dedication, who would like to do something other than devise methods of insulating while selling.

There may be other and simpler methods of utilizing these instruments of radio and television in the interests of a free society. But I know of none that could be so easily accomplished inside the framework of the existing commercial system. I don't know how you would measure the success or failure of a given program. And it would be hard to prove the magnitude of the benefit accruing to the corporation which gave up one night of a variety or quiz show in order that the network might marshal its skills to do a thoroughgoing job on the present status of NATO, or plans for controlling nuclear tests. But I would reckon that the president, and indeed the majority of shareholders of the corporation who sponsored such a venture, would feel just a little bit better about the corporation and the country.

It may be that the present system, with no modifications and no experiments, can survive. Perhaps the money-making machine has some kind of built-in perpetual motion, but I do not think so. To a very considerable extent the media of mass communications in a given country reflect the political, economic and social climate in which they flourish. That is the reason ours differ from the British and French, or the Russian and Chinese. We are currently wealthy, fat, comfortable and complacent. We have currently a built-in allergy to unpleasant or disturbing information. Our mass media reflect this. But unless we get up off our fat surpluses and recognize that television in the main is being used to distract, delude, amuse and insulate us, then television and those who finance it, those who look at it and those who work at it, may see a totally different picture too late.

I do not advocate that we turn television into a 27-inch wailing wall, where longhairs constantly moan about the state of our culture and our defense. But I would just like to see it reflect occasionally the hard, unyielding realities of the world in which we live. I would like to see it done inside the existing framework, and I would like to see the doing of it redound to the credit of those who finance and program it. Measure the results by Nielsen, Trendex or Silex—it doesn't matter. The main thing is to try. The responsibility can be easily placed, in spite of all the mouthings about giving the public what it wants. It rests on big business, and on big television, and it rests at the top. Responsibility is not something that can be assigned or delegated. And it promises its own reward: good business and good television.

Perhaps no one will do anything about it. I have ventured to outline it against a background of criticism that may have been too harsh only because I could think of nothing better. Someone once said—I think it was Max Eastman—that "that publisher serves his advertiser best who best serves his readers." I cannot believe that radio and television, or the corporations that finance the programs, are serving well or truly their viewers or listeners, or themselves.

I began by saying that our history will be what we make it. If we go on as we are, then history will take its revenge, and retribution will not limp in catching up with us.

We are to a large extent an imitative society. If one or two or three corporations would undertake to devote just a small fraction of their advertising appropriation along the lines that I have suggested, the procedure would grow by contagion; the economic burden would be bearable, and there might ensue a most exciting adventure—exposure to ideas and the bringing of reality into the homes of the nation.

To those who say people wouldn't look; they wouldn't be interested; they're too complacent, indifferent and insulated, I can only reply: There is, in one reporter's opinion, considerable evidence against that contention. But even if they are right, what have they got to lose? Because if they are right, and this instrument is good for nothing but to entertain, amuse and insulate, then the tube is flickering now and we will soon see that the whole struggle is lost.

This instrument can teach, it can illuminate; yes, and it can even inspire. But it can do so only to the extent that humans are determined to use it to those ends. Otherwise it is merely wires and lights in a box. There is a great and perhaps decisive battle to be fought against ignorance, intolerance and indifference. This weapon of television could be useful.

Stonewall Jackson, who knew something about the use of weapons, is reported to have said, "When war comes, you must draw the sword and throw away the scabbard." The trouble with television is that it is rusting in the scabbard during a battle for survival.

364

INDEX

Index

x

A NOTE *About the Author*

Edward R. Murrow *was born near Greensboro, North Carolina, in 1908. He graduated from Washington State College in 1930, and he was a member of Phi Beta Kappa. From 1932 to 1935 he was assistant director of the International Institute of Education. He joined the Columbia Broadcasting System in 1935, for which he worked until 1961. From 1961 to 1964 he served as director of the United States Information Agency. He was married and the father of a son. He died on April 27, 1965, on his farm in Pawling, New York. Seven weeks before his death he was made an Honorary Knight Commander of the Most Excellent Order of the British Empire by Queen Elizabeth II.*

Other titles of interest

THE WAR, 1939–1945
A Documentary History
Edited by Desmond Flowers
and James Reeves
New introduction by
John S. D. Eisenhower
1,142 pp., 20 maps
80763-7 $24.95

THE AMERICAN EARTHQUAKE
A Chronicle of the Roaring
Twenties, the Great Depression,
and the Dawn of the New Deal
Edmund Wilson
576 pp.
80696-7 $17.95

THE AUTOBIOGRAPHY OF
ELEANOR ROOSEVELT
498 pp., 24 pp. of photos
80476-X $16.95

FRANKLIN D. ROOSEVELT:
HIS LIFE AND TIMES
An Encyclopedic View
Edited by Otis L. Graham, Jr.
and Meghan Robinson Wander
512 pp., 250 illus.
80410-7 $22.50

THE GI's WAR
American Soldiers in Europe
During World War II
Edwin P. Hoyt
638 pp., 29 illus.
80448-4 $16.95

THE KOREAN WAR
Matthew B. Ridgway
360 pp., 55 photos
80267-8 $13.95

CONFLICT
The History of the Korean War,
1950–1953
Robert Leckie
480 pp., 60 photos, 1 map
80716-5 $16.95

THE MIGHTY ENDEAVOR
The American War in Europe
Charles B. MacDonald
621 pp., 78 photos, 10 maps
80486-7 $16.95

NUREMBERG DIARY
G. M. Gilbert
488 pp., 24 photos
80661-4 $16.95

THE PATTON PAPERS, 1940–1945
Martin Blumenson
944 pp., 31 photos, 5 maps
80717-3 $19.95

REMINISCENCES
General Douglas MacArthur
440 pp., 30 photos
80254-6 $15.95

ROOSEVELT AND
CHURCHILL: Their Secret
Wartime Correspondence
Edited by F. Loewenheim,
H. Langley, and M. Jonas
840 pp., 31 photos
80390-9 $17.95

STALIN
The History of a Dictator
H. Montgomery Hyde
679 pp., 76 photos
80167-1 $18.95

Available at your bookstore

OR ORDER DIRECTLY FROM

DA CAPO PRESS, INC.

1-800-321-0050